AN

CQ GUIDE TO

CURRENT AMERICAN GOVERNMENT

Spring 1988

Congressional Quarterly Inc.

Congressional Quarterly Inc.

Congressional Quarterly Inc., an editorial research service and publishing company, serves clients in the fields of news, education, business and government. It combines specific coverage of Congress, government and politics by Congressional Quarterly with the more general subject range of an affiliated service, Editorial Research Reports.

Congressional Quarterly publishes the *Congressional Quarterly Weekly Report* and a variety of books, including college political science textbooks under the CQ Press imprint and public affairs paperbacks designed as timely reports to keep journalists, scholars and the public abreast of developing issues and events. CQ also publishes information directories and reference books on the federal government, national elections and politics, including the *Guide to Congress,* the *Guide to the U.S. Supreme Court,* the *Guide to U.S. Elections* and *Politics in America.* The *CQ Almanac,* a compendium of legislation for one session of Congress, is published each year. *Congress and the Nation,* a record of government for a presidential term, is published every four years.

CQ publishes *The Congressional Monitor,* a daily report on current and future activities of congressional committees, and several newsletters including *Congressional Insight,* a weekly analysis of congressional action, and *Campaign Practices Reports,* a semimonthly update on campaign laws.

The online delivery of CQ's Washington Alert provides clients with immediate access to Congressional Quarterly's institutional information and expertise.

Printed in the United States of America

Library of Congress Catalog No. 61-16893
International Standard Book No. 0-87187-454-7
International Standard Serial No. 0196-612X

1414 22nd Street, N.W., Washington, D.C. 20037

Editor: Jane Gilligan
Contributors: Bob Benenson, Peter Bragdon, Martha Bridegam, Jacqueline Calmes, Nadine Cohodas, Rhodes Cook, John R. Cranford, Alan Ehrenhalt, Ronald D. Elving, John Felton, Jeremy Gaunt, Janet Hook, John Moore, Julie Rovner, Paul Starobin, Pat Towell, Tom Watson, Elizabeth Wehr
Graphics: Richard A. Pottern, Robert Redding, John B. Auldridge, Julie B. Booth
Index: Linda Busetti
Production: I. D. Fuller, Maceo Mayo

Photos: 11, 15, 52 - AP/Wide World Photos; 42, 110, 111 - Bettmann Newsphotos; 64 (Karnes) - Jim Burnett 40 - Columbia Pictures Industries; 28, 30, 34 - Paul Conklin; 67 - Tibor Gasparik; 36, 37, 43, 46 (plane), 50, 75 (Spratt), 106 (Biden), 114 - Ken Heinen; 14, 46 (truck), 61 (Boschwitz), 64 (Daub), 73, 80, 106 (Humphrey) - Sue Klemens; 65 (Lautenberg), 75 (McCurdy), 91, 96 - Marty LaVor; 94, 97 - Joseph McCary/Photo Response; 30 - Jeff MacNelly/Tribune Media Services; 76 - Rep. Patterson's office; 42 - Senate Historical Office; 20, 31 - Art Stein; 46 (man) - Rojer Tully; 6 - *The Washington Post;* 32, 48, 61 (Kerry), 65 (Bryan), 73 (Leath), 75 (MacKay), 79 - Teresa Zabala

TABLE OF CONTENTS

PRESIDENCY/EXECUTIVE

Powers of the President 1
Iran-Contra Affair 4
Covert Operations 14
Defense 17
Trade............................. 20
AIDS Testing 22

CONGRESS

Congressional Powers 23
Robert Byrd's Senate............... 28
Speaker Wright.................... 34
The Filibuster..................... 40
Transportation/Commerce 46
Economic Affairs.................. 52

POLITICS

Presidential Primaries............... 54
The Presidential Nominating Process . 56
Senate Elections 61
House Elections.................... 69
The Conservative Coalition.......... 73
Campaign Spending 80

LOBBIES

The Washington Lobby 83
Inside Congress.................... 88
Political Action Committees......... 89
Nuclear Energy Lobby 91
Vietnam Veterans 93
Tom Korologos.................... 96

SUPREME COURT

Judicial Powers 98
Bork Vote......................... 104
Robert H. Bork 107
Supreme Court Appointees 111
Supreme Court Agenda 114
Reagan's Judiciary................. 118
Biographies of Justices............. 120

APPENDIX

Glossary of Congressional Terms.... 125
How a Bill Becomes Law........... 135
Reference Guides................. 140
Text of the Constitution 142

INDEX.......................... 151

THE CQ Guide to Current American Government is prepared twice yearly as an up-to-date handbook for the study of American government. It contains the most useful and instructional of recent Congressional Quarterly news research material, rearranged and edited for students of government and politics.

The Guide is designed to serve two main functions. First, it provides students with current illustrations of the continuing interplay of forces that constitute our political system. It shows not only how the president, Congress and judiciary act and react to one another but how this traditional interplay is tempered and influenced by other vital forces such as politics, changing social pressures, new administrations, current issues and lobbying. A study of the balance of power among the three branches of government, for example, at once raises questions about the current status of that balance — especially between the president and Congress — and likely changes in the balance to come. Illustrations of these forces at work will help the student see and learn from the important differences that exist between theory and operation, between format and function.

Second, the Guide is a starting point for discussion and individual research in the day-to-day operations of government. Such research may be as informal as the careful reading of good newspapers. With reliable news sources, a good library and ample amounts of curiosity and imagination, students can find in daily events — whether in Washington, D.C., their own state capital or hometown — a rich supply of case studies of government and politics in action. In the process, they stand to gain greater sophistication, not only as students, but as citizens.

To facilitate additional research on topical events, citations have been provided to related and background articles in the Guide's basic sources of material, the CQ *Weekly Report* and the CQ *Almanac*. The *Weekly Report* and *Almanac* are available at most school and public libraries.

PRESIDENCY/EXECUTIVE

Powers of the President

The place of the executive branch in the new plan of government greatly troubled the framers of the Constitution. A longstanding fear of authority, arising from experience with England's monarchy, led them to consider first a plan in which the executive deferred to the national legislature. The final draft of the Constitution, however, provided for a more balanced system in which some powers were to be shared between the president and Congress. Explicit congressional powers were enumerated at length, but Article II on the presidency was short and somewhat vague.

The looseness of the constitutional grant of power to the president allowed strong 19th century chief executives such as Thomas Jefferson, Andrew Jackson and Abraham Lincoln to establish precedents that steadily enhanced the position. Laws that provided them special powers in emergencies further strengthened presidents' authority.

Presidential power grew rapidly in the 20th century, spurred by a major economic depression and two world wars, until it posed a threat to the viability of Congress as a coequal branch of government. As the volume and complexity of federal business increased, legislative initiative shifted from the Capitol to the White House. Congress with its antiquated procedures found that it often was no match for the tremendous resources of the executive branch.

The result was repeated clashes between Congress and the president, particularly over the spending, war and treaty powers, as legislators resisted executive usurpation of the powers assigned to them by the Constitution.

Authorities for Powers

Constitutional Grant of Power

In sharp contrast to the explicit power granted the legislative branch (almost half the words of the Constitution are devoted to the functions of Congress), Article II of the Constitution describes only briefly the powers of the president. It begins with the ambiguous sentence: "The executive power shall be vested in a President of the United States of America." But the nature of the president's authority has evolved only through practice.

The only authority for what has become presidential dominance in foreign affairs is contained in Section 2. In addition to appointing ambassadors and making treaties, the Constitution provides that "The President shall be Commander in Chief of the Army and Navy of the United States and of the Militia of the several states." Even those powers, however, were to be shared with the legislative branch; the Constitution gave Congress power to "provide for the common Defence," declare war, raise and support armies, ratify presidential treaties and confirm presidential nominations. Conversely, the Constitution requires Congress to share its legislative function by authorizing the president to provide Congress with certain information and to propose legislation.

The president's legislative role always has been important, but the complexity of running today's government has put the chief executive at the center of the legislative process. Political scientist Lawrence H. Chamberlain has observed that "When so much of the life of the individual is influenced by federal legislation, the attitude of the President toward this legislation and his skill in gaining legislative approval of his proposals are matters of practical interest to millions of people. . . ."

While the Constitution vests "all legislative powers" in Congress, it also directs the president to "give to the Congress Information of the State of the Union and recommend to their Consideration such Measures as he shall judge necessary and expedient." Congress has broadened this function to direct the president to present to Congress each year, in addition to the State of the Union message, two other general statements of presidential aims — an economic report including proposals directed to the maintenance of maximum employment, and a budget message outlining spending and revenue proposals. During a typical session, the president transmits to Congress scores of other legislative proposals, some initiated by the White House and others in conformity with various statutes. The president's responsibility for proposing legislation has become so important that one measure of his effectiveness is how successful he is in persuading Congress to adopt those proposals.

Article I of the Constitution gives the president an additional legislative power, that of the veto. Congress must submit every bill and joint resolution (except those joint resolutions proposing constitutional amendments) to the president, who may approve the measure, let it become law without his signature, or veto it and return it to Congress within 10 days. If a president disapproves a bill, Congress can override the veto only by a two-thirds vote of both houses. Because presidents usually find it relatively easy to muster the support of at least one-third plus one member of either the House or Senate, the veto has been used with deadly effect; fewer than 6 percent of all vetoes have been overridden.

In addition to the regular veto, the Constitution gives the president the special power of the pocket veto, which he may use at the end of a congressional session. Under this procedure the president, presented with a bill 10 days or less (Sundays excepted) prior to the adjournment of Congress, can merely ignore or "pocket" it, depriving Congress of an opportunity to override the veto.

Court decisions in 1974 and 1976 specified that a president's power to use the pocket veto was restricted to final adjournments of Congress and not to holiday recesses. This provision was reaffirmed in 1984 when a federal appeals court ruled that President Ronald Reagan had acted unconstitutionally when he pocket vetoed a bill between two sessions of the same Congress in November 1983. The Supreme Court declared the case moot in 1987 because the bill was invalid by the time the case reached the Court.

The first American presidents conceived of the veto as a device to be used rarely and then only against legislative encroachment on the prerogatives of another branch of government. Presidents increased use of the veto in the 19th century, often to prevent Congress from passing private bills benefiting specific individuals. In the 20th century presidents began to use the threat of a veto as a powerful tool of persuasion.

Another major power the Constitution granted to the president is the power to make appointments. Article II, Section 2 empowers the president to appoint, besides ambassadors, "other public Ministers and Consuls, Judges of the Supreme Court, and all other Officers of the United States," subject to Senate confirmation. In the case of high offices such as Supreme Court justices and Cabinet officers, the president is able to pick persons of his own philosophy who presumably will aid his program.

The president's patronage power — gained through making appointments to increase political strength — derives from the constitutional authority to appoint lower court judges and other federal officials.

Despite the chance to reward a friend or political ally, many members of Congress bemoan their task of recommending patronage recipients. The late Sen. Patrick McCarran, D-Nev. (1933-54) once said of judicial appointments, "It's the lousiest duty in the world because what you end up with is 100 enemies and one ingrate."

Powers Authorized by Congress

A number of the president's powers have been conferred by Congress. It was common at one time for Congress to grant special powers during emergencies. During World War I, for example, President Woodrow Wilson acquired sweeping control of the economy in what political scientist Rexford G. Tugwell has called "the most fantastic expansion of the executive known to the American experience." The numerous powers granted to him by Congress included prohibition of exports, takeover of the railroads and requisition of food and fuel for public use.

Statutes passed during World War I were still in effect as the United States prepared to enter World War II. In 1941 there were approximately 250 different laws delegating discretionary authority to the president and other executive officials. Congress also had given the executive emergency powers to deal with economic crises, most notably in the case of Franklin Delano Roosevelt and the great Depression. Scholars theorized that an activist president probably could find some legislative grant for any action he deemed appropriate in an emergency.

In 1976 Congress moved to reassert its authority in this area by subjecting to congressional review all states of national emergency declared by the president. The measure also terminated, as of Sept, 14, 1978, all existing powers of the president and federal employees that were based on national emergency declarations in effect in 1976. Four such states of emergency, dating back to 1933, were in effect when the legislation was approved.

Modern laws authorizing the president to assign federal contract awards and to choose the location of government installations have given the president the weapon of preferment, which allows the president to reward or punish members of Congress quite spectacularly. It became particularly important after World War II as federal budgets skyrocketed. Members of the powerful committees and subcommittees dealing with defense, for example, frequently received defense installations in their districts in return for their support for military requests.

Powers From Precedent

Certain presidential powers are considered part of the office today simply because they were assumed by strong presidents and then carried on by their successors. Executive orders, by which the president can alter legislation, fall into this category. There is no legislative or constitutional basis for such orders. An example of an executive order with far-reaching effect was President Ronald Reagan's decontrol of crude oil, gasoline and propane prices issued on Jan. 28, 1981, for which no concurring act of Congress was necessary.

The president also holds certain powers simply because of the presitge of his office and the respect with which it is generally approached. This gives the president the ability to shape public opinion through his command of television, radio and the press. Such techniques as live televised news conferences, introduced by John F. Kennedy, and televised addresses before Congress have enabled presidents to gain public support for their legislative programs. President Reagan used television to his advantage in gathering support for his Economic Recovery Program in 1981.

The prestige of the president's office also helps him in persuading members of Congress to go along with his programs. Breakfast at the White House, a walk in the Rose Garden or a publicity picture taken with the president all are flattering to members of Congress and useful in their re-election campaigns.

War Powers

Probably the most fateful of the president's powers is the authority to act as commander in chief in times of war. The president's war powers are ambiguously stated in the Constitution but, in presenting the new charter to the nation, the authors of *The Federalist Papers* — James Madison, Alexander Hamilton and John Jay — stressed that they construed the president's war powers narrowly.

Richard B. Morris, professor emeritus of history at Columbia University, told the Senate Foreign Relations Committee in 1971 that the Constitution's authors intended the presidential war powers to be "little more than the power to defend against imminent invasion when Congress was not in session."

Historically, however, the president has exercised much more than a defensive war-making power. Successive presidents — following the precedent of Lincoln's administration perhaps — have interpreted their authority in this realm broadly and dynamically. The list of specific actions taken by the White House under the authority of this constitutional provision is almost endless.

Throughout its history, the United States has been involved in more than 125 instances in which American troops have been sent into areas of conflict under presidential authority and without specific congressional approval. For example, in 1846 President James K. Polk unquestionably provoked Mexico into war when he ordered the army to occupy disputed territory along the Rio Grande River.

Recent years have seen increasingly frequent examples of presidential moves that involved the country in armed conflicts without the prior authorization of Congress. In 1950 President Harry S Truman ordered American armed forces in the Pacific to resist North Korea's aggressive drives into South Korea, thereby involving the United States in one of the most prolonged and expensive undeclared wars in its history. Beginning with President Dwight D. Eisenhower, a succession of chief executives expanded America's military commitments to the government of South Vietnam, thereby in time virtually guaranteeing massive American involvement in the conflict between North and South Vietnam.

Until it became clear that the war in Vietnam would not be easily or quickly won, most members of Congress thought that modern diplomatic and military conditions required that the president be free to conduct foreign policy and defend the nation. But as opposition to the war grew both among the public and on Capitol Hill, a number of members of Congress began to question the authority of the Lyndon B. Johnson administration to involve the United States so heavily in Vietnam. Many Americans came to equate White House reliance upon the armed forces to achieve diplomatic objectives — often with little or no consultation with Congress — as a symbol of the "imperial presidency."

In response, Congress sought to assume some of the responsibility for determining whether the United States should engage in armed conflict. On Nov. 7, 1973, Congress enacted, over President Richard Nixon's veto, the War Powers Resolution (PL 93-148). Intended to restrict the president's war-making powers, the measure set a 60-day limit on the president's authority to wage undeclared war and required him to report within 48 hours to House and Senate officers on any commitment of U.S. combat forces abroad. It also required the president to consult with Congress "in every possible instance" in advance of a troop commitment overseas.

Presidents Gerald R. Ford, Jimmy Carter and Reagan submitted reports to Congress under the War Powers Resolution in sending troops to Southeast Asia and the Middle East, but Congress never has tried to use its veto power to force a withdrawal of troops.

Moreover, that power was called into question by the Supreme Court's June 23, 1983, decision nullifying so-called "legislative veto" provisions in legislation.

Confrontation between the White House and Congress came in the wake of Reagan's 1987 Persian Gulf policy. Under his plan, U.S. warships in the Persian Gulf would provide protection for 11 Kuwaiti tankers that were being registered as U.S.-owned vessels entitled to fly the American flag. Kuwait had sided with neighboring Iraq in its war with Iran.

Liberals in Congress, critical of what they saw as Reagan's undue willingness to risk military involvement abroad, had tried to force the issue of whether the reflagging plan triggered the War Powers Resolution. The administration, which challenged the constitutionality of the resolution, argued that it was irrelevant because the escorting ships would not face "imminent involvement in the hostilities," the key condition of the act.

Spending Power

For the first 134 years of the republic, Congress held undisputed sway over the government's purse strings, except for scattered incidents of executive impoundment, where the president refuses to spend money Congress has appropriated. But the increasing complexity of both the economy and government led to fragmentation of congressional control over the budget and an expanded role for the executive. In 1921 Congress itself ceded coordination over government spending and revenue estimates to the executive branch, and the next half-century was marked by further erosion of the congressional budget-making power. Nonetheless, Congress clung jealously to its taxing and appropriating powers specifically granted by the Constitution.

Then in the late 1960s and 1970s an intense dispute between Congress and the Nixon administration over impoundment prompted Congress to try to reclaim some of its control over fiscal policy and spending priorities.

Although the Constitution gave Congress complete authority to appropriate federal funds, it left vague whether a president was required to spend the appropriated money or whether he could make independent judgment on the timing and need for outlays. The issue had been a nettlesome one throughout the nation's history; precedent for such impoundments apparently went back to the administration of Thomas Jefferson. But impoundments became a major dispute only when President Nixon refused to spend appropriated funds running into the billions of dollars.

Nixon argued that he was withholding funds to combat inflation, but opposition Democrats contended that Nixon was using impoundment primarily to assert his own spending priorities.

This conflict prompted Congress to enact the Congressional Budget and Impoundment Control Act of 1974 (PL 93-344) to reassert control over the federal budget. In full operation for the first time in 1976, the measure streamlined congressional procedures for handling spending and tax legislation and created a mechanism for congressional disapproval of presidential impoundments. The legislation called for the president, when deciding to withhold funds, to submit a report to Congress. If the withholding was intended to be temporary (a deferral), either chamber could disapprove it at any time. The funds then would have to be released for obligation by the agencies. If the withholding was intended to be permanent (a rescission), the president would have to obtain the support of both houses within 45 days of continuous session. Otherwise, the funds would have to be released.

Congress lost some of this control over spending with the Supreme Court's 1983 decision striking down the legislative veto. The ruling nullified Congress' power to halt deferrals without the president's consent. It did not affect recissions.

As part of the budget process, Congress could direct its authorizing and appropriating committees to enact a single omnibus bill reconciling the spending and revenue requirements with the levels set out in the budget resolutions. It was the reconciliation tool that the White House and Republican strategists seized upon in 1981 to achieve the Reagan administration's desired budget cuts.

Hearings Leave Reagan Down but Not Out

In the middle of his second term in office, an immensely popular Republican president is shaken by revelations that he secretly violated some of his most fundamental foreign policies and that his aides carried out possibly illegal covert operations.

That, in essence, was the Iran-contra affair. Was it a political scandal, in the mold of Watergate nearly a decade and a half before, showing that deception and incompetence had reached the highest levels of government? Or was it a natural part of the political process, the latest evidence that the executive branch and Congress go through periods of not trusting each other?

Multiple investigations, private and public, appeared to demonstrate that the Iran-contra affair was both. Frustrated with the standard procedures of government, zealous Reagan administration officials acted as if lofty goals — bringing democracy to Central America and winning freedom for Americans held hostage overseas — justified secrecy, skirting the law, and the misleading of Congress.

But because those goals were so admirable, each beholder judged for himself the seriousness of the scandal over the means used to achieve them. For some, the Iran-contra affair was more frightening than Watergate because it revealed that the entire U.S. national security apparatus had been distorted by flawed policies and actions. For others, the affair was overrated, a secondary matter blown out of proportion by "the media" and "liberals" who had never accepted the popularity of President Reagan.

With facts and revelations continuing to tumble out, it was impossible to tell which view ultimately would prevail. In the short term, however, the Iran-contra affair clearly curtailed the political effectiveness of the most popular president in a generation. The revelation that Ronald Reagan had been selling arms to Iran, the foreign government most hated by Americans, drove the president underground at a crucial point, just after the voters put the Democrats in charge of both houses of Congress. For all practical purposes, Reagan lost a full year of his presidency, as his administration and Congress were preoccupied with investigations and a bewildering array of charges and allegations.

Of all the revelations, perhaps the most important was that Reagan was not always the strong and effective leader that his aides had portrayed him to be. Nearly every report about the Iran-contra affair produced new evidence that Reagan could be easily manipulated by White House aides, that he asked few questions, and that he did not always understand the full implications of the decisions he was asked to make. Friends and supporters said Reagan's managerial weakness was actually a strength: He never got lost in "detail," and his greatest asset was a genius for articulating the hopes and aspirations of average Americans. Even so, Reagan promised to improve his management style, and he appointed new aides who seemed likely to avoid the shortcuts that were one hallmark of the Iran-contra affair.

From the congressional viewpoint, Reagan's most important promise was to end the practice of carrying out policies in total secrecy just because they might prove unpopular. Just four days after the select House and Senate committees investigating the Iran-contra affair finished their twelve weeks of public hearings, Reagan sent Congress a letter promising to keep it informed about all covert operations. His Aug. 7, 1987, pledge did little more than reaffirm existing law, but that was not the point. Critics said the president was acknowledging that he needed to cooperate more with Congress. Reagan's supporters said Congress, too, needed to be more receptive to the president's policies.

Mistrust between the two branches of government and the Reagan team's obsession for secrecy appeared to be the fundamental flaws that produced the Iran-contra affair. The administration used covert operations of dubious legality to implement policy in hopes of avoiding public debate and criticism. But when those operations were exposed, as they inevitably would be, the debate became more intense and more politically damaging than if the administration had openly confronted the underlying issues at the outset.

Lt. Col. Oliver L. North, a central figure in the Iran-contra affair, might have summed up the essence of the administration's troubles when he said he faced a choice between "lies and lives." To protect the lives of those with whom he was dealing in Iran and Central America, North said, he was forced to lie to Congress and to others in the administration whom he did not trust.

But Secretary of State George P. Shultz, one of those deceived by North, told the Iran-contra committees that government does not need to operate on that basis. "Nobody has to think they need to lie and cheat in order to be a public servant or to work in foreign policy," he said.

Roots of the Disaster

In many ways, the Iran-contra affair was a natural outgrowth of policies and procedures implemented early in the Reagan administration. National Security Council (NSC) staffers were confident, with some reason, that their actions simply carried out decisions that Reagan made throughout his presidency.

Once in the Oval Office in 1981, Reagan moved quickly to transform his broad philosophy of anticommunism into concrete foreign policy. Relying heavily on devices such as arms sales and military aid, the president bolstered friendly regimes that were fighting communist insurgencies. More controversial was his de facto introduction of the "Reagan doctrine": extending covert aid to a broad range of guerrilla groups that were attempting to overthrow Soviet-backed governments in the Third World.

Because of a convergence of events, the preeminent examples of both Reagan policies were to be found in Central America: in El Salvador, where Washington poured hundreds of millions of dollars to prop up weak civilian governments, and in Nicaragua, where he funded a rightist insurgency in hopes of toppling the revolutionary Sandinista regime, which had moved progressively to the left.

But Reagan confronted in Congress the still-powerful remnants of what some called the "post-Vietnam syndrome": a reluctance to make overseas commitments when U.S. interests were not clearly defined and when the means to be employed appeared to fall short of whatever goals were sought. Reacting to the Vietnam War, Congress in the mid-1970s had placed dozens of restrictions on many of the tools that presidents used to carry out their overseas policies, particularly foreign aid and the deployment of U.S. troops overseas. The Reagan administration chafed at those restrictions, but never found a successful way to avoid them until the Iran-contra operations.

Almost from the opening days of the Reagan administration, El Salvador was the focus of a struggle in Washington over the extent to which the United States should rely on military means to deal with international problems. Reagan sought to use U.S. military assistance to bolster a series of Salvadoran governments beset by guerrillas on the left and "death squad" terrorists on the right. During three years of legislative disputes, Congress curtailed aid and put human rights conditions on it, effectively shifting U.S. policy toward a middle ground of moderating and stabilizing the civilian leadership in El Salvador.

The experience with El Salvador set the tone for the rest of Reagan's dealings with Congress on foreign policy — from his deployment of U.S. Marines to shore up the government of Lebanon to his continual campaign on behalf of the Nicaraguan contras. Congress at first went along with those policies but then withdrew support when it became clear that the original goals were not met.

The administration's battles were not only with Congress: Reagan never was able or willing to quell infighting and turf battles within and between the various agencies that dealt with foreign policy. Possibly more than any other recent president, Reagan was badgered constantly by "leaks" of secret information, including details of high-level policy deliberations. Although executive branch officials routinely blamed Congress for leaks, there was little doubt that the vast majority came from within the bureaucracy.

Some White House aides also concluded that the agencies of government that normally carry out foreign policy — particularly the State and Defense departments — were unwilling to take risks despite the potential for extraordinary gains. "The cost of failure is too high for them," said Adm. John M. Poindexter, Reagan's national security adviser in 1986.

Frustrated by leaks and the recalcitrance of Congress and the bureaucracy, the White House turned increasingly to covert action, both the "normal" kind conducted by the Central Intelligence Agency (CIA) through standard procedures required by laws enacted in the 1970s, and a new variety under which the National Security Council staff both formulated covert operations and implemented them.

From the White House point of view, the key virtue of both kinds of covert action was secrecy. By going covert, the White House could reduce the prospect of what Poindexter called "outside interference" with its policies.

In the first category of covert action, Reagan expanded to a massive scale an on-going program of covert military aid to Moslem rebels in Afghanistan, and in late 1981 he ordered the CIA to fashion a serious fighting force out of the band of anti-Sandinista soldiers in Nicaragua. The administration also relied on covert action to accomplish political purposes: In 1984, the secret support by the CIA reportedly played a role in ensuring that moderate José Napoleón Duarte won the presidency in El Salvador. By 1987, Reagan had signed some three dozen "findings" authorizing CIA covert operations overseas, according to testimony to the Iran-contra investigating panels.

CIA-run operations had one major drawback, as far as the White House was concerned. By law, they had to be reported to Congress, where questions and objections likely would be raised. To get around that problem, the Reagan White House developed the concept of having the NSC staff conduct operations in secret, with involvement from the CIA and other agencies only as necessary and with no notice to Congress. North, an aggressive and tireless proponent of Reagan's policies, became a one-man covert action department, working out of his office in the Old Executive Office Building adjacent to the White House. By early 1986, North was managing a small network of private and public agents who were providing unofficial aid to the contras and helping sell U.S. weapons to Iran.

What Went Wrong

The Iran and contra operations carried the administration's fondness for covert action to the extreme, while demonstrating that secrecy and ideological zeal do not necessarily make for successful policy.

Testimony before the congressional committees showed that the Iran and contra operations ultimately failed, and were exposed, because of a series of fundamental flaws within the administration. Reagan's own investigatory commission, headed by former senator John Tower, R-Texas, said the basic fault was what it euphemistically called "management style" — the president's inability or unwillingness to grasp the details of his policies and to ensure that they were carried out properly.

Reagan's 'Management Style'

As testimony before the Iran-contra panels demonstrated, the president's loose control over the White House meant that determined aides had free rein to carry out what they perceived as his ideological agenda. It was that management style that gave Poindexter, by his testimony, reason to assume that he had the right to make decisions on the president's behalf. Internal memos made clear the fact that Poindexter, North, and others all were certain they had wide latitude to implement Reagan's policies, with or without his knowledge. Poindexter, for example, insisted that the diversion of Iranian arms sales funds to the contras was merely a "detail" of the president's stated goal of aiding the Nicaraguan rebels, and so Poindexter felt free to approve it on his own.

The president's style of management had been a constant source of controversy throughout his presidency, and the Iran-contra investigations produced a confusing and somewhat conflicting picture of Reagan the boss.

In its report, the Tower Commission portrayed Reagan as a hands-off manager, one who asked few questions about what was being done in his name and who had little understanding of how his policies were being implemented. But key aides, starting with former national security adviser Robert C. McFarlane, testified to the select committees that Reagan was

Lt. Col. Oliver L. North, standing left, was sworn in July 7, 1987, to testify before the House and Senate select committees investigating the Iran-contra affair by Sen. Daniel K. Inouye, D-Hawaii, standing far right.

more than a rubber-stamp president, that he did understand substance and did have general knowledge about his staff's activities. In particular, they pointed to the fact that Reagan occasionally overruled his own advisers, as when he decided to proceed with the Iranian arms deals over the objections of Shultz and Defense Secretary Caspar W. Weinberger.

The common ground in both versions was that the president set the overall direction and tone of his administration and knew that his aides were busy carrying out his policies but asked few questions about what they were doing.

Even after the main investigations were completed, it was not clear that Reagan fully understood what had happened. In his two formal speeches acknowledging mistakes — on March 4 and Aug. 12, 1987 — the president did not say what had gone wrong, and he attributed any failure to the implementation of policies, not to the policies themselves. In his August speech, Reagan said that at times he had been "mad as a hornet," but he did not say what he was mad at, the failures or the investigations and publicity about them.

Although Reagan said on several occasions that he accepted responsibility for what had gone wrong, he appeared to accept personal blame on only one count: allowing his emotional concern about the hostages to override his judgment that making concessions to Iran was wrong.

The president never acknowledged, as many Democrats had charged, that political considerations had been another driving factor behind the Iranian deals. Under that interpretation, the White House pursued the arms sales in hopes of getting the hostages released before the November 1986 congressional midterm elections. The primary evidence for this theory was North's frantic efforts a month before the election to make deals to free all the hostages. When Iran balked, the White House accepted a plan for the release of only one or two hostages, even though the plan contained elements violating U.S. policies.

Staff, Chief Advisers Faulted

As the Tower Commission noted, the White House staff failed to compensate for Reagan's weak grasp of details. McFarlane and Poindexter, in their daily briefings, apparently gave the president only the sketchiest information on which to make decisions. For example, Reagan apparently never read a lengthy memo justifying his Jan. 17, 1986, decision to proceed with direct arms sales to Iran.

Standard procedures for making and implementing decisions were skirted: Key actors, such as Shultz and Weinberger, were excluded when they voiced objections, and there were no periodic reviews to determine whether the adopted policies were working.

Some critics, including the Tower board, charged that Shultz and Weinberger also failed in their duties. Shultz ceded jurisdiction over the Iran project to the NSC staff in mid-1985. Weinberger loyally carried out orders to supply missiles for Iran, and he reacted aggressively only when necessary to protect his own turf as secretary of defense, not to protest a policy with which he disagreed, critics said.

In the most recent manifestation of another long-term problem, White House aides and CIA director William J. Casey appeared to fashion intelligence assessments to suit their policies, instead of the other way around. Shultz and Weinberger were especially vocal in noting that the White House based decisions on Israeli-supplied intelligence projections that were at odds with official positions of the U.S. government. Casey's precise role remained one of the mysteries of the Iran-contra affair. At the very least, he appeared to overstep the traditional CIA role of providing objective information to the president and became an active exponent of particular policies.

On a more practical level, the administration's covert operations faltered because of lack of experience and sophistication on the part of those who ran them.

As the chief operative, North also was the chief fumbler, according to all available evidence. Although he fancied himself as a smooth diplomat and covert action specialist, North had little background in either field, and it showed. Rep. Ed Jenkins, D-Ga., noted perhaps the most important weakness in North's actions: his habit of making false promises to the Iranians. By misleading those with whom he was negotiating, Jenkins said, North was creating expectations that would later come back to haunt the United States.

To assist him, North recruited private agents who also were inexperienced in diplomacy and covert operations and whose prime interest was in making money.

One of the most perplexing questions to arise from the Iranian dealings was why the White House relied so heavily on exiled Iranian businessman Manucher Ghorbanifar, a man known to top CIA officials as a "talented fabricator."

Ghorbanifar may have been representing Iran or Israel or both. But his first concern, according to the evidence, was financial gain.

Aiding the Contras

U.S. involvement with the Nicaraguan contras began in late 1981, when Reagan authorized the CIA to help form a paramilitary force of about 500 fighters to harass the Sandinista government. In private briefings to Congress, the administration insisted that it was not trying to overthrow the regime in Managua but was merely hoping to use the rebels to block the flow of weapons from Nicaragua to the leftist guerrillas in nearby El Salvador. Led by rightist military officers, the guerrillas soon became known as contras, short for "counterrevolutionaries."

In spite of growing skepticism in Congress, the CIA continued to fund the contras through 1982 and 1983, providing a total of about $90 million. Amid news reports about the "secret war" in Nicaragua, the full House voted in July 1983 to cut off that funding. That move failed, but it led that October to the imposition of an absolute $24 million limit on CIA aid to the rebels in fiscal year 1984.

Congress Bans Aid

In April 1984, the *Wall Street Journal* revealed that the CIA had hired Latin American agents to mine the harbors of Nicaragua on behalf of the contras. That report created an uproar in Congress, largely because leaders of the Senate Intelligence Committee insisted they had never been told about the mining.

Political support for aid to the contras drained rapidly, and in October 1984 Congress voted into law the most restrictive of several versions of the "Boland amendment." Named after House Intelligence Committee chairman Edward P. Boland, D-Mass., it barred all aid to the contras by the CIA, Pentagon, or other agencies "involved in intelligence activities." The effect of the amendment was to cut off official U.S. support from mid-1984 until August 1985, when Congress voted "humanitarian" or nonmilitary aid to the contras.

As it became clear in 1984 that Congress would block further contra aid, North privately began recruiting agents to help the rebels, in place of the U.S. government. One of his first recruits was retired Air Force major general Richard V. Secord, who North said was recommended by Casey.

The administration also began seeking out alternative sources of financing for the contras. McFarlane approached Saudi Arabian King Fahd, who eventually agreed to provide $1 million a month. Fahd later upped his contribution and by 1985 had provided nearly $32 million. The administration also approached Taiwan, which gave $2 million to the contras, and gave serious consideration to asking South Africa to aid the contras. At the State Department's request, Brunei agreed to donate $10 million, but the money was sent mistakenly to the wrong Swiss bank account and never reached the contras.

North Fills Void

With the CIA phasing out of the contra-aid program, North quickly phased himself in. Working closely with Casey, North provided the contras with intelligence information and advice on military tactics. Through private agents such as Secord, North also arranged for the contras to buy several major covert shipments of arms from China, Poland, and other countries. The contras paid cash for those arms, using money supplied by the Saudis. Secord and his partner, Iranian-American businessman Albert Hakim, soon built up a network of secret Swiss bank accounts, filled with the profits from their arms sales to the contras. They later used those accounts to handle some $30 million generated by the Iranian arms sales.

North also began working closely with a group of conservative activists in Washington who were experts at raising money and spending it. Relying on North's ability to tell the contras' story compellingly, Washington fund-raiser Carl R. "Spitz" Channell generated several million dollars in contributions from wealthy Americans, ostensibly for the contra cause. But much of the money went to support Channell's operations, along with a closely associated public relations firm headed by Richard R. Miller. Channell and Miller later pleaded guilty to tax fraud charges related to their contra-aid activities.

North testified that in January 1986 Ghorbanifar proposed aiding the contras with some of the profits from U.S. arms sales to Iran. North acknowledged that Ghorbanifar made the proposal as an incentive to encourage the Reagan administration to continue the sales. Poindexter quickly approved the idea but said he never told the president.

By the end of February 1986, the Secord and Hakim accounts were filled with millions of dollars generated by the various covert operations. Secord used some of the money to rent and buy airplanes and to hire pilots and support crews for a sophisticated operation that would deliver supplies to the contras inside Nicaragua. After many false starts, the air drops began in April and continued sporadically through the summer and into early fall. Secord testified that he spent about $3.5 million aiding the contras from the Iranian arms sale profits.

North's activities on behalf of the contras were an open secret in Washington and the subject of several newspaper stories in mid-1986. But when the House Intelligence Committee privately questioned him, North said he was complying with the Boland amendment. North later told the Iran-contra committees he justified that contention on the grounds that the Boland amendment barred involvement with the contras only by U.S. intelligence agencies, not by the NSC staff. Contra-aid supporters on the select committees embraced that justification, but Boland and other administration critics said North was violating at least the spirit of the law and probably was overstepping the letter of it. McFarlane said he assumed that the Boland law applied to the NSC staff, but Poindexter, his successor, said he had the opposite view.

On Oct. 5, 1986, Nicaraguan troops shot down a supply plane; all on board were killed except loading specialist Eugene Hasenfus, a U.S. civilian hired by the Secord network. Captured by Nicaragua, Hasenfus later claimed that the contra-aid supply network was run by the CIA.

The downing of the Hasenfus plane, coupled with revelation a month later of the arms sales to Iran, ultimately led to exposure of the private contra-aid network that North and Secord had built and managed. In testimony shortly after the Hasenfus plane went down, State Department and CIA officials insisted that the U.S. government had no involvement with it, either directly or indirectly. Those officials later acknowledged that their denials were misleading, at best.

Involvement with Iran

Like Nicaragua, Iran always had presented special problems for the Reagan administration. Reagan had been elected president in 1980 in part because the voters were disgusted with President Carter's inability to free the

Americans who were held hostage at the U.S. Embassy in Tehran, and because Reagan projected the image of someone who knew what to do.

But once the embassy hostages were freed — through no active involvement by Reagan — Iran practically disappeared from the new administration's map. Aside from ritual denunciations of terrorism and calls for an end to the Persian Gulf war between Iran and Iraq, the administration appeared to be acting as if the radical Islamic regime in Tehran did not exist. That attitude persisted in spite of clear evidence that Iran played a major role in the October 1983 terrorist bombing that killed more than 240 U.S. Marines stationed in Beirut on a futile "peace-keeping" mission.

As pro-Iranian groups in Lebanon kidnapped one American after another, Reagan seemed to stand by helplessly, just as Carter had done. When asked about the hostages, Reagan and his aides said they were doing everything possible short of making deals with the hostage-takers. They also insisted that Reagan faced a more difficult situation than did Carter, since the hostages in Lebanon were held by shadowy groups that did not advertise their whereabouts, while the embassy hostages had been under the effective control of a government with which the United States could negotiate.

Israeli Arms Sales

In the meantime, some administration officials apparently viewed with sympathy Israel's attempts to use selective arms sales to curry favor with conservative military elements in Iran. Israel had had close ties to Iran before Shah Mohammed Reza Pahlavi was ousted in 1979. According to various reports, Israel as early as 1981 began supplying small quantities of spare parts and other military gear to the Iranian army in hopes of bolstering the factions opposed to the excesses of the radical Islamic regime of the Ayatollah Ruhollah Khomeini. There also was speculation that Israel wanted to prolong the Iran-Iraq War, with the particular goal of sapping the military strength of Iraq, an Arab country.

While U.S. intelligence officials knew that Israel was supplying military items to Iran, the Iran-contra hearings left unclear whether Washington in the early 1980s gave formal approval or merely signaled Israel to be cautious. Under U.S. arms sale laws, Israel was required to get official permission from Washington before shipping American-made weapons to another country, but Israel apparently never did so.

The U.S. acquiescence in the Israeli sales was all the more ironic in that it occurred in spite of Reagan's embargo on direct arms sales to Iran and an aggressive campaign by the administration to halt arms exports by all countries to Iran. Under the rubric "Operation Staunch," the Reagan administration sent a series of special ambassadors to foreign capitals pleading for a halt to the arming of Iran. While it succeeded in blocking several planned shipments by West European countries, the effort had little overall impact on the flow of arms to Iran, which turned to China and Soviet-bloc countries for its military supplies.

Iran Policy Reappraised

As early as 1984, administration officials began raising questions about the underlying assumption of U.S. policy toward Iran: that little or nothing could be done to encourage moderation in Tehran until the aged Khomeini died. An NSC-initiated study examined that assumption in late 1984 and concluded that it was essentially correct.

The CIA in 1985 received new reports about potential instability in Iran, coupled with the possibility of renewed Soviet maneuvering to gain influence there. Based on those reports, the NSC produced a new study, on its own, which suggested a fundamental change in policy. The United States should encourage U.S. allies to help Iran meet its "import requirements," including those for weapons, in hopes of reducing Tehran's dependence on the Soviet Union. That proposal drew sharp rebukes from Shultz and Weinberger; the latter scribbled on his copy that encouraging arms sales to Iran was "absurd" and "roughly like inviting Quaddafi over for a cozy lunch."

The opposition by Shultz and Weinberger killed the NSC proposal for an official realignment of policy toward Iran; the study was never put in final form for submission to the president. But other events at the same time ensured that the essential thrust of the NSC draft became de facto U.S. policy. Throughout early and mid-1985, NSC consultant Michael Ledeen held a series of meetings with Israeli officials to discuss the need to gather more information about Iran. Those meetings apparently led Israel to conclude that Washington was ready for a broader review of its policy toward Iran. The White House also was impressed in June when a top Iranian official — Speaker of the Parliament Ali Akbar Hashemi Rafsanjani — played a role in freeing Americans taken hostage after the hijacking of a TWA jetliner to Lebanon.

The Iranian role in the TWA crisis, and the possibility that Iran might be willing to help gain the release of six other American hostages in Lebanon, proved irresistible to Reagan.

In spite of his tough talk about Iran and terrorism, Reagan by 1985 apparently was willing to take extraordinary steps to get the hostages released. Against the advice of many of his aides, the president had been meeting regularly with members of hostage families, many of whom made emotional pleas with him to be more aggressive in looking for ways to win freedom for the hostages. Several officials later said Reagan should not have met with the families because doing so put him under so much stress that he allowed his emotions to override his judgment.

It was in that context that a pattern began to emerge: Israel approached the United States with proposals for weapons sales to Iran, and White House aides presented the idea to Reagan as a diplomatic move aimed at bolstering moderates there. But the aides got the president's attention by holding out the prospect of winning freedom for the hostages.

Events moved rapidly during the rest of 1985, with the administration accepting dramatic changes in policy toward Iran. First, according to McFarlane's testimony, Reagan in August approved Israeli shipments of TOW antitank missiles to Iran. Two shipments in August and September, totaling 508 missiles, resulted in the release of one American hostage from Lebanon, the Rev. Benjamin F. Weir. Because Iran paid more than triple the market price for the missiles, the shipments also produced huge profits for the Israeli arms dealers who handled them.

November 1985 Hawk Shipment

Three months later, in November, Israel proposed and the White House approved a major shipment of Hawk antiaircraft missiles to Iran. That shipment became so fouled up that only 18 missiles ever arrived in Iran, and then only because the CIA, at North's request, provided one of its "proprietary" airlines to handle the job. No hostages were released in exchange for the shipment, although the White House had expected that all five Americans then held in Lebanon would be freed. Iran claimed the missiles were inadequate and demanded that the United States take them back, which it did in 1986.

The November shipment of Hawks later took on great legal and political significance, since Reagan had not given the legally required advance approval of CIA involvement and because Congress had not been told — as required by law — that Israel had transferred U.S.-made weapons to another country. To cover the CIA's tracks, Deputy Director John N. McMahon ordered the drafting of a presidential "finding" retroactively authorizing agency participation in the shipment. Poindexter testified that Reagan signed the finding on Dec. 5, 1985. But Poindexter said he destroyed the document a year later because its stated focus on releasing hostages might prove "embarrassing" to the president if ever revealed.

The November Hawk shipment was important in another respect: It marked the first involvement in the Iranian deals by North and Secord, who North had recruited to aid the contras. At North's request, Secord spent a week in Lisbon trying unsuccessfully to route the shipment from Israel through Portugal to Iran.

On Dec. 6, 1985, about 10 days after the Hawk shipment was completed, Reagan and his top aides held their first serious discussion about the Iran initiative. Shultz and Weinberger argued strenuously against proceeding with additional arms deals that Israel was planning, and they left the White House meeting assuming that there would be none. McFarlane, who days before had handed in his resignation because of longstanding turf battles within the White House, then flew to London for meetings with Ghorbanifar, whom Israel had been pressing the United States to use in its dealings with Tehran. McFarlane said he was shocked by Ghorbanifar's lies and misrepresentations, and he returned to Washington convinced that the Iran initiative should be ended. Hearing of Ghorbanifar's involvement, top CIA officials had him take a lie detector test, which he flunked.

But North argued for continuing the initiative, and Israel in January 1986 sent a representative to Washington who convinced Poindexter to carry on with the Iranian arms deals through Ghorbanifar. Israel's eagerness to get the United States involved was demonstrated by its willingness to risk sending another 500 of its TOW missiles to Iran in hopes of getting more U.S. hostages released. Poindexter later testified that he assumed Israel wanted the United States to give formal approval to the arms sales it had long been making to Iran. Shultz was more blunt, saying in a later White House meeting that Israel had "suckered" the United States into going along with its arms sales.

January 1986 'Finding'

After another inconclusive meeting among the president and his top aides, Reagan on Jan. 17, 1986, signed a finding that authorized the CIA, working through third parties, to sell arms to Iran. The third parties turned out to be Ghorbanifar and Secord. One important and unusual provision of the finding was a directive that Congress not be told about it.

A key factor in Reagan's decision apparently was an informal intelligence assessment, provided by Poindexter and CIA director Casey, concluding that Iran was the weaker of the two parties in the Iran-Iraq War. That assessment matched the official Israeli view of the war, but it was directly opposite of the position embraced by all U.S. intelligence agencies. In later private meetings, Reagan cited the alleged Iranian military weakness as one justification for the arms sales.

Reagan's signature on the Jan. 17 finding set off a series of U.S.-Iranian negotiations and arms deals. Early in 1986, North and Ghorbanifar were the principal actors, meeting secretly at various locations in Europe to arrange arms sales, supposedly to be accompanied by the release of hostages.

The first sale, of 1,000 TOW missiles in February, failed to produce a hostage release. Nevertheless, based on Ghorbanifar's assurances that Iran was ready for better relations, the White House moved ahead with plans for the next step up: a direct meeting in Tehran between high-level U.S. and Iranian officials. That meeting came in May, when McFarlane, North, and two other officials traveled to Tehran and spent three frustrating days negotiating with midlevel Iranian functionaries. McFarlane took with him a pallet of spare parts for Hawk missiles that Iran already owned. Negotiations about a larger shipment of parts collapsed because Iran was willing to release only two hostages and McFarlane insisted on the release of all five Americans then held in Lebanon.

The failure of the McFarlane mission dimmed White House enthusiasm for the Iran initiative, but only for a while. Casey, Poindexter, and others began talking about mounting a rescue mission to free the hostages, and North pursued another scheme of using Drug Enforcement Administration agents to locate the hostages and then bribe the Lebanese captors into releasing them.

In the meantime, some Iranian leaders appeared to be reconsidering the hardline stance that had led to collapse of the McFarlane mission. To get things moving again, Iran arranged in July 1986 for the release of another hostage, the Rev. Lawrence Jenco. In response, Reagan approved the shipment to Iran of another 12 pallets of Hawk spare parts.

Contact with 'Second Channel'

After months of searching for an alternative to Ghorbanifar as an intermediary with Iran, Secord and Hakim in August made contact with a so-called "second channel," who turned out to be a relative of Rafsanjani. He led an Iranian delegation to Washington for secret talks with North and others in mid-September, and those discussions led to one final arms sale in October: 500 more TOW missiles sent to Iran by Israel in exchange for release of hostage David P. Jacobsen.

As part of the October deal, the White House agreed to a nine-point plan, negotiated by Hakim, that included a promise to seek release of seventeen terrorists imprisoned in Kuwait for attacking Western embassies. Poindexter testified that he got Reagan's approval for that plan, even though it was contrary to the stated U.S. policy of demanding that Kuwait keep the seventeen terrorists in prison. The White House denied that Reagan ever approved the plan, however, and Shultz said Reagan was astonished to hear about it.

The dumping of Ghorbanifar relieved the United States of the necessity of dealing with an untrustworthy intermediary, but it may have planted the seeds for the ultimate disclosure of the Iranian arms deals. On November 3, 1986, one day after Jacobsen was released, a pro-Syrian newspaper in Lebanon revealed McFarlane's trip to Tehran. Rafsanjani immediately confirmed the report, insisting that Iran had rejected the U.S. overtures. The source of information for the Lebanese newspaper was not revealed, but many officials in Washington were convinced that Ghorbanifar had something to do with the disclosure — a charge he heatedly denied.

Aftermath of Disclosure

The administration's initial response to the disclosure was to deny that it had been dealing with Iran. Reagan told reporters there was "no foundation" to the reports. Poindexter also instructed White House spokesman Larry Speakes to say that the U.S. arms embargo against Iran remained in effect.

But as the days passed and as news reports produced a deluge of information — some accurate and some misleading — about U.S. dealings with Iran, administration officials became involved in a tug of war. Those who had opposed the initiative argued for prompt and full disclosure of the facts in hopes of reducing the ultimate political damage, while Poindexter insisted on trying to keep as much information secret as possible. Reagan, according to notes of White House meetings, apparently was caught in the middle. At one key session on Nov. 10, he told his aides: "We must say something but not much." White House officials later said Reagan feared that publicity would kill any chance of winning the release of more hostages.

One of the administration's problems at the time was a lack of hard information about what had happened. Because officials made decisions almost casually and kept few formal records, there were conflicting recollections about what happened when. In an attempt to put the facts together, North and others began work in mid-November on a chronology. By Nov. 20, the NSC staff had produced at least a dozen versions; some contained nearly all the essential facts and were labelled "maximum version," while others merely skimmed the surface.

McFarlane, later said that he assumed one purpose of the exercise was to "protect" the president by minimizing his role. None of the chronologies mentioned Reagan's approval of the 1985 Israeli shipments, and none reported that money from the Iranian arms sales had been diverted to Secord's contra-aid network. In fact, the chronologies did not mention Secord at all.

Reagan made two attempts to explain the arms sales, first in a speech from the Oval Office on Nov. 13 and then in a news conference on Nov. 19. From a political standpoint, both efforts were disasters, raising more questions than they answered. The president's aides watched in disbelief as Reagan insisted during the press conference that the United States had not worked with Israel during the Iran arms deals. Minutes after the questioning ended, the White House issued a statement retracting that claim.

Congress in the meantime was demanding information, and the administration agreed that Casey and Poindexter would privately, and separately, brief the House and Senate Intelligence committees on Nov. 21. The preparations for those briefings exposed, perhaps for the first time, the extent of uncertainty within the administration about the facts, especially about Israel's November 1985 shipment of Hawks to Iran.

At an important White House meeting on Nov. 20, called to review Casey's proposed written testimony, North suggested a change stating that no one in the U.S. government knew until January 1986 that the November shipment included weapons. In effect, North was asking his colleagues to stand by a cover story developed in 1985 that Israel had shipped oil drilling equipment to Iran. Poindexter and Casey, the only others in the room who knew for certain that North's suggested statement was wrong, reportedly said nothing.

North told the Iran-contra committees that he and Casey later met privately and "fixed" the testimony. He never explained just how it was fixed, but the next day Casey did not tell the Intelligence committees that Israel had shipped the Hawk missiles to Iran.

North also testified to the Iran-contra committees that he and Casey previously had devised a "fall guy plan" to limit the political damage should word of the diversion ever be made public. Under that plan, North was to take full responsibility, he said. But North said Casey told him that Poindexter also would have to share blame because North was not senior enough to have made all the decisions.

Looking for Facts

As an attempt to cover up the 1985 Hawk shipment a year before, the November 20 White House meeting failed, because State and Justice department officials raised the alarm. Hours after the meeting, Shultz went directly to Reagan and told him that parts of Casey's proposed testimony were untrue. Alerted by his aides, Attorney General Edwin Meese III gave Reagan the same message on Nov. 21 and got approval to conduct a "fact-finding inquiry."

The true nature and extent of Meese's inquiry was a matter of sharp debate during the Iran-contra hearings and may continue to be so for years to come. Meese insisted that he was merely trying to straighten out conflicts in the recollections of various top officials and that he had no reason to look for criminal wrongdoing. Critics said Meese and his aides were too slow to recognize that a coverup was under way. Warren B. Rudman, R-N.H., vice chairman of the Senate Iran-contra committee, charged that Meese had "telegraphed" his moves to North and Poindexter, who then destroyed or altered incriminating documents. As Meese was proceeding, North shredded dozens, if not hundreds, of memos, telephone logs, and reports. He also instructed his secretary, Fawn Hall, to make substantial changes in other memos discussing his involvement with the contras. Poindexter testified that he, too, destroyed documents, including the December 1985 finding by which Reagan retroactively approved the Israeli Hawk shipment.

Diversion Memo Discovered

However haphazard it may have been, Meese's investigation did turn up the most damaging document of all: a memo North had written the previous April saying that $12 million from a proposed Iranian arms sale would be used to aid the contras. Confronted with the memo on Nov. 23, North acknowledged that he had written it and that money had been diverted to the contras. He also pleaded with Meese to keep those facts secret.

Meese testified that he took the information to Reagan on Nov. 24, who agreed with him that it would be necessary to make the diversion public. At a White House press conference the next day, Reagan announced that he had not been "fully informed" about one aspect of the Iranian arms deals and that, as a result, Poindexter had agreed to resign and North had been fired. The last part apparently came as news to North, who already had sent Poindexter a computer message resigning his post. Reagan refused to answer questions, but Meese, taking over the press conference, revealed the diversion and estimated it at $10-$30 million.

As White House officials knew it would, the connection between Iran and the contras created a sensation, transforming a controversy about flawed policy into a major political scandal. Hoping to stem at least some of the inevitable criticism, Reagan appointed a prestigious board to review the facts, headed by Tower; other members were former senator and secretary of state Edmund S. Muskie and former national security adviser and retired lieutenant general Brent Scowcroft. At first, Reagan gave the panel only 60 days to investigate and issue a report, but the members found the task too big and demanded, and got, until the following February.

Reagan also chose as his new national security adviser Frank C. Carlucci, a long-time foreign policy official who was widely respected in Washington.

Pressure from Capitol Hill

The appointment of the Tower board did not accomplish its primary purpose, that of quelling the demands on Capitol Hill for separate inquiries. Under political pressure, Reagan agreed to request appointment of an independent counsel, or special prosecutor, and a three-judge panel chose retired federal judge Lawrence E. Walsh, an Oklahoma Republican.

Congress began its own multiple investigations. The House and Senate Intelligence committees held closed-door hearings with key participants throughout late November and early December. The House Foreign Affairs Committee held two dramatic days of public hearings, during which North and Poindexter cited their Fifth Amendment privileges in refusing to testify.

Congressional leaders also agreed in December to appoint select committees to hold full hearings into the Iran-contra affair. Republicans wanted a limited inquiry that would answer questions quickly and curtail the political damage to their party. Democrats, who had just taken control of the Senate, slowed the process and made it clear that any inquiry would be thorough and run well into 1987.

Senate leaders named Daniel K. Inouye, D-Hawaii, and Rudman to head their eleven-member committee, and House leaders put Lee H. Hamilton, D-Ind., and Dick Cheney, R-Wyo., in charge of their fifteen-member committee.

Even before the select committees could get their investigations fully under way, the public got two hefty doses of facts that answered many of the outstanding questions. First, after a partisan battle over the timing of a report, the Senate Intelligence Committee in late January 1987 made public a summary of its findings. Although crammed with details, the report contained no conclusions and thus was of limited help in advancing public understanding of what had happened and why.

Tower Commission Report

The Tower Commission report, released Feb. 26, 1987, provided a much more complete picture of the Iran-contra affair — in large part because the commission's computer experts had unearthed dozens of internal White House memos that documented the activities of North, Poindexter, and others on an almost daily basis.

While cautiously worded, the Tower report served up a damning indictment of failures by Reagan and his aides throughout the events of the Iran-contra affair. Reagan, the Tower board said, had not paid close attention to what his aides were doing and had not asked the kinds of questions that would have revealed problems in time to correct them. Given the president's inattention to detail — which the board gingerly described as his "management style" — the White House staff failed to take compensating steps, such as taking troublesome issues to him for his review.

Introducing the Tower board at a press conference minutes after getting the report, Reagan clearly was stunned and confused; he stumbled in reading a prepared statement and rushed from the room to avoid questions from reporters. But Reagan quickly recovered the next day, effectively firing his chief of staff, Donald T. Regan, who the Tower panel had criticized for allowing "chaos" to descend upon the White House following

President Reagan displayed a copy of the Tower Commission report during a televised address August 12, 1987. The president had promised to speak to the nation about the Iran-contra affair at the conclusion of the congressional hearings.

disclosure of the Iranian arms sales. Reagan named former Senate majority leader Howard H. Baker, Jr., R-Tenn., to take Regan's place — an appointment that produced sighs of relief all over Capitol Hill, where Baker was highly popular.

A week later, on March 4, Reagan made yet another effort to explain the Iran initiative. In a prime-time speech, he said he accepted responsibility for any failures, but he did not apologize, as many supporters had encouraged him to do. Reagan also insisted that any flaws were in the "implementation" of his policies, not in the policies themselves.

The president acknowledged for the first time that the United States had traded arms for hostages. Recalling his denial the previous November of arms-for-hostages swaps, Reagan said: "My heart and my best intentions still tell me that is true, but the facts and the evidence tell me it is not."

Congressional Hearings

From the outset, it was clear that the congressional investigation into the Iran-contra affair would be plagued with several problems, chief among them partisanship and the natural inclination of the public to compare it unfavorably with the Watergate probe of 1973-74.

Attempting to reduce partisan feuding, the congressional leaders agreed to limited agendas and tight time schedules for the investigations. The committees were to look into only the Iran arms sales and the administration's covert operations in support of the contras, and were to issue reports by late summer or early fall. They were not directed to examine the full range of administration foreign policies, nor where they to concentrate on other contra-related issues, such as alleged human rights violations by the contras or news media reports that certain contra leaders financed their operations with proceeds from drug smuggling.

Congressional leaders also made it clear that they did not expect the select committees to turn up evidence that might force the president from office — as the Senate Watergate committee had done more than a decade earlier.

The only issue that even raised the question of illegal action on the president's part was the diversion and whether he had approved it. Reagan insisted at every point that he knew nothing of the diversion until Meese told him about it on Nov. 24, 1986, but opinion polls consistently showed that a majority of Americans did not believe him. Poindexter was considered the only person who could provide solid evidence refuting Reagan, but few members of the select committees expected him to do so.

Partly for that reason, congressional Democrats sought early in 1987 to play down the prospects of a direct confrontation between Congress and the president. House majority leader Thomas Foley, D-Wash., a member of the select committee, noted that memories of the trauma caused by Watergate would make it more difficult to consider impeachment. Besides that, Foley and others noted, Reagan was a popular and likable president, and Nixon had been neither.

The select committees spent the first four months of 1987 getting ready for hearings, reviewing documents, and privately interviewing hundreds of witnesses. Among them was Poindexter, who told a small group of committee lawyers and members on May 2 that he had never told Reagan about the diversion. Under an agreement with Independent Counsel Walsh, the committees sealed Poindexter's testimony and kept it secret. Walsh wanted more time to gather evidence against Poindexter, who would be testifying to the committees in public under a grant of limited immunity.

Perhaps the most important decision the committees made during the start-up period was to hold joint public hearings, thus avoiding the spectacle of two panels competing for witnesses and news coverage.

The committees began their public hearings May 5 with testimony by Secord. In 12 weeks of hearings that lasted until early August, the committees heard from 32 witnesses, several of whom received limited immunity against prosecution for their testimony.

The hearings filled in many of the details of the Iran-contra affair, painting a picture of twin covert operations run by the NSC staff and private agents with little supervision by either the president or his senior foreign policy advisers. Nearly every day produced important revelations, ranging from Secord's estimate that only about $3.5 million actually had been diverted to the contras, to Hall's dramatic description of how she altered important memos at North's request and helped him shred dozens of other documents.

The strong partisan inclination of some committee members also produced a pattern resembling two sets of hearings: The six House Republicans, joined by Sen. Orrin Hatch, R-Utah, staunchly defended Reagan at every turn and sought to play down the severity of administration mistakes, while most Democrats and some Republican members of the Senate panel sought to conduct a more aggressive investigation.

The most interesting split was among the Republicans. The House GOP members were accustomed to their minority status and to using the political version of guerrilla warfare to get attention. Doing what came naturally, they attempted to derail the hearings from an investigatory track by making lengthy speeches defending Reagan and condemning Congress for interfering in his foreign policy. But three Republican senators — Rudman, William S. Cohen of Maine, and Paul Trible of Virginia — sought to distance their party from the failures of the Iran-contra affair. Rudman and Trible, in particular, targeted Secord and Hakim as likely villains and devoted much of their attention to the profits those two men may have made on the various arms deals.

Dramatic Testimony

For millions of Americans, however, the focal point of the hearings was North, who spent nearly six days at the witness table in July. Combative and articulate in his self-defense, North portrayed himself as a loyal soldier who had done only what was authorized and who had sought merely to serve his president. North's forceful presentation — aided by his appearance in a Marine Corps uniform adorned with medals — created a sensation. Opinion polls suddenly showed that many regarded him as a "hero," and popular magazines promoted "Olliemania." Hundreds of visitors, many wearing "Ollie North for President" T-shirts, waited in line for up to four hours to get into the hearings.

North's popularity put the committees on the defensive, especially the hard-driving lawyers who headed the investigation, Senate counsel Arthur L. Liman and House counsel John W. Nields, Jr. Republican defenders of Reagan were thrilled to find a witness who could articulate the president's foreign policy goals better than the president ever could. North received thousands of congratulatory telegrams, many condemning the committees.

North was followed to the witness table by Poindexter, who in a matter of minutes quelled the minuscule chance that Reagan would be impeached. Poindexter testified that he had never told Reagan about the diversion of funds to the contras. "On this whole issue, you know, the buck stops here with me," he said.

Poindexter testified that he viewed the diversion merely as an implementation "detail" of Reagan's overall policy of aiding the contras and so saw no need to tell the president about it. But Poindexter also said he realized that the diversion would be controversial if revealed; by not telling Reagan, Poindexter said he had hoped to protect the president politically.

Committee Republicans, some of whom had heard Poindexter testify nearly three months before in private, greeted the statement as the ultimate vindication of Reagan's position. Several Democrats expressed skepticism, and a few insisted that he was not telling the truth, but all acknowledged that there was no way of proving that Poindexter was lying.

Committee members were unanimous, however, in condemning Poindexter for keeping such important information from the president. "It's my view that presidents ought to be allowed to create their own disasters," Rudman lectured Poindexter. "Nobody else ought to do it for them."

The remaining weeks of the hearings continued to produce dramatic testimony: Meese's defensive explanation of his inquiry the previous November; Shultz's gripping description of a "battle royal" in the administration over how much information to make public; Regan's claim that he knew little about the Iranian arms deals, in spite of a widespread assumption that he had run the White House with an iron fist; and Weinberger's devastating critique of the White House contention that the United States could bolster Iranian moderates by selling them weapons.

Drawing Conclusions

In closing statements summarizing the hearings, the four leaders of the committees stressed the dangers of bypassing standard procedures, allowing unelected aides to have too much power, and putting public policy in the hands of private agents. The leaders also acknowledged that Congress shared a measure of the blame and said the hearings demonstrated the need for cooperation between the legislative and executive branches of government.

Concentrating their fire on White House aides and private agents, the committee leaders virtually ignored Reagan's role in the Iran-contra affair. Inouye said the hearings had told "a chilling story, a story of deceit and duplicity and the arrogant disregard of the rule of law." But he did not mention Reagan's involvement in any of those things. Hamilton criticized the president only for failing to make "clean and crisp" decisions and for not knowing what his aides were doing.

In the weeks following the hearings, the committees turned their attention to the drafting of a report. Members said they assumed they could get relatively quick agreement on the basic facts of what had happened but would face a political struggle when it came to drawing conclusions and making recommendations for corrective action.

There appeared to be broad agreement that the committees should not propose a wholesale rewriting of the laws dealing with the making and implementation of foreign policy. Instead, members said they were more likely to recommend limited steps such as tightening the requirements for presidents to tell Congress about covert operations, arms sales, and other foreign policy actions.

Reagan's Aug. 7 letter to leaders of the Senate Intelligence Committee promising to tell Congress in advance about covert operations was one attempt to head off restrictive legislation. But the president said that under "extraordinary circumstances" he might have to delay notice to Congress for two working days. Senate Intelligence chairman David L. Boren, D-Okla., who had sought a firm notification promise from the president, said the commitment demonstrated "a good first step" toward a better relationship between the White House and Congress.

Five days later, on Aug. 12, Reagan went on national television to review the lessons learned in the Iran-contra affair. While again taking responsibility for any mistakes made by his aides, the president appeared to minimize the seriousness of the Iran-contra affair and insisted he had already corrected any flaws in White House operations.

In response, Democratic leaders sought to remind the public that a Republican administration had made serious mistakes. But the Democrats also wanted to avoid appearing to be too eager to benefit from the president's troubles.

"Let there be no misunderstanding," Sen. George J. Mitchell, D-Maine, said in response to Reagan's speech. "The mistakes were not only in the execution of policies. The major mistakes were in the policies themselves. And the policies were the president's."

However, Mitchell immediately said that the Iran-contra affair "should be put behind us." ▮

Reagan Promises Congress He'll Tighten Covert Rules

Seeking to head off stiff new laws limiting his flexibility to carry out foreign policy, President Reagan promised to do a better job of telling Congress about covert operations.

The president's promise came in the wake of the Iran-contra inquiry, which showed that his administration exploited loopholes and inconsistencies in current laws governing covert actions and foreign arms sales.

Reagan and leaders of the Senate Intelligence Committee on Aug. 7, 1987, announced agreement on new covert operation standards and on procedures for telling Congress about them. As required by current law, that notice would be given in advance for most operations; but Reagan agreed to notify Congress within two days after ordering covert actions in emergencies.

In a letter, Reagan told Senate committee Chairman David L. Boren, D-Okla., and Vice Chairman William S. Cohen, R-Maine, that he supported six proposals to tighten regulations over covert operations. Reagan said he hoped the ideas would produce "a more positive partnership" between Congress and the executive branch.

Boren called the letter a "good first step" and Cohen said it showed a "change in attitude" by the president. But both said they would wait to see how Reagan implements the proposals before deciding whether to support legislation on the issue. Cohen said Reagan would have no reason to oppose legislation that went no further than Reagan's letter.

Others said Congress must act on its own rather than accept written promises. "Executive orders are not good enough," said Senate Majority Leader Robert C. Byrd, D-W.Va.

Covert Actions

As a result of revelations in the mid-1970s of abuses, Congress enacted two major requirements for covert operations by the CIA: They must be approved personally by the president, and they must be reported to Congress.

The Hughes-Ryan amendment of 1974 required the president to "find" that each covert operation is necessary for the national security, and it said all "appropriate" congressional committees must be notified. Congress modified that law in 1980, reducing to two (House and Senate Intelligence) the number of committees that must be told about covert operations.

Reagan issued his own guidelines in 1981 and 1985 governing covert actions, but some were skirted in the Iran-contra operations.

The major covert-action issues:

• **Notice to Congress.** As rewritten in 1980, intelligence law required the president to report covert actions in advance to the House and Senate Intelligence panels. However, in "extraordinary circumstances," the president could limit notice to the so-called "gang of eight": the Speaker and minority leader of the House, the majority and minority leaders of the Senate, and the chairmen and ranking minority members of the two Intelligence panels. Since 1980, Presidents Carter and Reagan had given the full Intelligence committees advance notice of most covert operations.

While demanding advance notice as a general rule, the 1980 law (PL 96-450) stated there might be cases in which the president could not or would not reveal covert actions beforehand. Then, he must report to Congress "in a timely fashion."

David L. Boren, D-Okla., chairman of the Senate Intelligence Committee, called the president's letter on covert notification a "good first step."

The "timely fashion" phrase never had been defined clearly. In the Iran case, the Reagan administration interpreted the law as giving the president the right to defer notice indefinitely. Reagan signed a finding on Jan. 17, 1986, authorizing arms sales to Iran, and did not tell Congress about it until the sales became known in November.

One obvious way of tightening the law would be for Congress to try to require the president to notify Congress in advance of all covert operations, without exception. Such a step would be extremely controversial, and any president likely would insist that it was an unconstitutional infringement on his executive powers.

Reagan promised to give advance notice. But if "exceptional circumstances" prevented prior notice, Reagan said he would report to Congress within two working days.

Boren called his pledge "the most important" item in Reagan's letter. The administration in the past had opposed putting in the law any inflexible notice requirement.

• **The NSC staff and covert operations.** Iran-contra committee members agreed unanimously on few things; one was that the National Security Council (NSC) staff should not run covert operations, as did Lt. Col. Oliver L. North. Reagan already had barred future NSC management of covert operations. But there was little agreement in Congress about whether such a ban should be put in law.

• **Retroactive findings.** Most legal experts who testified before the Iran-contra panels said the president should give formal approval to covert operations before they begin, not afterward.

In December 1985, however, Reagan signed a finding giving retroactive approval to the CIA's involvement in an Israeli arms shipment to Iran, according to former national security adviser John M. Poindexter. Reagan's letter said he opposed retroactive findings.

• **Written findings.** Reagan

Sidestepping a Mine Field: Executive Privilege

Executive privilege — the issue that took the Watergate case all the way to the Supreme Court in 1974 — never arose in the Iran-contra affair, simply because President Reagan chose to avoid the political struggle that helped doom President Nixon. Without so much as a legal brief being filed, Reagan agreed in the early stages of the Iran-contra affair to make his aides and papers available to investigating arms of Congress and the courts.

Appearing before reporters Dec. 2, 1986, Reagan promised to "cooperate fully" with Congress because of its "important oversight and legislative" functions. Although he did not say it in so many words, Reagan's statement meant that, for the purposes of Iran-contra inquiries, he was waiving his claim to executive privilege: the traditional assertion that presidents have a right to keep confidential all discussions with their aides and all papers relating to those talks.

Reagan avoided issue . . .

At the outset of the Senate Watergate Committee's inquiry in 1973, Nixon said he was waiving executive privilege for "any testimony concerning possible criminal conduct or discussions of possible criminal conduct."

But Nixon later fought requests by the committee and by the Watergate special prosecutor for tape recordings of his White House conversations. In July 1974, the Supreme Court ordered Nixon to turn those tapes over to the special prosecutor. While affirming the principle of executive privilege, the court ruled that the president's assertion of it "must yield to the demonstrated specific need for evidence in a pending criminal trial."

Two weeks after the court ruled, Nixon made public the transcripts of three incriminating tapes; three days later he resigned to avoid certain impeachment.

Reagan's disclosures had not been nearly so embarrassing or incriminating as Nixon's — if only because Reagan's personal involvement in the Iran-contra affair seemed to have been limited.

In carrying out his pledge of openness, Reagan allowed current and former administration officials to testify before congressional committees about their roles in the Iran-contra affair, including their discussions with the president. Some, including Secretary of State George P. Shultz and former national security adviser Robert C. McFarlane, did so several times, in front of standing committees and the select Iran-contra panels.

Within weeks of Reagan's statement, the White House sent boxes of classified papers to the Intelligence committees — although not without quibbling over what would be included. The Iran panels reviewed thousands of documents — most provided by the administration.

Leaders of the Iran-contra committees thanked Reagan for his cooperation, acknowledging that their investigation would have taken longer and been less complete without it. But some administration officials and supporters on the committees had expressed fear that Reagan's willingness to open his administration to scrutiny might be taken as a precedent.

"I'm very concerned about the eroding of executive privilege, what it means for the future," Henry J. Hyde, R-Ill., a member of the House Iran-contra committee, said July 30, 1987. Hyde said he was especially concerned about the impact on foreign leaders, "who might very well think twice about working cooperatively with us if they think that the advice they are giving or the positions they are taking will be a matter of public record."

Similar statements were made by two other Republicans on the House panel, ranking minority member Dick Cheney of Wyoming and Jim Courter of New Jersey. Administration witnesses, however, denied they were setting a precedent. Defense Secretary Caspar W. Weinberger testified July 31, 1987, that Reagan had ordered all officials "to be sure that we talked about this thing fully and frankly and set aside all of what I might call the normal rules." Reagan's order, Weinberger said, was only a "one-time exception" to the executive privilege rules.

Shultz was more blunt in telling the committees July 23 about his willingness to reveal his conversations with the president. "If I am testifying before you on some other subject some time and you try to use this as a precedent, I won't buy it," Shultz said. "I am just putting you on notice right now."

. . . that trapped Nixon.

While Cabinet secretaries routinely testify before committees — if not about their private advice to presidents — White House officials rarely make formal appearances on Capitol Hill. In the wake of Reagan's waiving of executive privilege, four former White House aides testified before the Iran-contra committees: Chief of Staff Donald T. Regan, national security advisers McFarlane and Adm. John M. Poindexter, and National Security Council staff member Lt. Col. Oliver L. North. The committees called no current White House officials, however.

Regan noted that only two previous chiefs of staff to sitting presidents had testified before Congress without invoking executive privilege. They were President Eisenhower's chief, Sherman Adams, queried about his acceptance of gifts from a friend who was under investigation by federal agencies, and Nixon's chief, H. R. Haldeman, called by the Senate Watergate Committee in 1973. "I wouldn't want you to get the notion . . . that I approve of chiefs of staff coming before the Congress and revealing intimate details of his advice to the president or what the president said to him," Regan said.

signed an order in January 1985, National Security Decision Directive 159, requiring that all covert action findings be in writing. However, some officials had testified that Reagan made "oral findings" that allowed covert operations to proceed without explicit written approval. Again, Reagan said all findings should be in writing except in emergencies; even then, records should be kept and findings should be signed as soon as possible.

• **Non-CIA covert operations.** In most cases, the CIA carries out covert operations. But North conducted what he said were several covert operations out of his NSC office; in one case, he used agents of the Drug Enforcement Administration to track down U.S. hostages in Lebanon. Some witnesses told the Iran-contra panels that the president could use any agency — even the Agriculture Department — to conduct covert actions.

Reagan in 1981 signed an executive order (No. 12333) saying that only the CIA can conduct covert operations unless the president "specifically designates" another agency. Reagan's letter promised that any non-CIA operations would be reported to Congress.

Ironically, existing law was inconsistent. Most lawyers had interpreted the law as requiring congressional notification of covert operations, regardless of which agency performs them, even though the law did not require presidential approval of non-CIA covert operations.

• **Periodic reviews.** In its February 1987 report a commission headed by former Sen. John Tower, R-Texas, criticized the administration for failing to make periodic reviews of the Iran arms sales once Reagan had given his approval. Reagan agreed with periodic reviews and said all covert actions should have "sunset" provisions terminating them at specified intervals unless they were renewed.

Arms Sales

Under normal circumstances, the United States sold weapons directly to foreign governments under the procedures of the Arms Export Control Act (PL 90-629). First enacted by Congress in 1968 and revised almost annually since, the law required notice to Congress of all major arms sales, and gave Congress a chance to reject them.

For the three direct arms sales to Iran in 1986, Reagan avoided the congressional notice requirements of the Arms Export Control Act by signing a "finding" authorizing the CIA to conduct a covert action. His basic authority for covert actions stemmed from his constitutional power as commander in chief and the 1947 National Security Act (PL 80-253), which created the NSC and the CIA.

Under the arms sale law, the president must report all major arms sales to Congress at least 30 days beforehand. That is in contrast to the "timely fashion" option in the 1980 law allowing the president to delay telling Congress about covert actions until after he has approved them.

In 1981, then-Attorney General William French Smith wrote a secret opinion saying that the president did not always have to use the arms export law to sell weapons overseas. Instead, the president could sell arms through the CIA — and thus avoid the tougher congressional-notice requirements of the arms sale law, that opinion said. Disclosed by the Iran-contra committees, the Smith opinion was written to justify a covert action unrelated to the Iran-contra inquiry.

Edwin Meese III, the current attorney general, relied on that 1981 opinion in advising Reagan to use a covert action — rather than the Arms Export Control Act — as the legal means to sell weapons to Iran.

To make such incidents more difficult, the farthest step Congress could take would be to bar the president from using covert actions to sell arms overseas, forcing him to adhere to the stricter notification requirements of the arms export act.

But because every president, including Reagan, had insisted that he had a constitutional power to carry out such foreign policies as selling arms, any attempt to legislate a flat ban would provoke a fierce political battle.

Short of such a sweeping action, there are several ways of making it more difficult for any administration to avoid telling Congress about foreign arms sales. One simple — but potentially controversial — way would be to tighten an existing requirement for reports to Congress on arms sales made through covert actions.

Existing law, first enacted in 1985, requires the president to report to Congress whenever he uses a covert action to transfer weapons to foreign governments or guerrilla movements, such as the contras. But he must do so only when providing a single piece of military equipment or a single contract for military services (such as training) valued at $1 million or more. Most weapons cost much less than $1 million apiece, so the law, in effect, applies only to sales of big-ticket items such as tanks and fighter planes. In particular, none of the weapons sold to Iran in 1986 would have been covered by this law.

Although Congress intended the $1 million reporting requirement as a restriction on presidential action, the administration also saw it as an explicit authorization for presidential action. In a Dec. 17, 1986, memo, Assistant Attorney General Charles J. Cooper interpreted the law as giving "unambiguous recognition" to the president's right to use covert actions to transfer arms overseas.

Congress also could try to change the "thresholds" under which regular arms sales must be reported. Under the Arms Export Control Act, the president had to tell Congress in advance about government-to-government sales valued at $14 million or more for any piece of "major defense equipment" or $50 million for a package of items. The law also required quarterly reports to Congress on all sales valued at $1 million or more.

Iran paid a total of about $35 million for the three shipments of U.S. arms in 1986, and the United States received only $12 million of that — both figures were well below the current limits for advance notice to Congress. Congress could lower the dollar figures to require more advance reports on more sales. But, even if the president used the arms-export law to make future sales such as the ones to Iran, he could still divide the sales to avoid the reports to Congress.

Other Suggestions:

• **Cracking down on leaks.** Witnesses and Iran-contra committee members suggested tougher penalties for persons who reveal classified information. Echoing a position long advocated by the CIA, some Republicans also proposed creating a joint House-Senate Intelligence Committee, with a dozen or so members and a small staff, to reduce congressional leaks. As an alternative to the joint committee, the current panels could limit access by members and staff to classified material and establish new procedures for punishing leakers. Leaders of both committees said they already had taken steps to prevent leaks.

• **Confirming the national security adviser.** This idea had been kicked around Capitol Hill for more than a decade but had picked up little support in the past. ∎

In Hill-Reagan Tug of War, the Tugs Get Harder

Struggles Over Gulf, Arms Control Issues

The stakes and the rhetoric both got higher in the Senate's evolving power struggle with President Reagan during the week of Sept. 21, 1987.

Galvanized by the capture of an Iranian minelayer Sept. 20 — the first successful U.S. military action against Iran — Senate Democrats seemed determined to establish Congress' right to end the policy of escorting Kuwaiti oil tankers in the Persian Gulf, though whether they would exercise that right was less clear. On Sept. 24, they introduced an amendment to the fiscal 1988-89 defense authorization bill (S 1174) that would allow Congress to end the escorting policy after 90 days.

Meanwhile, the White House and Senate Republicans were dug in to resist any such legislation, with the senators poised to filibuster the defense bill. The White House charged Sept. 25 that the proposed legislation could have the effect of "achieving the ayatollah's purposes," and branded it "highly irresponsible." *(Box, p. 18)*

At the same time, important facets of Reagan's approach to strategic weapons and arms control continued to face heavy going on the defense bill.

Reagan suffered no massive defeat to match the 58-38 vote by which the Senate repudiated on Sept. 17 a key administration position on the meaning of the 1972 treaty limiting anti-ballistic missile (ABM) weapons. But he came very close: Only a tie-breaking vote by Vice President George Bush staved off a bid to cut by $800 million the authorization for the strategic defense initiative (SDI), Reagan's nationwide ABM defense plan.

At week's end, critics were gearing up for another run at SDI with an amendment proposing a slightly smaller funding cut, in hopes of picking up the additional vote needed to win.

Also waiting in the wings was an amendment to require compliance with certain limits set by the unratified 1979 SALT II nuclear arms treaty. Charging that the Russians were violating several arms control agreements, Reagan in November 1986 scrapped the policy of informally observing those limits.

From the administration's standpoint, the outlook on the SALT II amendment was grim enough that when the Senate tried to work out an overall agreement on the defense bill's schedule, Republicans refused any limit on their right to offer gutting amendments in case the anti-administration SALT II measure should pass.

In sum, it was a remarkably vigorous assertion of congressional power over national security policy against an administration particularly loath to concede Congress much right to that role. Moreover, the Senate was confronting Reagan just when events had dealt him what would have seemed like a strong political hand.

The challenge to Reagan's unfettered freedom of action in the Persian Gulf followed — indeed, was triggered by — the capture of the Iranian minelaying ship, which had seemed a triumph: Militarily, it was carried off as smoothly as could be imagined; diplomatically, it was a coup in the administration's campaign to pressure Iran to accept a U.N.-sponsored cease-fire; politically, it was generally applauded.

Yet some of the senators who lauded the capture were among the architects of the effort to establish Congress' power to end the naval escorting.

By the same token, the Senate's challenges to Reagan on strategic weapons and arms control went unabated even in the immediate aftermath of an agreement with the Soviet Union to conclude a treaty abolishing intermediate-range nuclear force (INF) missiles — an agreement in which the Russians would give up three times as many nuclear warheads as the United States. *(1987 CQ Weekly Report p. 2233)*

Moreover, the Senate critics were not deterred by the widespread belief in Congress that Reagan's willingness to develop and deploy controversial new weapons — and particularly his push for SDI — were important incentives driving the Russians to conclude the INF deal and to discuss far-reaching cuts in other kinds of weaponry.

Taking a Swing at SDI

Bush's tie-breaking vote on Sept. 22 tabled (and thus killed) an amendment by J. Bennett Johnston, D-La., that would have cut the total funds authorized for SDI to $3.7 billion. In marking up the defense bill, the Armed Services Committee had included $4.5 billion for the program.

Reagan had requested $5.7 billion, of which the House had authorized $3.12 billion in its version of the defense bill (HR 1748).

Johnston's leadership of the attack on SDI funding symbolized one of the administration's political problems. For nearly a decade, proponents had argued that the common-sense appeal of a defense against nuclear missiles would fuel a political steamroller that would flatten any opposition based on arguments of arms control policy or nuclear strategy.

But like many supporters of his amendment, political centrist Johnston — who had emerged as a leading critic of Reagan's SDI program — did not argue against the concept of seeking an anti-missile defense, insisting during the debate that he was "pro-SDI."

Johnston argued for cutting the Armed Services' SDI recommendation by $800 million partly on grounds of overall budget limitations. Even with changes in the congressional budget targets that were incorporated in the debt-ceiling bill cleared for Reagan's signature on Sept. 23, the committee bill would put the defense budget some $11 billion over its allowed ceiling, Johnston contended.

But the main thrust of Johnston's attack was that the administration, seeking quicker SDI deployment, had reshaped its initial SDI plan. Those moves, Johnston argued, had diminished the effectiveness of the Reagan SDI program.

Refining the Vision

Since he inaugurated the program in 1983, Reagan had insisted that he was looking for an anti-missile defense that would protect the entire country, not just selected military installations.

Gulf Coup Brings Reagan No Political Payoff

Just when President Reagan's war of nerves in the Persian Gulf seemed to encounter increasing success militarily and diplomatically, it ran into growing opposition politically in the Congress. And those converging realities portend an intensifying confrontation between the two branches.

The military and diplomatic successes included:

- On Sept. 20, 1987, U.S. forces had scored a coup by seizing an Iranian mine-laying ship, giving the administration the evidence it had sought of Iran's responsibility for mines in the heavily traveled gulf.
- While neither U.S. allies in Europe nor in the gulf region would publicly align themselves with the convoying effort — a political embarrassment for Reagan from the start — several European countries had dispatched their own warships to the gulf to escort merchant ships flying their flag, and several of the gulf states reportedly had become more forthcoming in providing access to local facilities to U.S. and other Western forces.

But beneath the veneer of international successes, festered a serious problem at home: Reagan and his aides had not sold Congress on the wisdom of providing U.S. military escorts for 11 Kuwaiti-controlled oil tankers that were thinly disguised behind the American flag they flew as nominal property of a dummy U.S. corporation.

Though technically a non-belligerent in the seven-year-old Iran-Iraq War, Kuwait — like the other Arab states on the western side of the gulf — has supported Iraq.

Agreed to by the Reagan administration early in 1987, the re-flagging policy came to the focus of congressional attention only late in May, after the accidental Iraqi attack on the frigate *Stark*. From that point on, despite strong and widespread congressional hostility toward Tehran, re-flagging aroused strong opposition on Capitol Hill as provocative of Iran, and unduly risky of a clash between U.S. and Iranian military forces.

Hill efforts to dissuade Reagan from beginning to convoy the Kuwaiti ships came to naught, although the House voted July 8 to delay the program for three months. Senate action on a similar proposal was blocked by a GOP filibuster.

But most of the opposition to congressional action against re-flagging did not reflect support for Reagan's policy. Rather, members feared that once Reagan had publicly committed the country to the course, Congress would risk damage to U.S. prestige if it reversed him.

The convoy operations began in July 1987, with the largest tanker in the first convoy, renamed the *Bridgeton,* striking a mine enroute to Kuwait. Despite that incident, threats from Tehran, and a high level of Iranian military activity in the area, the Reagan team rejected demands that it accord Congress a say in how long the policy would continue by triggering the 1973 War Powers act.

Under this legislation, enacted over the veto of President Nixon and criticized as unconstitutional by every president since, the president must report to Congress within 48 hours of introducing U.S. forces into hostilities or a situation of "imminent hostilities." By 90 days after that, the president must withdraw U.S. forces, unless Congress declares war or passes a joint resolution letting them stay.

On Sept. 18, the Senate rejected 50-41 an amendment to the defense bill that would have triggered the provisions of the War Powers act. But two days later armed U.S. helicopters from the frigate *Jarrett*, using sophisticated night-viewing TV cameras, observed the 213-foot-long Iranian landing craft *Iran Ajr* laying mines in the gulf. After the helicopters attacked the ship, killing at least three men, the survivors fled and at first light the ship was seized.

Though the ship's capture was applauded in Washington, the episode highlighted the risk of U.S. involvement. And it undermined further the White House contention that hostilities in the gulf were not "imminent."

When the Senate resumed action on the defense bill Sept. 22, Lowell P. Weicker Jr., R-Conn., offered an amendment triggering the War Powers act. Majority Leader Robert C. Byrd, D-W.Va., sought a compromise with other Democrats and with John W. Warner, Va., the senior Republican on the Senate Armed Services Committee.

Several sources said the prospective substitute became weaker in a series of drafts on Sept. 23, but then the pendulum began swinging back toward tighter restrictions. On Sept. 24, the search for a bipartisan approach broke down, with the White House advising Warner to resist any bill that would let Congress force an end to the escorting.

As introduced by Byrd on Sept. 24, the substitute was a virtual revision of the War Powers act tailored to allow Congress to end only the practice of escorting Kuwaiti tankers. Under the War Powers act, the only option would be to force all U.S. forces to leave the gulf, which Byrd and his allies opposed.

On Sept. 25, the White House, threatening a veto, charged that Byrd's amendment would "pull the rug out from under the United States and our friends in the Persian Gulf.... Iran must be as overjoyed ... as our friends around the world are dismayed."

Since it would have to deal with tens of thousands of missile warheads and decoys within a few minutes, the system likely would rely largely on space-based lasers or atomic particle beams able to strike targets a thousand miles distant at the speed of light.

In 1986, however, the administration began to emphasize development of a first-phase SDI, consisting of heat-seeking missiles called "space-based kinetic kill vehicles" (SBKKVs) carried on satellites. Much less technically advanced than the laser-type weapons, they could be deployed a decade sooner — by the mid-1990s — according to their proponents.

"Phased deployment" advocates conceded that the heat-seeking rockets could deal with only about 20 percent of the nuclear warheads in a massive Soviet attack. But though this strategy could not physically block an attack, they contended, it could deter one. The argument was that an attack would make sense only if Soviet planners could count on wiping out the vast bulk of forces with which the United States could retaliate. By making that result uncertain, a "first-phase" defense consisting of missile-armed satellites would deter the Soviets, proponents said. Meanwhile, work would continue on the more effective beam-weapons for later deployment as a "second-phase" anti-missile defense.

The Issue Joined

Citing a report to the Pentagon by a technical advisory panel, Johnston contended that the SBKKV system had too many problems and could too easily be negated by the Soviets to warrant the expense of deploying it.

Moreover, he contended, far from being a way station toward deployment of more effective beam weapons, the SBKKV approach would sop up funds needed to develop the more advanced systems. "It is not a step. It is a choice," he insisted. "You cannot have both unless we have found some new pot of gold at the end of the rainbow."

The real reason for the administration's recent emphasis on the less effective, but more nearly ready, weapons was political, Johnston said. "The program was losing political momentum, so they shifted to early deployment," he claimed. "They want to get hardware projects in place to build up a political constituency for the program."

Pete Wilson, R-Calif., one of the Senate's most vigorous SDI proponents, countered that the two-phase approach had been approved in August by a top-level Pentagon committee. The phase-one system would provide a useful check on current Soviet missiles, he insisted. And by the time the Russians completed the expensive modifications they would need to overpower the SBKKVs, beam-weapon defenses would be ready for deployment.

"We need both" kinds of anti-missile system "at different times," Wilson insisted. Moreover, he argued, a vigorous SDI program might dissuade the Russians from beginning that expensive cycle of action and reaction. They might not make the huge investment needed to counter the phase-one defenses if they concluded that, before those new missiles were deployed, beam weapons able to knock them down would be ready for deployment.

Dan Quayle, R-Ind., another SDI backer, blasted Johnston's amendment as "a nice, polite, quiet way to kill SDI, because the practical effect . . . is to confine SDI to research."

While Johnston and several leading SDI proponents debated the strategic value of the current development timetable, other senators stressed political reasons for opposing Johnston's proposed cut.

J. James Exon, D-Neb., reasoned that if the Senate upheld the Armed Services panel's recommendation of $4.5 billion, a likely compromise in conference with the House would be about the amount Johnston proposed.

Contending that SDI had been an important incentive for Moscow to resume arms reduction negotiations, John W. Warner, R-Va., warned that if the Senate slices the program further, "it will be another indication that we are undercutting the efforts of our negotiators at the very time that they are making good progress."

But Johnston brushed that aside, calling the "bargaining chip" argument "the last refuge of big spenders."

Switches and New Faces

In 1986, when Johnston offered an amendment to reduce SDI funding in the fiscal 1987 defense authorization bill (S 2638) to $3.24 billion, it was tabled 50-49.

Since the absent Paula Hawkins, R-Fla. (1981-87), had announced her opposition to the amendment, the net change between the GOP-controlled Senate of 1986 and 1987's Democratic-controlled chamber was a one-vote gain for Johnston. That yielded the 50-50 tie that Bush had to break.

In the 1987 vote on Johnston's SDI funding reduction:

- Four votes against killing the SDI cut came from Democrats elected in November 1986 to replace Republicans (Brock Adams, Wash.; Thomas A. Daschle, S.D.; Wyche Fowler Jr., Ga.; and Terry Sanford, N.C.).
- Also voting against killing the SDI cut were Republicans Dave Durenberger, Minn., and John Heinz, Pa.
- On the other side of the ledger, Republican Christopher S. "Kit" Bond, Mo., elected in 1986 to replace a pro-Johnston Democrat, voted to table the SDI funding cut.
- And four senators who voted with Johnston in 1986 voted to kill his amendment this time: Democrats Lloyd Bentsen, Texas, and David L. Boren, Okla., and Republicans Nancy Landon Kassebaum, Kan., and Bob Packwood, Ore.

Bentsen, Boren and Kassebaum each later cited the need for bargaining leverage in the conference as the main reason for their shift. Asked whether they also had been influenced by ongoing negotiations with the Russians, each allowed that it had been a factor, though not an important one.

And Boren voiced the dilemma of members who saw SDI's chief immediate value as a bargaining chip but who were confronted by Reagan's resolute refusal to bargain it away. "I get frustrated sometimes with the fact that the president seems unwilling to play the card," he said.

A veteran staffer close to the Johnston effort attributed its near success to two factors. First, though Armed Services Chairman Sam Nunn, D-Ga., voted to table, he was not an active opponent. "You never did see him stand up" and defend the committee position, the source said.

Second, fewer members than in the past were receptive to arguments that by reining in an administration program, Congress risked undermining the U.S. negotiating stance with Moscow.

"The bogeyman is gone," the staffer declared: "The old 'Geneva' argument is dead."

Bush's vote was his seventh tie-breaker as vice president, his fifth on a defense issue. He voted for production funds for the MX missile in 1984 and for chemical-weapons production twice in 1983 and again in 1986. ▮

Odds Against Reagan in Trade Conference

There were increasing signs that President Reagan would wind up the loser if setting trade policy dissolved into a political fight between Congress and the White House.

Despite continued administration promises to work with Congress on the massive trade bill (HR 3), there were no signs of movement toward accommodation. On Oct. 13, 1987, Reagan renewed his threat to veto the measure if it was not altered. "I will not sign any bill that will hurt the American worker," he said.

HR 3 was passed by the House and Senate by 2-to-1 margins, and if anything the mood had hardened since then. After disappointing trade figures were announced Oct. 14, members seemed more inclined than ever to take action on their own.

"Year by year, trade deficit by trade deficit," said Senate Majority Leader Robert C. Byrd, D-W.Va., "the administration seems more interested in rhetoric than reality."

Reagan's concerns focused on congressional efforts to limit presidential discretion to retaliate against foreign actions that restrict U.S. business opportunities. But the administration found something objectionable in virtually every section of the bill.

With the numbers against him, the president needed to negotiate, but his team was in disarray, and members complained they were getting nothing but vague and confusing signals from the White House.

The bill was in a House-Senate conference committee in October 1987, and, despite a slow start, congressional leaders promised that HR 3 would find its way to the president's desk by February 1988 at the latest. And they confidently predicted strong, bipartisan support, enough to override a veto.

As Senate Finance Committee Chairman Lloyd Bentsen, D-Texas, put it: "In all candor, if he doesn't sign it, it'll be put into law anyway."

Both versions of the trade bill would stiffen penalties against perceived unfair trading practices abroad and grant more certain relief to import-injured industries.

The bills also seek to strengthen government-sponsored educational and training activities to improve the nation's competitiveness. And they would promote exports by negotiating stable exchange rates and debt relief for Third World countries and by enhancing government export assistance. *(House bill, CQ Weekly Report p. 811; Senate bill, p. 1633; major provisions compared, p. 1822)*

Gloomy Economic Report

As if Congress needed added impetus to act — propelled as it was for more than a year by billowing trade deficits — the nation's trade picture was not getting perceptibly better.

The day after the president's denunciation of the trade bill, the Commerce Department released trade figures for August 1987 showing only the slightest improvement from July, the worst month in history. If the trend held, the 1987 U.S. merchandise trade deficit would exceed the 1986 record of $166.3 billion.

An already jumpy Wall Street responded by driving down stock prices and pushing up interest rates on corporate and government bonds, while the value of the dollar fell overseas.

Economists cautioned that the numbers were changeable and that the two-year, 40 percent decline in the dollar's value masked increases in the volume of goods shipped abroad and decreases in imports.

Federal Reserve Board Chairman Alan Greenspan on Oct. 13 called the continued high trade deficit a "disappointing trend." But he said U.S. goods were claiming a larger share of the domestic market, which he called a further signal that the trade picture should improve.

And in any event, most economists contended that the foreign actions the trade bill would address accounted for only a small fraction of the imbalance between U.S. imports and exports.

Where Would It Lead

On and off Capitol Hill there was continued uncertainty about what would happen to many specific parts of the bill. Some of that uncertainty related to what Republicans and Democrats alike called vague, inconclusive and in some instances non-existent signals about the administration's viewpoint.

"In all candor, if he doesn't sign it, it'll be put into law anyway."

—Sen. Lloyd Bentsen, D-Texas

Many Democrats and their organized-labor allies were suspicious of administration promises to work toward a bipartisan compromise that could be enacted into law. They believed Reagan would veto any trade bill, no matter how accommodating they were.

Parallel doubts derived from confusion over just what it was that the Democrats — and particularly House Speaker Jim Wright, D-Texas — wanted from the bill.

Some Republican skeptics believed (or feared, depending on their hopes for the bill) that Wright wanted a presidential veto that would be sustained, giving Democrats a 1988 campaign issue.

Big Issues

There were, most members and staffers agreed, perhaps two dozen contentious issues. In many cases, the conflict would be greater between Congress and the administration than between the two chambers.

Three of the most crucial issues were how to respond to Japan and a few other countries that were seen as major offenders against the cause of free trade, how to guarantee that U.S. industries are aided when they are threatened by cheaper imports and whether to require advance notice of domestic plant closings.

Both bills have provisions that would mandate retaliation against countries that consistently deny fair access to their markets. And both versions are unacceptable to the White House.

The House retaliation provision, seen as the more protectionist, was crafted by Rep. Richard A. Gephardt, D-Mo., a presidential candidate. It targets countries that have large trade surpluses with the United States and have demonstrated a pattern of unfair practices. It passed the House by only four votes, as compared with its not-quite-parallel Senate provision, which had Minority Leader Robert Dole, R-Kan., as a cosponsor and passed 87-7.

A version of these provisions was seen as certain to survive in the bill, despite White House objections, along with some form of presidential waiver for national security concerns. The only question seemed to be how to preserve a semblance of the Gephardt language without losing GOP votes.

"Everyone has to come out a winner" on Gephardt, one Senate Democratic aide observed.

Both bills also provided for more certain relief — in the form of tariffs or quotas — for domestic industries injured by competing imports.

In this case the House bill was regarded as less objectionable in its grant of discretion not to act. But it would take the decision-making authority away from the president, which the administration would fight.

Though Bentsen was a strong supporter of the Senate language, he was opposed by two committee Republicans whose votes might be crucial to a veto override — John C. Danforth of Missouri, an original sponsor of the Senate bill, and Bob Packwood of Oregon. Packwood surprised many by voting — reluctantly — for the bill on the Senate floor.

For his part, Bentsen said, "I always thought this [provision] would be written in conference," suggesting that compromise is likely.

A provision only in the Senate bill that was at the top of administration and business-group hit lists would require public notice 60 days in advance of a plant closing or layoff of 50 or more employees.

Danforth, among other crucial Republicans, was adamantly opposed to this provision, but there were signs it might not be the killer it appeared to be.

Much of organized labor did not put the provision even near the top of its long list of trade bill issues.

If the trade bill accomplishes other labor aims — such as requiring strong retaliation and enhancing worker-training programs — and this provision stood in the way of bipartisan support for the bill, it seemed unlikely that the unions would fight hard to keep it.

A Veto Strategy

U.S. Trade Representative Clayton Yeutter and Treasury Secretary James A. Baker III insisted that the administration wants and needs a trade bill.

The Constitution gives Congress the last word on trade matters. But administration negotiators said they need a free hand in the worldwide talks under way in Geneva to reduce tariffs, expand protections for patents and other intellectual property rights, and reduce agricultural subsidies.

Whatever bill emerges from conference would give the administration the authority it wanted, with a guarantee that Congress would consider any agreement without trying to amend it.

What was unknown, however, was how much the administration would swallow on other issues to get this authority.

There were few outward signs of the cooperation that administration officials promised. For example, while business, labor and other lobbying groups peppered Congress with comments on the bill, the administration had not sent its own list.

Moreover, the administration lobbying team, which aside from Baker and Yeutter was to include Labor Secretary William E. Brock III, was greatly diminished with Brock's announced departure.

And Reagan's own words were seen as evidence that he — if not his chief negotiators — wanted a showdown.

Yeutter and others have denied they were pursuing a "veto strategy." But at the same time, Yeutter promised that he had a solid block of 34 Republican senators who he could count on to sustain a veto.

Nineteen Republicans voted for the bill on the Senate floor, but reserved the right to reject a conference agreement that showed no improvements. Twenty-seven others voted no.

Most of those "yes, but" senators were expected to support the general trade law changes the bill would contain, however.

And even some free-traders like Rep. Bill Frenzel, R-Minn., thought the conference would produce a bill that, on balance, would be acceptable. "A lot of things can be defanged," he said.

"I anticipate that the president will sign" the bill, John D. Dingell, D-Mich., chairman of the House Energy and Commerce Committee, said Oct. 13. "I do not see how he can do otherwise."

But Yeutter reminded reporters the same day, "The president doesn't have to sign anything." ∎

A 'Leave It to the States' Approach:

Administration AIDS Policy Comes Under Fire in House

As the House geared up for a potentially bruising fight over federal policy on AIDS testing, the Reagan administration was coming under attack from members on both sides of the issue for what they saw as a lack of leadership on the problem.

The latest skirmish was over legislation then pending in the Energy and Commerce Committee. The bill (HR 3071), sponsored by Rep. Henry A. Waxman, D-Calif., would authorize $400 million for voluntary AIDS testing, seek to create federal assurances of confidentiality of results, and extend anti-discrimination protections to those exposed to the AIDS virus who have not yet developed the disease. In a March 1987 ruling that government officials acknowledged applied to AIDS victims, the Supreme Court held that Section 504 of the Rehabilitation Act prohibits discrimination against people with contagious diseases.

At a hearing Sept. 21, 1987, before the Health Subcommittee that Waxman chairs, Otis R. Bowen, secretary of the Department of Health and Human Services (HHS), testified that the administration thought that this bill and several other measures seeking to deal with the AIDS epidemic were either unnecessary or premature. Most decisions about handling AIDS matters were best left to the states, Bowen said.

In addition to offering lengthy criticisms of HR 3071, Bowen also announced administration opposition to a series of initiatives proposed by subcommittee member William E. Dannemeyer, R-Calif., including ones requiring mandatory testing of certain groups of people.

Although Bowen strongly endorsed the goals of Waxman's bill, he said it "was not clear at this time" that funds in excess of the $90 million for testing requested by the administration for fiscal 1988 were needed.

As to confidentiality of test results, he said, "We do not believe that it is necessary to impose a federal presence in an area where states are actively working and experimenting unless we can propose a system that will not confuse the issue further."

The Discrimination Issue

But Bowen was most critical of the bill's anti-discrimination language. Arguing that "a convincing case has not yet been made" that new protections are needed, Bowen said, "At this time the primary role in determining whether protection is needed in addition to that provided by current law, including Section 504, should belong to the states."

House critics were quick to attack that position. J. Roy Rowland, D-Ga., a cosponsor of HR 3071, said the Bowen statement represented "another indication that efforts to develop an effective national policy are in disarray." Citing a "lack of cohesive direction in the fight against AIDS," Rowland argued in a statement that "the AIDS virus does not stop at state boundary lines. It is a national problem and we need a national strategy."

Waxman, too, chided the administration. "Every public health and medical expert who has testified before this subcommittee has agreed that strong confidentiality and nondiscrimination protections are essential to a successful testing program," he said in a statement. "The question for the administration is, 'Are you prepared to sacrifice the success of an AIDS testing program in order to wait for the states to act?' "

The comments did not go unnoticed at HHS, and Bowen Sept. 23 issued a statement charging that press coverage of his appearance before the subcommittee "left unclear that HHS is already taking steps to support states in their efforts to ensure confidentiality and to protect against discrimination for those with AIDS or [exposure to the virus], and that eventual federal action was not precluded.... But now is not the time to leap beyond our current supportive role nor to override states' current active efforts to protect confidentiality and prevent discrimination while encouraging testing, counseling and other steps to reduce the risk of additional infection."

Division Over Specifics

There seemed to be widespread agreement among subcommittee members that more testing was needed, that results should be kept confidential, and that those with AIDS should not be subject to discrimination because of their illness. But members were clearly divided over the specifics.

At the Sept. 21 hearing, Dannemeyer said he thought he could work out an agreement with Waxman over confidentiality provisions but argued that in its current form, the bill "is a surreptitious means of furthering the civil rights agenda of a select group and not the much-needed federal solution to the AIDS crisis."

And while the subcommittee's ranking Republican, Edward R. Madigan, Ill., said in an interview that he strongly supported more money for voluntary testing, he, too, was troubled by the anti-discrimination language.

"I have a lot of compassion for those with this problem, but I don't see how we can justify special protection," said Madigan. "What about other people with other kinds of illnesses? Why not spinal meningitis or cancer?"

A subcommittee counsel, however, said those with other illnesses were already protected under regulations governing enforcement of the Rehabilitation Act. To exclude carriers of the AIDS virus would constitute an exception, the counsel said.

Despite the differences, spokesmen for House Democratic leaders confirmed that their bosses would like to see an AIDS-testing bill on the floor before Congress adjourns in 1987.

But working out a compromise would not be easy, warned Madigan, "because you've got Henry Waxman on one side, Bill Dannemeyer on the other, and HHS [not doing anything]." ∎

CONGRESS

Congress Has Broad Authority To Regulate Fiscal Affairs, Commerce

The authors of the Constitution recognized that the new government needed an executive to carry out the laws and a judiciary to resolve conflicts in them. But Congress would be the heart of the new republic. The House of Representatives was the only part of the federal government originally elected by the people; consequently, Congress was the branch of government expected to respond directly to their needs.

It was thus to the national legislature that the framers entrusted most of the power necessary to govern the new nation. To Congress the Constitution granted "all legislative Powers." These included the power to tax, regulate commerce, declare war, approve treaties and raise and maintain armies.

The framers also gave Congress some authority over the other two branches. Congress was granted the power to establish whatever federal judicial system below the Supreme Court seemed desirable and to impeach and convict the president, federal judges and other federal officers for treason, bribery or other high crimes and misdemeanors. Each chamber has authority to seat and discipline its own members.

The exercise of these powers is subject to some limitation. The Constitution specifically prevents Congress from singling out individuals for punishment and from imposing a direct tax that is unapportioned or an indirect tax that is not uniform. The most significant constitutional limitations may be those added by the First Amendment, prohibiting Congress from interfering with the free exercise of speech, the press, assembly, or religion, and the Fifth Amendment, prohibiting the taking of life, liberty or property without due process of law.

Fiscal Powers

Perhaps the most important of the constitutional prerogatives granted to Congress are the powers to tax and to spend. Congress may use its power to tax both to raise revenue and as a regulatory device. The power to spend allows Congress to determine policy on almost every matter that affects daily life in the United States.

Taxation

Taxes on the income and profits of individuals and corporations have become the federal government's basic sources of revenue since the 16th Amendment permitting a general income tax was ratified in 1913. In addition, Congress has imposed an excess profits tax on corporations during wartime, levied a variety of excise taxes, authorized estate and gift taxes and imposed payroll taxes to underpin insurance and unemployment compensation systems.

Tax legislation must, under a constitutional provision, originate in the House of Representatives. Tax and tariff bills are handled there by the Ways and Means Committee. After the House acts, such bills go to the Senate where they are referred to the Finance Committee. Because that committee and the full Senate may amend the House version of a tax bill, the Senate plays an influential role in the consideration and adoption of tax legislation. In a departure from tradition and constitutional dictates, the Senate initiated a major tax bill in 1982. It was enacted, although some House members challenged the constitutionality of the legislation.

In the post-World War II era, initiatives on raising, lowering, or enacting new taxes generally have been taken by the executive branch; it has prepared the initial recommendations and Congress has acted on them. But there is no requirement that the executive initiate tax changes. Congress itself generated a major tax reform bill in 1969, a wide-ranging tax revision bill in 1976, and a massive tax code overhaul in 1986.

Appropriations

Revenue raised through taxation is not available in the Treasury to be disbursed by the executive branch to meet governmental needs simply as agency officials see fit. The Constitution gives to Congress the sole authority to determine how monies collected shall be spent and requires a regular statement of expenditures.

This appropriations procedure works in two steps after the president presents his annual budget requests to Congress. First, the various congressional committees consider the parts of the request that fall under their jurisdictions and report out bills authorizing expenditures and setting a ceiling on the amount of funds that can be spent for the programs. After the authorization becomes law, Congress actually provides (appropriates) the money to fund the programs. The amount of money appropriated often is less than the maximum amount specified in the authorization for the program. Although the Constitution does not require it, appropriations traditionally originate in the House and initially are considered by the relevant subcommittee of the House Appropriations Committee where the bulk of basic spending decisions are made — although both the full committee and the House may amend a bill before it is passed and sent to the Senate. The Senate reviews the House action and hears appeals from agencies seeking changes in the allotments accorded them by the House.

Budget Control

Congress, having long treated its taxing and spending powers separately, in 1974 enacted the Congressional Budget and Impoundment Control Act (PL 93-344) to provide a method of setting overall fiscal policy for the federal government, and in some respects constrain congressional committees from acting against the goals espoused in the budget.

The budget law set up House and Senate Budget committees to write annual budgets and keep track of Congress' performance in adhering to them, and it created a Congressional Budget Office to provide technical information about the economy and the budget that previously was available only from the president's budget agency, the Office of Management and Budget.

In December 1985, the perceived failure of the 1974 law to prevent steadily increasing, multibillion-dollar deficits led Congress to make radical changes in budget procedures that presumably would force a balanced budget by October 1990. The new law, known as Gramm-Rudman-Hollings (PL 99-177) for its Senate sponsors, set maximum annual allowable deficits for the years 1986-91, and mandated automatic, across-the-board spending cuts if Congress failed to meet those goals.

Assessments of Gramm-Rudman ranged from disgusted rejection to modest claims that its enforcement procedures had, for the first time, forced appropriators to respect spending limits set by the budget resolution.

In February 1986, President Ronald Reagan submitted a fiscal 1987 budget that appeared to meet the statute's deficit goal. But critics discerned — and the administration later conceded — that it substantially understated defense spending and so exceeded the target. And the fiscal 1987 budget resolution made none of the structural spending and revenue changes that budget experts said were essential to meet the law's declining annual deficit targets.

On July 7 the Supreme Court found that Gramm-Rudman's automatic spending cut mechanism violated the separation-of-powers doctrine, because it assigned executive-type responsibilities to the General Accounting Office, an entity under the legislative branch. The device that was supposed to compel meaningful budget compromises as an alternative to across-the-board cuts was thereby removed.

However, on Sept. 29, 1987, Reagan signed a new version of the Gramm-Rudman-Hollings anti-deficit law. The legislation eased the Gramm-Rudman targets of the 1985 law. Moreover, it revived the automatic spending cuts — this time to be initiated by the Office of Management and Budget — to achieve a balanced budget by 1993.

Many in Congress hoped the new measure would force Reagan to choose between defense cuts or tax increases. The widespread certainty that Reagan would never bend to new taxes fed the fear that he would let automatic cuts occur instead and blame Congress for the resulting harm.

Commerce Powers

Nearly as important as the powers to tax and spend is the power to regulate interstate and foreign commerce. Congress' exercise of its virtually exclusive authority in these areas has produced extensive government regulation not only of the actual transport of goods but also of their manufacture, sale and, in many cases, their purity and safety.

The Constitution gave Congress a broad and positive grant of power to regulate interstate and foreign commerce but left interpretation of the extent of the power to precedent and judicial determination. Although the Supreme Court initially gave Congress almost complete control over interstate commerce, the legislative branch seldom exercised its power. But with the passage of the Interstate Commerce Act of 1887, Congress moved decisively into the area of domestic regulation. The act, prompted by the individual states' inability to curb increasing abuses by railroads, ultimately was broadened to include regulation of trucking companies, bus lines, freight forwarders, water carriers, oil pipelines, transportation brokers and express agencies. The act, which established the Interstate Commerce Commission as the first regulatory agency, also led to creation of several other agencies that regulate various aspects of commercial transactions in the United States, as well as entire industries, such as communications and energy.

In 1890 Congress moved into federal regulation of commercial enterprise with enactment of the Sherman Antitrust Act "to protect commerce against unlawful restraints and monopolies." With the turn of the century, Congress began to regulate interstate commerce to protect the health and morals of the general populace. To this end, Congress banned interstate shipment of such items as lottery tickets, impure food and drugs and prostitutes.

Although the Supreme Court sanctioned most of these new uses of the interstate commerce power, it balked occasionally at certain regulations, such as the congressional attempt in 1916 to outlaw child labor by barring the shipment of goods made by children. It was this narrower view of the commerce power that prevailed when the Supreme Court reviewed and declared unconstitutional many of the early New Deal economic recovery programs. The confrontation resulted in the court's recognition of Congress' authority to regulate virtually all apsects of business and manufacture affecting interstate commerce.

Only once since 1937 has the court found an exercise of the commerce clause to be unconstitutional. In that same period it has sanctioned broadened uses of the commerce power. In the Civil Rights Act of 1964, Congress found justification in the commerce clause and the "equal protection" clause of the 14th Amendment for a ban on racial discrimination in most public accommodations. Congress used the commerce clause in 1968 as the basis for legislation making it a federal crime to travel in interstate commerce for the purpose of inciting or participating in a riot. The commerce clause is also the basis for the far-reaching federal clean air and water laws.

Foreign Policy Powers

While the president generally takes the initiative in foreign relations, Congress possesses several constitutionally granted powers that are indispensable to the success of the president's policies. These include the powers to raise taxes (to finance wars), create and maintain an armed force, regulate foreign commerce and ratify treaties. Except for votes on the Vietnam War in the 1970s, and Lebanon and Central America in the 1980s, Congress in the 20th century has chosen to use its powers to support the president in these matters rather than to challenge him.

While the Constitution gives Congress the power to declare war and "provide for the common Defence," both the initiation and conduct of war have come to be almost entirely directed by the president. In November 1973 Congress sought to restore some of its control over war efforts when it enacted, over President Nixon's veto, the War Powers Resolution (PL 93-148). In addition to certain reporting requirements, the measure set a 60-day limit on any presidential commitment of U.S. troops abroad without specific congressional authorization, unless troops were sent to respond to an "attack upon the United States, its territories or possessions or its armed forces." Unauthorized commitments could be terminated prior to the 60-day deadline through congressional passage of a concurrent resolution — a measure that does not require the president's signature to take effect.

Although Congress had never used that "legislative veto" authority to force a president to withdraw troops, the threat of a veto may have forced chief executives to consult more closely with Congress in taking military actions abroad. The Supreme Court's June 1983 ruling that legislative vetoes were unconstitutional dealt a blow to congressional influence over such commitments by nullifying that provision of the War Powers Resolution. In the wake of that ruling Congress wrestled with ways to develop an alternative method of influencing decisions. After the April 14, 1986, bombing of Libya, Congress again addressed the question of presidential prerogative. This time the debate centered on if and when the president should consult Congress in cases involving a U.S. response to terrorism.

Another area in which the Supreme Court's ruling could have a potentially far-reaching impact is congressional control of arms sales. In 1976 Congress enacted the Arms Export Control Act (PL 94-329), substantially expanding its power to veto arms sales to foreign countries through adoption of a concurrent resolution. Again, although most arms sales have raised little controversy, Congress has repeatedly challenged the president's judgment on specific sales to countries, particularly those in the volatile Middle East. As with the War Powers Resolution, Congress never has actually vetoed a proposed arms sale, but the possibility forced Presidents Jimmy Carter and Ronald Reagan to make compromises.

In spite of the Supreme Court's legislative veto ruling, congressional power over some other aspects of foreign policy has increased substantially. Legislative authority over the massive post-World War II foreign aid and military assistance programs is an example. The programs have required specific congressional authorizations and repeated congressional appropriations. Frequently Congress has disagreed with the president over the amounts and allocations for these programs, making its views known either through directives in the authorizing legislation, or by changing funding requests in appropriations bills.

The Constitution gives the president authority to make treaties with other countries if two-thirds of the Senate concur. For years this power served as a cornerstone of American foreign policy. Treaties forged peace agreements with other nations, supported U.S. territorial expansion, established national boundaries, protected U.S. commerce and regulated government affairs with Indian tribes.

Except for rejection of the Versailles Treaty after World War I, Senate action on treaties has not been a major factor in foreign policy. Although the Senate has killed several treaties by inaction, it had by the end of 1985 rejected only 20 treaties since 1789. However, the lengthy debates on the Panama Canal and U.S.-Soviet strategic arms limitation talks (SALT II) treaties in 1978 and 1979, respectively, were seen as Senate moves to expand its power in the foreign policy field.

In recent years the Senate's role has been eroded somewhat by the use of executive agreements instead of treaties with foreign countries; such agreements do not require Senate approval.

Confirmations of Nominations

Under the Constitution the Senate must approve all presidential nominations of federal officers. Most nominations involve promotions of military officers and Senate action is only a formality. But each year several hundred major nominations are subjected to varying degrees of Senate scrutiny. These include nominations to Cabinet and sub-Cabinet positions, independent boards and regulatory agencies, major diplomatic and military posts and the federal judiciary.

The Senate role in Supreme Court appointments has proved particularly important. It may not be able to dictate Supreme Court nominees, but historically the Senate has not been afraid to reject them. Slightly more than one-fifth of all Supreme Court nominations have failed to win Senate confirmation.

Appointments to lower federal courts are another matter. Traditionally the president has used this power — particularly those at the district court level — to please members of both chambers. Generally the president names as district court judge the person recommended by the House member of Congress from that district. These lower court appointments thus provide the president with his important patronage power — the opportunity to win the good will of a member of Congress or a vote on a crucial issue.

The Senate carefully considers nominations of Cabinet officers, but such officers usually are confirmed with little difficulty on the theory that the president should have great leeway in choosing the members of his official "family." There have been exceptions though. President Reagan first nominated Edwin Meese to be attorney general in January 1984. After 13 months — longer than any other Cabinet nominee in recent history — he was confirmed.

Presidential appointments to independent boards and commissions present a somewhat different situation. These agencies are created by Congress and are not subordinate to the executive branch. Congress expects these agencies to implement congressional goals and therefore it plays a large role in the selection process. Contests over these nominations have been frequent, although few nominees actually have been rejected.

Impeachment

Impeachment of federal officers is perhaps the most awesome, though the least used, power of Congress. The Constitution specifies that the House shall impeach (indict) federal officials that it believes guilty of treason, bribery or high crimes and misdemeanors. The charges are drawn up in an impeachment resolution, usually reported by the House Judiciary Committee. If the House adopts the resolution, the Senate holds a trial, with House members acting as prosecutors. If a president is impeached the chief justice presides at the Senate trial. Conviction requires two-thirds approval of the senators present. Punishment is limited to removal from office and disqualification for further federal office. There is no appeal.

The two most famous cases of impeachment resulted in acquittal after sensational trials. They involved President Andrew Johnson, accused of violating the Tenure of Office Act, and Supreme Court Justice Samuel Chase, accused of partisan conduct on the bench. Since 1789 only 14 federal officials have been impeached by the House. Of the 13 cases that went to Senate trial, two were dismissed before trial after the person impeached left office, six resulted in acquittal and five ended in conviction. President Nixon's resignation on Aug. 9, 1974, foreclosed House action on impeachment charges approved by the Judiciary Committee. U.S. District Judge Harry E. Claiborne was removed from office Oct. 9, 1986, for tax fraud. He was the first official to be removed from office in 50 years and the fifth in the history of the nation.

Constitutional Amendments

Congress shares with the states the power to propose amendments to the Constitution. Amendments may be offered by two-thirds of both chambers of Congress or by a convention called by Congress at the request of the legislatures of two-thirds of the states. Amendments must be ratified by the legislatures or conventions of three-fourths of the states. Congress has always specified ratification by the state legislatures, except for the 21st Amendment.

Although these constitutional provisions anticipated a substantial role for the states, Congress has dominated the amendment process. Not once have the states been successful in calling for a convention to propose an amendment to the Constitution. The states fell one short in 1969 when 33 of them called for a convention to write an amendment overturning the Supreme Court's "one person, one vote" decisions. As of 1985 the states were two short of the two-thirds required to call a constitutional convention to draft an amendment requiring a balanced federal budget.

Restrained use of the amendment procedure has enabled the Constitution to remain the fundamental law of the land even though the United States has been transformed beyond recognition since the Constitution was drafted. The states have ratified only 26 amendments. Included among those are the ten amendments comprising the Bill of Rights, extension of the right to vote to blacks and women and the guarantees of equal protection and due process of the law against them.

Altogether, Congress has submitted to the states only 33 amendments. The states failed to ratify seven of these, including a proposal to give the District of Columbia voting representation in Congress. The proposed amendment, approved by Congress in 1978, failed to win ratification by its 1985 deadline.

The Equal Rights Amendment, approved in 1972 by Congress, failed to win ratification by the extended deadline of June 30, 1982. Despite a massive lobby effort, only 35 states had approved the proposal, three short of the necessary 38. The congressionally approved extension and efforts by five states to rescind their ratification raised constitutional questions about the amendment procedure.

Election of the President

Congress under the Constitution has two key responsibilities relating to the election of the president and vice president. First it must receive and in joint session count the electoral votes certified by the states. Second, if no candidate has a majority of the electoral vote, the House must elect the president and the Senate the vice president.

In modern times the formal counting of electoral votes has been largely a ceremonial function. The House actually has chosen the president only twice, in 1801 and 1825. In the course of the nation's history, however, a number of campaigns deliberately have been designed to throw elections into the House. Apprehension over this has nurtured many electoral reform efforts. The most recent attempt came in 1979 when the Senate rejected a proposed constitutional amendment that would have abolished the electoral college system and replaced it with direct popular election of the president.

The 20th and 25th Amendments authorize Congress to settle problems arising from the death of a president-elect or candidate or the disability of a president. The 25th Amendment, ratified in 1967 to cover what its authors assumed would be rare occurrences, was applied twice in 12 months and gave rise to executive leadership unique in the nation's history. The amendment provides that whenever the office of vice president becomes vacant, the president shall appoint a replacement, subject to confirmation by Congress.

Gerald R. Ford was the first vice president to take office under the amendment. He was sworn in Dec. 6, 1973, to replace Spiro T. Agnew, who had resigned after pleading no contest to a charge of federal income tax evasion. Little more than a year later, Nelson A. Rockefeller was sworn in Dec. 19, 1974, to succeed Ford. Ford had become president upon the Aug. 9, 1974, resignation of President Nixon. Thus neither of the nation's two chief officials in 1975 and 1976 was elected by the people.

Congressional Ethics

The Constitution empowers each member of Congress to seat, unseat and punish its own members. The House and Senate have the power to determine whether a member fulfills the constitutional requirements for service, to settle contested elections and to censure members for misconduct. Some of these powers come into conflict with the right of voters to decide who will represent them. As a result Congress has been cautious in using its authority. While it has acted often to determine the winner in contested elections, it has rejected the clear choice of the voters, for lack of the requisite qualification, in fewer than 20 cases since 1789.

Censure Proceedings. Congress has shown like restraint in expelling or punishing members for disorderly or improper conduct. Expulsions have numbered 15 in the Senate and four in the House, including the expulsion of Rep. Michael "Ozzie" Myers, D-Pa., in the fall of 1980. Seven senators, 22 representatives and one territorial delegate have been formally censured by their colleagues. In 1979-80 the House censured Charles C. Diggs Jr., a Michigan Democrat who resigned in June 1980, and Charles H. Wilson, D-Calif., both for financial misconduct. In July 1983 Reps. Daniel B. Crane, R-Ill., and Gerry E. Studds, D-Mass., were censured for sexual misconduct with teen-age congressional pages.

One historical reason for the comparatively few instances of congressional punishment of its members had been the difficulty in determining what constitutes conflict of interest and misuse of power. But an increasing incidence of scandals in the 1960s led to creation of ethics committees in both houses to oversee members' conduct.

By the mid-1970s Congress' reputation suffered as a number of current and former members were accused of criminal or unethical behavior. In 1976 Rep. Wayne L. Hays, D-Ohio, was forced to resign under threat of a House probe into charges that he kept a mistress on the public payroll. The same year the House voted to reprimand Robert L. F. Sikes, D-Fla., for financial misconduct.

Shortly after Congress convened in 1977, special committees in both the House and Senate began drawing up new codes of ethics adopted by both chambers in March. The new rules were codified into law and extended to top officials in the executive and legislative branches in 1978.

Still more scandal was unveiled in 1980 through a government undercover investigation of political corruption — known as "Abscam" — in which law enforcement agents, posing as businessmen or wealthy Arabs, attempted to induce some members of Congress and other elected officials to use their influence, for pay, for such things as helping Arabs obtain U.S. residency, get federal grants and arrange real estate transactions.

The expulsion of Ozzie Myers, which resulted from his Abscam conviction, was something of a milestone for a House that had long been the butt of derisive jokes about lax punishment of wayward members. The other congressmen involved in the scandal escaped expulsion. Two of the convicted House members resigned: John W. Jenrette Jr., D-S.C., on Dec. 19, 1980, and Raymond F. Lederer, D-Pa., on May 5, 1981. Three others were defeated for re-election: Richard Kelly, R-Fla., John M. Murphy, D-N.Y., and Frank Thompson Jr., D-N.J. The lone senator convicted in the Abscam scandal, Harrison A. Williams Jr., D-N.J., resigned on March 11, 1982, hours before the Senate was expected to vote on his expulsion.

In the wake of the Abscam convictions, both the House and Senate ethics committees considered revising their codes of conduct.

Power of Investigation. The power of Congress to undertake investigations — perhaps its most controversial of legislative branch power — is not specified in the Constitution. It is based instead on tradition and the belief that investigations are indispensable to the legislative process. Yet, the Supreme Court never has questioned the right of Congress to conduct investigations.

No period of American history has been without congressional investigation. The first was held in 1792, to investigate the massacre of U.S. soldiers in Indian territory. Since then, congressional probes have gathered information on the need for possible future legislation, tested the effectiveness of past legislative action, questioned executive branch actions and laid the groundwork for impeachment proceedings. Investigations have elevated comparatively minor political figures to national fame, broken the careers of important men and women and captivated millions of newspaper readers and television viewers.

Members' Pay

A very ticklish power held by Congress is that of setting members' salaries. Although Congress traditionally has tried to bury its own salary increases in general pay raises for federal workers, increases nevertheless have led to public criticism.

In December 1982, in a break with nearly two centuries of tradition, Congress decided to pay House members more than senators, while the latter could earn unlimited amounts in outside income, including honoraria.

Effective Dec. 18, 1982, House members' salaries were raised to $69,800. Salaries for senators remained at $60,662.50, but they were allowed to earn as much as they chose in outside honoraria. Outside earnings for representatives continued to be limited by the House rules to 30 percent of members' salaries.

The Senate voted to raise members salaries to the House level of $69,800 in June 1983. But amid public criticism of senators' outside income, they agreed to place a cap on Senate honoraria effective Jan. 1, 1984, that was equal to the House limit. However, in December 1985 the honoraria limit was raised by Congress from 30 percent of their annual salaries to 40 percent. The new cap on the amount members could collect from speeches and articles did not affect House members because they were bound by a House rule adopted in 1981 setting the limit at 30 percent.

In 1985 the annual 3.5 percent pay increase came on top of a 4 percent raise that federal white-collar employees and Congress received in 1984. The 1985 raise boosted the salaries of senators and representatives from $72,600 to $75,100.

In January 1987, President Reagan proposed increasing the annual salaries of members of Congress to $89,500 — a 16 percent increase from the 1986 salary of $77,400. The proposal fell far short of the 74.4 percent congressional salary hike recommended in December 1986 by a federal commission.

In February, the House followed the Senate's lead in rejecting the salary increase for members. However, the House cleared the measure one day after a 30-day deadline set in law for disapproving pay proposals, and the pay hike went into effect. If the maximum honoraria limit were met, House members could earn a maximum of $116,350 a year and Senators $125,300.

Byrd Struggles to Lead Deeply Divided Senate

Urges Party Unity To Build a Record

"There should be more political discipline in this body, because after all . . . there has to be party leadership. A party has to be held responsible for the governance of a nation."
—Senate Majority Leader Robert C. Byrd (April 18, 1980)

Seven months later, the voters did hold Byrd's Democratic Party "responsible for the governance of a nation" and decided it had failed. The keys to both the White House and the Senate went to the Republicans.

Republican Ronald Reagan still had 19 months on his White House lease in July 1987, but voters had returned control of the Senate, and thus the Congress, to the Democrats. For Byrd, the 1986 elections heralded a second stint as majority leader — and a second chance to prove that Democrats could govern.

His performance in the 100th Congress indicated that Byrd still swore by his words from 1980. If anything, the later losses only reinforced the West Virginian's emphasis on party discipline and leadership, by showing what happened when they were lacking.

Whether Byrd was doing a better job of selling that message, or whether his fellow Democrats simply were shocked into line by the past defeats, Byrd got credit for early shows of party unity and legislative activism that took both Democrats and Republicans by surprise.

But the initial good reviews for both Byrd and his Democratic counterpart in the House, Speaker Jim Wright of Texas, had a wait-and-see tone, conditioned with warnings of tougher battles to come. Those battles had begun — on the budget, defense, foreign policy and campaign finance.

After initial disarray, Senate Republicans mounted a formidable opposition. Relations between House and Senate Democrats proved fragile, as illustrated by the five-week struggle to agree on a fiscal 1988 budget. Within the Senate, Byrd chastised Democrats for one disciplinary problem, spotty attendance, and irritated some colleagues with his actions on arms control and campaign finance.

But he enjoyed their continued support on the floor. Through June 26, 1987, the average Senate Democrat had voted with his party 87 percent of the time on roll calls in which a majority of one party opposed a majority of the other, a Congressional Quarterly analysis showed. Republicans had a 79 percent party-unity score.

The problem was that the Democrats' 54 votes often were not enough. Byrd needed 60 votes both to break a filibuster and to waive objections that a bill exceeds budget limits. Republicans, mustering at least 41 of their 46 votes, had blocked Byrd's initial efforts to craft a record that his party could boast of in 1988.

"I understand that I am not very well-liked around here anyhow. I did not get elected to be liked here. I got elected because I thought I could do a job."
—Robert C. Byrd, D-W.Va.

The bigger hurdles ahead were President Reagan's vetoes. Democratic senators were losing hope that former Senate Majority Leader Howard H. Baker Jr., the Tennessee Republican who became Reagan's chief of staff in 1987, could prod the president toward consensus.

Byrd needed support from up to 13 Republicans to override a veto with the required two-thirds vote, or 67 when all senators were present. Early in 1987, his reputation and Wright's were enhanced when Congress renewed the Clean Water Act (HR 1) and authorized highway and mass transit programs (HR 2) over Reagan's veto. But those bills had support across party lines because they meant federal projects for hundreds of districts.

Republicans were less likely to buck Reagan on such things as spending and tax bills, and arms limits.

As Byrd maneuvered in 1987, at stake was not only his party's future as a presidential-election year approached, but also Byrd's own. Re-election to a sixth term as senator was all but certain. Less so was the Democrats' willingness to re-elect him as their leader in the 101st Congress.

Party Unity

"One of the fundamental objectives of every leader should be that of unity for the common cause." (May 2, 1980)

That statement, like the previous one from April 1980, is part of Byrd's ongoing orations that are to be compiled into a book on Senate history. Because his 1980 views on Senate leaders and parties were formed before Byrd experienced six years in the minority and challenges to his leadership in 1984 and 1986, those speeches were useful guides to what was constant and what was changed in his leadership style.

The quote above made clear that party unity was not a new objective.

But veteran senators detected greater effort and urgency than before.

Some members and observers said Democrats would be more unified now regardless of Byrd's actions. The glue that bound them, they said, was a mix — awareness of their narrow margin of control, desire to confront a president weakened by scandal, and eagerness to promote a Democratic agenda after six years in waiting.

"I'd give Byrd high marks, very high marks, for knowledge of the process, for his determined approach to providing a floor presence, and for personal knowledge of issues as they come to the floor," one senator said. "But I'd give him marginal marks on his ability to lead. He is perceived as somewhat of a weak leader. He doesn't have the force of personality to coalesce the members behind his command."

But Louisiana Democrat J. Bennett Johnston, who aborted an attempted coup against Byrd in 1986, noted Democrats' unity so far and said, "I think you've got to give the leader credit when things go well — and blame when they don't, even if he's not the author of all the good and all the bad. That's the way leadership works."

"Byrd has welded the group into more unity than I've seen here in my nine years," Nebraska Democrat J. James Exon said. "It's Byrd's call that people have elected the Democrats as a majority and we have an obligation to lead. And to lead with as scant a majority as we have calls for rallying behind the leader on crucial votes."

The Democrats' slim 54-46 edge contrasted with the overwhelming 62-38 margin of Byrd's first Congress as majority leader in 1977-78, and with the 59-41 split of his second.

"We had the numbers then. We could afford to be a little independent," Byrd said. "But being in the minority for six years . . . we learned that we don't have the luxury of each going his own way, and we do have to look at things together as a party. Because, while a given senator may be reelected on his own, quite independent of his party, at the same time he is a committee chairman or a subcommittee chairman because the party has control of the Senate."

"So," he added, "it's important that our party stay in control. Otherwise, we go back to being the ranking members and having far less influence and impact on national programs and the direction of our country. That's the penalty if we don't stick together."

In the past, such an ominous warning wouldn't have worked on Byrd's colleagues. "We figured we had the majorityship by the divine right of kings earlier," Johnston said. "Nobody really, seriously, considered a threat by the Republicans to be credible. Now it is, and we're more careful."

Besides their numbers, another big change since Democrats last ruled the Senate was Republican occupancy of the White House. From 1977-81, Byrd and then-Speaker Thomas P. O'Neill Jr. of Massachusetts had to help a Democratic president, Jimmy Carter, pass his legislative program. In the 100th Congress, Byrd and Wright had to develop Congress' own agenda as an alternative to Reagan's.

And they had to do so quickly, before the partisan strains of 1988 barred all progress. "Byrd's goal was to get what's getable early and build momentum," said David Pratt, until 1987 a top Byrd aide.

Byrd's good relations with Wright helped. The men bridged the traditionally jealous House and Senate, smoothing the way for priority legislation. In the past, a political and cultural gulf divided Byrd and O'Neill.

While Wright's West Texas is farther from West Virginia than O'Neill's Boston, its isolation and conservative politics mark it as much closer to Byrd's home. Wright campaigned for Byrd's first election to the Senate. While O'Neill was a gregarious pol from a city machine, both Wright and Byrd are introspective workaholics, self-made men who bucked the establishment to win office.

Byrd knew the House; he was elected to it in 1952 and served three terms, the last two with Wright. Wright, for his part, was said to understand the Senate better than O'Neill and thus to appreciate that its peculiar rules could leave the leader captive to the whims of a single member. "We both understand this Hill very well," Byrd said.

In December 1986, Byrd told a party conference he and Wright would work closer than any leaders since Senate Majority Leader Lyndon B. Johnson and Speaker Sam Rayburn, Texas Democrats who shared power from 1955-61. For Byrd, that prospect held special meaning: In his 1980 speeches, he counted the House-Senate partnership as a major reason for Johnson's effectiveness.

Months before Wright became Speaker in 1987, Byrd trekked to the House to discuss future strategy. Coordinating, they broke with recent practice and put members to work from Congress' start Jan. 6, instead of waiting for the president's State of the Union address at month's end.

Together they delivered the party response to Reagan's Jan. 27 speech on national television. "That sent out a very positive message" about party unity, said Kirk O'Donnell, director of the Democratic-oriented Center for National Policy and former counsel to O'Neill. So did their decision to combine the House and Senate panels investigating the Iran-contra scandal.

"Jim Wright wants to be a forceful leader, so I think he seeks out Byrd and I think Byrd has been pleasantly surprised," said Sen. Lloyd Bentsen, a Texas Democrat. "O'Neill was more interested in the House, by itself. Now both leaders have a deep desire to coordinate on a common Democratic program."

But institutional strains were inevitable. Days after the leaders' joint TV appearance, House members were lambasting Byrd for not blocking a Republican amendment to a homeless-aid bill that would have canceled a congressional pay raise. As Byrd noted, Senate rules permit unrelated amendments to almost any bill, unlike House rules. After some House maneuvering, the pay raise took effect after all.

Significantly, Wright wasn't the only new leadership figure Byrd faced upon his return to power. Of the Senate Democrats who became committee chairmen, only John C. Stennis of Mississippi and William Proxmire of Wisconsin had chaired major committees when Democrats last controlled the Senate.

In 1977, Byrd was a new leader sharing power with titans like John L. McClellan of Arkansas, Warren G. Magnuson and Henry M. Jackson of Washington, and James O. Eastland of Mississippi.

In 1987, he had a decade as leader behind him and was senior to most chairmen. Supporters said Byrd showed greater ease and confidence in his job as a consequence.

At the same time, senators noted, the new chairmen were more independent than the old bulls, and less easily swayed by his calls to fall in line for the good of the party or the institution.

"The old guard acted more like a Senate club," said Ohio Democrat Howard M. Metzenbaum. "Each was a force in and unto himself, but they were team players. Byrd didn't have

The new leadership team of Senate Majority Leader Byrd and House Speaker Jim Wright has been a cartoonist's delight.

to make his case for something. With this new young breed, he has to."

But Byrd said, "I don't detect a greater independence. I detect out of these chairmen as great a desire to cooperate with the leader as I ever detected back in those days."

Meanwhile, his deference to chairmen in part reflected his view of his own role. "He recognizes the type of leadership the caucus wants, and that's a shared leadership with the chairmen," a senior party aide said.

At the same time, Byrd "has pushed the committee chairmen to get legislation through their committees and out on the floor," Democrat Wendell H. Ford of Kentucky, chairman of the Rules and Administration Committee, said. That panel produced the campaign-finance bill Byrd wanted despite Ford's reservations.

Bentsen, chairman of the Finance Committee, said Byrd persuaded key senators to work late into 1986, at holiday time, so trade legislation would be ready when Congress convened.

Caucuses and Power Shared

"I have lived through periods here when there were just too many caucuses.... When I call a conference I expect it to be of importance sufficient to justify the attendance of senators who are busy and who have other things to do." (April 18, 1980)

Party caucuses were one subject on which Byrd clearly had changed his mind since 1980. While in the minority, Byrd borrowed from the Republicans' practice and scheduled weekly Democratic policy luncheons. He continued the caucuses in 1987, and there he made his case for unity.

In the minority, Byrd said, "by necessity we had to come together . . . and decide how and where we were going to apply whatever pressure we could to influence the directions of policy."

"I found [caucuses] to be a very useful process," he said. "And so now the entire Democratic conference is my policy committee."

"He's been much more of a good leader in the caucus," said Democrat Lawton Chiles of Florida, whose dissatisfaction with Byrd's style led him to mount a last-minute assault in 1984. "He tries to convey that we're not in the minority anymore, we can't go off in a dozen different directions."

In his days as minority leader, Byrd took other steps to encourage Democrats' participation and thus their identity as a group, Ford said — providing opportunities for all to manage legislation on the floor and appointing members to policy-making task forces, for example. "Trying to give everybody a responsibility by delegating, he brought us closer together," Ford said.

"Most of us had gotten into the position that 'we know Byrd will do it, we know Byrd will get it done,' so we hadn't been carrying our share of the load," Ford said. "When we were in the minority and he gave everybody responsibilities, we started learning how to carry our part of the burden. I think it's indicated by the number of times we've held together. And that's an accolade we ought to give Byrd."

To Republicans, Byrd's use of caucuses as a leadership tool was just one debt he owed to their past and present leaders, Baker and Robert Dole of Kansas.

"I think Byrd observed under Baker a growing discipline of Republicans in the minority and then as a majority," Oregon Republican Mark O. Hatfield said. "He saw that as a certain objective, though I'm not sure he succeeded when Democrats were in the minority like Howard Baker did."

"He shows more interest in the substance of legislation," said New Mexico Republican Pete V. Domenici. A notable example was the campaign-finance bill, which Byrd had all but taken over from sponsor David L. Boren, an Oklahoma Democrat.

"He takes the lead on a lot more things," Domenici said, "following in the footsteps of our two leaders. And that's a very big change."

The Minority's Role

"Its role is not to obstruct, but it has a certain adversary role and it is a built-in opposition role." (April 18, 1980)

If Byrd learned a few things from Republicans, they also acknowledged having gained new understanding of him — and of the majority's role.

"That is clearly because we had to run the place for six years," Domenici said. "We now understand what Democrats are going through."

"It's like running a class, with kids raising their hands all the time," said Alan K. Simpson of Wyoming, second-ranking Republican leader. "It's a crazy business, and it used to drive me bonkers. How do you accommodate 100 people? He accommodates his people, but he also accommodates ours."

"I have a different feeling toward him. When you're the leader, you're the leader and you don't allow the minority party to determine what's going to come to the floor." Simpson said the "grudging respect" he had for Byrd in 1979 had mellowed into a "very authentic respect."

Though Republicans might understand better why Byrd does what he does, that doesn't mean they always like it. His mastery of Senate rules could leave them sputtering. They complained of Reagan-bashing in Byrd's scheduling of measures the president opposed. Even Simpson was enraged when Byrd implied in May 1987 the Republican efforts to block a fiscal 1988 defense bill (S 1174) were unpatriotic in the wake of the Iraqi attack on the U.S. frigate *Stark* that killed 37 servicemen.

Each week, Majority Leader Byrd presides over a luncheon caucus of Senate Democrats, like this one June 30.

Minority members also resented his effort to push a campaign-finance bill, seeing it as a strictly partisan gambit to depict their party as anti-reform while limiting its fund-raising ability.

But the party fought back. And despite Simpson's observation that the majority leader decides what bills come to the floor, Republicans had shown that was not always so.

In May 1987, they blocked both the defense bill and a bill making supplemental appropriations for this fiscal year (HR 1827). The appropriations bill finally passed June 2, but the defense bill had been stalled since May 20, when Byrd fell one vote short on a third attempt to end the filibuster. Republicans opposed a provision barring the administration from conducting space tests of anti-missile systems without Congress' approval.

In June, they blocked the campaign-finance bill, five times defeating Byrd's motions to choke off their filibuster. But Byrd felt he had won something in the bargain: proof of Republican obstructionism.

In 1987, as in 1980, Byrd drew a firm line between obstructionism and what he saw as the minority party's proper role — opposition to the majority's program. Opposition does not prevent action; obstructionism does.

Republicans denied that they had a strategy of obstructionism. "If there is, I don't know it," Domenici said.

In fact, Republicans confessed to an embarrassing disunity early in 1987, when dissidents helped Democrats override Reagan's vetoes. They said the recent bloc voting simply reflected the partisan nature of the issues Byrd had raised — notably the defense and campaign-finance bills.

"The Republicans sort of went along for a while and were surprised the Democrats were voting in such numbers together," said Republican Richard G. Lugar of Indiana. "The shock of this occurring for four months finally led Republicans to say, 'Well, now we have to pull up our socks on a couple of issues.' But there's certainly not much of a monolithic strategy there."

Scheduling and Attendance

"It is extremely difficult to deal with the wishes and needs of 99 other senators, attempting to schedule legislation, because almost in every case, at any time it is scheduled, it inconveniences some senator, and I cannot fire any of them. . . . I often say, when I am to fill out a form and the form says 'occupation,' I should put 'slave.'" (April 18, 1980)

Scheduling is both the most tedious and most important aspect of a majority leader's job. Dole also compared himself to a slave during his two years as majority leader. But responsibility for the schedule means more than adjusting Senate hours to senators' busy lives. It is the power to set the legislative agenda.

A measure of the schedule's importance was the number of senators who mentioned it when asked to appraise Byrd's leadership to date.

Freshman Democrat Thomas A. Daschle of South Dakota said Byrd's scheduling of early votes on the highway and water bills, and on the subsequent veto overrides, took advantage of Democrats' "initial euphoria" at being back in power. The successes then enhanced their sense of unity.

Both sides saw improvements in

the hours the Senate kept, compared with Byrd's last stint. "I think he's making a determined effort not to keep us around here late on silly things. That's quite a difference from the way it was [when Democrats last had control]," said Republican John H. Chafee of Rhode Island. "It was really miserable around this place. I think he learned a lot seeing the way Howard Baker did it, and Bob Dole."

At the start of the 100th Congress, Byrd ruled out night sessions and agreed to three-day weekends, with Mondays off, at least until July. But he insisted Fridays would be workdays, in a break with the Tuesday-to-Thursday schedules of recent years.

Republicans applauded the arrangement. Byrd's problem had been in his own ranks. The absence of seven Democrats, including three presidential contenders, proved embarrassing on Friday, May 29, 1987, when Byrd failed by five votes to get the 60 needed to override budgetary objections and pass the supplemental spending bill.

In the oft-recounted floor scene that followed, Byrd lashed out at absentees and retaliated by scheduling two more votes that afternoon. "Bed-check votes," snapped Democrat Patrick J. Leahy of Vermont, noting that senators have duties off the floor to committees and their constituents.

Byrd retorted: "This senator is not going to stand supinely by in silence and quaking with fear and have others say, 'Well, I'm going home. Let's don't have any votes on Fridays.' "

Despite his admonition, 25 senators were missing for the day's final vote, including seven more Democrats.

That was not to say members didn't care about absenteeism. Senators' attendance, measured by presence for roll-call votes, had improved in recent years as challengers used incumbents' records to damaging effect.

"That gives the majority leader a very strong weapon," Lugar said. "On the other hand, if he misuses it, if it is obvious that there is simply the threat of votes when there is nothing of consequence, then there are going to be some problems."

In the following weeks, Byrd continued to hold votes on Fridays. There was some grousing when he forced senators to meet on a Saturday, June 27, for debate on a trade bill. But generally, Democrats supported Byrd's push for action. "A leader's position is not to be liked, it's to lead," said first-term Democrat John B. Breaux of Louisiana. "If you're never going to do anything to make anybody mad, you're not going to get anything done."

A Tenuous Hold

"Lyndon Johnson could not lead this Senate today as he led the Senate in his day.... It is a different Senate." (April 18, 1980)

In an extraordinary aside during the May 29 flap, Byrd acknowledged, "I do not expect to get kudos from anybody. I understand that I am not very well-liked around here anyhow. I did not get elected to be liked here. I got elected because I thought I could do a job. This is a challenge, and I do not back off from a challenge."

Most senators already had heard a similar statement the night before, when Byrd addressed a gala audience celebrating his and his wife Erma's 50th wedding anniversary. Still, many confessed surprise for weeks afterward.

For Byrd, an orphan who was raised by an aunt and uncle, the Senate was home and its members were family; in 1980, he called them "brothers." To have believed they did not like you "must hurt," Domenici said. "We're politicians," Breaux said, "We all want to be loved."

Byrd is a loner, and a non-stop laborer; he does not mix with senators in the gym or on the golf course. But if they do not like him, senators respect him — for his command of history and Senate rules, for rising from poor butcher to senator (and then earning a law degree at night school) and for his reverence for their institution.

Byrd knew perhaps better than anyone that the metaphor of the family was no longer an apt one for the Senate — as he believed it was when he arrived in 1959 and Johnson was majority leader.

"I think you've got to give the leader credit when things go well — and blame when they don't, even if he's not the author of all the good and all the bad. That's the way leadership works."

—Sen. J. Bennett Johnston, D-La.

In 1987, members showed little allegiance to party or institution. Newcomers were no longer admonished to be seen but not heard and, given the proliferation of subcommittees, it would be pointless: Four first-year Democrats were subcommittee chairmen.

That was why Byrd insisted Johnson's iron hand would no longer work. On May 2, 1980, Byrd listed the necessary traits for a leader: patience, good temper, fairness, knowledge of the members and ability to organize them.

Then he added: "It would be well if he could also have the attribute of being a forceful, eloquent and articulate speaker, but not every man can be so equipped."

Though Byrd did not apply that test to himself, Chiles and Johnston did it for him in 1984 and 1986. The episodes bared something of a contradiction: While Democrats might complain of Byrd's weaknesses as a national spokesman, and drew unflattering comparisons with the glib and telegenic Dole, many senators actually preferred a leader like Byrd who was willing to do the drudge work and cede the center stage on various policy debates.

However, despite his ease in weathering the past challenges, most Democrats interviewed said they expected others in the future.

"Not by me," Chiles said, "not if he's doing the job he's doing now." But Johnston said, "I said at the time I withdrew that I'd be a likely candidate at some point in the future, and that's still valid."

The man considered Byrd's heir apparent, Daniel K. Inouye of Hawaii, 62, was not likely to challenge Byrd since the two are allies. Inouye entered the leadership with Byrd in 1977, in the No. 3 post of conference secretary.

In 1986, they ran as a team, along with Majority Whip Alan Cranston of California, the No. 2 Senate Democrat. Cranston, 73, was not viewed as a potential successor, given his age.

Byrd, 69, sidestepped recurring questions about rumors started in 1986 that he told senators he wanted just one more two-year term as leader.

Still, some members privately speculated about a scenario under which Byrd, once re-elected senator, would forgo the leadership to become chairman of the Appropriations Committee, where he had kept a second-ranking seat. Under this scenario, the current chairman, 85-year-old Stennis, would move aside and keep only his ceremonial post of Senate president pro tem — assuming he seeks and wins re-election in Mississippi in 1988. Stennis dismissed such rumors as unfounded.

However fanciful, such talk was regarded by some as a sign that Byrd's hold on the majority leader position was tenuous.

"He's done a lot for his state, and I think he'd like to wind up his career doing more for a state that's been good to him," Ford said.

"That kind of gives me a gut feeling that he may spend the next term being a good senator and chairman of the Appropriations Committee and helping West Virginia" get federal funds. But, Ford added, "one of the best ways to help West Virginia is to be majority leader."

"I would be foolish to say today that I will or won't [seek the leadership], and I'm just not going to do it," Byrd said. "We have much more important problems and that's what I'm giving my attention to." ▮

Speaker Jim Wright Takes Charge in the House

Seizes the Initiative In Setting the Agenda

A few hours before President Reagan went to Capitol Hill in January 1987, to deliver his State of the Union address, Jim Wright was spotted on the floor of the House of Representatives. The newly elected Speaker was alone in the chamber. As if he were preparing for visitors to his own home, he straightened some chairs.

That painstaking attention to detail was emblematic of the degree of control over the House and concern about its image that the Texas Democrat had brought to the No. 1 leadership job.

In his first six months in office, Wright had largely stuck to an agenda he laid out moments after being named Speaker. He had personally attended to policy questions that his predecessor would have left to others. He had pulled all available levers of power to get his House in order.

Amid this flurry of activity, Wright had clearly placed a great premium on being seen as a strong Speaker as well as on actually exercising the powers of the office.

"He wants to be perceived as someone who's got all these issues in the proper place, at the proper time, and that he's the one who's calling the shots," said Joe Moakley, D-Mass., a senior member of the Rules Committee.

Having an aggressive, purposeful leader generally suited rank-and-file Democrats, who believed that a well-managed House would showcase their party's ability to govern in the 1988 election campaign.

But Wright's assertive leadership style "has its pluses or minuses, depending on whether you happen to agree with the Speaker," said John D. Dingell, D-Mich., the Energy and Commerce Committee chairman who agreed with Wright more often than not.

In 1987, Democrats had mostly seen the pluses, because Wright, in setting his agenda, generally had not been forcing unwelcome issues on his followers. To be sure, he had prodded Democrats to switch their longstanding strategy and support a tax increase to reduce the deficit, despite Reagan's continued opposition.

But for the most part, Wright had used the power of the speakership to propel issues about which there was wide consensus among Democrats — water projects, highway funding, aid to the homeless and a trade bill very similar to one that had passed in May 1986.

"All the victories we've had are sweet victories, but water projects, the homeless — that's high visibility, that's easy," said Dan Rostenkowski, D-Ill., chairman of the tax-writing Ways and Means Committee. "The tough things are yet to come."

Welfare reform was proving to be easier said than done. A renewed confrontation with Reagan was inevitable over arms control.

And since Congress had approved a budget resolution (H Con Res 93) calling for $19 billion in new taxes, the House had to address the more divisive question of which taxes to raise.

The institutional challenge for Wright was whether he would be able to maintain a balance between exerting the kind of strong leadership he admired and learned from his Texas mentor, former Speaker Sam Rayburn, and practicing the kind of politics of inclusion and consultation that is now *de rigueur.* As Wright knew, the contemporary House could no longer be led, Rayburn-style, through private dealings with a few powerful, senior members.

"Even if a Speaker wanted to impose an agenda, he doesn't have the tools to do it," said Matthew F. McHugh, D-N.Y. "The key point for Jim is, will he consult in a way that gives members the feeling that his agenda is the product of those consultations?"

Flexing New Muscles

Wright was officially installed as Speaker on Jan. 6, 1987, in a reshuffling of the Democratic leadership that was triggered by the retirement of Speaker Thomas P. O'Neill Jr. of

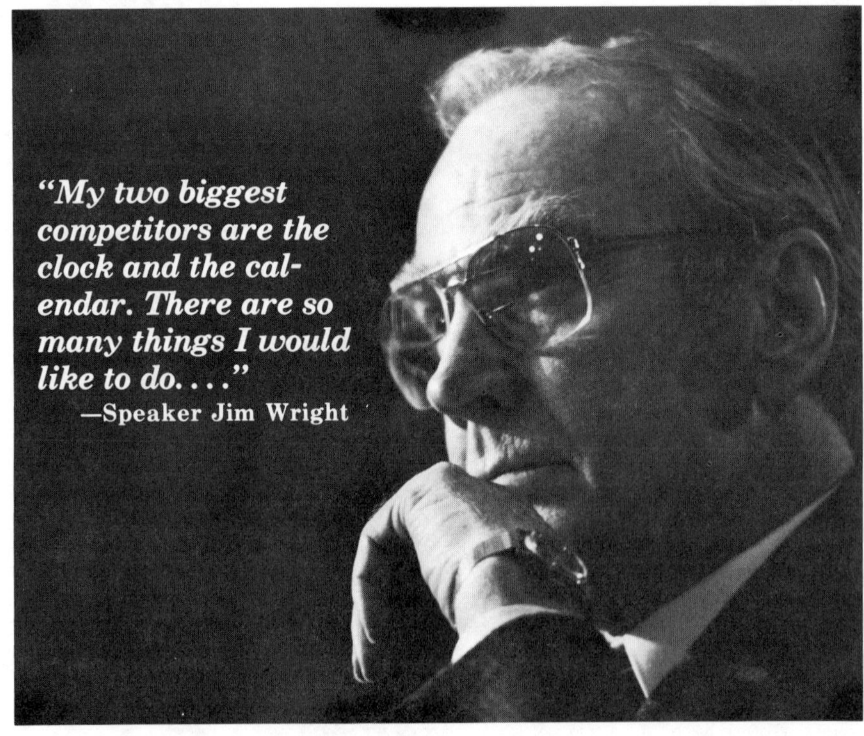

"My two biggest competitors are the clock and the calendar. There are so many things I would like to do. . . ."
—Speaker Jim Wright

Massachusetts at the end of 1986. Also thrust into new jobs were Majority Leader Thomas S. Foley of Washington, who had been majority whip, and Tony Coelho of California, who succeeded Foley as whip. *(Foley and Coelho, box, next page)*

In July 1987, it remained too early for a definitive assessment of Wright's leadership style as Speaker. Many members said he was still enjoying the good will of a honeymoon period. The phrase "Speaker Wright" did not yet come naturally to many of his colleagues.

But Wright had tried hard to make his mark — early and often. Wright had asserted himself aggressively in internal House matters. Putting his imprint on the Steering and Policy Committee, the leadership panel that makes committee assignments, he dropped O'Neill's practice of allowing freshmen, women and black members to choose their own representatives to the panel. Instead, Wright selected them.

He also had backed a proposal to have the Speaker appoint Democratic members of the House Administration Committee, which doles out such gratitude-inspiring perks as office space and parking spots.

Wright's ambitious legislative agenda reflected his determination to change the pace of the House floor activity, which in the past typically was very light until spring or later. He had made aggressive use of the Rules Committee to restrict debate and to speed action on the bills he had identified as top priorities.

The aura of accomplishment created by Wright and his leadership team had been bright enough to distract from their blemishes. No one took much notice when a deadline was missed. And his successes might help him escape lasting damage to his prestige from controversy surrounding his intervention with federal banking regulators on behalf of Texas savings and loan and real estate interests. *(1987 CQ Weekly Report pp. 1390, 1110)*

From O'Neill to Wright

O'Neill certainly was never a weak Speaker, but there were striking contrasts between his leadership style and Wright's. Particularly in the last two years of his tenure, O'Neill preferred to delegate responsibility and to pick his personal fights carefully. His idea of leadership did not require mastery of legislative technicalities.

Wright was far more interested in the particulars of legislation and involved in more issues. He did his homework and could discuss fine points of various bills with the subcommittee chairmen charged with drafting them.

For example, he had helped broker legislation (HR 2470) to protect Medicare beneficiaries against catastrophic health-care costs. He personally saw to it that the bill included coverage for prescription drugs — an add-on that he viewed as a way to put a Democratic stamp on a proposal that originated in the Reagan administration. *(1987 CQ Weekly Report p. 1437)*

"He wants to be perceived as someone who's got all these issues in the proper place, at the proper time, and that he's the one who's calling the shots."

—Rep. Joe Moakley, D-Mass.

More controversial was Wright's involvement in legislation (HR 27) to bail out the federal agency that insures savings and loan deposits. He lobbied the Banking Committee to support a version of the bill regarded as more favorable to ailing thrift institutions — of which there were many in Texas, hard hit by the slump in the oil industry.

He later switched his position on the legislation, but criticism resurfaced when the national news media reported on his intervention with federal bank regulators on behalf of three fellow Texans. Wright said he was only doing his congressional duty to help his home state.

On fiscal matters, Wright monitored the budget resolution with an attentiveness bred during his dozen years on the Budget Committee. He and Senate Majority Leader Robert C. Byrd, D-W.Va., were de facto members of the conference committee, personally intervening to break an impasse between House and Senate Democrats.

"Jim is more involved in every issue at some point," said one Budget Committee Democrat. "Tip had an understanding of what was going on, but it was a back-channel appreciation. Jim is more up-front."

O'Neill was more inclined to wait for consensus to emerge, giving wider latitude to committee chairmen to set their own agendas. O'Neill did assert himself and push the House in his direction on issues he cared about, but his hand often was less evident than Wright's.

"Tip wanted to give the impression of a kind of consensus," even when he was dictating the outcome, said one senior Democrat. "Jim wants to give the appearance of direction even when there is some consensus. He wants to have the reputation as well as the reality of being a strong Speaker."

Admirers and adversaries alike already were calling Wright "the strongest Speaker since Sam Rayburn." But they probably forgot that similar superlatives were applied to O'Neill during his first year as Speaker.

In 1977, O'Neill pushed through a new congressional ethics code. He, too, supported the idea of making House Administration a leadership-dominated committee. And just as Wright won kudos for his handling of a multifaceted trade bill, O'Neill was hailed for maneuvering President Carter's energy program through a maze of competing committee jurisdictions to approval by the House in August 1977. By then, *The Washington Post* was downright fulsome in its praise for the Speaker, running an article headlined, "Tip O'Neill: A Legend Being Born." *(1977 CQ Almanac p. 12)*

The Wright Time for Activism

But the circumstances in 1977 were very different from those in 1987. O'Neill was serving with a Democratic president, Jimmy Carter, and was throwing the weight of his leadership behind the White House's agenda. Wright was crafting his own Democratic program as the agenda of opposition.

Foley, Coelho Stick to What They Do Best . . .

In the six months since House Democrats promoted Thomas S. Foley of Washington to majority leader and elected Tony Coelho of California as majority whip in January 1987, the two have helped the Democratic leadership project a new, take-charge image.

But in many ways, their roles had not changed much since the reshuffling in January, which also put Jim Wright of Texas in the Speaker's office. *(Wright, p. 34)*

In the 99th Congress, Foley was whip and made regular appearances on the House floor to announce the legislative schedule. Behind the scenes, he was heading a task force to consider changes in the budget process. In the 100th Congress he still did both.

In the 99th Congress, Coelho more often than not was buttonholing colleagues on the floor as he sought backing for his bid to become whip — the House Democrats' third-ranking leader, chief vote-counter and floor manager. He was still on the prowl, only in 1987 he was soliciting support for leadership positions on key bills.

Majority Leader Thomas S. Foley, D-Wash., right, confers with colleagues, including Dan Glickman, D-Kan., center.

Despite their new titles and responsibilities, Foley remained the voice of caution in the leadership and Coelho the hard-charging party operative.

Yet while the personalities in the leadership might be familiar, both Democrats and Republicans said the chemistry at the top had been transformed by the rearrangement of its elements.

"It's a much more aggressive and energetic team than Democrats have had in years," said Newt Gingrich, a conservative Republican from Georgia. "The score this year is that the Democratic House leadership knows what it's doing, has the muscle to do it, and is doing it."

Said Coelho, "It's not business as usual, and the public perceives it."

Adjusting to New Roles

Both Coelho and Foley had important adjustments to make in their new leadership posts.

Until January 1987, Coelho had presided over his own domain as chairman of the Democratic Congressional Campaign Committee (DCCC). As whip, he had to be a team player on a three-man squad, and he began as odd man out, because Wright and Foley already had worked together for years.

Foley moved from a job with fairly clear-cut responsibilities to one that was ill-defined. The majority leader's office is "more open-ended," Foley said, "It is, to some extent, defined by relationship to the Speaker."

Foley had had to accommodate a Speaker who was more personally involved in agenda-setting and legislative detail than his predecessor, Thomas P. O'Neill Jr. of Massachusetts. And at times, members detected some tensions as all three leaders adjusted to their new jobs and to one another.

Relations initially seemed strained, particularly between Foley and Coelho. An ambitious fifth-termer, Coelho had hinted at a future rivalry with Foley by telling some people privately that "he does not want to wait 20 years to become Speaker," as one associate put it.

For the most part, however, members said the leadership seemed to be strengthened by the fact that Foley and Coelho had such different styles and temperaments. As they carved out roles to match, tensions eased.

Wright had become Speaker just as Democrats had gained control of both chambers of Congress for the first time in six years, House Republicans were at a loss for an effective opposition strategy, Reagan was at the weakest point in his administration, and Democrats believed the public's support for an activist government was on the rebound.

"We were in a holding action.... Now we are able to move forward in legislation," said James J. Howard, D-N.J., chairman of the Public Works Committee. "Thank God we've got someone like Jim Wright — a doer."

Although Wright's activism was abetted by circumstances, it was hard to imagine any situation in which a man of his background and character would be a caretaker Speaker. Having been elected majority leader in 1977, Wright had been waiting 10 years for his chance to move up. That was a good long time to think about what he would do in the No. 1 job.

His taste for legislative detail was cultivated during 22 years on the Public Works Committee; O'Neill's background had been on the Rules Committee — a leadership panel that deals with the substance of legislation only on the margins.

Wright was a decisive man by nature, not one to be paralyzed by a choice among multiple options. He had a sense of urgency about his goals that could make him impatient with the time-consuming activities of coddling and consulting colleagues.

"My two biggest competitors are the clock and the calendar," he said in an interview. "There are so many things I would like to do....

"The trouble is you have only so

. . . As New House Leadership Team Settles In

Coelho brought to the whip's job the same energy and determination he showed as the DCCC's most successful fund-raiser. His high-octane approach was well-matched to Wright's ambitious agenda for the 100th Congress.

Coelho presided over a growing whip's organization that included nearly one-third of the Democratic Caucus. It was made up of 11 deputy whips, including chief deputy David E. Bonior of Michigan; 44 at-large whips appointed by the leadership, and 22 regional whips elected by members of the area they represent.

Coelho also had expanded the practice of naming task forces to plot strategy on key issues, such as the budget or U.S. policy in Nicaragua. At last count, there were 14 such task forces.

Division of Labor

As majority leader, Foley replaced Wright as the leadership's representative on the Budget and Intelligence committees. He also was appointed to the select committee investigating the Iran-contra affair.

A contemplative man, Foley tended to play the devil's advocate in leadership councils. That could infuriate shoot-from-the-hip types like Wright and Coelho, but he was generally appreciated for injecting a dose of caution into the leadership.

Foley also is a consensus builder, and he used that skill to great acclaim in 1985 when he headed a task force that crafted House Democrats' strategy for handling the Gramm-Rudman-Hollings budget bill.

In 1987 he was leading another task force on the budget process.

"Tom can lock up people in a room and craft a good compromise, understand arcane views, and then go out and give a 30-second sound bite," said Dennis E. Eckart, D-Ohio. "Tony will find you the votes for it. . . . They seem to have gotten very compatible now in their compartments."

Their different styles also were an asset when the leadership was trying to whip the rank and file into line on key votes.

"Some people are offended at being whipped too hard, and Foley works with them," said Buddy MacKay, D-Fla. "There are other people whom you really have to shove, and Tony works with them."

Practicing the art of persuasion, Majority Whip Tony Coelho, left, presses a point with Les AuCoin, D-Ore.

Before Foley's election as majority leader, some members wondered whether he was too conciliatory to be the kind of partisan spokesman Democrats had come to expect of their majority leader. Similarly, members wondered whether Coelho, as whip, would tone down the strident partisanship he brought to the job as DCCC chairman. Some members believed his concentration on political fund raising for the previous six years had left him unprepared for managing the Democrat's agenda.

However, neither had radically changed his political persona. They might instead have changed Democrats' ideas about how a whip and leader should operate.

many weeks in the legislative year, and so many days in the legislative week, so many hours in the legislative day."

Working With the Senate

For one haunted by the limits of time, maintaining a schedule could be an obsession. One of Wright's biggest frustrations was seeing his control over scheduling dissipate as bills move to the Senate. *(Byrd's Senate, p. 28)*

"That's frustrating, but there isn't anything I can do about it," he said. "Senate rules are tilted toward not doing things. House rules, if you know how to use them, are tilted toward allowing the majority to get its will done."

House Democrats had on occasion tried to help their Senate colleagues move things along. Faced with a close Senate vote on overriding Reagan's veto of highway legislation (HR 2), Rep. Charlie Rose and other North Carolina Democrats were dispatched to talk to wavering Sen. Terry Sanford, D-N.C., who first voted to sustain Reagan's veto, then reversed himself to provide for the override.

The top three Democratic leaders from both the House and Senate met every other week to coordinate strategy, bringing with them the committee chairmen involved in issues at hand. But however useful such meetings are, they could not always pry legislation from inter-chamber logjams.

Wright's pet initiative to aid the homeless emerged from conference long after the winter chill passed.

And the image of his party as a bunch of can-do, able governors was jeopardized when House and Senate Democrats fell to squabbling in conference over the fiscal 1988 budget resolution. Wright flinched when a *Washington Post* editorial dubbed members of his party "flubbocrats."

"Democrats were looking great for the first five months of the year. Now we are getting panned," Wright said in a letter to House Democratic budget conferees.

Within his own domain of the House, Wright had gone to great lengths to keep major legislation moving. He announced a schedule in January 1987, at a weekend retreat for House Democrats, and hit within a week or so for most items.

He missed the mark on some matters, such as welfare reform and foreign aid bills, which were slated for May floor action. Still, members of both parties appreciated his efforts to increase the predictability of floor activity. Scheduling is the one job of leadership that affects all members all the time; it sets the parameters of their lives outside the House chamber. In discussing Wright's record so far, a striking number of members remarked on his ability to "make the trains run on time."

While talking with a visitor, Speaker Jim Wright fiddles with Chinese metal balls that are said to have a calming influence.

The Reign of Wright

But Wright had grander ideas about what he wanted to accomplish. He wanted to be known as a policy maker, not just a master of procedure.

Indeed, he sometimes seemed to view his office as on a par with the presidency. For select bills, he had turned into a ceremonial occasion the Speaker's routine job of signing legislation before sending it to the White House. He sometimes talked as if the House were an administration; he believed it had a responsibility to produce a program, not just legislation, and that the Speaker was well-positioned to coordinate that program.

"The House should develop a program of action . . . rather than leaving the making of policy to a fragmented group of 21 standing committees without any cohesion," said Wright. "There has to be a sense of coordinated policy, a cohesive pattern to what the institution does."

One problem with viewing the speakership like the presidency is that committee chairmen are not Cabinet officers. They are not appointed by the Speaker, and they cannot be dismissed by him.

Many members believed that Wright, in his efforts to coordinate the agenda, ran the risk of stepping on the toes of committee chairmen.

Rostenkowski had urged Wright to set up a "chairman's council," which he believed would give the leadership the pragmatic advice it needed from the people responsible for actually putting together legislation.

Wright acknowledged the potential for riling committee chairmen jealous of their turf. But some of Wright's closest allies were chairmen.

Jack Brooks, chairman of the Government Operations Committee, is dean of the Texas delegation and a member of Wright's inner circle. After being elected Speaker, Wright entrusted to Brooks the chairmanship of an in-house personnel committee that controls patronage jobs such as elevator operators, doorkeepers and pages. The patronage chairmanship previously had been held by Moakley, an O'Neill lieutenant.

Energy and Commerce Chairman Dingell, once considered a potential challenger for the speakership, had forged a close and powerful alliance with Wright. That paid off handsomely early in 1987 when the Speaker helped Dingell get three Democrats of his choice assigned to Energy and Commerce, strengthening his position on environmental issues that were dividing the committee.

Public Works Chairman Howard also was very close to Wright, after working with him on the committee for 12 years. He found himself referring to a compendium of Wright's speeches so often that he kept a copy on his desk at all times. It was appropriate that the first two major bills cleared this year were public works measures — a Clean Water Act renewal (HR 1) and the highway bill.

If Wright had had his way, the year's third bill would have been a massive one to repair the nation's infrastructure. Howard said he was not ready to introduce such a bill, but promised it would be "the most important public works project probably in the history of the world."

Wright's taste for grand public works programs reflected his populist streak. He was optimistic about government's ability to solve economic and social problems, and he was inclined to think big.

If a politician "seeks only a limited amount, it's a cinch he won't achieve more," Wright said. Quoting the 16th-century Danish astronomer Tycho Brahe, Wright added, "Make no little plans. They have no magic to stir men's blood."

The Tax Man Cometh

It was not surprising that of all the committee chairmen, Rostenkowski had the most problematic relations with Wright. He is the chairman who has to write the tax legislation to pay for Wright's expansive notions of the good that government can do. Rostenkowski also was the one man who acknowledged interest in being Speaker long after Wright was generally regarded as O'Neill's heir apparent.

While other committees' agendas were probably no different now from what they would have been if O'Neill were still in charge, Wright's accession had changed Rostenkowski's work.

"If Jim Wright was not as strong as he has been with respect to raising revenues ... we wouldn't be talking about it now," said Rostenkowski.

Left to his own devices, Rostenkowski, understandably concerned about the political difficulties of putting together a bill that would pass the House, let alone one that would become law, would have adhered to O'Neill's strategy of withholding support for a tax increase until Reagan was on board.

But Wright was convinced that more revenues were urgently needed to reduce the deficit and that they would not be raised if no one pushed Reagan.

Some members were still dubious about the wisdom of crawling out on this political limb. Many winced back in December 1986 when, within hours of being elected Speaker by the Democratic Caucus, Wright called for delaying a scheduled tax cut for the wealthiest Americans. But by midyear, both the House and Senate had passed a budget resolution calling for $19 billion in new taxes.

Juggling Factions

Wright's aggressive position on tax issues had won plaudits from liberals, such as Democratic Study Group activists, whose greatest frustration with O'Neill was his refusal to consider raising taxes.

In the past Wright had differed with the liberal wing of his party over defense issues, such as the MX missile. But while his views in the past were regarded as too hawkish for some liberals, he had voted with them consistently in 1987.

The potential for conflict with his left flank might not be tested until after Reagan leaves office. In the 100th Congress, the president's positions on key defense and foreign-policy issues had so alienated Democrats that the moderate and liberal wings of the caucus were generally united in opposition to the administration.

Wright had made arms control a leadership priority. The leadership essentially took over the handling of arms control amendments to a supplemental appropriations bill (HR 1827). But the amendments ultimately were dropped in conference with the Senate, and liberal activists might want the leadership to push harder the next time the issue comes up.

Wright ran the risk of alienating what might seem his natural constituency within the caucus — Southerners — if he pushed liberals' priorities too far. Some conservative Democrats already were restive at the prospect of repeated votes on arms control matters and labor bills that had little chance of being signed into law.

"Some of these bills will never see the light of day," said one Southern Democrat. "Why put these members, particularly new members, on the spot?"

On budget issues, however, Wright had managed to build bridges to moderates who felt frozen out under O'Neill.

"I felt the leadership [before] was out of touch with the realities of being a Democrat in the Sun Belt," said Buddy MacKay, D-Fla.

Jim Wright: A Self-Portrait

But under Wright, MacKay said, "I feel there's a greater sensitivity to the views of those of us who are centrists in the party, and there's less attention paid to people who are the purists, the zealots on either extreme."

MacKay praised Wright for supporting, against the wishes of senior Appropriations Committee members, his amendment to cut the supplemental appropriations bill to within limits set by the House budget resolution.

He also cited Wright's role last year when, as majority leader, he helped pressure Appropriations Chairman Jamie L. Whitten into dropping a proposal to resurrect the multibillion-dollar revenue-sharing program. The Mississippi Democrat had quietly slipped the proposal into an omnibus spending bill; he dropped it at the leadership's bidding. *(1986 Almanac p. 219)*

"That was the first time I saw the leadership assert itself on behalf of fiscal discipline during my tenure as a House member," said MacKay. "At that point I began to think we've got some good times ahead of us."

Many Southerners said they were pleased with the change in the leadership's image that had come with Wright's ascension. After years of having to distance themselves from O'Neill, they said Wright was playing well in their home districts.

"In the South, Jim Wright is selling big," said North Carolinian Rose. "That makes my life easier."

While Wright might help give the Democratic Party a more moderate image than O'Neill, some Republicans said he had arrested the Democrats' search for new ideas.

"On every tactical level, Wright is doing a superb job," said Newt Gingrich, R-Ga. "The problem for Democrats is that, faced with a temporary Republican disarray, they are reverting to the party of Jimmy Carter — higher taxes, more spending, weaker defense, big labor bills."

Both sides were portraying Congress' public face as the Democrats' most visible campaign billboard for the 1988 elections.

The record Wright helps Democrats compile might make its way into the platform on which the party's presidential candidate would run. A Democratic president, in turn, could help enact the legislative agenda that remained largely stymied by the threat of a presidential veto.

"Part of what Wright has in mind and what the Democrats are looking for," said Thomas Mann, executive director of the American Political Science Association, "is to define a credible agenda for the 101st Congress, when they hope political conditions will make it more likely their legislation will actually emerge and be signed by the president."

But ironically, if a Democratic president were elected, it would render Wright's take-charge style less appropriate. The locus of Democratic Party leadership would shift to the White House, and Wright would be in less of a position to call the shots.

He conceded that his role would change if a Democrat were elected, but he said, "I sure would like to try it." ■

'Trivialized' Filibuster Is Still a Potent Tool

Filibusters aren't what they used to be a generation ago, when Strom Thurmond was a freshman senator.

In 1957, when the South Carolinian fought alone against a civil rights bill, he prepared for two days beforehand, drying out in the Senate steam room so bathroom calls wouldn't force him to surrender the floor. He lost the fight, but won the record for the longest filibuster by a single senator — 24 hours and 18 minutes.

Those were the old days, and they're long gone. In 1987, Thurmond, who switched from Democrat to Republican in 1964, was in effect participating with other Republicans in two filibusters at once, against defense and campaign-finance bills. But the effort demanded little. Often, the filibusterers did not even have to be on the floor, nor did the bills they were opposing.

Once reserved for the most bitter battles of historic dimension — slavery, war, civil rights — the filibuster has evolved into a tactic so routine that one senator, Republican Dan Quayle of Indiana, said, "It's been trivialized." Majority Leader Robert C. Byrd, a West Virginia Democrat, complaind the strategy is used "promiscuously."

Historically, the rare filibuster provided the Senate's best theater; practitioners had to be ready for days or weeks of freewheeling debate, and all other business was blocked until one side conceded.

Today, drama is rare; as soon as a filibuster is threatened or begun, the majority works either to get the necessary votes to invoke the 70-year-old cloture rule, which chokes off debate, or to negotiate a compromise.

Most of that action occurs behind the scenes. Meanwhile, leaders often shelve the disputed bill temporarily, with members' unanimous consent, so the Senate can turn to other matters — a tactic known as "double-tracking."

"Double-tracking has made it possible to keep going" on Senate business, said Connecticut Republican Lowell P. Weicker Jr. But, he added, it also "has kept the filibuster from being a real filibuster."

Visitors to the Senate gallery who expect a real-life version of Jimmy Stewart's climactic oration in the movie "Mr. Smith Goes to Washington" will be disappointed. They are likely to look down on an empty floor and hear only the drone of a clerk reading absent senators' names. "The modern-day filibuster," Quayle said, "means putting in quorum calls."

Debate and Deliberation

Throughout the Senate's history, perhaps nothing about the institution has so exasperated its members as the filibuster. It delays action and frustrates the majority's will. Yet no practice is more jealously guarded. *(Filibuster history, p. 44)*

The right of unlimited debate is what most differentiates the Senate from the House. Although the term "filibuster," derived from a word for pirates or soldiers of fortune, originated in the House, that chamber rarely experienced one. Given its size, the House has strictly enforced debate limits to maintain order.

Both chambers had adopted debate limits during the First Congress, but the Senate's were soon abandoned. Ever since, the Senate has proudly claimed to be the more deliberative body. In George Washington's often-cited metaphor, it is the saucer where passions cool.

What troubled many senators in 1987 was the conviction that the modern filibuster impedes rather than encourages deliberation. Often a bill never makes it to the floor for debate, blocked either by a filibuster of a motion to bring it up or by the mere threat of a filibuster. Critics said that frequent resort to the filibuster, even over what Iowa Republican Charles E. Grassley called "piddly little issues," had diminished its value.

"The filibuster has become a disservice to the institution and to the orderly consideration of issues here," said Democrat Dennis DeConcini of Arizona.

In large part, the change dated to

The contemporary filibuster lacks both the duration and the drama of the classic version, which Hollywood adapted for Jimmy Stewart's climactic scene in "Mr. Smith Goes to Washington."

1975, when the Senate ended years of infighting and agreed to reduce the number of votes needed for cloture from two-thirds of those voting to three-fifths of the full Senate — or from 67 votes when all members were present to 60. Ironically, once the new rule made it easier to silence a filibuster, filibusters and threats of filibusters became a common weapon of senators hoping to spotlight, change, delay or kill legislation.

In the 100th Congress, the Senate had 15 cloture votes as of September 1987 — as many as occurred in the first 27 years after the cloture rule was adopted in 1917. Of the 245 cloture votes in the past 70 years, 58 percent had been in just the dozen years since the 1975 rule change.

1987: The Majority Doesn't Rule

Not only had filibusters become more common, but in this Senate they also had been more routinely partisan than ever before.

With both parties jousting for advantage in the 1988 presidential election, nearly every major issue provoked a partisan standoff. Democrats hold a 54-46 majority, but that was six votes short of the number needed for cloture. Meanwhile, the Republican minority had been united enough to deprive Democrats of the extra votes.

Consequently, the majority party had prevailed on just one of the year's 15 cloture votes. Its sole victory involved a proposal much desired by both parties — a $12,100-a-year pay raise for members of Congress.

Clear party splits like those on the 1987 cloture votes were fairly rare in Senate history. Traditionally, the Senate had been divided along party lines only on such obviously partisan matters as a 1975 fight to fill a seat left open by a disputed New Hampshire election.

In 1987, the Senate had four successive partisan filibusters. In May, on three votes to end Republicans' filibuster against the fiscal 1987 defense authorization bill (S 1174), Democrats voted in rare unanimity, but they fell one vote short of the 60 needed for cloture when no more than five Republicans would join them.

On five cloture votes in June, all but three Democrats voted to end a Republican filibuster against a campaign-finance bill (S 2), while all Republicans but two opposed cloture. Byrd's high point was 52 votes for cloture, on the first tally.

Then on three votes in July, no more than four Democrats opposed motions to end Republican filibusters of proposals to delay an administration pact with Kuwait, under which Kuwaiti oil tankers would travel the Persian Gulf under protection of the U.S. flag. But no more than six Republicans broke ranks, so 57 votes were the most garnered for cloture.

An earlier Republican filibuster in March, against a measure blocking aid to Nicaraguan rebels, survived three cloture votes. Those were roughly party-line votes also, but defections on both sides, and particularly among Democrats, were greater than for the three later issues.

All year, the Senate sputtered and stalled as a result of actual or incipient filibusters. The defense and campaign-finance bills were both victims of ongoing filibusters; Byrd set them aside to take up other matters, but he vowed to return to both.

A filibuster threat against a bill for catastrophic-illness insurance (S 1127) prevented Byrd from bringing that measure to the floor before the August recess. Other threats waited in the months after the Senate returned. Vulnerable were Democratic labor bills, including one requiring workers to be notified of job-related health hazards (S 79); Reagan's nomination of Robert H. Bork to the Supreme Court; and the so-called "Grove City" bill that would overturn a 1984 Supreme Court decision limiting the reach of four civil-rights laws (S 557).

"The problem with the Senate today," said Democrat David Pryor of Arkansas, "is that the filibuster is very, very debilitating. And the threat of a filibuster is almost as deadly."

One benefit of the increased use of filibuster tactics in recent years, according to former Senate parliamentarian Robert B. Dove, was the impetus it provided for compromises. On the other hand, said Dove, now a consultant to Republican leader Robert Dole of Kansas, the frequent resort to filibusters "carries with it something that is not good for the Senate — a bill that doesn't have 60 votes can't pass."

Put another way: In this Senate, the majority often did not rule.

And because Democrats had been unable to muster enough Republican votes to get 60 for cloture, "cloture just isn't a weapon," Dove said.

"It's very hard to invoke cloture when the majority party only has a relatively small majority," Democrat William Proxmire of Wisconsin said "Part of the time I've been here, we've had a Democratic Party that had 65, 67 senators. Then, of course, it was relatively easy, at least easier, to put cloture into effect. But when you don't have that, you don't have filibusters that are prolonged very long, because the majority knows there's no way to break it. You have to give in."

The Limits of Force

Why give in, some asked. Why not break the filibusterers physically, much as Strom Thurmond or Jimmy Stewart were broken? Why doesn't Byrd keep the Senate running night and day, in the hope that some Republicans will relent?

That simply wouldn't work, members of both parties agreed. First, Republicans' numbers are too great.

"Even if he [Byrd] gets to the defense bill, there are enough senators who will filibuster the bill itself. And an amendment, no matter what it is, will get filibustered," Quayle said. "So you really cannot pass a bill if you have a dedicated, hard-core minority that is dead set against it, assuming they can muster 41 votes from time to time [to defeat a cloture motion]."

Also, the issues involved were so partisan that defections were unlikely. "If Byrd kept us up all night, it'd be the same thing. He wouldn't get the votes then, either," Thurmond said.

Another consideration was time. John B. Breaux, a Louisiana Democrat, said, "Byrd's thought is, 'I know they can find enough people to oppose this. Why waste time when I can move on to something else? At least let me be constructive.' "

For instance, after putting the Senate through five cloture votes over 11 days, Byrd pulled the campaign-finance bill from the floor when a major trade bill was ready for debate.

Leaders also knew that brute force was a double-edged sword. If Byrd kept the Senate in non-stop to crush a GOP filibuster, Democrats had to stay nearby for quorum calls and other procedural moves, or risk losing control of the floor. "All Republicans would need is three people at a time, in shifts at four-hour intervals," Dove said. "But 51 Democrats would have to be on call, while the other Republicans sleep."

"If Byrd starts doing that," Quayle said, "he might not be majority leader for long."

Proxmire recalled the majority's anguish during a 1960 civil-rights bill filibuster. Eighteen Southerners had formed two-man teams, and talked non-stop in relays. To thwart them,

For the Senate's talkers and listeners alike, filibusters used to be exhausting. Left, Strom Thurmond during his 1957 record-setter; top right, Hugh Scott in 1964; bottom, William Proxmire in 1960.

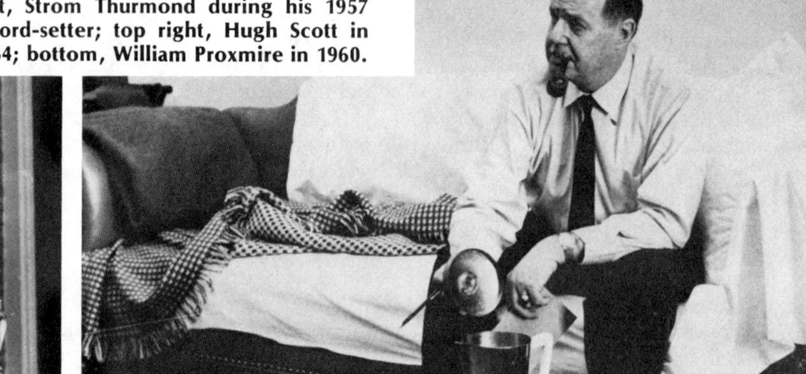

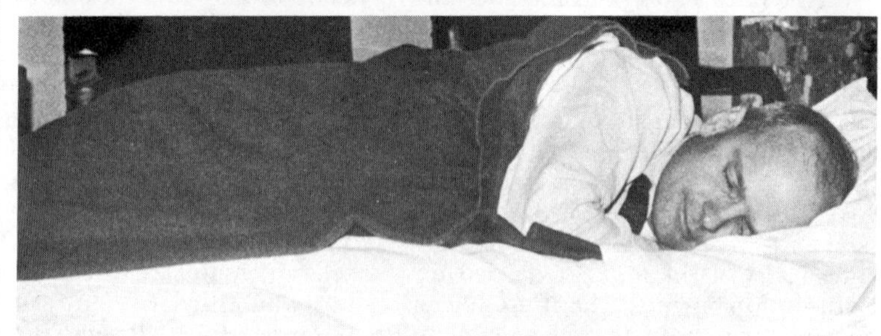

Majority Leader Lyndon B. Johnson, a Texas Democrat, kept the Senate going around the clock for nine days. That was a record for the longest continuous session in Senate history (157 hours, 26 minutes), but Johnson ultimately had to abandon the bill. Later that year a weaker version passed.

"We slept on cots in the Old Supreme Court chamber [near the Senate floor], and came out to answer quorum calls," Proxmire says of the bill's proponents. "It was an absolutely exhausting experience. The Southerners who were doing the talking were in great shape, because they would talk for two hours and leave the floor for a couple days."

"The only way to break a filibuster is to invoke cloture," said Murray Zweben, Senate parliamentarian from 1975-81. "If you have just one or two guys, you can break them down physically, but if you've got a whole group, they just take turns."

Even two could find strength in numbers, as Democrats Howard M. Metzenbaum of Ohio and James Abourezk of South Dakota did in 1977 when they opposed an energy bill deregulating natural-gas prices.

While one senator rested or plotted, the other forced action on one amendment after another. Byrd, then a first-year majority leader, failed to overcome the duo by force — a 37-hour session. Days later, he succeeded through stratagem, orchestrating a series of fatal parliamentary rulings with the presiding officer, Vice President Walter F. Mondale. Even so, the bill that passed was a compromise that met some of the foes' concerns.

Dove, an assistant parliamentarian at the time, says Metzenbaum and Abourezk were successful enough that leaders really have not forced confrontations of the classic sort since.

But that was not a new development. Although filibusters were popularly thought of as endurance contests, in the Hollywood mold, Senate majorities historically have not found force an effective way to subdue a minority. The potential gain is not considered worth the losses of time, tempers and pending legislation in many cases.

And in the gentlemen's club that has been the Senate, some tactics for breaking filibusterers are simply off-limits. Floyd M. Riddick, Senate parliamentarian from 1965-74, recalled one incident during a 1950 filibuster of a public-power bill.

Tennessee Democrat Estes Kefauver was several hours into a night-shift filibuster when his aide came to the desk to talk to Riddick, then an assistant parliamentarian. The aide said Kefauver desperately needed to go to the men's room to adjust a urine bag hidden in his trousers. How, the aide asked, could the senator do so without losing the floor? Riddick advised Kefauver to ask for a quorum call. Although one or two rival senators were present, no one objected.

"It was really entertaining, knowing what the situation was, to see him try to walk off that floor," Riddick told an oral-history researcher in 1978. In a recent interview, Riddick said Thurmond likewise had to leave the chamber during his record-setting filibuster — despite his advance preparation in the steam room. Then, too, no one objected. "The Senate is a clubby place," Riddick said, laughing. "They're all friendly, you know."

Perhaps not all. In 1908, Wisconsin Republican Robert M. LaFollette Sr. was filibustering late at night, sweating in the 90-degree heat of the chamber and sustaining himself on turkey sandwiches and eggnog. But on tasting one eggnog, he threw it aside and cried that it was drugged. The drink was found to contain a potentially fatal amount of poison, but no culprit was ever fingered.

But for many of the best-known filibusterers, the suffering or deprivation were self-induced, not a result of the majority's tactics. Some senators, like Thurmond in 1957, knew their fight was doomed. But the object was to dramatize a point.

Thurmond had opposed the decision of his fellow Southerners, led by Richard B. Russell of Georgia, to acquiesce in passage of the 1957 civil-rights bill. The legislation was tame enough for the others to accept. And, Thurmond said, Russell figured the victory would help Johnson in his 1960 bid to be the first Southerner since the Civil War to win the Democratic presidential nomination.

"The problem with the Senate today is that the filibuster is very, very debilitating. And the threat of a filibuster is almost as deadly."

—Sen. David Pryor, D-Ark.

Thurmond said he urged Russell to reconsider, "and he said he couldn't do that. 'But you can speak as long as you want to,' Russell said. I said, 'I know that I can speak as long as I want to, but you're not going to get any results.' " In the end, Thurmond said, "I thought I did get across a message to the nation."

Proxmire holds the Senate's fourth-place filibuster record, at 16 hours and 12 minutes, for an all-night 1981 speech opposing the Reagan administration's proposal to raise the nation's debt limit to more than a trillion dollars. "All I wanted to do," he said, "was dramatize that historic date, and say why I thought it was a terrible mistake for the Congress to permit the debt to get that big."

Post-Cloture Filibuster

Democrats' current difficulty in winning cloture votes, while striking for the partisanship it bares, was not unanticipated in 1975 when senators eased the cloture threshold from a high of 67 votes to a flat 60.

The historical record suggested that the change would be of slight help to filibuster foes: In past years, few cloture motions had drawn 60 or more votes. Nevertheless, as Riddick said, "If you decrease the number of votes needed to invoke cloture, you're going to have more attempts."

Of 245 cloture votes since 1917, 103 were in the 58 years before the 1975 rule took effect and 142 occurred since. And the efforts were more successful: Cloture petitioners won about 22 percent of the time from 1917-75, compared with 41 percent since the 1975 change.

A largely unforeseen consequence was the reaction of those conducting filibusters. "Once it was easier to get cloture," Riddick said, "they had to come up with other ways to give the minority a way to prolong debate."

The tactic was the post-cloture filibuster, and the pioneer was Democrat James B. Allen of Alabama, a frequent obstructionist. In 1976, he opposed an antitrust bill and, when the Senate invoked cloture against further debate, he demanded action on the many amendments he had filed previously. He required that each be read aloud, sought roll-call votes and quorum calls, objected to routine motions and appealed parliamentary rulings.

Allen was exploiting a gaping loophole in the cloture rule: Though it limited debate after cloture to 100 hours, the time spent on other parliamentary tactics did not count.

Several major measures died at the end of that Congress under the threat of such filibusters. So in 1977, Byrd proposed limits on the post-cloture filibuster. While unsuccessful then, his cause gained adherents later that year after the wrenching Metzenbaum-Abourezk filibuster against gas deregulation. In 1979, the Senate modified its rule to provide that all action, not just debate, would come under the 100-hour post-cloture limit.

The 1980s' debate over televising the Senate was the next opening to review the cloture rule. Senators had resisted following the House's lead in allowing live coverage because its proceedings were so much slower and more staid. Various rule changes were proposed to quicken the Senate's pace, and to limit filibusters, as a condition for allowing cameras inside. But in the end, the only major reform was a reduction from 100 hours to 30 in the time for post-cloture debate.

Changing Times

In recent years, as the filibuster became less associated with civil rights opposition, more senators embraced the tactic on occasion.

Even Pryor, a leading advocate of debate limits, once threatened to read 1,000 rice recipes unless an agriculture bill was changed to his liking. "That's what all the guys do," he said. "They say, 'I don't like these filibusters. I don't like these rules. But as long as they're here, I'm going to use them.' "

Since proponents of change generally come from the majority party, members' willingness to limit minority rights often depended on which side they were on at the time.

For example, when Republicans had a majority before the Democrats' 1987 takeover, Quayle espoused a proposal to bar filibusters against the motion to proceed to a bill. Increasingly, filibusterers blocked both the motion to proceed to a bill and the bill itself, prolonging debate and forcing at least two cloture votes.

Since Quayle was not in the 100th Congress minority, he no longer wanted to restrict that practice. "You have a different view of rules changes when you're in the minority than you do when you're in the majority," he said, grinning.

Still, some members and observers saw signs that Senate fidelity to its tradition of extended debate had been waning. The 1975 and 1979 rule changes were seen as evidence of that.

Also, since the 1970s the Senate passed a number of bills providing for expedited debate on specific issues, in effect circumventing Senate rules. It had, for example, set deadlines in law for votes on the MX missile and contra aid. But the most far-reaching provisions to speed action were part of the 1974 Congressional Budget and

Dilatory Debate: A Tactic as Old as the Senate

The Senate was just six months old in 1789 when delaying tactics were first used, by opponents of a bill to locate the nation's capital on the Susquehanna River. A disgusted Sen. William Maclay of Pennsylvania wrote: "I gave my opinion in plain language that the confidence of the people was departing from us, owing to our unreasonable delays."

Maclay's warning had no effect, nor have similar admonitions to the present day. "The more one reads about the procession of alarms on this score since 1789," a bemused historian wrote in 1922, "the more astonished he becomes at the vast volume of public confidence the national legislature there must have enjoyed at the start. Otherwise, the reservoir would have been drained dry long, long ago!"

By 1840, dilatory debate was common enough that Henry Clay of Kentucky was demanding "a rule which would place the business of the Senate under the control of a majority." But what are considered the first full-fledged filibusters occurred the next year, when Democrats and Whigs squared off first over the appointment of official Senate printers and then over the establishment of a national bank.

Slavery, Civil War, Reconstruction and blacks' voting rights in turn were the sparks for the increasingly frequent and contentious filibusters of the 19th century. Opponents had no weapon against them; proposed rules to restrict debate were repeatedly rejected. The majority's only recourse was to win unanimous consent for a time limit on considering a bill, on a case-by-case basis.

Minor curbs were adopted early in the 20th century. But they did not hinder Republican filibusterers from killing two of President Wilson's proposals to put the nation on a war footing — a 1915 ship-purchase bill and a 1917 bill to arm merchant ships.

As a political scientist in 1881, Wilson had celebrated "the Senate's opportunities for open and unrestricted discussion." After the 1917 defeat, he railed, "The Senate of the United States is the only legislative body in the world which cannot act when the majority is ready for action. A little group of willful men ... have rendered the great government of the United States helpless and contemptible."

Public revulsion forced the Senate to yield. On March 8, 1917, it finally adopted a cloture rule, requiring a vote of two-thirds of the senators present to end a filibuster.

The rule's framers predicted it would be little used, and for years that was the case. The first successful motion, in 1919, ended debate on the Treaty of Versailles. Nine more motions were voted on through 1927, and three were successful. Over the next 35 years, until 1962, only 16 were voted on and not one was adopted.

In large part, that reflected the politics of civil rights. Southern Democrats successfully filibustered legislation against the poll tax, literacy tests, lynching and employment discrimination, by building an anti-cloture coalition that included Westerners and some Republicans. In return for their allies' votes against cloture on civil-rights filibusters, the Southerners supported Westerners' highway and water projects and Republicans' fights against labor legislation.

At the same time, those factions were careful not to abuse the right to filibuster, for fear the frustrated majority would succeed in making cloture easier to invoke. That effort began in 1949; nearly every two years when the Senate adopted its rules for a new Congress, Northern Democrats and moderate Republicans tried to reduce the cloture threshold.

Slowly, the anti-cloture coalition began to dissolve. A signal of its demise was the 1962 vote to end a filibuster against a proposed communications satellite — the first successful cloture vote since 1927. Then in 1964, the Senate for the first time invoked cloture on a civil rights bill. During 74 days of debate, the longest filibuster in Senate history, West Virginia Democrat Robert C. Byrd, now the Senate's majority leader, gave one of the longest speeches by an individual — 14 hours, 13 minutes. The bill, he objected, "cannot be justified on any basis — legal, economic, moral or religious."

A year later, cloture was approved for another civil rights measure, the Voting Rights Act. And in 1968, a 34-day filibuster of an open-housing bill was stopped.

By the 1970s, the liberals' victories on civil rights had cooled their ardor for cloture reform. Moreover, they had become the ones doing much of the filibustering — against President Nixon's Vietnam policies, weapons systems and anti-busing proposals.

In 1973, for the first time in years, the new Senate did not fight over the cloture rule. But in 1975, the liberals tried again — and won. Now three-fifths of the Senate, or 60 votes, could shut off a filibuster instead of up to 67, two-thirds of those present and voting.

Impoundment Control Act.

That law limits debate on the annual budget resolution and any amendments, requires committees to report their share of budget-cutting or tax proposals to the Budget Committee by a certain date, and restricts floor debate on the resulting deficit-reduction package, known as a "reconciliation bill," to 20 hours.

Most significantly, it immunizes the reconciliation bill against filibusters, making that bill an end-of-year magnet for a variety of proposals that otherwise might fall to filibusters.

For different reasons, the annual continuing appropriations resolution was another such magnet. The "CR" combines all appropriations for the federal government when Congress fails, as it usually does, to enact the 13 individual spending bills before the start of a fiscal year.

The CR and whatever measures are attached get expedited treatment in the Senate not because of a law but because of circumstances. Debate occurs at year's end, when members are eager to go home. And few want to be held responsible for the embarrassment of the government shutting down if the bill does not pass.

Another development that pointed to eroding respect for extended debate was the absence, for the first time in decades, of senators who supported all filibusters and never voted for cloture. These typically were Southerners who, when they weren't fighting civil rights bills, were trading "no" votes on other cloture motions with allies who would back them later against civil rights.

By now, the cloture opponents have died, retired or been converted. Among the converts are Byrd, Thurmond and Democrats John C. Stennis of Mississippi and Ernest F. Hollings of South Carolina. For several, a 1971 cloture vote to end liberals' filibuster against the draft was their first.

"I knew things were shifting when John Stennis voted for cloture," said Zweben. "Then I knew the ball game was changing."

Byrd, meanwhile, bragged of his record for sponsoring cloture motions. As a party leader since 1971, first as whip and then as leader, Byrd offered 61 of the 245 cloture motions voted on — one-fourth of the total.

The 100th Senate included at least two members who would always vote *for* cloture, DeConcini and Democrat Claiborne Pell of Rhode Island.

The routine practice of seeking cloture as soon as debate begins also showed slipping respect for filibusters. "Years ago, even Lyndon Johnson wouldn't try to get cloture until after a week," Thurmond said. "But now, after one day, if the leaders see you are really going to fight, they'll apply cloture immediately."

Similarly, if cloture is rejected, the majority often tries again and again. "There used to be an unwritten rule that three [cloture votes] was enough," Dove said. "The 1975 fight for the New Hampshire Senate seat blew that tradition."

The six votes on that controversy, all unsuccessful, set a record. It was tied in 1978, during debate on a labor-law revision. But Byrd broke the record in September 1987 after a seventh cloture vote on the campaign-finance bill.

Riddick, in his 1978 oral history, said, "In my humble opinion, the framers of that [cloture] rule never intended that you would run ad infinitum with different cloture motions. . . . If they had a point of order on such a basis early in the history of the rule, I'm inclined to believe the Senate would have established the precedent that you wouldn't be permitted more than one vote to invoke cloture on a particular question."

But, Riddick continued, under Majority Leader Mike Mansfield, a Montana Democrat and Byrd's predecessor, the practice began "that you would keep on trying, as long as you felt there was a chance, or as long as you felt it was necessary to convince the country that you were trying to bring the issue before the Senate so as to get a vote."

While Mansfield would not file additional cloture petitions unless he was gaining support, Byrd pressed seven votes against the campaign-finance filibuster without winning one new ally. His aim was "to convince the country," in Riddick's phrase, that Republicans were blocking campaign reform.

For all senators' grousing about filibusters, few expected that Senate rules would be changed any time soon. But a wild card was the growing number of House members winning seats. They tended to be younger, activist and accustomed to the House's faster pace.

Nine of the 13 new senators elected in 1986 were former House members, bringing the total to 39 — 29 of whom arrived in the past decade.

"We need to expedite the procedures to get things done around this place," said freshman Democrat Timothy E. Wirth of Colorado.

Pryor, a House member from 1967-73, had proposed four reforms, including a one-hour limit on debate on a motion to proceed. "It's the former House fellows I'm concentrating on to get support," he said. "And I'm getting support from most."

A current House member, New York Democrat Thomas J. Downey, said he teased Democratic senators: "We get a bill out of the House, and then we have to figure out how to help them get it out of the Senate. . . . The 19th-century rules they live by are absurd for the 20th century."

Pryor agreed: "The 20th century has left this place behind." It's an oft-stated complaint — Senate rules are too archaic for the modern world. As one historian wrote, "In our day, with a larger House and Senate, with greater interests at stake, with this immense volume of business pressing for attention, it is right and necessary that the majority should cut down some of the privileges the minority have so long enjoyed. . . . The time for dilatory motions, for refusals to answer roll calls, for time-consuming debate, has gone by."

The year was 1893. ∎

Deregulation: New Doubts, Damage Control

Deregulation of the airline, railroad and trucking industries and divestiture of the telephone system have led to unanticipated problems for Congress to solve.

Deregulation in the 1970s was the bipartisan solution to fears that excessive government control was choking the American economy.

But during the 1980s, faith in the magic of the free market had diminished. In 1987, "deregulation" brought to mind airplanes lined up on runways, poorly maintained trucks and lousy telephone service.

Some in Congress were clamoring for action to fix the problems they claimed were deregulation's unexpected offspring. And, while there was little sentiment to return to the regulated ways of the past, enthusiasm was lacking for new deregulation proposals, such as calls by shippers to eliminate all remaining controls on the trucking industry.

"A few years ago, it seemed that virtually everyone around here was chanting the sacred mantra: 'deregulation, deregulation, deregulation,' " said Senate Commerce Committee Chairman Ernest F. Hollings, D-S.C. "Our policy makers were mesmerized by its ring and placed great faith in it.

"Now," he continued, "we are seeing that all of deregulation's great promises have not come to pass, and that any benefits we have derived have been accompanied by problems."

Growth in Mergers

In the late 1970s, Congress passed laws relaxing government control over prices and competition in the airline, railroad and trucking industries. And the federal courts ordered the breakup of the Bell telephone system, which had operated as a regulated monopoly.

Proponents predicted competition and innovation would flourish as regulated businesses faced the test of the marketplace.

But all did not go as planned. Besides the gripes about bad service, mergers and bankruptcies had been rampant. In the rail and airline industries, and in a key segment of the trucking industry, top firms had a greater market share than they enjoyed before deregulation. Some shippers complained they were being gouged on rates by monopoly railroads. Predictions that divestiture would end the dominance by the American Telephone & Telegraph Co. (AT&T) of the long-distance market were wrong.

As a result, prospects were ripe for legislation intended to soften deregulation's harsh effects. Bills were introduced to crack down on deceptive airline advertising and scheduling practices and to compensate customers for unhonored tickets issued by bankrupt carriers.

Sens. Brock Adams, D-Wash., and John C. Danforth, R-Mo., were pushing legislation (S 861) to tighten truck safety standards, and lawmakers in both the Senate Commerce and House Energy and Commerce committees were sponsoring plans to make it easier for rail shippers to win rate reductions from the Interstate Commerce Commission (ICC).

The telephone arena was relatively quiet. But observers expected debate to heat up over existing proposals — as considered by the courts — to allow regional phone companies to enter new lines of business, such as equipment manufacturing.

Hesitancy to 'Reregulate'

By 1987, discontent had not produced a stampede to slap controls back on industry. For one thing, many business leaders and economists maintained deregulation had improved the efficiency of the economy. For another, the structure of deregulated industries had changed so greatly it would be difficult to return to the old ways without massive disruption.

In the airline industry, for example, carriers had created a new "hub and spoke" routing system that sent most flights through a handful of large airports. Rail deregulation had spawned the growth of "short-line" firms that operated marginal routes that were not profitable for big companies to maintain.

"You can't unscramble the egg," said Danforth, ranking member of the Senate Commerce panel. "We've set in motion forces that aren't going to be reversed."

Nor did "reregulation" hold much political appeal. "Young Democrats,

Democrats of my generation," said Rep. Ron Wyden, D-Ore., who was elected in 1980, "don't want to just flail out blindly and say, 'Let's regulate for regulation's sake.' "

"We were still in a basically conservative cycle in the country," said Stuart Eizenstat, domestic policy adviser to President Jimmy Carter and consultant to several 1988 Democratic presidential candidates. "To justify putting [regulation] back on would require a showing of a real pattern of abuse, sufficient to overcome the conservatism of the era."

Second Thoughts

Still, some lawmakers had regrets about supporting deregulation — regrets that, at the very least, made them skittish about embarking on new deregulation voyages. Many of the complaints had a populist flavor, coming from lawmakers from rural areas who contended constituents were being neglected by deregulated industries.

A free-market enthusiast, Rep. Glenn English, D-Okla., backed the 1978 law (PL 95-504) to lift strict government controls on airline routes and fares. "It was to be a great experiment resulting in competition throughout the airline industry," he recalled. *(1978 CQ Almanac p. 496)*

In 1987 English was convinced that safety and service had deteriorated and wished he had his vote back. "In my 12 years in the U.S. House of Representatives," he told colleagues, "without question that is the worst vote I have cast."

A bill (HR 2545) introduced by English would return the industry to its pre-1978 regulated status, although an aide said the measure was offered mainly to stir debate. Supporters included Rep. Mickey Edwards, his Republican colleague from Oklahoma.

As transportation secretary in the Carter administration, Brock Adams helped push, despite serious misgivings, the 1980 trucking deregulation law (PL 96-296), which made it much easier for new firms to compete with established carriers. *(1980 Almanac p. 242)*

Seven years later, Adams said safety was suffering as financially pressed companies skimped on maintenance and required drivers to stay behind the wheel for dangerously long stretches of time.

"I've got grave doubts" about the 1980 law, Adams said in an interview, adding that the "logical" next step would be legislation to make it more difficult for new firms to enter the industry.

Some lawmakers, such as Rep. Mike Synar, D-Okla., said Congress did the right thing in passing the deregulation laws but that the Reagan administration had failed to enforce health and safety standards and had taken a much too lenient approach toward mergers.

"A few years ago, it seemed that virtually everyone around here was chanting the sacred mantra: 'deregulation, deregulation, deregulation.' . . . Now, we are seeing that all of deregulation's great promises have not come to pass, and that any benefits we have derived have been accompanied by problems."

—Sen. Ernest F. Hollings, D-S.C.

On the Defensive

Attacks on deregulation had sparked a defensive reaction from business leaders and those in the Reagan administration nervous that Congress would reimpose economic controls.

"In an increasingly competitive world economy, we can't afford to impose a single penny's worth of excessive regulation," Transportation Secretary Elizabeth H. Dole said in a March 24, 1987, speech to the National-American Wholesale Grocers' Association.

At Dole's urging, shippers and representatives of the airline and rail industries had formed a coalition, the Transportation Reform Alliance, to counter criticism of deregulation.

Leaders of the alliance pointed to such benefits as discount airline fares and said rail and trucking deregulation had substantially reduced shippers' costs of transporting goods — savings that had been passed on to consumers.

Increasing industry concentration should not cause concern because "the threat of new entrants will keep incumbents in check," said Daniel Witt, project director for Citizens for a Sound Economy, a conservative group active in the coalition.

Safety concerns also had been exaggerated, coalition officials claimed. For example, they said that although the number of truck accidents had gone up since deregulation, the accident rate — accidents per driving miles — had actually gone down. Others disputed that claim, however.

While Dole warned in her speech of a "serious reregulatory threat from Capitol Hill," not everyone was as alarmed.

"After a wave comes in, you often get a little backsliding before the next wave hits the beach," said Stanton P. Sender, assistant general counsel for Sears, Roebuck and Co. "I don't see Congress going back."

Business support for deregulation had in the past been buttressed by consumer groups. But now some were having second thoughts.

"Maybe we've gone too far with the theory without looking at the practical consequences," said Gene Kimmelman, legislative director for the Consumer Federation of America. He said consumer activists did not, for example, expect increased competition to jeopardize safety. *(Box, p. 49)*

Consumer leaders supported many of the legislative initiatives to cure ailments associated with deregulation, including proposals to require airlines to disclose their performance records. Leaders also had called for much tougher enforcement of antitrust laws.

Deregulation Trend

Regulation's classic rationale was to protect key industries from destructive competition that could lead to bankruptcies, excessive concentration and other economic problems. But critics contended that, because entry into a line of business was restricted, prices were higher than necessary. They said lifting of controls posed no great threat as long as the antitrust laws were strictly enforced.

With help from Sen. Edward M. Kennedy, D-Mass., and other liberals, airline regulations were the first to go. The 1978 law abolished rules administered by the Civil Aeronautics Board (CAB) since 1938, as well as the CAB itself.

The CAB had told airlines which cities they could serve, and which routes they had to fly. Fares were set by formulas, and the agency could prevent new companies from entering the business. Deregulation eliminated or substantially eased all of these restrictions, and much lower fares were expected to result.

Also with an assist from Kennedy, a trucking law was enacted in 1980. The bill swept aside ICC rules, dating back 45 years, that had originally been sought by the industry as protection against economic ruin. During the Great Depression, a combination of low entry costs attracting many newcomers and the decline in freight forced many firms out of business.

In addition to easing entry restrictions, the deregulation law provided carriers greater operating and pricing freedom.

The 1980 rail deregulation law, also known as the Staggers Act, drew on support from the rail industry, which was in desperate economic straits. Industry and Carter administration officials said greater freedom to set rates was crucial to rail's survival in the threat of competition from the more nimble trucking industry. Rail labor also supported the law.

Opposition originally stemmed from coal producers, utilities that depended on coal, agricultural shippers and consumer organizations. They were concerned that monopoly railroads would be allowed to raise rates excessively. The final package, however, included key concessions that allowed the ICC to review rates charged by "market dominant" railroads.

The stimulus for telephone divestiture was an antitrust suit filed by the Justice Department against AT&T. Some in Congress also pursued divestiture but their efforts slowed after AT&T agreed in 1982 to shed its 22 local phone companies. The agreement, which took effect Jan. 1, 1984, called for the consolidation of the local entities into seven regional Bell operating companies (BOCs). *(1982 Almanac p. 331)*

AT&T was left free to pursue the long-distance service market and other opportunities. The BOCs were restricted from manufacturing telephone equipment, offering long-distance service and providing information services, such as electronic publishing. The courts set these limits to keep the BOCs from subsidizing new ventures with revenues from local phone operations and from using the local phone network to crush smaller competitors.

The Airline Story

Airline deregulation was greeted with a proliferation of new carriers hoping to make a buck.

Few of them were in business in 1987. Of the 234 carriers certified since deregulation, only 74 were operating and a mere nine controlled more than 90 percent of the market, according to Airline Economics Inc., a Washington, D.C.-based consulting firm. Analysts said larger firms, with established facilities at major airports, had a crucial advantage when the industry shifted to nationwide hub-and-spoke networks.

But one consequence of a more concentrated industry, Airline Economics predicted, would be a decline in the use of discount fares and a gradual increase in average fares over the next 10 years.

There was some evidence to back up complaints that deregulation had caused carriers to abandon service to small communities in favor of more popular, profitable routes.

Between 1978 and 1984, the number of communities reached by scheduled airlines fell to 541 from 632, depriving 91 cities and towns of air service, according to a study by the General Accounting Office (GAO), the investigative arm of Congress.

"You can't unscramble the egg. We've set in motion forces that aren't going to be reversed."

—Sen. John C. Danforth, R-Mo.

While the number of aviation accidents had not increased since deregulation, there had been an upward swing in the number of reported near midair collisions. Financial pressures had resulted in pilots working longer hours and in reduced outlays for equipment maintenance, according to the Office of Technology Assessment, a congressional research agency.

Airline industry officials said the government deserved blame for increased congestion because it had failed to use revenues from ticket taxes to fund expansion of airports and the air traffic control system to keep pace with growth in passenger traffic. Congress had held down spending in the face of pressure to reduce the federal deficit.

Industry leaders also said the air travel system had yet to recover fully from the jolt it received in 1981 when President Reagan fired more than 11,000 striking controllers.

Spurred by a rash of passenger complaints about shoddy airline service, the House approved legislation (HR 3051) intended to protect consumers from such problems as excessive delays and lost baggage. The bill would require airlines to disclose their on-time performance records and other data.

Proponents said such information would help passengers learn which airlines provide good service, thereby giving carriers an incentive to improve their records. They described this as a market-based approach in keeping with the goal of deregulation to increase industry competition. The measure won bipartisan support on the floor. Ron Packard, R-Calif., said it would be politically difficult for any lawmaker to oppose the bill because of intense consumer anger at the airlines.

Although the Reagan administration had yet to take a formal position on the legislation, several committee members said they would not be surprised by a veto threat. Department of Transportation (DOT) leaders in the past had said they would prefer to handle consumer problems through new regulations rather than legislation.

In the Senate, a similar disclosure bill (S 1485) was approved July 14, 1987, by the Senate Commerce, Science and Transportation Committee.

Air Travel for the Masses: Could Be a Myth

"The great thing about [airline] deregulation is that the benefits went to the masses."
—Thomas G. Moore, Council of Economic Advisers

Flying was not just for the rich anymore, Moore was saying, a view shared by many policy makers and those in the airline industry.

It had been a potent argument for deregulation. Nearly everyone wanted a transportation system accessible to rich and poor alike. But some said the "democratization" claim was based more on myth than on reality.

That was the conclusion reached by the Consumer Federation of America (CFA) in a reassessment of deregulation done at the request of Congressional Quarterly. Leaders of the consumer group backed the 1978 airline deregulation law but had since then contended consumer benefits were "highly uneven and have been vastly overstated."

In particular, CFA leaders found virtually no evidence that more people of modest means were flying after than before deregulation. And the numbers never had been high.

Researchers compared the popularity of flying for different income levels in 1980-81, when deregulation was just getting under way, and in 1984, a time of hot competition. The numbers were based on consumer surveys of "households" done by the Bureau of Labor Statistics, and did not include business spending. No data were available for 1985 and 1986. *(See chart)*

For the poorest households — those on the bottom fifth of the income ladder — the percentage that reported at least one air-fare expenditure increased slightly, from 4 percent to 4.5 percent. For the second and third poorest segments of the population, there was no increase. The greatest increase was recorded for the wealthiest 40 percent of the households.

While the analysis did not cover business spending, there was no reason to suspect a great increase in the percentage of low-income workers flying on the company payroll, said Mark N. Cooper, CFA's research director.

CFA also found evidence that refuted the frequent claim that passenger traffic had increased dramatically as a result of deregulation. Before deregulation, from 1974-80, the annual growth rate was 6.3 percent. Afterwards, from 1980-86, the passenger load grew at an annual rate of 7.4 percent.

Cooper did not examine the impact of fare changes. But not even the most optimistic studies of deregulation claimed that the greatest benefits had come from lower fares.

A widely circulated analysis published by the Brookings Institution concluded that consumers had netted $6 billion in annual "welfare" gains from deregulation. However, some two-thirds of that amount was attributable to the availability of more flights. Only about one-third was linked to lower fares. And, as co-author Steven Morrison acknowledged, the calculation did not take into account the disadvantages of cancellations or delays.

CFA officials continued to believe that deregulation had brought benefits to travelers who were flexible about the routes and the times they had to fly. Such people were able to take the greatest advantage of discount tickets.

But, said Cooper: "We do find it bothersome that some have romanticized about deregulation to the point where grossly unrealistic claims have been made in its name and the real problems that have arisen in its aftermath have been completely ignored."

Household Spending on Air Fares

Income Group	Percent Reporting Air-Fare Expenditure 1980-81	1984
Bottom Fifth	4.0	4.5
Second Fifth	5.1	4.7
Third Fifth	6.6	6.6
Fourth Fifth	6.5	7.7
Top Fifth	14.7	15.3

SOURCE: Consumer Federation of America; Bureau of Labor Statistics, *Consumer Expenditure Survey*

That bill was denounced by DOT leaders as administratively onerous. One provision, not contained in the House panel's bill, would require DOT to calculate a "minimum realistic time" for each domestic flight. Travel times displayed on computerized reservation systems used by ticket sellers would have to reflect the DOT calculations.

On another matter, the House voted Oct. 7, 1987, to delete a provision in a bill that would give the FTC authority to regulate airline advertising. The provision had been included in a version of the bill approved July 14 by the Energy and Commerce Committee, which has primary jurisdiction over the FTC. Public Works and Transportation Committee members argued that the power should remain with the DOT, over which their committee has jurisdiction. Energy and Commerce members had maintained that DOT had failed to protect consumers from a steady stream of false ads for cheap fares.

The House also had approved a bill (HR 1101) that would require airlines that merge to extend financial benefits to workers hurt by the transaction. Senate Commerce had approved a measure (S 724) that would shift from the DOT secretary to the secretary of labor the authority for determining whether to require payment of such benefits. Proponents cited the past unwillingness of DOT to mandate payments.

The Senate Commerce bill also would speed up a planned transfer of authority to approve mergers from

DOT to the Department of Justice, which advocates expected would take a more critical look at merger requests. The transfer would take place upon enactment of the law rather than in 1989, as required by current law.

Congress was also expected to extend for another 10 years, and perhaps expand, a DOT program to guarantee service to small communities that enjoyed service by government-certified carriers before deregulation. Airlines serving 150 communities in 40 states were currently getting $30 million in annual subsidies.

Trucking Troubles

The trucking industry had experienced some of the same problems as the airline sector. Critics said the fleet was aging for lack of money to buy new equipment and that operators were working too many hours. "Corners are being cut by financially strapped firms and the accident rate is rising," charged Nicholas A. Glaskowsky, author of a study on deregulation for the Connecticut-based Eno Foundation for Transportation Inc.

Tens of thousands of firms had entered the industry since deregulation. Competition was particularly intense in the so-called "truckload" sector, involving direct hauls from the pickup site to the destination point.

But different conditions prevailed for what were known as less-than-truckload (LTL) operations. These transported small lots from their origin to their ultimate destination point through as many as half a dozen trucking terminals. This segment had become increasingly concentrated as large firms exploited nationwide networks of terminals.

Some analysts had raised concerns about large carriers using their pricing freedom to push smaller firms out of the business, but the GAO said in a February 1987 study that there was no "conclusive" evidence of so-called "predatory" pricing. The GAO did note that market shares of the largest LTL firms had increased in all regions of the country since 1980.

Many shippers said deregulation had allowed them to cut costs. Trucks owned and operated by shippers were no longer restricted from hauling other firms' goods, for example. Before, "private fleet" trucks would make the first leg of a journey with full loads but would have to make the "back-haul" empty.

Although shippers wanted Congress to remove remaining trucking controls, safety-related legislation continued to dominate the agenda.

"In my 12 years in the U.S. House of Representatives, without question that [vote for airline deregulation] is the worst vote I have cast."

—Rep. Glenn English, D-Okla.

In 1986, lawmakers passed a measure (PL 99-570) that increased funding for roadside inspections of trucks and buses and required states to make license applicants take tests in the type of vehicle they planned to drive. *(1986 Almanac p. 92)*

1987's Adams-Danforth bill would eliminate exemptions from safety rules provided to trucks operating in certain metropolitan areas known as "commercial zones."

The measure also would direct DOT to look into the possibility of requiring trucks to have anti-lock brakes, designed to prevent skidding, which are widely used in Europe.

In addition, the bill would require the transportation secretary to examine the possibility of installing on-board computerized devices that would record drivers' hours. The sponsors were concerned about widespread falsification of written logs as drivers exceed legal hours-of-driving limits. However, DOT officials had dropped objections to considering such a rule.

House Public Works staffers also were drafting legislation to delete the commercial-zone exemption.

Lobbyists trying to drum up interest in another round of deregulation acknowledged that safety was uppermost in lawmakers' minds. The safety question had been "like a chicken bone caught sideways down our throat as we've tried to talk to members about deregulation," said Bruce Gates, lobbyist for the National-American Wholesale Grocers' Association. "Every member has got his story about the trucker that bore down on him on I-95. . . . They immediately assume this link between safety and economic regulations."

The Teamsters union, which had lost trucking industry members since deregulation, and the American Trucking Associations were opposed to further deregulation.

Rail Monopolies

Deregulation was widely credited with improving the financial state of the rail industry, and many analysts said safety conditions had improved as firms had become healthier.

But critics countered that the recovery had been accomplished partly by the industry's practice of charging higher rates to those "captive" shippers unable to transport their products by truck or another rail carrier.

Leaders of the Consumer Federation of America said, for example, that electricity costs were inflated because utilities had to pay unreasonably high costs for coal shipments.

Many lawmakers, including Rep. John D. Dingell, D-Mich., chairman of the Energy and Commerce Committee, had lambasted the ICC for ignoring provisions of the Staggers Act intended to prevent rate gouging. Although the law allowed the ICC to determine "rate reasonableness" when a railroad enjoyed market dominance, Dingell and others claimed the criteria used by the agency to make this determination were skewed in favor of the railroads.

Labor groups also were upset about an exemption from job protection requirements that the ICC had applied since 1980 to sales of branch lines by major carriers to new short-line railroads. New carriers did not have to make severance payments to laid-off workers — a requirement that was in place for mergers between existing firms and in cases of track abandonments. The ICC said many short-line sales would not take place without the exemption, resulting in the abandonment of low-density lines.

Despite rapid growth of the short-line sector, the top six rail carriers had substantially increased their share of freight revenues since deregulation — from below 70 percent of total revenues in 1980 to nearly 90 percent at the end of 1986. Big carriers had also bought firms in the trucking and maritime industries, leading some large shippers to fret about the dangers of reduced competition.

Identical measures (HR 1393 and S 676) had been introduced in the House and Senate to change the tests by which the ICC determined whether a rate charged by a monopoly railroad was reasonable. The burden of proof would shift to the railroad. Rep. Rick Boucher, D-Va., and Sen. John D. Rockefeller IV, D-W.Va., were the leading sponsors.

In 1986, the Energy and Commerce Committee narrowly rejected efforts to attach similar provisions to legislation providing for a public sale of the Conrail freight railroad. Lobbyists representing the shippers claimed they lost only because sympathetic members did not want to make the Conrail bill more controversial. *(1986 Almanac p. 279)*

A shippers' representative said members seemed more receptive to their complaints in 1987 because of increased skepticism about the merits of transportation deregulation. At the urging of Luken, leaders of shipper and railroad groups were meeting to try to reach agreement on a compromise package to meet concerns of captive shippers.

However, Danforth said he did not see broad support in Congress for revisions favored by the captive shippers. The Reagan administration had said it saw no need to change the law.

There also was strong support within the Energy and Commerce Committee for action to close the ICC's labor-protection exemption for short-line sales. A labor-protection provision included in the Conrail bill passed the House in 1986 but died in conference. The Reagan administration strongly opposed the plan.

Doubts About Divestiture

In the telephone industry, AT&T held a share of over 80 percent of the long-distance market even though other carriers widely advertised their services. Long-distance rates had declined, but not enough to offset increases in local phone rates, according to the Consumer Federation of America. A study released December 1986 by the group found the average rsidential phone bill was almost 20 percent higher since the breakup.

"We were told that widespread, cutthroat competition would drive down telephone prices and bring information-age gadgets to all consumers," said the study's authors. "Instead, consumers must pay significantly more to get the same old service they had prior to the breakup."

Others pointed out that local rates had stabilized after an initial spurt and listed such benefits as the ability of consumers to purchase their own phones rather than to have to rent them year after year from the old Bell system. "No fair-minded person can deny, I think, that there has been a freer market, with more diversity, more innovation, and more sophistication in telephone apparatus and service in the last two or three years than in the preceding 30 or 40," declared Judge Harold H. Greene of the U.S. Court of Appeals for the District of Columbia, which had jurisdiction over the AT&T antitrust settlement.

Yet in a blow to the regional telephone companies, Judge Greene refused to lift existing restrictions that prevented the firms from manufacturing telephone equipment or offering long-distance telephone service. In the Sept. 10, 1987, ruling, Greene rejected the contention of the BOCs and the Reagan administration that competition in the telecommunications industry had increased so much that the curbs were no longer necessary.

House Energy and Commerce Committee Chairman Dingell reacted angrily to the ruling, saying that "a single unelected, unaccountable federal judge has transformed himself into a regulator without portfolio, arrogating the power to determine whether and when the American people will be allowed to receive the advanced new services that are already available in countries with more enlightened telecommunications policies." Dingell, who supported shifting supervision of the companies to the FCC, said he hoped that the judge's ruling "will at last produce consensus on the need for legislation." ▮

Democrats: Snared in a Gramm-Rudman Trap?

The trap set by Congress for President Reagan in the new Gramm-Rudman-Hollings anti-deficit law could snap shut on Democrats instead.

The legislation was meant to force the president into budget negotiations on a tax increase and defense spending restraints as part of a deficit-reduction plan — or else take the consequences of automatic budget cuts called for by Gramm-Rudman.

It passed with strong bipartisan support. But Reagan and leading Republicans signaled that they would not consider new taxes even if that meant the across-the-board Gramm-Rudman cuts in both defense and domestic programs would take effect.

Arithmetic suggested that defense might not fare much worse under automatic cuts than under conventional legislation in the Democrat-led Congress. And politics suggested that Republicans did well.

Under automatic cuts, they got the reductions in domestic programs that Reagan sought, no tax increase and many opportunities to blame Democrats for salvaging the military.

Democrats would be left with the black mark of pushing a tax increase and none of its deficit-fighting benefits, since no one considered higher taxes possible without GOP assent.

"It may have put [Reagan] back in the driver's seat," suggested Sen. Pete V. Domenici, R-N.M. Domenici, convinced Reagan was so opposed to a tax increase that he would accept automatic cuts instead, voted against the bill. *(1987 CQ Weekly Report p. 2309)*

'Nuts' to Taxes, Defense Cuts

Whether Democrats would get all the blame for Gramm-Rudman's depredation of federal programs was, of course, imponderable. Republicans played a prominent role in writing and passing it; Reagan signed it into law, however unhappily, and prominent GOP sponsors looked on as he did so. The sole Democrat to appear at the Sept. 29, 1987, signing ceremony was Sen. Ernest F. Hollings of South Carolina.

But, as one top Democratic House aide remarked, "Our fingerprints are all over it."

President Reagan with administration officials and members of the Senate at the Gramm-Rudman bill-signing ceremony Sept. 29. The president castigated "big spenders"; Minority Leader Robert Dole gave a thumbs down when asked if he was one. From left, Office of Management and Budget Director James C. Miller III, and Sens. Bob Packwood, John H. Chafee, Pete V. Domenici, Ernest F. Hollings and Phil Gramm.

"We've given the president a free ticket out of town," complained Rep. Vic Fazio, D-Calif. Fazio warned that despite the seeming mildness of defense cuts under the automatic process, their impact would disturb even critics of military programs.

Sen. J. Bennett Johnston, D-La., repeatedly warned colleagues that Reagan would simply demand extra defense money in a 1988 supplemental appropriations bill, Gramm-Rudman limits notwithstanding.

At the Sept. 29 signing, Reagan vowed to fight tax increases and further reductions in the growth of defense spending. Both options, he declared, were "nuts."

Two days later, on Oct. 1, GOP members of the House Ways and Means Committee refused in a closed-door session to vote for any part of an $8 billion package in extensions and revisions of existing taxes proposed by committee Chairman Dan Rostenkowski, D-Ill. The tax-writing panel was to contribute $12 billion in new revenues to a $23 billion deficit-reduction ("reconciliation") bill that was supposed to be the alternative to automatic cuts.

Only after reconciliation would Congress tackle another important piece of fiscal legislation, a 1988 continuing appropriations resolution that would, among other things, establish the level of defense spending for the fiscal year that began Oct. 1.

Democratic leaders said that the size of the defense budget would be set in the continuing resolution after they knew whether Reagan would permit a tax increase. If he did, they said, the defense total would be higher than if he did not.

Meanwhile, on Oct. 20 the first round of automatic cuts, totaling $23 billion, was to go into effect. On Nov. 20, if no alternative had become law, the cuts would become permanent.

Revenue Options

Ways and Means Republicans reiterated Reagan's demand that Congress cut more from domestic programs and forget about taxes.

Rostenkowski responded that Republicans should tell him just which programs they would cut and by how much. But the gridlock on the deficit reflected bipartisan reluctance to cut much more from domestic spending.

In his tax plan, Rostenkowski confronted committee Republicans with nearly $3 billion in unpopular user fees and tax increases that had appeared in Reagan's own fiscal 1988 budget. This section would eliminate remaining Medicare tax exemptions for state and local government employees, impose payroll taxes on employers for employees' cash tips, repeal gasoline and other highway tax exemptions for state and local governments and bus operators, and tax certain student earnings, among other things.

The plan also incorporated an additional $3 billion in revisions of estate-tax and estimated tax-payment rules for corporations. These two changes, as he told reporters, were introduced earlier as separate bills (HR 1311, HR 1581) by Rostenkowski and ranking committee Republican John J. Duncan of Tennessee.

Other items in the plan would extend existing telephone excise taxes, freeze estate and gift tax rates that are scheduled to decline, and continue an expiring portion of the federal unemployment tax.

Republican Reluctance

Notwithstanding the GOP tinge to the package, Rep. Hal Daub, R-Neb., said Republicans would not supply votes for taxes "to get Democrats off the hook."

The GOP response did not disturb more partisan committee members such as Rep. Charles B. Rangel, D-N.Y. "We don't really need Republicans," Rangel said. "If they tell us to go to hell, we still have to come up with something."

Rostenkowski preferred bipartisan legislating but said he could move a bill out of his committee with Democratic votes alone.

In the private session he told members he would accept additions to the bill, including tax benefits, but only if costs are offset with additional tax revenues. The same requirement for "revenue-neutrality" would prevail in the Senate Finance Committee.

Rostenkowski also believed that Reagan would come around. "I think when we get a bill to his desk and he looks at the alternative, he'll sign it."

Automatic Cuts' Impact

If the $23 billion in automatic cuts (known as a "sequester") went into effect, $11.5 billion would be subtracted from domestic spending and the same amount from military programs.

The total to be cut translated into 8.5 percent reductions in domestic spending, under early estimates of the House Budget Committee, and 6 percent to 10 percent cuts in military expenditures.

The percentage reductions would be calculated from current levels of spending, as set by appropriations bills, with allowances for future inflation. The inflation allowance was an important change from the original Gramm-Rudman law. It, along with the new version's higher deficit targets, made automatic cuts significantly less harsh than they would have been under the old version.

Rostenkowski reported "a strong feeling among Ways and Means Republicans that a sequester under these circumstances is not all that bad." Liberal Democrats also might not be upset if Reagan vetoed tax legislation.

"It's OK with me. He vetoes it and I get the defense cuts I wanted," said Rep. Fortney H. "Pete" Stark, D-Calif., a Ways and Means member.

For military expenditures the percentage reductions could vary because the Gramm-Rudman legislation gave Reagan latitude to determine the total amount of spending from which the $11.5 billion was subtracted, by exempting or shielding certain accounts. If he did not make any exemptions, the percentage cut would be 6 percent. If he exempted military personnel accounts, as permitted, the cut into remaining programs would be about 10 percent.

The president, if Congress approved, might also vary the percentage reductions in non-personnel accounts, taking more from some and less from others.

Defense Options

Because of the variability in Reagan's options, because of peculiarities in the rates of spending in different military accounts, and because of some confusion about what the law required, there were several answers to the question: How much defense spending would be left after automatic cuts? But the House Budget Committee estimate was that automatic cuts would have to bring defense outlays — money actually spent in a given year, down to $280.3 billion.

What would vary, depending on options Reagan chose, would be defense budget authority, which referred to the amount of money that might be obligated in a given year.

If the president made no exemptions, the automatic cuts would set defense budget authority at $285 billion for fiscal 1988.

If he exempted personnel accounts, as the new law let him do, the budget authority number would be pushed down to $280.5 billion.

If Reagan, for example, were to exempt personnel and fully fund his controversial strategic defense initiative and make up the difference from other accounts (and if Congress let him do so), the budget authority total would drop to $275 billion.

These figures compared with the fiscal 1987 appropriated level of $291.4 billion in budget authority and $284.4 billion in outlays.

The fiscal 1988 budget resolution (H Con Res 93) had stipulated that if Reagan accepted a larger tax increase than was under consideration, defense spending would be set at $296 billion in budget authority and $289.5 billion in outlays.

Absent any new taxes, the resolution assumed lower defense levels of $289 billion in budget authority and $283 billion in outlays.

Speaking at an Oct. 1 breakfast, House Budget Committee Chairman William H. Gray III, D-Pa., speculated that "maybe $23 billion is not a strong threat ... there's a question of whether [Reagan's] favorite child is really threatened" by automatic spending cuts. ∎

POLITICS

Presidential Primaries

Although they have existed for almost a century, primaries only recently have emerged as a dominant factor in the process by which candidates obtain the presidential nominations of major parties. After many years of ebbing and surging as an alternative to the smoke-filled-room system, presidential primaries flourished in the 1960s and 1970s. They helped to produce a few nominees who otherwise would have been unlikely prospects to capture the highest award a party can bestow.

Presidential primaries originated as an outgrowth of the Progressive movement in the early 20th century. Progressives, populists, and reformers in general were fighting state and municipal corruption. They objected to the links between political bosses and big business and advocated returning the government to the people.

Part of this "return to the people" was a turn away from what were looked upon as boss-dominated conventions. It was only a matter of time before the primary idea spread from state and local elections to presidential contests. Because there was no provision for a nationwide primary, state primaries were initiated to choose delegates to the national party conventions (delegate-selection primaries) and to register voters' preferences on their parties' eventual presidential nominees (preference primaries).

Florida enacted the first presidential primary law in 1901. The law gave party officials an option of holding a party primary to choose any party candidate for public office, as well as delegates to the national conventions. However, there was no provision for placing names of presidential candidates on the ballot—either in the form of a preference vote or with information indicating the preference of the candidates for convention delegates.

Wisconsin's Progressive Republican politician, Gov. Robert M. La Follette, gave a boost to the presidential primary following the 1904 Republican National Convention. It was at that convention that the credentials of La Follette's Progressive delegation were rejected and a regular Republican delegation from Wisconsin was seated. Angered by what he considered his unfair treatment, La Follette returned to his home state and began pushing for a presidential primary law. The result was the 1905 Wisconsin law mandating the direct election of national convention delegates. However, the law did not include provisions for indicating the presidential preference of delegates.

La Follette's sponsorship of the delegate-selection primary helped make the concept a part of the Progressive political program. The growth of the Progressive movement rapidly resulted in the enactment of presidential primary laws in other states.

The next step in presidential primaries—the preferential vote for president—took place in Oregon. There, in 1910, Sen. Jonathan Bourne, (1907-13), a Progressive Republican colleague of La Follette, sponsored a referendum to establish a presidential preference primary, with delegates legally bound to support the winner of the preference primary. By 1912, with Oregon in the lead, 12 states had enacted presidential primary laws that provided for either direct election of delegates, a preferential vote, or both. The number expanded to 26 states by 1916.

Primaries and Conventions

The first major test of the impact of presidential primary laws — in 1912—demonstrated that victories in the primaries did not ensure a candidate's nomination at the convention. Former president Theodore Roosevelt, campaigning in 12 Republican primaries, won nine of them, including a defeat of incumbent Republican president William Howard Taft in Taft's home state of Ohio. Roosevelt lost only three — to Taft by a narrow margin in Massachusetts and to La Follette in North Dakota and Wisconsin.

Despite this impressive string of primary victories, the convention rejected Roosevelt in favor of Taft. Taft supporters dominated the Republican National Committee, which ran the convention, and the convention's credentials committee, which ruled on contested delegates. Moreover, Taft was backed by many state organizations, especially in the South, where most delegates were chosen by caucuses or conventions dominated by party leaders.

On the Democratic side, the convention more closely reflected the results of the primaries. Gov. Woodrow Wilson of New Jersey and Speaker of the House Champ Clark of Missouri were closely matched in total primary votes, with Wilson only 29,632 votes ahead of Clark. Wilson emerged with the nomination after a long struggle with Clark at the convention.

After the first wave of enthusiasm for presidential primaries in the early years of the 20th century, interest in them waned. By 1935, eight states had repealed their presidential primary laws. The diminution of reform zeal during the 1920s and the preoccupation of the country with the Depression in the 1930s and war in the 1940s were apparently leading factors in this decline. Also, party leaders were not enthusiastic about primaries; the cost of conducting them was relatively high, both for the candidates and the states. Many presidential candidates ignored the primaries, and voter participation often was low.

But after World War II interest picked up again. Some politicians with presidential ambitions, knowing the party leadership was not enthusiastic about their candidacies, entered the primaries to generate a bandwagon effect. In 1952 Sen. Estes Kefauver, D-Tenn, (1949-63), riding a wave of public recognition as head of the Senate Organized

Crime Investigating Committee, challenged Democratic party leaders by winning several primaries, including an upset of President Harry S Truman in New Hampshire.

With the growing demand for political reform in the 1960s and early 1970s, the presidential primaries became more attractive as a path to the nomination. John F. Kennedy, then a relatively obscure U.S. senator from Massachusetts, helped to popularize that route with his successful uphill fight for the Democratic nomination in 1960. An unbroken string of Kennedy victories helped force the withdrawal of his chief rival in the primaries, Sen. Hubert H. Humphrey of Minnesota.

The Democrats Begin to Tinker

Despite the Progressive reforms, party leaders until 1968 remained in firm control of the nominating process. With only a handful of 15 to 20 primaries regularly contested, candidates could count on a short primary season. They began in New Hampshire in March, then tested their appeal during the spring in Wisconsin, Nebraska, Oregon and California before courting the party leaders.

But in 1968 the Democrats launched reforms in an effort to reduce the alienation of liberals and minorities from the Democratic nominating system and to allow the people to choose their own leaders. The Republicans seldom made any changes in their rules. This era of grassroots control produced for the Democrats presidential candidates such as George McGovern, a liberal from South Dakota who lost in a landslide to Nixon in 1972, and Jimmy Carter, who beat incumbent president Gerald R. Ford in 1976 but lost to Ronald Reagan in 1980.

With the record high of 37 primaries held in 1980, the opportunity for mass participation in the nominating process was greater than ever before. President Carter and Republican nominee Reagan were the clear winners of the long 1980 primary season. Although Carter received a bare majority of the cumulative Democratic primary vote, he amassed a plurality of nearly 2.7 million votes over his major rival, Sen. Edward M. Kennedy of Massachusetts. With no opposition in the late primary contests, Reagan emerged as a more one-sided choice of GOP primary voters. He finished nearly 4.6 million votes ahead of George Bush, who eventually withdrew from the race.

Disheartened by their nominee's massive defeat in 1980, the Democrats revised their nominating rules for the 1984 election. The party created "superdelegates"; that is, delegate seats were reserved for party leaders who were not formally committed to any presidential candidate. This reform had two main goals. First, Democratic leaders wanted to ensure that the party's elected and appointed officials would participate at the convention. Second, they wanted to ensure that these uncommitted party leaders could play a key role in selecting the presidential nominee if no candidate was a clear frontrunner.

The Democrats' new rules had some expected, as well as unexpected, results. For the first time since 1968, the number of primaries declined and the number of caucuses increased. The Democrats held only 25 primaries in 1984. Yet, like McGovern in 1972 and Carter in 1976, Colorado senator Gary Hart used the primaries to pull ahead (temporarily) of former vice president Walter F. Mondale, an early front-runner whose strongest ties were to the party leadership and its traditional core elements. In 1984 the presence of superdelegates was important because about four out of five backed Mondale.

Critics regarded the seating of superdelegates as undemocratic and called for reducing their numbers. Instead, by adding 75 superdelegate seats, the Democratic National Committee (DNC) increased their numbers from 14 percent of the delegates in 1984 to more than 15 percent for 1988. Moreover, another 150 new delegate seats have been set aside for party leaders, but these delegates may be bound by the results of primaries and caucuses. All 362 members of the DNC will be guaranteed seats, as will all the Democratic governors and about 80 percent of the Democrats in Congress.

The Republican party does not guarantee delegate seats to its leaders, nor has the party created superdelegates. However, its rules permit less rigid pledging of delegates.

Growth of Regional Primaries

In addition to the Democrats' internal party concerns with the nominating process, other critics often cited the length of the primary season (nearly twice as long as the general election campaign), the expense, the physical strain on the candidates, and the variations and complexities of state laws as problems of presidential primaries.

To deal with these problems, several states in 1974-75 discussed the feasibility of creating regional primaries, in which individual states within a geographical region would hold their primaries on the same day. Supporters of the concept believed it would reduce candidate expenses and strain and would permit concentration on regional issues.

The idea achieved some limited success in 1976 when two groups of states—one in the West and the other in the South—decided to hold regional primaries. However, they chose the same day, May 25, to hold their primaries, thus defeating one of the main purposes of the plan by continuing to force candidates to shuttle across the country to cover both areas. Attempts were also made in New England to construct a regional primary. But New Hampshire could not participate because its law requires the state to hold its primary at least one week before any other state.

As of late 1987, 38 states planned to hold some form of presidential primary in 1988. This marked a sharp increase from the 25 in 1984, but the timing of the primaries was likely to have greater consequences than the increase in their numbers. More and more states, hoping to increase their impact on the presidential campaign, decided to hold their primaries early in the year. On March 8, three weeks after the New Hampshire primary, 20 states were lined up to hold primaries or caucuses. This so-called "Super Tuesday," largely dominated by southern states, would be the closest thing to a national primary the presidential nominating process had ever seen. Victories or strong showings in Iowa and New Hampshire would generate momentum; the payoff in Super Tuesday states would be delegates.

The Game Is the Same, But Not So the Rules

The presidential nominating process calls to mind the cliché about the weather. "If you don't like it now, just wait 10 minutes and it'll change." For nearly two decades now, the nominating process has been changing as regularly and reliably as the weather.

The impetus for change came from the Democrats, who began revising their delegate-selection rules after the party's tumultuous 1968 convention, in which Hubert H. Humphrey was nominated without having to run in a single primary.

Rewriting their rules every four years since then, the Democrats transferred power in their nominating process from party kingmakers to the grass roots. To a significant degree, the Republican nominating process was affected as well. In many states where Democratic-controlled legislatures had established presidential primaries for their party, the GOP had been pushed to hold a primary also.

Throughout the 1970s, there was a steady growth in presidential primaries — the number swelled from 17 in 1968 to 37 in 1980. During the 1980s, the Democrats established whole new blocks of delegates, culminating in 1984 with the creation of hundreds of uncommitted "superdelegate" slots for Democratic members of Congress and state party leaders.

But at no time in the present era of mass participation had there been a change as potentially revolutionary as the one-day, 20-state event on March 8, 1988, known as "Super Tuesday." It is the closest thing to a national primary that the country has ever seen.

Big, Early and Unpredictable

Democratic state legislators across the South were the instigators of the big Super Tuesday vote. Weary of taking a back seat to the early "media fishbowl" events in Iowa and New Hampshire and tired of being saddled with liberal presidential nominees who were a drag on state and local Democratic tickets in the South, the legislators created a massive, one-day primary that will include virtually every state in the region, plus several on its fringe.

The South is so big and its voting so early that it certainly will have a significant impact on the 1988 nominating process. No one was at all sure, however, exactly what that impact would be.

Many Southerners hoped that Super Tuesday would not only force candidates to come South and "talk Southern," but that it also would relegate the Iowa and New Hampshire events to the status of small-scale warm-up acts.

Yet Super Tuesday could just as easily end up enhancing the clout of Iowa and New Hampshire. A burst of momentum based on victories in those two states could enable the winners to sweep straight through the vast block of states voting March 8.

There was even the prospect that Super Tuesday could backfire altogether for its Democratic instigators. Part of their aim in pushing for a regional vote was to create an event so exciting and important that it would attract the South's conservative whites, a group that had largely been lost to the GOP in recent presidential elections.

But with Georgia Sen. Sam Nunn's Aug. 27, 1987, decision not to seek the Democratic nomination, conservative Southern Democrats could lose interest in their party's nominating contest if they viewed it as dominated by left-of-center candidates. The conservative Democrats might end up voting on the GOP side in the March 8 primaries, or they might skip Super Tuesday altogether. Either outcome would be a bad omen for Democratic chances of carrying the South in November 1988.

Knockout or Stalemate?

With the impact of Super Tuesday so uncertain, speculation about how the 1988 nominating process would play out runs the gamut: A fast-starting candidate could score a quick knockout on Super Tuesday, or there could be a lengthy, even stalemated contest that goes on through the spring to the national convention.

During the present era of presidential primaries — there were tentatively 38 scheduled in 1988 — the conventions merely served as backdrops for the coronation of the candidate who emerged on top in the primaries. And the results in the "media fishbowl" states of Iowa and New Hampshire set the tone for the entire primary season. Every presidential

nominee in the last dozen years won either Iowa or New Hampshire, and finished no lower than second in the other.

Usually the nominating contests had continued through the "trench warfare" period of March and April, when most of the major Frost Belt industrial states vote, into the final round of primaries in May and June, anchored by the vote in California at the end. But it had generally been clear much earlier which candidate would win the nomination.

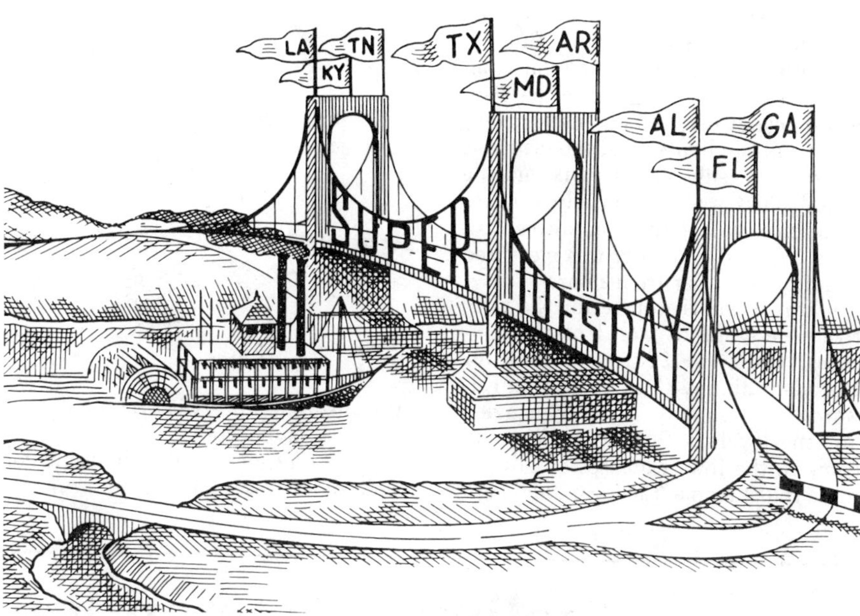

Follow the Rules

There had never been a nominating year with as many delegate-selection events concentrated at the beginning of the calendar as was the case in 1988. In 1972, only two primaries were held before the middle of March; by 1984, there were seven. For 1988, 20 states had set primaries before March 15. Add in early caucus activity in a half dozen or so other states, and more than half the country would vote before the ides of March.

That made one thing certain about 1988: The candidates' delegate totals would be more important at an earlier stage of the process than ever before. So, too, would the rules by which they were allocated.

Democratic and Republican candidates operated under similar ground rules when it came to the calendar order of states' votes and the campaign finance laws that regulated fund raising and spending.

But the candidates operated on vastly different playing fields when it came to winning delegates. In the Republican Party, the accent was on winner-take-all systems of delegate selection. In the Democratic Party, the emphasis was on proportional representation, with the delegates divided to reflect a candidate's share of the primary or caucus vote.

The result was that a Republican candidate who registered a string of early successes in the "media fishbowl" and Super Tuesday states in 1988 was more apt to score a quick knockout than a Democratic candidate who got off to a similarly fast start.

On Super Tuesday alone, seven of the Republican primaries offered the possibility of winner-take-all, including contests in the two largest Southern states, Texas and Florida. Meanwhile, virtually every Democratic delegate that day was allocated on the basis of proportional representation.

Democratic primaries in Illinois (March 15), Pennsylvania (April 26) and New Jersey (June 7) are direct-election, or district winner-take-all, contests that offer a victorious candidate the chance for a large windfall of delegates. But those states stood virtually alone as exceptions to the Democratic rule of proportional representation.

Independent Operators

Another potential brake on any quick Democratic decision in 1988 were the "superdelegates," a block of more than 600 uncommitted party and elected officials that included all Democratic governors and members of the Democratic National Committee, plus four-fifths of the party's members of Congress. Superdelegates were to occupy 15 percent of the delegate seats at the Democratic convention in Atlanta.

In 1984, the large House component of superdelegates was chosen before the Iowa caucuses in an event that was dubbed by some as the "first primary." They gave Walter F. Mondale a lead in the delegate count that he never relinquished.

But in 1988, no candidate would get an early boost from the congressional superdelegates; they were not to be selected until late April, after much of the country had already voted.

A Crucial Fraction

Those who vote in the primaries and caucuses are only a fraction of the number who cast ballots in the November presidential election. When both parties together last held competitive nominating contests in 1980, fewer than 33 million votes were cast in the presidential primaries — 19.6 million on the Democratic side, 12.9 million on the Republican. Activity in caucus states probably did not involve more than 2 million more voters.

By comparison, more than 86 million voters turned out that November to elect Ronald Reagan as president, roughly two-and-a-half times the number that took part in the nominating process that year.

Rules governing voting participation played a role in the comparatively low turnouts for the nominating process. Every primary is not as open as a general election, where any registered voter can participate. There were about 20 states where primary or caucus participation is limited to registered party members in 1987; in several other states, registered independents are allowed to participate but lose their nonpartisan status when they do so.

The Gate-Crash Factor

Still, the vast majority of registered voters across the country could participate in a presidential primary or caucus if they wanted to. The fact that more did not generated the conventional wisdom that the nominating process was dominated by ideological activists — liberals on the Democratic side, conservatives on the Republican.

There was no question that the nominating process was greatly influenced by dedicated party activists and by interest groups that were capable of mobilizing their members. But the primaries and caucuses were far from a closed universe; when a delegate selection event received extensive attention from candidates and the media, it often drew substantial rank-and-file input. That was particularly true for primaries, where the commitment of time required of a voter was measured in minutes rather than hours.

But it was also true for the relatively low-turnout world of the caucuses. Back in 1980, strategists for President Jimmy Carter and Sen. Edward M. Kennedy carefully singled out the loyalists they thought would come to the Iowa caucuses and determine the outcome. Each candidate approached the vote with about 35,000 identified supporters.

But on caucus night, thousands of rank-and-file voters poured into the caucus meetings. At least 30,000 more voters showed up than either side had expected, producing a turnout not much smaller than an average Democratic gubernatorial contest in Iowa. If another such rank-and-file explosion occurred in Iowa in 1988, there would be no telling how the nominating process would unfold.

Following are the Preliminary Spending Limits by state for 1988 presidential candidates as set by the Federal Election Commission; the Delegate Selection Calendar for 1988, listing primary and first round caucus dates and candidate filing deadlines; and the Summary of State Rules and Statistics, listing each state's form of delegate selection and system for allocating delegates to candidates. ∎

Preliminary Spending Limits

Listed below are preliminary spending limits in each state for candidates pursuing the 1988 presidential nominations, as determined by the Federal Election Commission (FEC). The figures are keyed to the voting-age population of each state.

The limitations apply only to campaigns that choose to accept federal funds; campaigns opting to forgo federal funding may spend unlimited amounts of money. According to FEC calculations, if the presidential election were held in 1987, candidates for party nomination would be able to spend almost $27 million, and party nominees would be able to spend nearly $45 million in the general election. Official spending computations will be available in early 1988.

	Voting-Age Population	Expenditure Limitations
Alabama	2,938,000	$ 1,044,987.84
Alaska	358,000	444,600.00
Arizona	2,405,000	855,410.40
Arkansas	1,728,000	614,615.04
California	19,949,000	7,095,460.32
Colorado	2,396,000	852,209.28
Connecticut	2,438,000	867,147.84
Delaware	475,000	444,600.00
Florida	9,071,000	3,226,373.28
Georgia	4,422,000	1,572,816.96
Hawaii	773,000	444,600.00
Idaho	682,000	444,600.00
Illinois	8,471,000	3,012,965.28
Indiana	4,013,000	1,427,343.84
Iowa	2,095,000	745,149.60
Kansas	1,792,000	637,378.56
Kentucky	2,715,000	965,671.20
Louisiana	3,150,000	1,120,392.00
Maine	871,000	444,600.00
Maryland	3,359,000	1,194,729.12
Massachusetts	4,480,000	1,593,446.40
Michigan	6,675,000	2,374,164.00
Minnesota	3,075,000	1,093,716.00
Mississippi	1,842,000	655,162.56
Missouri	3,733,000	1,327,753.44
Montana	588,000	444,600.00
Nebraska	1,154,000	444,600.00
Nevada	740,000	444,600.00
New Hampshire	769,000	444,600.00
New Jersey	5,761,000	2,049,072.48
New Mexico	1,023,000	444,600.00
New York	13,437,000	4,779,272.16
North Carolina	4,740,000	$ 1,685,923.20
North Dakota	484,000	444,600.00
Ohio	7,905,000	2,811,650.40
Oklahoma	2,379,000	846,162.72
Oregon	1,990,000	707,803.20
Pennsylvania	9,031,000	3,212,146.08
Rhode Island	751,000	444,600.00
South Carolina	2,460,000	874,972.80
South Dakota	503,000	444,600.00
Tennessee	3,572,000	1,270,488.96
Texas	11,792,000	4,194,178.56
Utah	1,046,000	444,600.00
Vermont	401,000	444,600.00
Virginia	4,337,000	1,542,584.16
Washington	3,271,000	1,163,429.28
West Virginia	1,415,000	503,287.20
Wisconsin	3,508,000	1,247,725.44
Wyoming	348,000	444,600.00
Territories		
American Samoa	19,000	444,600.00
District of Columbia	495,000	444,600.00
Guam	75,000	444,600.00
Puerto Rico	2,038,000	724,875.84
Virgin Islands	64,000	444,600.00

General Election Spending Limits

Candidate Limit	$ 44,460,000.00
National Party Committee Limit	$ 7,905,299.22

Delegate Selection Calendar for 1988

This calendar includes 1988 primary and first-round caucus dates as well as candidate filing deadlines. The list is necessarily tentative; some states have not yet set firm dates for their delegate-selection activity.

The dates listed for decisions by secretaries of state or election boards are, in many cases, the final date by which they must decide which candidates will go on their state's primary ballot; the ballot-placement decision could be made earlier than the date listed.

The primary and first-round caucus dates are listed in **boldface.** States in which presidential and congressional primary voting occurs on the same day are noted with an asterisk (*).

DECEMBER 1987

Date	State	Event
14th	VA	filing deadline
15th	MS	secretary of state decision
18th	NH	filing deadline
28th	IL	filing deadline
	MD	secretary of state decision (R)/filing deadline (R)
29th	SD	filing deadline
30th	RI	secretary of state decision

JANUARY 1988

Date	State	Event
4th	MA	filing deadline
	MD	secretary of state decision (D)
	TX	filing deadline
5th	AR	filing deadline
	FL	secretary of state decision
	MA	secretary of state decision
	MO	filing deadline
	NC	filing deadline
	TN	filing deadline
	VA	election board decision
7th	NC	election board decision
8th	KY	nominating committee decision/filing deadline
	RI	filing deadline
11th	MD	filing deadline (D)
12th	TN	secretary of state decision
13th	OK	filing deadline
14th	MI	**county conventions (R)**
	AL	filing deadline (R)
15th	AL	filing deadline (D)
	GA	secretary of state decision
	MS	filing deadline
	SC	filing deadline (R)
18th	VT	filing deadline
27th	HI	**caucus (R)**
29th	MI	**state convention (R)**
	CT	secretary of state decision
	LA	filing deadline
	WI	nominating committee decision

FEBRUARY

Date	State	Event
1st	AZ	filing deadline (D)
	CA	secretary of state decision
	KS	filing deadline (D)
	SC	filing deadline (D)
6th	WV	filing deadline
8th	IA	**caucus**
	HI	filing deadline (D)
10th	GA	nominating committee meeting
11th	NY	filing deadline (R)
15th	NM	nominating committee decision
16th	NH	**primary**
	CT	filing deadline
	NE	secretary of state decision
	PA	filing deadline
	WI	filing deadline
18th	OH	filing deadline
19th	PR	secretary of state decision
23rd	MN	**caucus**
	SD	**primary**
25th	MI	filing deadline (D)
	NY	filing deadline (D)
27th	KS	**CD conventions (R)**
28th	ME	**caucus**

MARCH

Date	State	Event
1st	VT	**non-binding primary**
4th	DC	filing deadline (D)
	IN	filing deadline
5th	KS	**state convention (R)**
	SC	**primary (R)**
	WY	**caucus**
	CA	filing deadline (D)
8th	**Super Tuesday**	
	AL	**primary**
	AR	**primary** *
	FL	**primary**
	GA	**primary**
	HI	**caucus (D)**
	ID	**caucus (D)**
	KY	**primary**
	LA	**primary**
	MD	**primary** *
	MA	**primary**
	MS	**primary** *
	MO	**primary**
	NV	**caucus (D)**
	NC	**primary**
	OK	**primary**
	RI	**primary**
	TN	**primary**
	TX	**primary *; caucus (D)**
	VA	**primary**
	WA	**caucus**
	Am. Samoa	**caucus (D)**
10th	AK	**caucus (D)**
11th	NE	filing deadline
12th	SC	**caucus (D)**
13th	ND	**caucus (D)**
15th	IL	**primary** *
19th	KS	**caucus (D)**
20th	PR	**primary**
22nd	Dems Abroad	**primary**
23rd	CA	filing deadline (R)
24th	MT	filing deadline
25th	ID	secretary of state decision
26th	MI	**caucus (D)**
29th	CT	**primary**

APRIL

Date	State	Event
2nd	VI	**caucus (D)**
4th	CO	**caucus**
5th	WI	**primary**
14th	NJ	filing deadline
16th	AZ	**caucus (D)**
18th	DE	**caucus (D)**
19th	NY	**primary**
	VT	**caucus (D)**
20th		**Democratic House superdelegates selected**
	ND	filing deadline
24th	Guam	**caucus**
25th	UT	**caucus**
	ID	filing deadline
26th	PA	**primary** *
	VT	**caucus (R)**

MAY

Date	State	Event
3rd	DC	**primary** *
	IN	**primary** *
	OH	**primary** *
10th	NE	**primary** *
	WV	**primary** *
17th	OR	**primary** *
24th	ID	**primary** *

JUNE

Date	State	Event
7th	CA	**primary** *
	MT	**primary** *
	NJ	**primary** *
	NM	**primary** *
14th	ND	**primary** *

JULY

18th-21st	**Democratic National Convention in Atlanta**

AUGUST

15th-18th	**Republican National Convention in New Orleans**

Summary of State Rules and Statistics

Open — Voters may participate in either party's event.
Closed — Event restricted to registered party voters.
* — Open to independents, but not to members of the other party.
C(D)/P(R) — Democratic caucus and Republican primary.
P(D)/C(R) — Democratic primary and Republican caucus.
DE — Direct election of delegates independent of vote for candidates (winner-take-all possible).
PR — Proportional representation system.
BPR — "Bonus" proportional representation; candidate receives a bonus delegate for each district won.
WTA — Winner-take-all system.
NFS — No formal system for allocating delegates to candidates; method determined by participants.

	Delegates		Form of Delegate Selection	Method of Allocation		REGISTERED VOTERS		
							Percent	
	Dem.	Rep.		Dem.	Rep.	Total	Dem.	Rep.
Alabama	61	38	Open Primary	PR	PR/WTA	2,341,264	—	—
Alaska	17	19	Closed Caucus	BPR	NFS	257,429	22	21
Arizona	40	33	Closed Caucus	PR	NFS	1,464,071	43	46
Arkansas	43	27	Open Primary	PR	PR	1,188,831	—	—
California	336	175	Closed Primary	PR	WTA	12,121,051	51	38
Colorado	51	36	Closed Caucus	BPR	NFS	1,807,156	31	33
Connecticut	59	35	Closed Primary	PR	PR	1,672,949	40	27
Delaware	19	17	Closed Caucus	PR	NFS	293,119	44	35
Florida	146	82	Closed Primary	BPR	WTA	5,631,188	57	36
Georgia	86	48	Open Primary	BPR	WTA	2,575,819	—	—
Hawaii	25	20	Closed Caucus	PR	NFS	419,794	—	—
Idaho	23	22	Open C(D)/P(R)	PR	PR	514,801	—	—
Illinois	187	92	Open Primary	DE	DE	6,003,811	—	—
Indiana	85	51	Open Primary	PR	WTA	2,878,498	—	—
Iowa	58	37	Open Caucus *	PR	NFS	1,544,902	35	31
Kansas	43	34	Closed Caucus	PR	NFS	1,102,641	29	42
Kentucky	60	38	Closed Primary	PR	PR	1,936,025	68	28
Louisiana	71	41	Closed Primary	PR	WTA	2,139,861	78	14
Maine	27	22	Open Caucus *	PR	NFS	773,966	34	30
Maryland	78	41	Closed Primary	DE/PR	WTA	2,139,690	67	25
Massachusetts	109	52	Open Primary *	BPR	PR	2,933,364	47	13
Michigan	151	77	Open Caucus	PR	NFS	5,597,748	—	—
Minnesota	86	31	Open Caucus	PR	NFS	2,447,273	—	—
Mississippi	45	31	Open Primary	PR	WTA	1,643,191	—	—
Missouri	83	47	Open Primary	BPR	PR	2,775,654	—	—
Montana	25	20	Open Primary	BPR	NFS	443,935	—	—
Nebraska	29	25	Closed Primary	PR	DE	849,762	42	51
Nevada	21	20	Closed Caucus	PR	NFS	367,596	50	43
New Hampshire	22	23	Open Primary *	PR	PR	551,257	30	37
New Jersey	118	64	Open Primary *	DE	DE	3,647,886	34	20
New Mexico	28	26	Closed Primary	PR	NFS	499,180	60	34
New York	275	136	Closed Primary	BPR	DE	7,650,666	47	33
North Carolina	89	54	Closed Primary	BPR	PR	3,080,990	69	27
North Dakota	20	16	Open C(D)/P(R)	PR	PR	—	—	—
Ohio	174	88	Open Primary *	BPR	WTA	5,856,552	31	20
Oklahoma	51	36	Closed Primary	PR	WTA	2,014,578	67	30
Oregon	51	32	Closed Primary	PR	PR	1,422,226	48	40
Pennsylvania	193	96	Closed Primary	DE	DE	5,384,375	54	42
Rhode Island	26	21	Open Primary *	PR	PR	524,662	—	—
South Carolina	48	37	Open C(D)/P(R)	PR	WTA	1,184,133	—	—
South Dakota	19	18	Closed Primary	PR	PR	428,097	43	49
Tennessee	77	45	Open Primary	PR	PR	2,543,597	—	—
Texas	198	111	Open P & C(D)/P(R)	PR	PR/WTA	7,340,638	—	—
Utah	27	26	Open Caucus	PR	NFS	763,057	—	—
Vermont	19	17	Open Caucus	PR	NFS	328,466	—	—
Virginia	85	50	Open P(D)/C(R)	PR	NFS	2,546,345	—	—
Washington	72	41	Open Caucus	PR	NFS	2,230,254	—	—
West Virginia	44	28	Open Primary *	DE	DE	946,039	67	31
Wisconsin	88	47	Open Primary	PR	WTA	—	—	—
Wyoming	18	18	Closed Caucus	PR	NFS	187,302	33	59

GOP Faces Tough Odds in Bid to Regain Senate

Democrats' '88 Aim Is to Tighten Grip

A Minnesota cartoonist recently lampooned the 1987 Senate GOP as a banged-up boxer, collapsed in a locker-room daze while his trainer shouts: "Up and at 'em, I'm here to get you in shape for the '88 fight!"

The trainer in the drawing was Minnesota's junior senator, Rudy Boschwitz. The cartoon's framed original hangs in the headquarters of the National Republican Senatorial Committee (NRSC), where Boschwitz is the boss.

It's a tough job, but Boschwitz asked for it; he earned it by campaigning and raising money for Republican Senate candidates in 1986. He has the task of retrieving GOP fortunes from that year's debacle — a loss of eight seats and the Senate majority.

"After a year like we had, you look back and think that anything you didn't do, you should have," said Jann Olsten, formerly Boschwitz' top Senate aide and now NRSC executive director.

The hangover from 1986 dominated Republican preparations for 1988. Once the envy of the political fund-raising industry, the NRSC had collected only half what it had at a comparable point in the last cycle. And candidate recruitment was hampered by the lesser allure of serving on the weak side of the aisle.

In fact, despite heavy emphasis on encouraging candidates in 1987, the Republicans had thus far failed either to field their first choice or to find a strong substitute in several key states, including Virginia, Tennessee, Michigan, Maine, West Virginia, New York and Montana.

Their ballot picture was clouded further by the possibility of additional retirements among incumbents and of bloodlettings in a minimum of two party primaries — in Nebraska and Wisconsin.

And in at least two top-targeted states — New Jersey and New Mexico — the GOP might be counting on political novices to unseat Democratic incumbents.

The Democrats had their disappointments as well, including no-go decisions by a governor, a former governor and an at-large House member who were being urged to try for the Senate. But it was the Republicans who were looking to catch up.

The NRSC itself had been bloodied by a briefing memo, written by one of its researchers, urging Ohio candidates to attack incumbent Democrat Howard M. Metzenbaum as a communist sympathizer. Boschwitz had to apologize to Metzenbaum on the floor of the Senate. The Senate later adopted a resolution urging members and campaign committees to avoid negative and personal attacks during election campaigns. *(1987 CQ Weekly Report p. 2194)*

And shortly before Boschwitz took over the NRSC, the committee caught flak from GOP contributors who were angry that NRSC officials gave themselves big bonuses just after the party's loss of Senate control in November 1986.

Conversely, the recent past was a welcome topic at the Democratic Senatorial Campaign Committee (DSCC) in 1987, where the new chairman, Massachusetts' junior senator, John Kerry, could build on the 1986 success of his predecessor, George J. Mitchell of Maine.

Like Boschwitz, Kerry actively pursued the job as a first step into the Senate leadership and onto the larger national stage. But Kerry had had smoother sailing. A first-term senator who personally refused contributions from political action committees, Kerry had proven himself as a party rainmaker.

DSCC fund raising was still humbled by that of the NRSC, but it had increased by half over the comparable point in 1985. At midyear, the DSCC had raised $2.65 million, the NRSC $10.6 million.

In 1988, Kerry's committee might even be able to contribute the maximum amount allowed by law to each of its candidates. In 1986, while the NRSC "maxed out" in all races, the DSCC could do so only in the most competitive ones.

As chairman of the National Republican Senatorial Committee, Minnesota's Rudy Boschwitz confronts widespread skepticism that the GOP can retake the Senate.

Massachusetts Sen. John Kerry takes no PAC money for his campaigns, but he has been an effective fund-raiser for the Democratic Senatorial Campaign Committee.

Democrats Seek to Bolster Senate Margin . . .

18 DEMOCRATIC-HELD SEATS

	Incumbent		First Elected	1982 Percentage	Outlook
FLORIDA	Lawton Chiles	Vulnerable	1970	62%	GOP Rep. Connie Mack, reversing his earlier decision, now says he will run.
NEW JERSEY	Frank R. Lautenberg	Vulnerable	1982	51%	Republicans have an attractive, if untested, candidate in retired Army Brig. Gen. Pete Dawkins, who won the Heisman Trophy while at West Point.
OHIO	Howard M. Metzenbaum	Vulnerable	1976	57%	Metzenbaum will face a vigorous challenge no matter who emerges from the Republican primary, which pits downstate Rep. Bob McEwen against Cleveland Mayor George Voinovich.
WISCONSIN	No Incumbent	Vulnerable			William Proxmire's retirement has spawned large fields in both parties, including congressmen and other prominent officials.
MISSISSIPPI	John C. Stennis	Potentially Vulnerable	1947	64%	Stennis will be a heavy favorite if he chooses to run, but at age 86, he may retire. If he retires, House Minority Whip Trent Lott, R, and Democratic Rep. Wayne Dowdy likely would try to move up.
MONTANA	John Melcher	Potentially Vulnerable	1976	55%	Leading Republican contenders include state legislators Tom Hannah and Jack Ramirez.
NEW MEXICO	Jeff Bingaman	Potentially Vulnerable	1982	54%	With the state's two GOP congressmen declining to challenge Bingaman, the party's candidate may be Richard Montoya, who resigned as assistant secretary of the interior to prepare his bid.
NEW YORK	Daniel Patrick Moynihan	Potentially Vulnerable	1976	65%	Two potential GOP challengers are Rudolph W. Giuliani, the U.S. attorney in Manhattan, and Ronald S. Lauder, U.S. ambassador to Austria and heir to the Estée Lauder perfume fortune.
ARIZONA	Dennis DeConcini	Probably Secure	1976	57%	Unless former GOP Gov. Lamar Alexander decides to run in Tennessee, Sasser appears secure. Significant Republican candidates may surface in some of the other states, but none of the seats seems likely to switch control. In North Dakota, Burdick may face a vigorous primary challenge from Rep. Byron L. Dorgan, but Democrats are likely to retain the seat.
HAWAII	Spark M. Matsunaga	Probably Secure	1976	80%	
MAINE	George J. Mitchell	Probably Secure	1982 *	61%	
MARYLAND	Paul S. Sarbanes	Probably Secure	1976	64%	
MASSACHUSETTS	Edward M. Kennedy	Probably Secure	1962	61%	
MICHIGAN	Donald W. Riegle Jr.	Probably Secure	1976	58%	
NORTH DAKOTA	Quentin N. Burdick	Probably Secure	1960	63%	
TENNESSEE	Jim Sasser	Probably Secure	1976	62%	
TEXAS	Lloyd Bentsen	Probably Secure	1970	59%	
WEST VIRGINIA	Robert C. Byrd	Probably Secure	1958	69%	

On the Brink

By historical precedent, a party losing majority control has its best chance of regaining it in the very next election. But by the same precedent, if a deposed party fails to regain control at its first opportunity, it is usually consigned to the wilderness for an extended period. *(Box, p. 66)*

In October 1987 the wilderness seemed just over the horizon for the GOP. Early evidence from the 33 states electing senators in 1988 offered little hope for a renewed Republican majority.

The Democratic margin had been 54-46 since March 1987, when Nebraska's Republican Gov. Kay A. Orr appointed her former campaign manager, David Karnes, to replace the late Edward Zorinsky, a Democrat.

At a remove of 13 months, the likeliest scenario for 1988 would have the Democrats losing three or four seats at most, while taking away three or more held by Republicans in 1987. In that event, they would retain control with their current margin — give or take a seat. Hardly anyone expected a more pronounced shift absent a presidential landslide.

All of this had to be rather disappointing to the GOP. Not long ago, the

. . . While GOP Clings to Hopes of Recapture

15 REPUBLICAN-HELD SEATS

	Incumbent		First Elected	1982 Percentage	Outlook
NEBRASKA	David Karnes	Highly Vulnerable	1987 *	—	Karnes faces a tough fight for the GOP nomination from Rep. Hal Daub. The winner probably will have to take on popular former Democratic Gov. Robert Kerrey.
NEVADA	Chic Hecht		1982	50%	Democratic Gov. Richard H. Bryan is expected to announce his candidacy soon. Polls have shown Bryan with as much as a 3-to-1 lead over Hecht.
MINNESOTA	Dave Durenberger	Vulnerable	1978	53%	Durenberger's all-but-announced Democratic opponent is state Attorney General Hubert H. "Skip" Humphrey III.
RHODE ISLAND	John H. Chafee		1976	51%	Chafee's Democratic challenger, Lt. Gov. Richard A. Licht, is expected to run a strong, well-organized campaign.
VIRGINIA	No Incumbent				The Democrats will have a decided edge if former Gov. Charles S. Robb announces his candidacy for the seat left vacant by the retirement of Paul S. Trible Jr.
CALIFORNIA	Pete Wilson	Potentially Vulnerable	1982	52%	The Democratic field includes Lt. Gov. Leo T. McCarthy and state Secretary of State March Fong Eu.
CONNECTICUT	Lowell P. Weicker Jr.		1970	50%	Potential Democratic challengers include state Attorney General Joseph I. Lieberman and Reps. Sam Gejdenson and Bruce A. Morrison.
DELAWARE	William V. Roth Jr.		1970	55%	Longtime Democratic fund-raiser Samuel Beard has announced his candidacy. Lt. Gov. S. B. Woo and other Democrats are also considering entering the race.
WASHINGTON	Daniel J. Evans		1983	55%	Four Democrats from the House — Don Bonker, Al Swift, Mike Lowry and Norman D. Dicks — are anxiously waiting to see if Evans will seek re-election. Swift has said he will run regardless.
INDIANA	Richard G. Lugar	Probably Secure	1976	54%	The incumbents in these states look strong, although significant Democratic challengers may emerge. In Vermont, GOP Rep. James M. Jeffords is favored to succeed retiring Sen. Robert T. Stafford. Wallop's re-election would be jeopardized only if former Democratic Gov. Ed Herschler were to run.
MISSOURI	John C. Danforth		1976	51%	
PENNSYLVANIA	John Heinz		1976	59%	
UTAH	Orrin G. Hatch		1976	58%	
VERMONT	No Incumbent				
WYOMING	Malcolm Wallop		1976	57%	

** Mitchell was appointed to the Senate in 1980; his first election was in 1982. Karnes was appointed to the Senate in 1987.*

party could look to 1988 as a year in which to anoint President Reagan's successor, solidify Senate control and set the table for a takeover of the House in the 1990s.

Instead, a GOP deeply divided over the Reagan succession had to struggle to avoid further erosion in the Senate and to maintain numerical respectability in the House. *(House Elections, p. 69)*

The Senate element of that reality had to be especially frustrating, because the Democrats would appear to offer the fatter target in 1988. They had to defend 18 seats, the GOP just 15.

But while re-election by its nature is a hazard, incumbency is still an asset. Notwithstanding the occasional massacre (such as in 1980, when 13 incumbents fell), most senators still get re-elected (three-quarters won in 1986).

For 1988, the Democrats seemed better positioned to protect their own. About half of their incumbents were strong re-election favorites, and none seemed highly vulnerable. In contrast, several GOP senators looked shaky.

"We think we can win it," said Tom Mason, NRSC communications director, "in the same way Mitchell was thinking about it two years ago.

In Nebraska, Republican Sen. David Karnes, top, faces a primary against Rep. Hal Daub, middle; waiting in the wings is former Democratic Gov. Robert Kerrey.

But environmental factors will determine the size of the change."

From the other side, of course, the same race looks different. "The Republicans have no chance of winning control," said Robert Chlopak, executive director of the DSCC. "There's a slim chance of a pickup [of seats] for them and a good chance of a pickup for us."

Does Opportunity Knock?

Boschwitz' challenge might be better understood by narrowing it to a dozen races: six targeted Democratic seats (Wisconsin, Ohio, New Jersey, Florida, New Mexico and Montana), and six key seats he had to defend on his side of the aisle (Nevada, Nebraska, Virginia, Rhode Island, Minnesota and Washington).

First, the GOP targets:

Wisconsin: Democratic incumbent William Proxmire had served in the Senate longer than any Wisconsinite. As he retires, he opens a new era in his state's politics. First-term Gov. Tommy G. Thompson, a Republican, had said he would not run. Will he change his mind and claim the seat that early polls said he could win? If not, there would be big fields on both sides.

Four of the state's nine congressmen were considering the race (two from each party), and at least three would probably run. Others running or contemplating the race included a former governor, a lieutenant governor, four state senators, two former statewide candidates and at least one county executive. This might be the least predictable seat of the 1988 cycle.

Ohio: Democratic incumbent Metzenbaum always looked like a big target to Republicans, who tended to be perennially perplexed at how Ohio could send such a liberal to Washington. But the latest crop of challengers was a cut above. Downstate congressman Bob McEwen had strong backing in the Legislature, while Cleveland Mayor George Voinovich could dilute Metzenbaum's strength in critical Cuyahoga County.

New Jersey: Democratic incumbent Frank R. Lautenberg had been dutiful, if somewhat dull, in his first term. The GOP looked first to popular Gov. Thomas H. Kean, but he declined to run. Republicans still liked to talk about this race, though, because they recruited a "star-quality" candidate in retired Brig. Gen. Pete Dawkins, a decorated veteran of the Vietnam War and a former Heisman Trophy winner at West Point.

Dawkins was untested as a politician, however, and had had little to do with New Jersey since his college days. Lautenberg would be well organized and fully financed. This is a race that may well depend on the presidential winds.

Florida: Veteran Democratic incumbent Lawton Chiles is well liked by most Floridians who know him, but many don't. Republicans were fond of repeating that 40 percent of the voters were not voting in Florida when Chiles was first elected. The incumbent also made his fund-raising task more challenging by refusing all contributions from out of state, all contributions from political action committees and all contributions greater than $100.

Nonetheless, the GOP went months without a clear candidate before Rep. Connie Mack reversed field and announced Sept. 19, 1987, that he would run after all. At the moment, clouds over first-term Gov. Bob Martinez and his service tax were darkening the landscape for the GOP.

New Mexico: Democratic incumbent Jeff Bingaman had not become a household word in Washington, but he might surprise Republicans who included New Mexico on their best-target lists.

Elected over an incumbent in 1982, Bingaman had apparently escaped a challenge from either of the state's two GOP congressmen. The party's chosen challenger might be Richard Montoya, who resigned as assistant secretary of the interior the summer of 1987 and moved back to New Mexico.

Montana: Democratic incumbent John Melcher was thought to be a goner in 1982, but he came back with a series of folksy ads about "Doc" Melcher (he is a veterinarian). Again a prime Republican target in 1988, Melcher was already on the air in 1987 with the ads.

Republicans had elected only one Montana senator since popular elections for the Senate began in 1914. Their best 1988 prospect, Bud Leuthold, former president of the National Association of Wheat Growers, bowed out. Contenders then included state legislators Tom Hannah and Jack Ramirez. But with Democratic Gov. Ted Schwinden retiring, many with aspirations for statewide office were thinking about a race for governor.

Another Democratic senator whom Republicans would like to tar-

Perhaps the most vulnerable GOP senator up in 1988 is Nevada's Chic Hecht, left, who trails his likely Democratic challenger, Gov. Richard H. Bryan, in current polls.

get is Daniel Patrick Moynihan in New York, but mob-busting U.S. Attorney Rudolph W. Giuliani had yet to signal real interest in the race. In Tennessee, former Gov. Lamar Alexander would pose a formidable challenge to Jim Sasser, but Alexander had steadfastly refused to run.

Mississippi had become an instant target when John C. Stennis, at 86 the senior member of the Senate, announced his retirement Oct. 19, 1987.

North Dakota might offer the GOP some opportunity, if incumbent Quentin N. Burdick and Democratic congressman Byron L. Dorgan duel each other into vulnerability. But as yet, no Republican emerged to take on either.

The other seven Democratic incumbents looked so secure that no significant challenger had been found.

Big Flank to Guard

Meanwhile, Boschwitz must look to his own fences, including:

Nevada: Republican incumbent Chic Hecht had the unpleasant distinction of trailing Nevada Gov. Richard H. Bryan in test polls by as much as 3-to-1. Boschwitz had been to Nevada to bolster his colleague and help raise money. He predicted Hecht would run a stronger race than was expected. Bryan was expected to announce for the seat in October 1987.

Nebraska: Republican incumbent Karnes, 38, might be the only GOP senator with a tough primary. Republican congressman Hal Daub, a four-termer from Omaha, declared for the seat and began airing TV ads. So had Karnes. Whichever of them survived would probably have to face former Democratic Gov. Robert Kerrey, who had yet to declare but who dominated in polls pitting him against either Karnes or Daub.

Virginia: If Proxmire's retirement made Wisconsin a toss-up state, Trible's made Virginia a cakewalk for popular former Gov. Charles S. Robb, a Democrat, who might announce his candidacy after the state's legislative elections in November. If Robb did not run, a likely pairing would be between congressmen Stan Parris, a Republican from Alexandria, and Rick Boucher, a Democrat from coal- and tobacco-producing southwestern Virginia.

In the meantime, Virginia was the leading breeder of rumored celebrity GOP candidacies. The current crop includes Lt. Col. Oliver L. North, former Navy Secretary John F. Lehman Jr., retired Gen. Alexander M. Haig Jr. and evangelical broadcaster Pat Robertson — the latter two of whom were then GOP presidential candidates.

Rhode Island: Republican incumbent John H. Chafee, a moderate-to-liberal voice in his party, had had a roller-coaster electoral career in his heavily Democratic state. He barely survived in 1982 despite a big spending advantage. His opponent this time will be Lt. Gov. Richard A. Licht, nephew of the man who took the governor's office from Chafee in 1968. Licht the younger had been in elective office since 1974 and was considered a strong campaigner.

Minnesota: Republican incumbent Dave Durenberger alienated some in his own party with his handling of the Senate Intelligence Committee when he chaired it during the early stages of the Iran-contra affair in late 1986. He also had been unusually public about his personal life, ventilating his separation from his wife in national and Minnesota press alike.

Still, polls showed Durenberger retaining his personal popularity in the state as he headed into a confrontation with challenger Hubert H. "Skip" Humphrey III, who is Minnesota's attorney general. Durenberger was elected to the Senate in 1978 when Skip Humphrey's mother decided not to run for the rest of her late husband's Senate term.

Washington: Republican incumbent Daniel J. Evans had a long

New Jersey Democratic Sen. Frank R. Lautenberg, left, is preparing to meet the GOP's Pete Dawkins, a decorated Vietnam veteran and former Heisman Trophy winner.

Senate Control: The Rule of Two or Twelve

The Senate was designed to be a deliberative body, constitutionally resistant to change. That characteristic was evident not only in the chamber's pace of legislating, but also in its resistance to partisan upheaval.

Majority control of the Senate had changed hands only 14 times since 1854, the year the Republicans supplanted the Whigs as the Democrats' main rivals. And when a change occurred, it often was just a blip that was "corrected" in short order.

By historical precedent, the commonest interval between a party's losing control of the Senate and gaining it back had been the shortest possible interval — two years. When the takeover party extended control beyond that minimum, it usually held sway for a dozen years or more.

If the two-year interval holds in 1988, the GOP would regain the Senate majority it lost in 1986. But Republicans were not relying on history to do their work for them. Nor did they fear a historical curse.

"I don't place much stock in the averages," said Jann Olsten, executive director of the National Republican Senatorial Committee. "What really matters is what's going on in the world that first Tuesday in November."

If Not Now, When?

But the precedents did illustrate the patterns and pendulum swings of American political decisions.

Two-year switchbacks in party control had occurred four times since the beginning of the Republican-Democratic rivalry.

A switchback after four years happened only once, and a switchback after six years only twice. There were no switchbacks at intervals of eight years or 10 years. The long-majority regimes stretched to 12 years, 14 years (twice), 18 years (twice) and even to a remarkable 26 years.

Overall, periods of continuous majority for one party or the other lasted an average of 12.4 years, or about six Congresses.

Thus, the 2-or-12 guideline: When a party took the Senate, it ran the greatest risk of losing control when first forced to defend its majority; a party clearing that hurdle usually had been on its way to protracted control.

The Past as Prologue?

Sixty-seven Congresses had been elected since the Republican-Democratic rivalry began in the middle of the last century. The Republicans had controlled the Senate in 36 Congresses, the Democrats in 31 (although the Democrats had a 27-18 edge in this century).

In 30 of these Congresses, the Senate was elected under the original system — each state's senators were chosen by vote of its state legislature. Beginning with the 64th Congress, elected in 1914, voters chose their senators directly.

But either way, direct or indirect, the 2-or-12 pattern has held.

From Abraham Lincoln's election in 1861 until Woodrow Wilson's election in 1912, Republicans held the Senate majority with but two interruptions: 1879-81 (when feeling was running high for silver coinage) and 1893-95 (accompanying Democrat Grover Cleveland's return to the White House).

But both interruptions ended with Republicans snatching back the reins after just one term in the back seat.

The other two instances of a two-year switchback came in the midst of a Democratic hegemony as sustained as that of the post-Civil War GOP.

Seizing the Senate in Franklin D. Roosevelt's landslide presidential victory of 1932, the Democrats held it until Ronald Reagan became president in 1980 — with the exception of 1947-49 (an interlude of postwar backlash) and 1953-55 (the first two years of Republican Dwight D. Eisenhower's presidency).

track record of success in politics, including three terms as governor before he came to the Senate in 1983. But he had made surprisingly few moves to demonstrate interest in a 1988 re-election bid. He scarcely began to raise money, and told the state he would not announce his plans until his birthday (Oct. 16). He had even hedged on that date as well.

The NRSC continued to believe Evans would run. Even if he did, one or more Democrats might be willing to bet their House seats that Evans had had his day. Each of the state's five Democratic congressmen except House Majority Leader Thomas S. Foley was considering the race. This could be the most bruising Democratic primary outside of North Dakota.

Other Stones Being Turned

Democrats also had their eyes on Connecticut, where the two-term attorney general, Joseph I. Lieberman, was said to be close to declaring against incumbent Lowell P. Weicker Jr. As usual, there was a lack of enthusiasm among GOP conservatives for the liberal Weicker's views, but the three-term veteran had overcome that obstacle before.

Another medium-to-long shot would be the so-called California hot seat, to which no senator from either party had been re-elected since 1952. Occupied in 1981 by Republican Pete Wilson, the seat would be sought by several Democrats, led by Lt. Gov. Leo T. McCarthy. This might well be 1988's most media-intensive Senate race, and thus the most expensive.

Republicans counted on incumbent Orrin G. Hatch to hold Utah, particularly since former Gov. Scott Matheson declined to run.

Democrats also hold out some hope that Ed Herschler, just retired as Wyoming's Democratic governor, might take on Republican incumbent Malcolm Wallop.

The other five GOP seats offer little opportunity for takeaways.

The Coattail Question

The only chance for a dramatic shift in the partisan makeup of the Senate would seem to lie in an unexpectedly lopsided presidential victory for either party.

Although no one anticipated that

Democrats have high hopes for two challengers to GOP senators: Rhode Island's Lt. Gov. Richard Licht, left, and Minnesota's Attorney General Hubert H. Humphrey III.

the presidential winner in 1988 would even approach Ronald Reagan's 1984 tally of 59 percent, Republican chances of gaining ground in Senate races could be greatly improved if the party sustained its record of success in White House contests: The GOP has won four of the last five races, three times by Electoral College landslides.

More to the point, each of the last three Republicans elected president (Reagan, Nixon and Eisenhower) brought a net gain of Republican seats in the Senate when he first took office (an average gain of six). In the case of Reagan and Eisenhower, the gain was enough to tip Senate control to the GOP. Even in 1976, the one presidential election the GOP had lost since 1964, the GOP managed a tie in the Senate contests.

If the GOP continued to occupy the White House, its new vice president would also be available to break ties in the new Senate. That meant Republicans could resume control if they could just climb back into a 50-50 deadlock. To reach that point, the GOP would need a net gain of just four seats.

Taking the opposite extreme, if the Democrats reversed their presidential fortunes and scored a solid White House victory, the successful national ticket could carry Democrats home in a handful of tight contests — raising their Senate number into the high 50s.

That would considerably fortify the Democrats' ability to run the Senate and enhance their prospects for maintaining control well into the 1990s.

So, although it did not seem that control of the Senate would be at stake in 1988, some kind of pronounced shift in the rather shapeless presidential contest could significantly affect the Senate elections.

Mulling the Message

Though the Democrats' national tickets were perceived as damaging their senatorial candidates in four of the last five presidential years, party officials offered reasons why 1988 should be different.

"I don't see any Democratic [presidential] nominee making tax increases an issue in 1988," said the DSCC's Chlopak, "and the Republicans can't make it stick. I don't see the typical liberal-conservative or Democrat-Republican issues dominant."

Indeed, Republicans could sound a bit exasperated about the difficulty of identifying a national GOP theme in the closing phase of the Reagan administration.

"We have a retiring president [and] a vice president, a Senate minority leader and other party leaders engaged in a primary fight," noted the NRSC's Olsten. "If a national theme for Republicans were to evolve, where should it come from?"

"There is a Republican message out there that most people would see as positive," Olsten insisted. "How you deliver it is the key."

One thing seemed certain: The matter of which party should control the Senate was not likely to be at the center of public debate.

In 1984 and 1986, Republicans leaned heavily on the issue of Senate control.

It seemed to work in 1984, when President Reagan was sweeping to his second landslide. But in 1986, despite Reagan's October blitz of key states, the message seemed to have lost its muscle.

Democrats eventually won the tight contests by keeping their emphasis on issues that were closer to home.

That blueprint was one that both party committees were likely to recommend to their 1988 candidates. Despite the fretting in Washington over who would control the Senate, "if you're talking about voters in a particular state," said Olsten, "I don't think Democratic or Republican control is very meaningful to them." ∎

Two Republicans will vie for the right to meet Ohio Democratic Sen. Howard M. Metzenbaum. They are Cleveland Mayor George Voinovich, left, and Rep. Bob McEwen.

1988 Congressional Election Calendar

State	Primary Date [1]	Candidate Filing Deadline
Alabama	June 7/June 28	April 8
Alaska	Aug. 23	June 1
Arizona	Sept. 13	June 30
Arkansas	March 8 */March 22	Jan. 5
California	June 7 *	March 11
Colorado	Aug. 9	June 15
Connecticut	Sept. 14	Aug. 13 (D)/ Aug. 6 (R) [2]
Delaware	Sept. 10	July 29
Florida	Sept. 6/Oct. 4	July 15
Georgia	Aug. 9/Aug. 30	June 3
Hawaii	Sept. 17	July 19
Idaho	May 24	April 15
Illinois	March 15 *	Dec. 14, 1987
Indiana	May 3 *	March 4
Iowa	June 7	April 1
Kansas	Aug. 2	June 10
Kentucky	May 24	Feb. 24
Louisiana	Oct. 1/Nov. 8 [3]	July 29
Maine	June 14	April 1
Maryland	March 8 *	Dec. 28, 1987
Massachusetts	Sept. 20	June 7
Michigan	Aug. 2	May 31
Minnesota	Sept. 13	July 19
Mississippi	March 8 */March 29	Jan. 8
Missouri	Aug. 2	March 29
Montana	June 7 *	March 24
Nebraska	May 10 *	March 11
Nevada	Sept. 6	July 6
New Hampshire	Sept. 13	June 10
New Jersey	June 7 *	April 14
New Mexico	June 7 *	March 1
New York	Sept. 13	July 14
North Carolina	May 3/May 31	Feb. 1
North Dakota	June 14 *	April 20
Ohio	May 3 *	Feb. 18
Oklahoma	Aug. 23/Sept. 20	July 13
Oregon	May 17 *	March 8
Pennsylvania	April 26 *	Feb. 16
Rhode Island	Sept. 13	June 30
South Carolina	June 14/June 28	April 30
South Dakota	June 7/June 21	April 5
Tennessee	Aug. 4	June 2
Texas	March 8/April 12 *	Jan. 4
Utah	Sept. 13	April 15
Vermont	Sept. 13	July 18
Virginia	June 14	April 15
Washington	Sept. 20	July 29
West Virginia	May 10 *	Feb. 6
Wisconsin	Sept. 13	July 12
Wyoming	Aug. 16	June 17

Date	State and Event
March 8	Arkansas primary *
	Maryland primary *
	Mississippi primary *
	Texas primary *
March 15	Illinois primary *
March 22	Arkansas runoff
March 29	Mississippi runoff
April 12	Texas runoff
April 26	Pennsylvania primary *
May 3	Indiana primary *
	North Carolina primary
	Ohio primary *
May 10	Nebraska primary *
	West Virginia primary *
May 17	Oregon primary *
May 24	Idaho primary
	Kentucky primary
May 31	North Carolina runoff
June 7	Alabama primary
	California primary *
	Iowa primary
	Montana primary *
	New Jersey primary *
	New Mexico primary *
	South Dakota primary
June 14	Maine primary
	North Dakota primary *
	South Carolina primary
	Virginia primary
June 21	South Dakota runoff
June 28	Alabama runoff
	South Carolina runoff
Aug. 2	Kansas primary
	Michigan primary
	Missouri primary
Aug. 4	Tennessee primary
Aug. 9	Colorado primary
	Georgia primary
Aug. 16	Wyoming primary
Aug. 23	Alaska primary
	Oklahoma primary
Aug. 30	Georgia runoff
Sept. 6	Florida primary
	Nevada primary
Sept. 10	Delaware primary
Sept. 13	Arizona primary
	Minnesota primary
	New Hampshire primary
	New York primary
	Rhode Island primary
	Utah primary
	Vermont primary
	Wisconsin primary
Sept. 14	Connecticut primary
Sept. 17	Hawaii primary
Sept. 20	Massachusetts primary
	Washington primary
	Oklahoma runoff
Oct. 1	Louisiana primary [3]
Oct. 4	Florida runoff

NOTES

* *Presidential primary is held on the same day.*

[1] *Where two dates are listed, the first is the primary and the second is the runoff primary. Runoffs are required in these states when no candidate wins a majority in the primary.*

[2] *Connecticut's filing deadline falls 14 days after each party's state convention. The Democratic convention is scheduled for July 30, 1988; the GOP convention is slated to begin July 22 and end July 23, but it could run until July 24, in which case the GOP filing deadline would be Aug. 7.*

[3] *Louisiana's primary includes all candidates of both parties. The top two vote-getters in each race meet in the general election, regardless of party. A candidate receiving more than 50 percent of the primary vote is elected without a general election.*

SOURCE: Federal Election Commission

Once a Key Force in Elections, House Is Now Just a Sideshow

With the 1988 presidential nominations up for grabs in both parties, it made sense that the House elections would not be the focus of the nation's political attention. But it was a bit surprising how little was being said publicly about the 1988 House battles, even by the party officials who were charged with planning strategy for them.

The Democratic and Republican congressional campaign committees, known earlier in the 1980s for coining catchy slogans and waging fiercely partisan rhetorical battles, seemed to have lost their zeal for public muscle-flexing.

Not too many years ago, Michigan Rep. Guy Vander Jagt, chairman of the National Republican Congressional Committee (NRCC), was projecting a partisan realignment that would vault the GOP into a House majority. But after huge expenditures to recruit, train and finance Republican challengers during the 1980s, the goal of a GOP House majority was still far away. Democrats had a 258 to 177 advantage.

In 1987, Vander Jagt was nearing the end of his 12th year heading the NRCC. He still maintained that the GOP could capture the House by convincing voters that its Democratic majority was responsible for policy stalemates and ethical problems in the chamber. But he admitted that this was "a civics lesson about Congress" that "will be difficult to get across in a presidential-election year."

And although the Democratic presidential aspirants were trying to convey a sense of urgency about the need to elect an activist Democratic administration in 1988, the Democratic Congressional Campaign Committee (DCCC) had rather modest goals: Deputy Director Tom O'Donnell said that barring a huge Democratic wave, "we're looking at a net gain of a couple of seats."

To a great extent, the caution of the committees was simply a function of political reality. A wide-open race for the presidency pushed campaigns for the House so far out of the spotlight that it became quite difficult for congressional challengers to raise money in their districts.

In addition, House challengers had found Washington-based political action committees (PACs) increasingly wary of bucking the odds; eager to go with a winner, PACs usually supported incumbents. Competition for many House seats was further discouraged by congressional district boundaries that often strongly favored incumbents.

Yet the campaign committees were at least partly responsible for the lack of early excitement about the 1988 House elections. Instead of moving early and forcefully to shape the debate on national policies — as they did earlier this decade — the committees so far had not played much of a role in defining the post-Reagan political agenda. Committee officials in both parties seemed content to serve as technicians, providing voter data, issues analysis and media services to candidates in carefully selected priority districts.

Getting Organized

Organizational matters were a priority for both committees during the summer.

In the first half of 1987, the NRCC took in about $6.1 million, almost 33 percent less money than it collected during the same period in 1985. As a result, officials looked for waste to trim, a new experience for a group that had typically been flush with cash. Executive Director Joe

Once Upon a Time . . .

. . . House elections played a major role in shaping the election-year agenda. In 1980, the National Republican Congressional Committee captured attention with its ad parodying House Speaker Thomas P. O'Neill Jr. and the Democratic Party as "out of gas." The NRCC's "Vote Republican. For a Change." slogan helped elect Ronald Reagan and a GOP Senate majority.

House Departures

(as of 10/2/87)

RETIRING

	Date Announced	Began Service	Age
Marilyn Lloyd (D-Tenn. 3)	July 13, 1987	1975	58
Melvin Price (D-Ill. 21) [1]	—	1945	82

ELECTED TO OTHER OFFICE

	Began Service	Age	Office
Bill Boner (D-Tenn. 5) [2]	1979	42	Nashville Mayor

ANNOUNCED FOR OR MAY SEEK OTHER OFFICE

	Began Service	Age	Office
Hal Daub (R-Neb. 2)	1981	46	Senate
Byron L. Dorgan (D-N.D. AL)	1981	45	Senate
Richard A. Gephardt (D-Mo. 3)	1977	46	President
James M. Jeffords (R-Vt. AL)	1975	53	Senate
Jack F. Kemp (R-N.Y. 31)	1971	52	President
Bob Livingston (R-La. 1) [3]	1977	44	Governor
Connie Mack (R-Fla. 13)	1983	46	Senate
Bob McEwen (R-Ohio 6)	1981	37	Senate
Jim Moody (D-Wis. 5)	1983	52	Senate
David R. Obey (D-Wis. 7)	1969	49	Senate
Buddy Roemer (D-La. 4) [3]	1981	43	Governor
Toby Roth (R-Wis. 8)	1979	48	Senate
F. James Sensenbrenner Jr. (R-Wis. 9)	1979	44	Senate
Al Swift (D-Wash. 2)	1979	52	Senate
W. J. "Billy" Tauzin (D-La. 3) [3]	1980	44	Governor
James A. Traficant Jr. (D-Ohio 17)	1985	46	President

[1] *Price plans to retire, but he has not made a formal announcement.*
[2] *Boner won the Nashville mayoralty Sept. 22. He will vacate his House seat when he is sworn in as mayor Oct. 5.*
[3] *If member does not win other office, he retains House seat.*

Gaylord noted that the committee's goal for 1988 was "more services for less cost with fewer people."

The NRCC's fund raising was set back by the Iran-contra scandal, and also by a flap involving a separate party campaign group — the National Republican Senatorial Committee (NRSC). GOP contributors fumed when it was revealed that NRSC officials gave themselves big bonuses in 1986, following the party's loss of Senate control. *(Senate outlook, p. 61)*

1987 brought a major transition at the DCCC. California Rep. Tony Coelho, who took over a weakling DCCC in 1981 and made it a respectable force in House campaigns, moved up to majority whip. The man then in charge at the committee became Arkansas Rep. Beryl Anthony Jr.

The DCCC raised $2.9 million in the first half of 1987, $500,000 more than during the same period two years earlier. But because the NRCC still enjoyed a substantial advantage in terms of money and technical expertise, new DCCC Executive Director Richard Bates looked for ways to cut administrative overhead so more money could be funneled into campaigns.

Theme Wars Fade

From the late 1970s into the mid-1980s, the NRCC set the tone for national House politics. Sharp criticisms of Jimmy Carter's administration earned Vander Jagt and his committee much publicity; in 1980, the NRCC's theme — "Vote Republican. For a Change." — scored big with voters who saw Carter as ineffective and the federal government as intrusive. Largely on the strength of the new GOP blood that Vander Jagt helped bring into the House — 38 Republican freshmen in 1978 and 52 in 1980 — he was a contender for House minority leader in 1981.

The long-dormant DCCC soon awoke under Coelho's aggressive leadership. While the NRCC labored during the 1982 recession with a "Stay the Course" theme, the DCCC waged a nationwide attack on Reagan's economic policies, and "Stay the Curse" became the Democrats' unofficial battle cry. The party regained 26 seats that November.

But the last two House campaigns lacked such sweeping themes and dramatic seat shifts. In 1984, the NRCC hoped their House candidates would benefit from Reagan's popularity, but the presidential landslide brought the GOP only 14 new seats in the House.

In 1986, history suggested that Democrats would capture many GOP House seats; the party controlling the White House for six years had usually fared very badly in its second midterm election. But the DCCC's efforts were overshadowed by the battle for Senate control, and Democrats ended up gaining only five House seats.

Go Your Own Way

Developing dynamic national themes for the 1988 House elections would be even more difficult than in the last two cycles because of the formlessness of the presidential campaign.

For the first time since 1960, there were open presidential contests in both parties; for the first time since 1952, there was no clear favorite in either party. Officials at the House campaign committees had no specific ideas about what image their standard-bearers would project, and they seriously doubted that the presidential nominees would have much in the way of coattails in November 1988.

In reaching for themes for 1988, some Democratic House strategists were turning to an old reliable — Ronald Reagan. Though it was not clear that touting Reagan as either a hero or a villain had ever changed many votes in House campaigns, Reagan was the focus of the Democrats' first venture at 1988 agenda-setting: a series of commercials that blamed him for the federal budget deficit. The ads were

Hopefuls Courting PACs Find Them Wary

Though it was still more than a year until the next general election, in October 1987 many of the candidates who had committed to 1988 House challenges were already making the circuit of political action committees (PACs), trade associations and interest groups in Washington.

These candidates were being greeted with a harsh reality: In an era when incumbents won well over 90 percent of their re-election contests, challengers had to do a major selling job before PACs would commit their money and influence to them.

David Worley

David Worley, who said he would run against Republican Rep. Newt Gingrich in Georgia's 6th District, visited labor PACs in April and July. Although Gingrich is a conservative activist with a record that labor activists regard as anti-union, the labor groups did not rush to Worley's cause.

"Labor wants to get rid of Gingrich," said Worley, who at age 28 had never run for elective office. "But they need to see if I'm viable." Their caution stemmed partly from Gingrich's track record at the polls. In four re-elections, his average winning tally had been over 60 percent.

But even if an incumbent's electoral history indicated vulnerability, the PACs that opposed his policies would not automatically sign on with his challenger.

In his first three House contests in Indiana's 3rd District, GOP Rep. John Hiler received no more than 55 percent of the vote; in 1984, during the Reagan landslide, he won only 52 percent. But in 1986, several prominent local Democrats decided not to run, and the nomination went to Thomas W. Ward, a small-town lawyer whose only previous electoral experience was a third-place finish in the 3rd District's House primary in 1982.

Thomas W. Ward

Though Hiler's conservative record was opposed by a number of liberal PACs, many snubbed the little-known Ward. "People didn't know [me]," Ward noted. "The potential money people said, 'Who is Tom Ward?' Many people wrote off the Indiana 3rd." But Ward proved to be a capable and vigorous campaigner, and was able to change a few minds. "As a sense grew in the district that this guy does have a chance, they started to take note," Ward said.

Thanks to his fund-raising success late in the campaign, Ward was able to make a final push that brought him tantalizingly close to victory: He lost the election, after a recount, by 47 votes.

Ward recalled the frustration of not having enough money to convince the PACs that his campaign was a good investment. "Everyone wants something hard and fast. They want to see a poll, something in black and white." But the expense of producing such evidence of electability — including polls and district voting profiles, usually developed in coordination with paid consultants — was a major hurdle for challengers like Ward.

As Maryland Democratic Party Chairman Rosalie A. Reilly put it, "Before you're off the ground, you're already spending $25,000. It isn't a situation where you can pay $10 to find out your chances."

Rowland: Flunked 'Plane Fare' Test

It was not even always the case that PACs would respond generously when challengers presented them with data that seem promising.

In 1984, Connecticut Republican John G. Rowland ran a strong grass-roots campaign and unseated Democratic Rep. William R. Ratchford. But in February of that year, Rowland had taken what he thought were encouraging polls to about 30 PACs in Washington. He got the cold shoulder. "I didn't raise enough money to pay for the plane fare back," he said.

While upset winners such as Rowland suddenly found themselves popular among PACs, losing challengers seeking rematches had to prove themselves all over again. But for those who lost narrowly, there was at least some consolation: The PAC doors closed to them the first time were more likely to be open in the second campaign. Ward, who was running again in 1988, said that "it's quite a bit different this year than last." About his 1986 near-upset, he said, "A lot of people are sorry they missed it."

run in July 1987 in cities that the president visited to promote his economic policies.

But while the deficit was an issue that touched all voters, other 1988 issues mentioned by national Democratic strategists, such as trade and the uneven economic recovery, would not have salience in every region, much less in every congressional district.

The lack of a "boilerplate" Democratic message was evident in discussions with some of the party's candidates who already had launched their 1988 bids. While their pitches fall within a broad "time for a change" framework, they aimed carefully for specific constituencies.

David Worley, a 28-year-old lawyer running against Republican Rep. Newt Gingrich in Georgia's 6th District, planned to target young, suburban voters with "quality-of-life" issues. "People our age can't hope to have their parents' standard of living," he said.

Thomas W. Ward, who lost Indiana's 3rd District race to GOP incumbent John Hiler by 47 votes in 1986, planned again to emphasize the conservative incumbent's resistance to federal economic development aid in a district burdened with closed plants.

Richard "Buck" O'Brien, who won 47 percent of the vote against Montana Republican Ron Marlenee in 1986, would once more blame the economic problems of the agricultural and mining sectors in the 2nd District on the Republicans. "This administration has destroyed the economies of the resource states," he said.

A New Mood

The NRCC clearly was in no rush to establish a post-Reagan agenda. "We are letting the hand play out, see how they're falling for a while," said Gaylord. By October 1987, the committee had not yet run issue-oriented advertising for 1988.

Vander Jagt acknowledged that the widespread public disenchantment with government that spurred earlier GOP House gains was not so strong anymore. "It is going to be difficult to come up with a unifying theme," he said. "I contrast [1988] to 1980, with the high inflation, interest rates, unemployment. There was a feeling that we needed a change."

While "government is the problem" statements went over well in conservative districts — many of which were already held by Republicans — they were of little help to GOP candidates in traditionally Democratic or closely competitive districts.

Not surprisingly, the Republican candidates who had succeeded in such districts in 1986 had been moderates — such as Constance A. Morella of Maryland's 8th District, Patricia F. Saiki of Hawaii's 1st District, Jack Buechner of Missouri's 2nd District and Christopher Shays of Connecticut's 4th District. All of them had state legislative experience before entering Congress, and they came to Washington with a more positive attitude about what government could accomplish than did many of the conservative House Republicans first elected with Reagan in 1980.

The Limits of Recruiting

Beyond agenda-setting, the task of recruiting candidates was widely regarded as one of the committees' most important functions. But in fact, the impact of recruiting on the partisan balance in the House was rather limited.

The best House challengers were, of course, the ones who were highly motivated, and no recruiting was needed to get them going. A potential candidate who required lots of encouragement and hand-holding from his party committee was probably not a winner.

In a House district where a party's prospects seemed promising, several ambitious candidates were likely to throw their hats in the ring. In such situations, the party committees generally adopted a hands-off posture, even when they regarded one particular candidate in a crowded field as having the best chance in the general election.

The NRCC occasionally tried to play a role in seeing that a "star" got the nomination — Saiki and Morella were two candidates who were so favored in 1986. But to have gotten the NRCC's pre-primary support, a candidate had to be "head and shoulders above the rest," and had to have active support from members of the state's congressional delegations and from local party officials, according to Gaylord.

Recruiters did play an important role in lining up candidates for districts where their party faced long odds. If on Election Day the mood of the electorate was running strongly for or against one party, some of those long shots ended up scoring upsets. But since the 1988 presidential election was expected to be a close, no-coattails affair, nearly all of the long shots recruited by the House committees for 1988's House races would lose.

In the nuts-and-bolts categories of overseeing House campaigns — committee staffing, computer technology and the like — the DCCC made great strides toward approaching the NRCC's level.

In 1986, the DCCC joined the NRCC in providing daily issues updates and other information to candidates equipped to receive the on-line computer service. Also, the Democrats opened the Harriman Communications Center in their headquarters; like the Republicans, they had television and radio studios available for producing political ads.

In 1987, the NRCC had eight regional operatives who acted as talent scouts and gatherers of political gossip. The Democrats, who had no field operatives as late as 1984, had three in 1986 and had five for 1988.

Several times each election cycle, the parties held "campaign schools" in Washington, where prospective and active candidates received instruction on strategy, advertising, organization and issues. Candidates also got advice on campaign consultants, managers and other political operatives.

In the general election, the committees offered computerized data bases that helped nominees identify likely supporters and contributors, target direct mailings, and learn about opponents' issue stands and voting record.

An Inexact Science

Despite their stated commitment to contesting as many districts as possible, the committees were wary of wasting money on lost causes. The field operatives played a key role in helping Washington-based strategists pick the most promising nominees, but in each campaign, the party prioritizers overlooked a few golden opportunities.

In 1986, for example, DCCC officials saw Democrat Ben Jones as having little chance of beating Republican incumbent Pat Swindall in Georgia's 4th District. Jones, an actor who played an auto mechanic named Cooter in the "Dukes of Hazzard" TV show, had no elective experience, and he was a recovering alcoholic running against an incumbent with a squeaky-clean image. But Jones turned out to have a knack for keeping Swindall off balance, and he held the freshman Republican to 53 percent.

Jones, who planned to challenge Swindall again in 1988, accepted the DCCC's logic in not targeting his race last time, but not without a tinge of bitterness. "I understand why the DCCC had to have priorities," Jones said. "I was one of the few people who would have bet on me. [But] I would have won if I had another week and another $25,000."

When Republican John G. Rowland challenged a Democratic incumbent for the 5th District of Connecticut in 1984, he said he was on the NRCC's "junior varsity" for much of the campaign, and earned his way to the "varsity" only shortly before the election. Rowland ended up winning with 54 percent.

Despite the apparent themelessness of the 1988 House elections and the likelihood that few seats would shift party control, it was the success and near-success of long shots such as Rowland and Jones that continued to inspire competition for House seats. In an election year when party strategists, consultants and the media would be focusing most of their attention on the White House and the rest of it on the Senate, the House elections might end up offering some interesting contests that go almost completely unnoticed. ▮

Changing South Perils Conservative Coalition

Fifty years ago the summer of 1987, Franklin D. Roosevelt tried to persuade Congress to pass a bill "packing" the Supreme Court with liberal justices and found to his displeasure that it could not be done, despite overwhelming Democratic majorities in both the House and the Senate. He had discovered a new political phenomenon — the "conservative coalition" of Republicans and Southern Democrats.

In 1987, the same coalition that frustrated FDR remained a household name on Capitol Hill. From the days of Roosevelt to those of Ronald Reagan, one simple rule explained much of what happened in Congress: Liberal Democrats rarely had governed, even when their party had been the clear majority in both chambers. They were not able to govern because conservative Southerners in their own party, allied with Republicans across the aisle, had mustered the votes to stop them.

The conservative coalition had led a long and active life. But it might be dying. Every year since 1957, Congressional Quarterly has charted the percentage of votes on which a majority of Southern Democrats and a majority of Republicans vote together against a majority of Democrats from outside the South.

For the first half of 1987, the number was 7.5 percent — by far the lowest figure ever recorded.

The implications of this were enormous. Without a viable conservative coalition, a future Democratic president potentially would have more control over Congress than any of his predecessors. A Republican president would have virtually none. House and Senate Republicans, unable to win by forging alliances across the aisle, would be drawn more and more to the tactics of obstruction. The end result might well be a showdown over rules changes designed to prevent the obstruction from taking place.

All of this was conjecture. What was clear in 1987 was that Southern Democrats simply were not casting many votes with Republicans anymore. That had been evident on nearly all the important issues that came before Congress that year.

Democrats Cutting Ties To Old Allies in GOP

Democrats Sticking Together

When the Senate Democratic leadership brought a budget resolution to the floor May 1987, every single Democrat voted for it. The previous month, House Democratic leaders had passed their version of the budget easily — thanks largely to the help of Southern Democrats, who backed it by a margin of 71-9. Six years earlier, it was defections by those same Southerners that led to passage of President Reagan's economic program.

Meanwhile, both chambers were working on a defense authorization bill. Over the years, support for defense spending was perhaps the strongest common element cementing the conservative coalition. This time, though, Southern Democrats provided the decisive votes as the House on May 12, 1987, cut funding for Reagan's strategic defense initiative (SDI) to a level nearly 50 percent below what the president had asked for.

The next day, Senate leaders brought out a defense bill with language blocking Reagan from testing an SDI system in ways he would like to do. The crucial amendment on that subject — written jointly by Democrats Carl Levin of Michigan and Sam Nunn of Georgia — provoked a Republican leadership filibuster that enlisted all but a handful of GOP senators and not one Democrat.

That dispute was as good a symbol as any of the new arrangement in Congress: Democrats working together across regional and ideological lines, and Republicans united as a partisan

"The Boll Weevils are under the ground, but they are waiting, and sooner or later we will sing our mating song, and they will come out again."

—Rep. Trent Lott, R-Miss.

"The Democratic leadership would have to go totally crazy in a liberal direction for there to be a conservative coalition again."

—Rep. Marvin Leath, D-Texas

bloc against them. It was a far cry from the conservative coalition in its heyday.

One did not have to focus on major issues to see the coalition declining. It happened on procedural votes as well. In the 97th Congress, House Democratic leaders could not be sure that most Southern conservatives would back them on the day-to-day procedural questions that often determined control of the House. "I've got a lot of good friends out there," Speaker Thomas P. O'Neill Jr. once complained, "who won't even give me a vote to adjourn."

In the 100th Congress, that was no longer a worry for the Democratic leadership. On rules for floor debate, recommittal motions and numerous other procedural questions, even the most conservative Southerners were lining up on the leadership side.

"We always help them get the bills up," said Rep. G. V. "Sonny" Montgomery of Mississippi, chairman of the Veterans' Affairs Committee, who was a ringleader of the Southern defection to Reagan in 1981. "We realize they need help on procedure.... I have to have loyalty to the Democratic Caucus. They gave me a chairmanship. And I do have loyalty. I try to help them where I can."

A Temporary Decline?

It was possible, of course, to find short-term explanations for what had been going on between the parties in 1987, and to predict that the pendulum would swing back before too long.

These were, after all, the closing days of an administration whose popularity was in decline, and the local pressures that induced some Southern Democrats to side with the president in 1981 were then absent.

Southerners in the House had been affected by the arrival of a new Southern Speaker, Jim Wright of Texas, and some admit that they were giving him what amounted to a first-year leadership honeymoon.

Beyond that, some Southerners argued that the number of House Republicans — 176 — was simply too small to tempt conservative Democrats to join forces with them. There was nothing wrong with the conservative coalition, they insisted, that 20 more Republicans in the House could not cure.

One who believed that was Trent Lott of Mississippi, the House GOP whip and a man who had been working the conservative coalition, as aide and member, for more than 20 years.

"In 1981," Lott said, "we could go to Southern Democrats and offer them political cover with their constituents, help from the administration and, most of all, we could offer them victory. People don't like to stick their necks out and lose."

In a July 1987 floor speech that quickly made the rounds of the Southern delegations, Lott made fun of the disappearing "Boll Weevils," the Southern Democrats who backed the Reagan program in 1981 but then voted routinely with Speaker Wright. "Have all the Boll Weevils turned into cicadas?" Lott asked sarcastically, referring to the insects that appear at 17-year intervals.

In his view, the decline of the conservative coalition was a fact of current politics, not a trend in history. "The potential for a conservative coalition is there," Lott insisted. "The Boll Weevils are under the ground, but they are waiting, and sooner or later we will sing our mating song, and they will come out again."

Perhaps Lott was right. But the future might disappoint him. There was evidence that the decline of the conservative coalition represented something more than short-term politics. It had been going on, with occasional interruptions, for more than 15 years.

In 1971, in the middle of President Nixon's tenure in office, the conservative coalition emerged on 30 percent of the votes in Congress. By 1986 it was 16 percent. In 1987 it was down to 7.5 percent.

And many of the Southern Democrats who abandoned coalition politics made it clear they did not expect to return to it any time soon. In the words of Texas Democrat Marvin Leath, once an important Reagan ally, "The Democratic leadership would have to go totally crazy in a liberal direction for there to be a conservative coalition again."

South No Longer Solid

All of this suggested that the conservative coalition might be falling apart because of broad changes in American politics — institutional changes in the House and Senate, and demographic changes in the constituencies that members from the South represented.

One point was indisputable. There were fewer conservative Southern Democrats in the 100th Congress because there were fewer Southern Democrats, period.

In 1937, in the 75th Congress that balked at Roosevelt's court-packing, there were 120 House seats in the 13 Southern states (the old Confederacy, plus Kentucky and Oklahoma). A full 117 of those 120 were in Democratic hands. On their own, Southern Democrats possessed more than half the votes needed to carry a majority of the House on any question.

In 1987 those same states had 124 seats. But only 85 of them were Democratic. More than a quarter had fled to the GOP side of the aisle.

Most of the time, trading a Southern Democrat for a Southern Republican did not cost conservatives any ideological support. If anything, the new GOP member usually voted to the right of his predecessor. But the gradual erosion of Southern Democratic representation chipped away at the Southern subculture that used to be crucial to maintaining a conservative coalition in Congress.

Sen. Thad Cochran, a Mississippi Republican, recalled that joining the House as a Southerner in 1973 was something like joining a fraternity. The regulars congregated every afternoon in the House chamber along "redneck row," just in front of the rail on the aisle that separates the Republican and Democratic sides.

"Southern Democrats ate together, stood around the rail together, sat together in the House, swapped stories, played cards," Cochran recalled. "They got along with the leadership, but they voted the way they wanted to."

Sen. John B. Breaux of Louisiana was elected to the House as a Democrat the same year Cochran was elected as a Republican. "The Southern railbirds were a very powerful group in those days," Breaux said. "They were old, and they were senior, and they were chairmen. It was a very static thing. You followed the Southern leadership to make sure you weren't eliminated from participating."

If anyone symbolized the Southern subculture in the House, it was Montgomery of Mississippi, the genial and courtly conservative who had been one of the best-liked House members since his arrival in 1967.

Montgomery was one of the first to concede that being a Southerner in Congress did not mean what it meant 20 years ago. "When I first came here," he estimated, "there were about 100 Southern Democrats who voted conservatively. Now it's about 30-35.... Redneck row is still there. That

New Leaders: National Democrats From South

Unlike their predecessors of a generation ago, most of the Southern Democrats in the House had no ideological preconceptions that led them to vote conservatively when their constituents did not demand it.

On some issues, nearly all of them conceded, they found it politically helpful to cast conservative votes. Many of them were still sympathetic to the cause of Nicaragua's contras. Most were extremely nervous about appearing to side with labor in its periodic tilts with the business community.

But for the most part, such stances were a matter of pragmatism, not philosophy.

"I don't see myself as a conservative," said Democratic Rep. Dave McCurdy of Oklahoma, who had served since 1981. "Many of the Boll Weevils [who voted for President Reagan's economic package in 1981] became extensions of the Republican Party. They were taken for granted. Some of us didn't come here to be taken for granted."

Rep. Buddy MacKay

Actually, McCurdy himself became something of a leader of Southern Democrats in the six years since he arrived in Congress at age 30. Early in 1985, he was instrumental in rounding up votes for the successful challenge to Melvin Price, D-Ill., who was deposed as Armed Services chairman. Later in the 99th Congress, McCurdy took the lead in seeking a compromise on aid to the contras that could attract Southern Democratic support.

When newly arrived Southern Democrats were asked whom they looked to for guidance on foreign policy or defense votes, most of them mentioned either McCurdy or John M. Spratt Jr., a cerebral South Carolina Democrat who joined him on Armed Services in 1983 and who often served as a mediator between Armed Services members and more liberal Democrats outside the committee. Few mention G. V. "Sonny" Montgomery, D-Miss., or other senior Armed Services conservatives.

Rep. Dave McCurdy

When it came to economic matters, many of the newcomers said they listened to Buddy MacKay, a Florida Democrat elected in 1982.

In his first term, MacKay organized a budget study group frequented by, although not limited to, Southerners. The group continued to meet ever since.

MacKay challenged the power structure of the Appropriations Committee by winning adoption of an amendment cutting over $2 billion — more than 20 percent — from the fiscal 1987 supplemental-spending bill. Southern Democrats went along with him by a margin of 4-1. *(Supplemental-funding bill, Weekly Report p. 772)*

Rep. John M. Spratt Jr.

McCurdy, Spratt and McKay were not "Southern Democrats." They were national Democrats from Southern districts.

To the extent that they were regional leaders, it was because they balanced regional political needs with the task of setting goals for the party on a national basis — a job the leading Southern Democrats of past years never worried about doing.

hasn't changed. It's just that the numbers aren't there any more."

Nor was there a clear idea of who, if anyone, was the leader of the Southern bloc. Pressed for an answer to that question, many Southern Democrats named Montgomery. But nearly all agreed that nobody led this group the way it was led in the 1950s by Rep. Howard W. Smith of Virginia, the chairman of the Rules Committee, or in the early 1970s by Joe D. Waggonner Jr. of Louisiana, a Democrat who was perhaps President Nixon's closest personal ally in the House.

"There is no Joe Waggonner," a Democratic House leadership aide says. "Sonny Montgomery could do it, but he just doesn't like a visible role."

But it was more than just a matter of style. Leaders had to have followers. And the incoming generation of Southern House Democrats showed little interest in following traditional conservative leadership.

Liz J. Patterson of South Carolina was an example. For most of this century, her 4th District had been a bastion of conservative Democratic strength. It was represented in the 1960s by Robert T. Ashmore and in the 1970s by James R. Mann, and both were reliable supporters of the conservative coalition.

When Mann departed in 1979, the district elected Republican Carroll A. Campbell Jr., who voted to the right of Ashmore and Mann. But Patterson, who restored Democratic control of the 4th in 1986, had little in common with either of her Democratic predecessors. She cast her share of conservative votes in 1987, especially on fiscal matters, but as a supporter of legalized abortion and the Equal Rights Amendment, and a skeptic about the Reagan defense buildup, she was more interested in what her party leaders thought than in following any Southern conservative line.

"In the cotton fields," she said, "a Boll Weevil destroys. I want the Democratic Party to grow. I'm not in here to kill."

Senate Southerners: Still Leaders

In the Senate of a generation ago, Southern Democrats were not exactly a subculture or a "third force." They were the leaders. Seniority brought them control of most of the important committees, and they used it for their own purposes, sometimes cooperating with their national party but more often frustrating it.

In 1972, most of the important Senate committee chairmanships were in Southern Democratic hands, and few of the chairmen responded to what were then the concerns of the national Democratic Party.

Mississippi's James O. Eastland, chairman of the Judiciary Committee, was the scourge of the civil rights movement and an obstacle to liberal judicial nominees. Georgia's Herman E. Talmadge, at Agriculture, focused on Southern crop subsidies and ignored the nutrition and hunger issues that were coming to occupy much of the Democratic Party outside the South.

The Appropriations chairman, John L. McClellan of Arkansas, was a fiscal scrooge who did not like to vote for any substantial new forms of domestic spending. And Armed Services Chairman John C. Stennis of Mississippi, while universally respected, as he is now, was largely out of step with his party's growing skepticism toward the Pentagon and its priorities.

In 1987, after six years as part of the minority under Republican control, Southern Democrats regained their crucial role as Senate leaders. Of the 15 standing committees, eight had Southern chairmen. But these chairmen had little in common with the ones who held power in 1972.

The only Southerner who was a chairman then and remained one now is Stennis. But at age 86, he was in no way a controversial figure; as chairman of Appropriations, he simply presided over spending decisions laid out by party leaders and others across the ideological spectrum.

The other Southern chairmen were all bona fide national Democrats. Trade was perhaps the party's leading issue going into the 1988 elections, and it was Lloyd Bentsen of Texas, the head of the Finance Committee, who managed the trade bill that passed the Senate on July 21, 1987, by a 71-27 vote, without a single Democratic dissent.

Lawton Chiles of Florida brought a fiscal 1988 budget resolution to the floor in May, and every Senate Democrat voted for it.

Ernest F. Hollings of South Carolina, the new Commerce chairman, was an independent man with more than his share of personal quirks, but few of them were ideological. He was as much a member of his national party as were Howard W. Cannon of Nevada or Warren G. Magnuson of Washington, who chaired the committee during the last Democratic majority in the 1970s.

But perhaps the most important exhibit is Nunn, who remained to the right of his party on many important issues but who in his role as Armed Services chairman had led the Democratic challenge to Reagan's request for funds for SDI. Nunn's leadership on that pivotal question of defense policy coincided with his emergence as a contender for the 1988 Democratic presidential nomination, despite his reluctance to seek it actively.

The last Georgia senator to run for president, Richard B. Russell in 1952, was nothing more than a regional favorite son. Nunn, if he had decided to seek the presidency, would have instantly become the favorite candidate of a diverse array of Democrats, many of them Northerners and many with records far more liberal than his.

Some Republicans felt there still was a potential Senate coalition of Republicans and Southern Democrats, and that Nunn would be cutting himself off from it by going national. "I wonder if Sam's new image of moderation will cost him the leadership of whatever Southern bloc still exists," said Cochran of Mississippi. "He may be drifting off and lose his credibility with the real Southern conservatives."

However, that is not the way most Southern Democrats seemed to feel. In their view, Nunn was providing the political cover that allowed them to vote against the Reagan position on defense and foreign-policy issues without having to worry unduly about offending conservative sensibilities back home.

"It's very helpful to me," said one cautious Southerner, "to have a man of Sam's intellectual stature taking positions that go against some of the momentary whims in the country."

"In the cotton fields, a Boll Weevil destroys. I want the Democratic Party to grow. I'm not in here to kill."

—Rep. Liz J. Patterson, D-S.C.

A Different Breed

Equally decisive for some Southern senators were the 1986 election results. Democrats not only took back four Southern seats that had been in Republican hands, but elected several challengers who made no real pretense of being conservatives.

The most striking example was in Georgia, where the winner was Democrat Wyche Fowler Jr., who had spent nearly a decade in the House representing inner-city Atlanta and compiling a generally liberal voting record.

Fowler's narrow victory over GOP Sen. Mack Mattingly owed much to the weaknesses of Mattingly's campaign. Still, it was not lost on Democrats all over the South that Fowler carried 109 of his state's 159 counties, rolling past the Republican easily in rural south Georgia territory where it had been assumed that no Atlanta liberal could possibly succeed.

Moreover, Fowler campaigned in those south Georgia counties by talking about the need for government to spend more money on education and economic development — something virtually no Georgia candidate of the past would have dared to do.

In the 1960s, sensitivity about the

federal government's role in civil rights had generated hostility to nearly all federal social spending on the part of conservative Democrats throughout the South. Candidates succeeded by warning that new federal programs represented new potential for federal intrusion into Southern lives. It was 20 years ago the summer of 1987 that Congress defeated President Lyndon B. Johnson's bill providing $40 million in federal money for rodent control after Southern Democrats derided the measure as nothing but a "civil rats bill." That legislation was a clear victim of the conservative coalition. In 1987, Southerners of even the most conservative bent voted routinely for federal funds for a diverse array of social programs. Republicans opposed many of these initiatives, but they rarely attracted more than a token amount of support on the other side of the aisle.

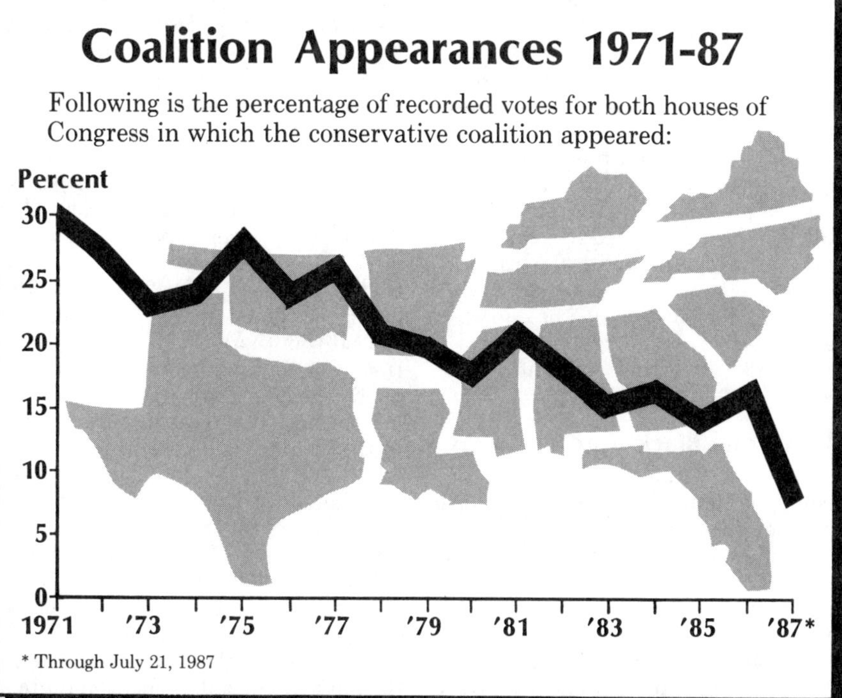

The Changing South

The changes in the way Southerners behaved in Congress were related to changes far beyond the walls of the institution. The districts that Southern Democrats represented were considerably different from the ones that sent them to Washington a generation ago.

Well into the 1960s, most Southern congressional districts were overwhelmingly rural, with a one-party political system, and, in the Deep South, an all-white electorate. All those things had changed. The one-man, one-vote requirement imposed by the Supreme Court in the 1960s had not only made districts equal in population, but ended the rural dominance of Southern congressional representation.

In the early days of one man, one vote, many Southern states preserved rural districts by filling them out with just enough urban constituents to meet population standards. But in 1987, with the state legislatures themselves reapportioned to reflect urban interests, it was more often the other way around. When Georgia redistricted for the 1980s, Atlanta became the hub of the congressional map; most of the state's 10 districts radiate out from the Atlanta metropolitan area.

One Democrat who had to deal with that change was Ed Jenkins, whose 9th District historically had been based in the mountainous northeast corner of the state.

When Phil Landrum, Jenkins' predecessor and mentor, first won this seat in 1952, the 9th had 243,000 people, nearly all of them in farm counties or small textile towns. The district included Gwinnett County, on the northeast outskirts of Atlanta, but even Gwinnett was still rural and contained only 32,000 people.

In 1987, the boundaries of the 9th are similar. But the demographics are completely different. Jenkins represented 551,000 people as of the 1980 census; in 1987 he represented more than 600,000, and an estimated 200,000 of them were in Gwinnett, whose population had exploded in the 1980s with the arrival of transient suburbanites.

In Jenkins' view, it would be politically impossible to represent such a heterogeneous district by being a diehard Southern conservative. "These people are turning over all the time," he said. "You have them one year and the next year they are gone. They're from all over the United States.... You know you are not going to have 90 percent approval. You hope for 60-40. You are going to moderate your views somewhat to reflect the population in your district."

Patterson's district, across the Savannah River in South Carolina, had not been subjected to the kind of population surge that has hit Jenkins' district. Greenville, the largest city, had fewer than 60,000 people; Spartanburg, the only other population center, has 43,000.

But the towns themselves had changed dramatically since the days when they were represented by Boll Weevils Ashmore and Mann. In 1967, Greenville was a textile town; in 1987 it was a small corporate headquarters city, with a disproportionate share of interstate banks. Spartanburg remained tied to textiles, but the foreign firms that had moved there brought in something completely new — an ethnic population of Swiss, Germans and French.

Those changes did not force anyone representing the district to become a liberal, but they did dictate a more cosmopolitan outlook and close ties to other members whose districts had similar needs, whether they were from the South or elsewhere in the country.

When Patterson came to Washington in 1987, she joined the Committee on Banking, Housing and Urban Affairs — something her predecessors would have been unlikely to do. "If I had come here 10 or 12 years ago," she said, "I wouldn't have asked to go on the Banking Committee."

Even in parts of the South where demographics had not changed dramatically, members were developing new kinds of constituencies. When Dave McCurdy of Oklahoma's 4th District won his first nomination in 1980, he was a 30-year-old lawyer and novice candidate up against a veteran state legislator. He built support among young professionals, the University of Oklahoma community, blacks and small business. Those were the constituencies he cultivated as an incumbent.

Rather than limit himself to wooing the district's traditionally important blocs — farmers and the oil industry — McCurdy tried to create new ones, not only for political purposes but for economic development. "My game plan for my district," he said, "is moving away from energy and agriculture and attracting scientific research."

The Pivotal Black Vote

It went without saying that for many Southern Democrats, the constituency that changed their lives the most in recent years was the black community. Substantial numbers of blacks were voting throughout this century in Tennessee, North Carolina and other "Outer South" states, but where the black population was largest — in states such as Mississippi, Alabama and South Carolina — the Southern Democrats of a generation ago were playing to an essentially all-white electorate. The Voting Rights Act of 1965 changed that situation forever.

The black vote still varied enormously, even within individual states. Rep. Tim Valentine, in central North Carolina's 2nd District, represented a constituency 40 percent black; fellow-Democrat James McClure Clarke, in the western part of the state, had a district just 6 percent black.

But in the vast majority of districts across the South, a Democratic incumbent knew two things: Blacks would provide the base of his support against any Republican, and they could cause him trouble in a Democratic primary if they turned against him.

For both reasons, the black community and its wishes had to be listened to. It was a sign of the times in 1983 when Southern Democrats voted 78-12 in favor of the national holiday honoring the Rev. Dr. Martin Luther King Jr. *(1983 Almanac p. 600)*

One of the Democrats supporting that holiday most enthusiastically was Mississippi's Wayne Dowdy, who came to the House in a special election in 1981.

Dowdy spoke in the drawl of rural white Mississippi, but black votes had been the basis of his House career. He was elected to the House four times, but only once — in 1986 — had he carried a majority of whites in his district. In his first campaign, he lost the white vote decisively, but his popularity in black precincts — where he offered a passionate defense of the Voting Rights Act — brought him victory by 912 votes.

Dowdy talked candidly about how the black community affected his work as a legislator. "The Voting Rights Act," he said, "gives me the luxury of being independent of the typical Southern conservative position. You couldn't be on the right half of the spectrum and win a primary in my district. The most important vote in the primary is blacks, teachers and labor. And they wouldn't support anyone that's overly conservative."

"There's no organization for conservatives in the Democratic Party in Mississippi," Dowdy added. "They used to have the courthouse crowd, but that's been busted up."

Blacks, teachers and labor were the most important element in quite a few Southern Democratic primaries. In some, they were the only organized element that existed. Members from the South were nearly unanimous in arguing that there was no political network remaining in the Democratic Party back home that could help them if they looked for support on the right.

"In lots of districts in Texas," said Rep. Martin Frost, who came from suburban Dallas, "conservative Democrats don't vote in the Democratic primary anymore. That doesn't mean they vote in the Republican primary. They aren't voting."

"Either there will be Republicans representing Dallas in Congress in the future," Frost predicted, "or there will be national Democrats. There's no room left for conservative Democrats."

Rising Republicanism

The moderate voting record that solidified Dowdy within the Democratic Party brought him significant Republican opposition in three out of four campaigns. Although he was an easy winner in 1986, he knew that the Republican Party was a viable entity in his district, and he could not take the general election for granted.

Here, too, Dowdy typified the change over the past 20 years. Until the 1970s, few Southern Democrats gave even the remotest thought to a Republican challenge. Even in 1987, few faced truly difficult GOP opponents. But many cast their votes with the idea of a challenge in mind.

And this had been an important factor in the demise of the conservative coalition. If the rise of the two-party South had been a source of pride to Republican strategists, it had also weakened them when it came to forming legislative alliances.

Southern Democrats used to vote with Republicans on key issues in the expectation that national GOP leaders would discourage challenges to them at election time. In 1987, there were no such guarantees.

"You see conservative Republicans going after a conservative Democrat simply because they want the seat," said Jenkins. "I understand that. It's natural. But what happens is, after you've had a hard race, and Republicans have put money in there, you begin to say, 'These are not my friends.' "

For many members like Jenkins, the pivotal event was the 1984 Republican challenge to Rep. Jack Hightower of Texas, one of the most popular of the Southern Democrats. Hightower was a genuine Boll Weevil — during his last two years in the House he voted with the conservative coalition 88 percent of the time. But he was unseated by a GOP opponent who accused him of failing to support school prayer, even though he had voted for school-prayer amendments numerous times in his 10-year House career.

Some of Hightower's friends had never forgotten what happened to him. "People from the South talk about Hightower all the time," said one Texas colleague. "Not just Texas — people from all over the South. He came back up here after the election and talked about what a mean, scurrilous campaign the Republicans had run against him. He told everybody that no matter how conservative they voted, Republicans would lie, cheat and steal to beat them. What's the percentage for some of these people to do business with the Republicans when they see the treatment Hightower got?"

No Republican Alternative

The 100th Congress had been marked not only by the refusal of Southern Democrats to join a conservative coalition, but the reluctance of Republicans even to promote one. That attitude was symbolized by the decision of GOP leaders not to offer any alternative to the Democratic budget resolution in spring 1987.

If no Republican alternative existed, there was no way even the most conservative Democrat could vote for it. Some of the Southerners were sounding rather bitter about this; they felt that Republican apathy was what was really killing the coalition.

"Republicans have been engaging more in rhetoric than in meaningful alternatives," Jenkins insisted. "They want to make difficult votes for us, rather than get things passed." He and other Southern conservatives used to vote occasionally in favor of GOP amendments to slash spending for social programs unpopular among constituents. Jenkins saw those amendments as partisan "cheap shots" and always voted "no."

Some who tried to practice coalition politics in recent months returned to their own side complaining that the GOP was unwilling to negotiate in good faith. "Republicans have abused the possibilities of compromise," said John M. Spratt Jr., D-S.C. "McCurdy worked with them on contra aid to develop an agreement and felt he got taken. Every time he tried to make a deal, the Republicans got what they wanted from him and then they didn't deliver on their end."

"The Voting Rights Act gives me the luxury of being independent of the typical Southern conservative position."

—Rep. Wayne Dowdy, D-Miss.

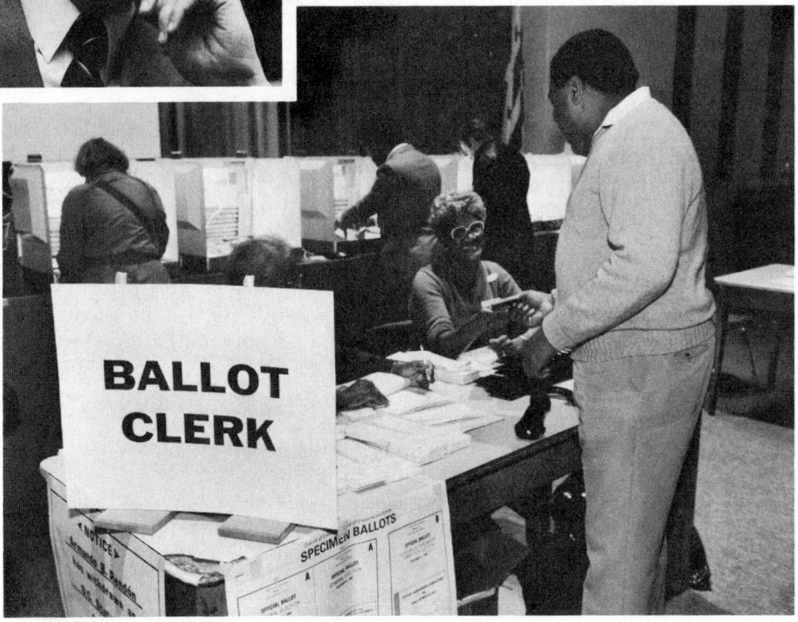

Protecting GOP Interests

It was not at all clear, though, whether Republicans were contributing to the decline of the coalition or simply responding to it. If, for a variety of complex reasons, the majority of Southern Democrats were no longer interested in voting with them, Republicans had little choice but to design a strategy focused on their own side of the aisle.

Lott, while he talked optimistically at times about a return to the Boll Weevil alliances of 1981, seemed to acknowledge at other moments that those days were gone. "They can vote with us, they can switch, or we will try to beat them," he argued. "While I support a conservative coalition, what I really want is a Republican majority."

A strategy built on anticipation of controlling the House might not seem very appealing to Republicans who reflected that their party had not won control since 1952 and would need a gain of 42 seats to take over. On the other hand, it might simply be a realistic admission that the prospects for coalition politics were now bleak, no matter how hard Republican House members might try to revive it.

In the Senate, Republicans possessed a weapon that their House counterparts could not employ: the filibuster. And it was a powerful weapon. It took only 41 votes to prevent the Democratic leadership from cutting off debate, and there were 46 Republicans in the chamber. Barring significant GOP defections, sustaining a filibuster did not require a single Democratic ally. Given that situation, it was understandable that Senate Republicans went to the extraordinary step this year of blocking Democrats from taking up the defense authorization because it contained language Reagan objected to.

That maneuver was interpreted variously as a display of petulant bad sportsmanship by a party rudely returned to minority status and as a symbol of emotional GOP commitment to SDI. But it might be viewed as the launching of a new strategy by a minority party that could no longer attract Democratic votes and could prevent passage of Democratic bills only by obstructing them.

The strategic importance of such tactics was conceded even by those Republican senators who found them distasteful. Cochran, a member of the Republican leadership, admitted that the filibuster on the defense bill "doesn't make us look awfully good." On the other hand, he admitted, "the filibuster gives the Republicans a reason to stick together."

Could Coalition Rise Again?

The one difficult question left unanswered about the demise of the conservative coalition was what might happen if a liberal Democrat became president and started proposing things unpalatable in much of the South. Would that turn the cicadas back into Boll Weevils?

Some Southerners thought so. "If you had a Michael Dukakis or a Mario Cuomo as president," Frost speculated, "and you had a clear-cut liberal agenda, you might have a conservative coalition again." Dowdy agreed. "For a Southerner," he said, "it's easier politically to be a Democrat with a Republican president and heckle from the sidelines."

In 1987 most Southern Democrats seemed to regard that as a remote possibility. "Clearly," said Rep. David E. Price of North Carolina, "a liberal Democratic president pushing a liberal agenda would create a lot of new strains for us. But we aren't going to have that kind of president." ∎

Where Have All the Dollars Gone?

In 'Permanent Campaign' Era, Members' Funds Find Many Uses

In 1985 and early 1986, Florida Democrat Sam Gibbons, then in his 12th House term, confronted what he thought might be the most serious re-election campaign of his career. It involved a new emphasis on fund raising, extensive public-opinion polling, a nationally known media consultant and an overall price tag exceeding $550,000.

What it did not involve, in the end, was an opponent. Gibbons was essentially elected when the candidate filing deadline passed in July 1986. Because no Republican opposed him, Gibbons' name did not even appear on the ballot.

But if he was alone in seeking to represent the Tampa-based 7th District, Gibbons was not alone in pursuing his campaign strategy, which could be called a strategic defense initiative applied to politics. A look at spending records for the last election cycle turned up numerous incumbents who made large "defensive" expenditures and ended up facing little or no opposition. There were 333 House incumbents who received 60 percent of the vote or more in 1986; they spent an average of $274,766 during their campaigns, according to the Federal Election Commission (FEC).

The reasons for these expenditures varied from district to district, but Gibbons' experience offered some insight into why and how so many incumbents came to wage costly "permanent campaigns," regardless of the nature of their opposition.

Once Burned, Twice Wise

What moved Gibbons to increase his campaign budget was his 1984 election. That year he was caught off guard when a little-known former local judge ran television ads against him and capitalized on President Reagan's political strength. Gibbons saw his winning tally drop just below 60 percent. That might not seem like thin ice to many, but for Gibbons, it was his worst-ever re-election showing, and it encouraged Republican talk of targeting the 7th in 1986.

"When you get down in the 50s you don't have to move too many figures before you are in real trouble," said Gibbons' son Clifford, who served as a paid consultant to the campaign and had been mentioned as a possible House aspirant when his father retires.

As a result of the 1984 scare, Gibbons decided immediately to start preparing for 1986. "We essentially ran a full-fledged campaign assuming that we had a strong opponent and assuming that the opponent was going to use everything in their artillery against us," said Clifford Gibbons.

Concerned by his 59 percent tally in 1984, Florida Rep. Sam Gibbons invested in a sophisticated campaign operation for 1986. He ended up spending more than $550,000, though he drew no GOP foe.

When hit with negative ads in 1984, Gibbons was flat-footed. "We saw that we got burned by that stuff and didn't have the ability to respond to it in such a short period of time," said the younger Gibbons.

To prevent that from happening again, Gibbons hired the dean of Democratic media consultants, Bob Squier — who normally concentrated on statewide contests — and he produced ads in 1985 that conveyed a positive image of the incumbent.

"The budget for the campaign almost quadrupled when you considered television," Clifford Gibbons said. "We began to figure out a whole new dimension in how to run a campaign in terms of cost."

In addition to TV ads, Gibbons ventured into another area that had boosted incumbents' spending and discouraged some potential candidates from undertaking campaigns: polling. While increasingly sophisticated survey methods made it possible to gauge voter attitudes more accurately, the information came with a significant price tag. For instance, FEC records show that Gibbons paid $18,000 for surveys in May 1985.

The extensive polling reinforced Gibbons' notion that he should prepare thoroughly for 1986, because the surveys confirmed the rapidly changing demographics in Florida. So many new voters arrived in the state each month that even established political figures like Gibbons were unknown by a sizable share of the electorate.

Such population changes were perhaps one of the main reasons that many seemingly strong incumbents spent heavily on their campaigns.

"In a state where there is going to be big change, they may have worries about reapportionment," said Herbert E. Alexander, a campaign finance expert and director of the Citizens' Research Foundation at the University of Southern California. With the approach of the 1990 census and subsequent redistricting, incumbents might seek to boost their visibility in case their districts are altered or eliminated.

The total cost of Gibbons' 1986 campaign was held down because he did not actually need to air the TV ads that Squier produced. But the polling and other efforts to beef up his cam-

Largess Helps Charities and Other Causes

Charity might begin at home, as the saying goes, but it did not necessarily end there, particularly for politically secure incumbents who could afford to be generous with the money in their campaign funds. Through expenditures that often appear only tenuously related to their political futures, a number of members built good will at home or furthered a favored cause with their funds.

Rep. James H. Quillen, one of the most influential Republicans in Tennessee after more than three decades of political involvement, was one member who could truly claim to have given at the office. Quillen reported expenditures of $459,119 for the 1985-86 election cycle, a surprising sum for an incumbent who was in no danger of losing his seat. But the figure is somewhat misleading, because a huge chunk of it went to meet an expense not usually associated with campaigning: Quillen used $250,000 from his campaign fund to help endow a chair in geriatrics at the Quillen-Dishner College of Medicine at East Tennessee University in his district. He also gave money from his personal funds.

With $250,000 in campaign funds, Rep. James H. Quillen helped endow a chair at the school that bears his name.

According to Quillen, the president of the university first asked him if he would be interested in raising money for the chair to be named in honor of his wife, who overcame a cerebral aneurysm and stroke suffered in 1981. That Quillen would be interested came as no surprise to those who saw his efforts to promote the school, which was named for him and a generous donor.

"I think that the need to research the problems of the aged is most important," Quillen said, pointing out that this was the only time he had used his funds for such a purpose.

The contribution was not without political benefit. Vice President George Bush made an appearance in the district when the money had been raised to endow the chair (nearly $2 million altogether). Photos of Quillen and Bush made the front page of several newspapers in upper East Tennessee.

"If you look at it from a campaign standpoint, it was the best investment I have made," Quillen said, "but I didn't look at it that way."

Youth Programs, Afghan Rebels Get Help

Most charitable contributions paled in comparison with Quillen's. While Florida Democrat Sam Gibbons was oiling his campaign machinery in the last election cycle, he was also showing himself to be something of a sports fan. According to reports filed with the FEC, Gibbons supported the Children's Fishing Club of Florida with a $35 contribution, gave $500 to District 6 Little League in Tampa and sponsored an under-10 soccer team for $2,000.

Georgia Democrat Charles Hatcher had shown some similar inclinations, donating $100 to a softball team for a trip to national playoffs. But some of his expenditures were more a reflection of his rural south Georgia district. At one point he used $119.50 to purchase a steer for a 4-H club.

And there were other disbursements that were more ideological than the purchase of a steer. Texas Democratic Rep. Charles Wilson had been a staunch supporter of aiding rebels fighting the Soviet-backed government of Afghanistan, arguing at one point that that country was "the only place in the world where we are killing Russians."

Wilson put his campaign money where his mouth was: The Committee for a Free Afghanistan received $750 from Wilson's campaign treasury in the last election cycle. Some of his other contributions were closer to home, including a $100 donation to the Lufkin, Texas, Community Police Dog Fund.

paign and visibility had a significant impact. Gibbons purchased an IBM computer for $8,679, he opened a new campaign office, he paid for giant billboards all around the district, and he made $1,000 contributions to candidates for the state Legislature, county commissioner, education commissioner and county property appraiser.

Gibbons' effort had the intended effect. "He had the most beautiful signboards all over the county. . . . It was very impressive," said Margie Kinkaid, chairman of the 7th District Republican Party. Because of Gibbons' aggressiveness, she said, "it made sense not to push it that time."

As for Gibbons, the 1986 strategy was a blueprint for the future. "It was a good dry run in terms of how to do a campaign," his son said. "I think we're going with that continuing strategy."

Food, Games, Gifts and More

Although television ads, polling and other sophisticated technology accounted for a hefty share of Gibbons' expenses, technology was not the driving force in many of the costly campaigns run by secure incumbents.

Tennessee Republican John J. Duncan, for instance, had stayed in the public eye in part by satisfying the public palate. He fed as many as 36,000 of his constituents at his bienniel barbecue held in the Knoxville coliseum, at a cost of roughly $50,000. That event — and Duncan's $20,000 donation to the Knox County

Republican Party — contributed to a campaign budget that exceeded $300,000 in 1986. Duncan had never even seen the man who filed against him in 1984 and 1986; he tended to feed more people at his barbecues than his Democratic foes mobilized against him at the polls.

Texas Democrat Charles Wilson made sure there was competition in his district every year, in the form of a domino tournament. More than 300 people from local senior citizens' centers show up at the Lufkin, Texas, civic center to play Texas 42, a variation of the game. The two winners of the tournament, which cost several thousand dollars, got a trip to Washington, D.C., compliments of the campaign.

Reports filed with the FEC showed a broad range of other expenditures that added to the campaign budgets of electorally secure incumbents. Democratic Rep. Charles Hatcher of Georgia dipped into his treasury at Christmas time to purchase pecans for his state's delegation, at a cost of $116 in 1986. In early 1985 Louisiana Democratic Rep. Jerry Huckaby spent $2,032 to purchase charms for his constituents.

Louisiana Republican Rep. Bob Livingston did not have to worry about an opponent in the last election cycle; he also did not have to worry about scraping together the $252.50 needed to purchase tickets to the Sugar Bowl, a college football game held in New Orleans.

Republican Rep. Robert E. Badham of California did have some opposition in 1986, but he still had room in his budget for entertainment-related expenses, such as a $617 reimbursement for his wife's formal attire to attend several functions in 1986.

Constant travel between Washington and the district had left many an incumbent weary, but Texas Democratic Rep. Wilson had a remedy. His FEC reports show that he had used several hundred dollars from his campaign to pay dues to comfort clubs for airline travelers, such as United Airlines Red Carpet Club and the Pan Am Clipper Club.

And there were others who used the campaign treasury to do even more traveling. In the last election cycle, Democratic Rep. E. "Kika" de la Garza of Texas spent some campaign funds during trips to San Francisco, Washington state, Brazil and Japan.

Campaign funds also had proven helpful for incumbents who had more than just their political futures at stake. New York Democrat Mario Biaggi, who had been indicted in two separate federal investigations, used nearly $100,000 in the first half of 1987 to pay legal fees. His New York colleague, Democrat Robert Garcia, who reportedly was also under investigation, had used his campaign treasury to reimburse himself for more than $20,000 in legal fees.

All in the Family

The current system of financing political campaigns had many critics, who said it encourages individuals and groups to try to endear themselves to incumbents with campaign contributions. FEC reports showed that the system also allowed members to endear themselves to one another.

Texas' de la Garza, chairman of the House Agriculture Committee, had worked hard to establish good rapport with members of his committee. He added to the price tag of his unopposed campaign in 1986 by contributing to 10 Democrats on the panel. Kansas Democrat Dan Glickman, for example, received $250 from de la Garza in October 1986. The secure Glickman had little need for the money; later that month, he contributed the same amount to Democratic Rep. Thomas A. Daschle's Senate campaign in South Dakota.

Making in-House contributions was a practice not confined to senior members. Tennessee Democratic Rep. Bart Gordon did not wait long after his initial election in 1984 to begin sharing his campaign funds. Gordon, a protégé of House Speaker Jim Wright, D-Texas, contributed $1,000 to the Wright Appreciation Fund in 1985. Gordon also gave to House candidates in 1986, including Democrat Tom McMillen, who won an open seat in Maryland, and Kathleen Kennedy Townsend, who lost to Maryland GOP Rep. Helen Delich Bentley.

Occasionally, political contributions made by an incumbent did not seem to be tied either to Washington or the district. Gibbons, for example, gave $1,000 to Evan Bayh, who in 1986 campaigned successfully to become secretary of state in Indiana. Gibbons and Bayh's father, former Democratic Sen. Birch Bayh, are longtime friends.

Members' Choice

The range of expenditures allowed under House rules was fairly broad, although the Committee on Standards of Official Conduct attempted to clarify the definition of political expenses in a 1986 report. *(1986 Almanac p. 46)*

The committee ruled that "any use of campaign funds which personally benefit the Member rather than to exclusively and solely benefit the campaign is *not* a 'bona fide campaign purpose.' " In practice, however, determining what is a "bona fide" expense is generally left to the member.

There were those who were disturbed by this, including some who helped provide the funds that incumbents spread around. "I think there is a concern on the part of our members that there is not a tight enough definition," said David Michael "Mick" Staton, a former GOP House member (1981-83) who manages political action programs for the U.S. Chamber of Commerce.

Staton had encouraged business political action committees to follow a set of guidelines when evaluating a candidate; the guidelines included assessing whether a contribution was actually needed by a candidate. He cited the purchase of clothing or raffle tickets as examples of expenditures that could be disturbing to contributors.

Temptation to Spend

While few members would admit to raising or spending more money than they needed for their campaigns, changes in campaign finance laws in 1979 might have increased the incentives for newer members to spend.

In 1979 Congress passed election law amendments (PL 96-187) forbidding incumbents sworn in after Jan. 7, 1980, to convert campaign funds to personal use when they retire. Thus, newer members might be encouraged to spend whatever money they collect.

For incumbents sworn in on or before that date, the amendments included a "grandfather" clause that allowed them to convert their political funds to personal use when they leave the House. That clause had prompted some to criticize campaign funds as a potential "political IRA [Individual Retirement Account]," said Randy Huwa of Common Cause.

But as the spending habits of Gibbons and many other senior members showed, the temptation to hoard campaign funds for use in retirement often gave way to the incumbent's desire to spend money now to stay on good terms with the voters.

"Whether you have an opponent or not, your campaign strategy is in place," said Clifford Gibbons. "Now, essentially it is a full-time operation." ▮

LOBBIES

The Washington Lobby: A Continuing Effort To Influence Government Policy

Of all the pressures on Congress, none has received such widespread publicity and yet is so dimly understood as the role of Washington-based lobbyists and the groups they represent. The popular image of a rotund agent for special interests buying up members' votes is a vast oversimplification. The role of today's lobbyist is far more subtle, his or her techniques more refined.

Lobbyists and lobby groups have played an increasingly active part in the modern legislative process. The corps of Washington lobbyists has grown steadily since the New Deal, but especially since the early 1970s. The growth in the number of lobbyists has paralleled the growth in federal spending and the expansion of federal authority into new areas. The federal government has become a tremendous force in the life of the nation, and the number of fields in which changes in federal policy may spell success or failure for special interest groups has been greatly enlarged.

With the drive to reduce federal spending that gained impetus during the Reagan administration, the competition for the dwindling supply of federal dollars has become more intense. Lobbyists have to compete with one another to safeguard traditional spending in their area of interest or to gain some portion of the smaller federal pool of funds. Thus commercial and industrial interests, labor unions, ethnic and racial groups, professional organizations, citizen groups and representatives of foreign interests — all from time to time and some continuously — have sought by one method or another to exert pressure on Congress to attain their legislative goals.

The pressure usually has selfish aims — to assert rights or to win a privilege or financial benefit for the group exerting it. But in other cases the objective may be disinterested — to achieve an ideological goal or to further a group's particular conception of the national interest.

Lobbying: Pros and Cons

It is widely recognized that pressure groups, whether operating through general campaigns designed to sway public opinion or through direct contacts with members of Congress, perform some important and indispensable functions. Such functions include helping to inform both Congress and the public about problems and issues, stimulating public debate, opening a path to Congress for the wronged and needy, and making known to Congress the practical aspects of proposed legislation — whom it would help, whom it would hurt, who is for it and who against it. The spinoff from this process is considerable technical information produced by research on legislative proposals.

Against benefits to the public that result from pressure activities, critics point to certain serious liabilities. The most important is that in pursuing their own objectives, the pressure groups are apt to lead Congress into decisions that benefit the pressure group but do not necessarily serve other parts of the public or the national interest. A group's power to influence legislation often is based less on its arguments than on the size of its membership, the amount of financial and manpower resources it can commit to a legislative pressure campaign and the astuteness of its representatives.

Origins of Lobbying

Representatives of special interests haunted the environs of the First Continental Congress, but the word "lobby" was not recorded until 1808 when it appeared in the annals of the 10th Congress. By 1829 the term "lobby-agents" was applied to favor-seekers at the state capitol in Albany, N.Y. By 1832 it had been shortened to "lobbyist" and was in wide use at the U.S. Capitol.

Although the term had not yet been coined, the right to "lobby" was made implicit by the First Amendment to the Constitution, which provided that "Congress shall make no law . . . abridging the freedom of speech or of the press; or the right of the people peaceably to assemble and to petition the Government for redress of grievances." Among the Founding Fathers, only James Madison expressed concern over the dangers posed by pressure groups. In *The Federalist* (No. 10), Madison warned against the self-serving activities of the "factions." "Among the numerous advantages promised by a well-constructed union," he wrote, "none deserves to be more accurately developed than its tendency to break and control the violence of faction. . . . By a faction, I understand a number of citizens, whether amounting to a majority or minority of the whole, who are united and actuated by some common impulse of passion, or of interest, adverse to the rights of other citizens, or to the permanent and aggregate interests of the community." A strong federal government, Madison concluded, was the only effective counterbalance to the influence of such "factions."

Sources of Pressure

Traditionally, pressure groups in the United States have been composed of similar economic or social interests. Classic examples of such traditional lobbies are those representing farmers, business executives and labor union members. Each group has specific interests that usually draw the support of a large majority of its members.

As the federal government broadened its activities, a new type of pressure group developed — the coalition of diverse economic and social interests brought together by concern for a certain issue. Most major legislation is backed by alliances of interest groups on one side and opposed by alliances on the other. Such lobby coalitions, while having the advantages of bigger memberships and more financial resources for lobbying, may be difficult to control because of the differences of opinion that are likely to arise within any coalition. Despite these inner tensions, lobby coalitions nonetheless have been instrumental in obtaining passage of much major legislation, such as the civil rights and Alaska lands bills.

A notable effort that did not succeed was the coalition for ratification of the Equal Rights Amendment (ERA), which failed to win ratification by the deadline of June 30, 1982. Only 35 states approved it, three short of the necessary 38. Also traditional secular and religious advocates for the underprivileged that have formed a coalition for the poor — such as the National Conference of Catholic Bishops, the National Low Income Housing Coalition and the Food Research and Action Center — have been challenged by the budget cutbacks of the conservative administration of Ronald Reagan.

Executive Branch. Equally prominent among forces exerting pressures on Congress is the executive branch. Executive lobbying activities have been described as the most pervasive, influential and costly of any of the pressures converging on Capitol Hill.

Although every president since George Washington has sought to influence the content of legislation, it was not until the administration of Dwight D. Eisenhower that a formal congressional liaison office in the White House was created. In addition, each executive department has a congressional liaison office charged with selling the department's legislative program to Congress.

While senators and representatives sometimes criticize what they regard as excessive executive pressures, they tend on the other hand to complain of lack of leadership when executive influence is missing. The inter-branch pressure process also works in reverse. Members of Congress exert pressure on executive agencies, if only through inquiries that demonstrate an interest on the part of the body that must pass agency appropriations.

Foreign Interests. Since World War II, lobbying by foreign interests and by American groups with foreign members or interests has become an increasingly important factor in Washington legislative and executive decision making. Foreign-oriented lobbying is based on international politics, world trade and many American domestic issues, for any action by the U.S. government may have foreign or global implications.

As of Dec. 31, 1986, 824 active registered agents representing the interests of foreign principals (governments, political parties, corporations and individuals) are listed with the Justice Department under the Foreign Agents Registration Act, despite Congress' narrowing of the act's coverage in 1966. Counting partners and associates who may participate in representing overseas clients, the number of individuals listed as being in the service of foreign "principals" swelled to over 8,000.

Public Interest Lobbies. Finally there is a collection of groups with no single special interest to promote or protect. These self-styled citizens' or public interest lobbies are concerned with a vast array of issues, and usually have large numbers of individual members. Two of the oldest public interest lobbies are the League of Women Voters and Americans for Democratic Action. Their activities set the pattern for the public interest groups that followed in this relatively new lobbying development.

Two groups, Common Cause and Public Citizen, have attracted wide attention over the last decade and have come almost to characterize liberal public interest lobbies. Developed by Ralph Nader, Public Citizen groups pursue a broad agenda of substantive economic, consumer, environmental, legal and social policy issues. Common Cause has focused on issues of political structure and procedure.

Conservative public interest groups have gained in prominence in recent years as well. Evangelical lobby groups, including the Moral Majority and Christian Voice, have joined other more traditional conservative groups, including the Conservative Caucus, in legislative fights against abortion, homosexual rights, and the Equal Rights Amendment, and in favor of budget-balancing, an anti-communist foreign policy and heavier defense spending. This loose coalition of conservative groups has come to be called The New Right.

Pressure Methods

A Washington lobby group is out to get results. It pursues them wherever results are likely to be found in the governmental process. Many organizations, directed by professionals in the art of government, focus major efforts at key points where decisions are made and policy interpreted into action. If a group loses a round in Congress, it may continue the fight in the agency charged with implementation of the legislation or in the courts. A year or two later, it may resume the struggle in Congress. This process can continue indefinitely.

Whether they focus on Congress or the executive branch, lobbyists use the methods they deem appropriate for the circumstances within the limits of their resources, group policies and ethical outlook.

Bribery

Bribery of members of Congress was a well-documented occurrence in the 19th and early 20th centuries. When Congress in the 1830s became embroiled in President Andrew Jackson's battle with the Bank of the United States, it was disclosed that Daniel Webster, then a senator from Massachusetts, enjoyed a retainer from the bank. On Dec. 21, 1833, Webster complained to bank President Nicholas Biddle: "My retainer has not been renewed or refreshed as usual. If it is wished that my relation to the Bank should be continued, it may be well to send me the usual retainers."

Col. Martin M. Mulhall, a lobbyist for the National Association of Manufacturers (NAM), stated publicly in 1913 that he had bribed members of Congress for legislative favors, had paid the chief House page $50 a month for inside information from the cloakrooms, and had influenced House leaders to place members friendly to the NAM on House committees and subcommittees. In a subsequent congressional probe, six members were exonerated but one was censured and resigned.

After World War II, direct vote-buying by lobbyists was replaced, for the most part, by more sophisticated techniques. Indirect, grass-roots pressures and political support became more powerful tools of persuasion. But bribery did not disappear altogether and the Abscam scandal that surfaced in 1980 demonstrated its persistence. The government undercover investigation of political corruption — known as "Abscam" — in which agents of the

Ex-Members as Lobbyists

Among the most influential and active lobbyists in Washington are former members of Congress, who, after leaving office, are hired as lobbyists for private organizations.

In some cases, former members become permanently associated with a single organization whose views they share. On the other hand, some former members work for many different organizations as lobbyists, frequently changing or adding employers from year to year.

Because of their service in Congress, former members of the House or Senate enjoy several advantages in lobbying activities. They have an excellent knowledge of the legislative process and frequently a good "feel" for the operations of the House or Senate, which help them decide precisely when and what kind of pressure to exert on behalf of their clients. They often enjoy easy access to congressional staff members and members who are friends and former colleagues. This enables them to see and speak with key legislative personnel, perhaps the chairman of a committee or subcommittee, at the proper time. The ordinary lobbyist might spend weeks trying to obtain an appointment. Former members also frequently have an expert knowledge of the subject matter of legislation through having dealt with it while in Congress.

The privileges of being admitted to the floor and adjacent halls of the House and Senate, which is granted in each chamber to former members of that chamber, is used relatively little by former members directly for lobbying purposes, although it is useful for maintaining contacts and acquaintances. In the House, use of the floor by former members for lobbying purposes has been circumscribed by House Rule 32 and a chair ruling in 1945 by Speaker Sam Rayburn, D-Texas. Under the "Rayburn rule," a former member is forbidden the privilege of the floor at any time the House is debating or voting on legislation in which he is interested, either personally or as an employee of some other person or organization.

No similar formal rule exists in the Senate. But as a matter of custom it is considered improper for a former senator, or any other non-member granted the privilege of the floor, to use that privilege to lobby for legislation.

Federal Bureau of Investigation, posing as businessmen or wealthy Arabs, attempted to bribe members of Congress and other elected officials to help Arabs obtain U.S. residency, get federal grants and arrange real estate deals, resulted in the convictions of seven members of Congress — six representatives and one senator. The charges ranged from bribery to conspiracy.

Campaign Support

Campaign contributions to members of Congress serve two important functions for lobbying organizations. Political support may not only induce a congressman to back the pressure group's legislative interests in Congress but also helps assure that members friendly to the group's goals will remain in office.

While corporations have been barred since 1907, and labor unions since 1943, from making direct contributions to campaigns for federal office, contributors have found numerous ways to get around the restrictions. Although unions are prohibited from using dues money to assist political candidates in federal elections, it is legal for them to set up separate political arms, such as the AFL-CIO's Committee on Political Education (COPE), which collect voluntary contributions from union members and their families and use the funds for political expenditures calculated to benefit senators and representatives friendly to labor. It is also legal for unions to endorse political candidates.

Similarly, while corporations are prohibited from making direct campaign contributions, they can set up corporate political action committees (PACs) to seek contributions from stockholders and executive and administrative personnel and their families.) Corporate PACs have proliferated in recent years and their influences rival, if not surpass, those of labor. Twice a year union and corporate politial action committees may seek anonymous contributions by mail from all employees, not just those to which they are initially restricted.

The same general resources for political support and opposition are available to members of citizens' groups and, indeed, to a wide range of organizations seeking to exert political pressure on members of Congress.

In approaching the typical member, a pressure group has no need to tell the member outright that future political support or opposition, and perhaps future political expenditures and the voluntary campaign efforts of its members, depend on how the member votes on a particular bill or whether, over a long period, the member acts favorably toward the group. The member understands this without being told. He or she knows that when the vital interests of some group are at stake in legislation, a vote supporting those interests would normally win the group's friendship and future support, and a vote against them would mean the group's enmity and future opposition.

Lobbyists themselves frequently deny that this is the intention of their campaign support. But lobbyists do admit that political support gives them access — that they otherwise might not have — to the legislator to present their case.

Grass Roots Pressures

Except on obscure or highly specialized legislation, most lobby campaigns now are accompanied by massive propaganda or "educational" drives in which pressure groups seek to mobilize public opinion to support their aims. In most cases, citizens are urged to respond by contacting members of Congress in support of or opposition to a particular bill.

The most outstanding example of a successful grass-roots lobbying group is the National Rifle Association (NRA). Despite polls showing a majority of Americans favoring some strengthening of gun controls, and despite periodic waves of revulsion brought on by the shooting of public figures, efforts aimed at stricter gun control legislation have been consistently subdued by the NRA, and other similar groups.

NRA has all the advantages of a successful grass-roots lobby organization going for it: a large, well-organized, passionately concerned constituency, concentrated on a single issue.

"In politics you learn to identify the issues of the

highest intensity," said Rep. Dan Glickman, a Democrat from Kansas. "This issue [gun control] is of the highest intensity. Those people who care about guns, care very strongly, almost to the exclusion of other issues."

Even in the aftermath of the assassinations of President John F. Kennedy, the Rev. Martin Luther King Jr. and Sen. Robert F. Kennedy, D-N.Y. (1965-68), the gun lobby, through an outpouring of mail opposing tighter gun controls, was able to bottle up proposals for tough controls. All that was passed in 1968 was watered-down legislation not vigorously opposed by the NRA. And it was widely perceived that the only real legislative impact of the shootings of John Lennon in December 1980 and President Reagan in March 1981 would be to diminish NRAs chances of rolling back the 1968 law.

Disadvantages. Despite the frequent success of grass-roots lobbying, such an approach has several inherent limitations that make its use questionable unless it is carefully and cleverly managed. If a member's mail on an issue appears artificially generated, by a professional public relations firm for instance, the member may feel that the response is not representative of the member's constituency. Such pressure mail is easily recognized because the letters all arrive at about the same time, are mimeographed or printed, or are identically or similarly worded.

G. Colburn Aker, a Washington lobbyist, said: "Anybody who believes you can use advertising or public relations techniques to create a groundswell that doesn't have a good basis to begin with is misconceiving the power of those techniques."

But others say a sense of insecurity has pervaded Congress recently, especially among the large number of relative newcomers. Skittish members are more eager to avoid controversy. Norman J. Ornstein, a politics professor associated with the American Enterprise Institute, agreed that the dramatic turnovers in the past few elections have taught many politicians to practice "damage limitation" — never taking a chance of making someone angry. But Ornstein said that as lawmakers gather experience they likely will learn when it is safe to trust their own judgment.

Direct Lobbying

Much lobbying still is conducted on a face-to-face basis. In a study of pressures on the Senate, Donald R. Matthews, a political scientist, observed that the vast majority of such lobbying was directed at members "who are already convinced." He added: "The services a lobby can provide a friendly senator are substantial. Few senators could survive without them. First, they can perform much of the research and speech-writing chores of the senator's office. This service is especially attractive to the more publicity-oriented senators. Members of the party that does not control the White House also find this service especially valuable, since they cannot draw upon the research services of the departments as much as can the other members. But most senators find this service at first a convenience and soon a necessity."

Once established, Matthews has said, "Senator-lobbyist friendships also tend to reinforce the senator's commitment to a particular group and line of policy. . . . Relatively few senators are actually changed by lobbyists from a hostile or neutral position to a friendly one. Perhaps a few on every major issue are converted and this handful of votes may carry the day. But quantitatively, the conversion effect is relatively small."

Ensuring continued access to members of Congress requires considerable tact on the part of the lobbyist. Lobbyists must be particularly wary of overstaying their welcome and appearing overly aggressive. Rep. Emanuel Celler, D-N.Y. (1923-73), wrote: "The man who keeps his appointment, presents his problem or proposal and lets the congressman get on with his other work comes to be liked and respected. His message has an excellent chance of being effective. The man who feels that it somehow adds to his usefulness and prestige to be seen constantly in the company of one legislator or another, or who seeks to ingratiate himself with congressional staffs, gets under foot and becomes a nuisance. He does his principal and cause no good."

Above all, the lobbyist must be certain that the information he gives the member is accurate and complete. In their book, *Interest Groups, Lobbying and Policymaking*, Norman J. Ornstein and Shirley Elder quoted a member of Congress: "It doesn't take very long to figure which lobbyists are straightforward, and which ones are trying to snow you. The good ones will give you the weak points as well as the strong points of their case. If anyone ever gives me false or misleading information, that's it — I'll never see him again."

Strategic Contacts. In fights over a specific bill, most direct approaches by lobbyists are likely to center on a few strategic members instead of a large part of the membership of the House or Senate. Generally the key members sit on the committees that have jurisdiction over the legislation in question. As one former member of the House said in 1970, "The committee system is still the crux of the legislative process and is still the basis for congressional action. Laws are not really made here on the floor of the House or on the floor of the other body. They are only revised here. Ninety percent of all legislation that has been passed was passed in the form reported by the committee to the floor."

The committee's power to prevent legislation or to determine its nature narrows down the number of targets for the great majority of specialized interests. Their Washington representatives become experts not only in their field but also on the House and Senate committees that deal with that specialty. This focus in some cases narrows still further to certain subcommittees.

Pressure groups pay their Washington staffs to keep them abreast of developments in government that could affect their constituents. These agents make it their business to watch the work of committees in which they have an interest, to establish and maintain working relationships with key members and staff members and to stay informed on potential and actual legislative developments.

Testimony at Hearings

Another useful technique for lobbyists is testimony at congressional hearings. The hearing provides the lobbyist with a propaganda forum that has few parallels in Washington. It also provides access to key members whom the lobbyist may not have been able to contact in any other way. On important legislation, lobbyists normally rehearse their statements before the hearing, seek to ensure a large turnout from their constituency on the hearing day, and may even hand friendly committee members leading questions for the group's witness to answer.

The degree of propaganda success for the hearing, however, is likely to depend on how well the committee's controlling factions are disposed to the group's position. In his book, *House Out of Order*, Rep. Richard Bolling, D-Mo.

(1949-83), says that within congressional committees "proponents and opponents of legislation jockey for position — each complementing the activities of their alter egos in lobbies outside." He points out: "Adverse witnesses can be kept to a minimum, for example, or they can be sandwiched among friendly witnesses in scheduled appearances so that their testimony does not receive as much attention from the press as it deserves. Scant attention will be given, for example, to a knowledgeable opponent of the federal fallout shelter program if he is scheduled to testify on such legislation on the same day as are Dr. Edward Teller, an assistant secretary of Defense and a three-star general. The opponent is neatly boxed in."

Regulation of Lobbying

In the 19th and 20th centuries, abundant evidence accumulated that venal, selfish or misguided methods used by pressure groups could often result in legislation designed to enrich the pressure group at the expense of the public or to impose the group's own standards on the nation.

The first regulation of lobbyists occurred in 1876 when the House passed a resolution requiring lobbyists to register during the 44th Congress with the Clerk of the House. Since the advent of the 62nd Congress in 1911, federal legislation to regulate lobbyists and lobbying activities has continued to be proposed in practically every Congress. Yet only one comprehensive lobbying regulation law and only a handful of more specialized measures have been enacted.

The principal method of regulating lobbying has been disclosure rather than control. In four laws, lobbyists have been required to identify themselves, whom they represent and their legislative interests. In one law, lobbyists also have been required to report how much they and their employers spend on lobbying. But definitions have been unclear, and enforcement has been minimal. As a result, the few existing disclosure laws have produced only limited information, and its effects have been questionable.

One reason for the relative lack of restrictions on lobbies has been the difficulty of imposing meaningful restrictions without infringing on the constitutional rights of free speech, press, assembly and petition.

Other reasons include a fear that restrictions would hamper legitimate lobbies without reaching more serious lobby abuses; the consolidated and highly effective opposition of lobbies; and the desire of some members to keep open avenues to a possible lobbying career they may wish to pursue later.

The two major lobbying laws that Congress has succeeded in enacting have dealt with lobbyists in general who meet certain definitions of lobbying. The Foreign Agents Registration Act was first enacted in 1938 amid reports of fascist and Nazi propaganda circulating in the United States in the period before World War II. It has been amended frequently since then, and its history is as much a part of this country's struggle with internal security as it is a part of efforts to regulate lobbying.

The one existing omnibus lobbying law, the Federal Regulation of Lobbying Act, was enacted in 1946 as part of the Legislative Reorganization Act. It requires paid lobbyists to register with the House and the Senate and to file quarterly reports with the House. However, large loopholes in the law exempt many interests from registering. The 1954 U.S. Supreme Court decision in *United States v. Harriss* further limited the scope of the law.

Since then congressional committees have investigated the situation and proposed replacements for the 1946 act. Both the House and Senate passed versions of a new bill in 1976 but conferees were not able to resolve differences between the two versions before Congress adjourned. Although various versions of a lobby disclosure bill have been introduced each year since then, including one passed by the House in 1978, no bill has been enacted.

Committee Remains Silent on Boner Case:

GOP Critics of Ethics Panel Are Rebuffed Again by House

The House had given its ethics committee a second vote of confidence after the latest attack from conservative Republicans protesting the panel's record of policing members' conduct.

By a 111-291 vote Aug. 5, 1987, the House rejected a resolution directing the Committee on Standards of Official Conduct to reopen an investigation of Fernand J. St Germain, D-R.I., chairman of the Banking Committee.

The committee in April had closed a 14-month inquiry into published allegations that St Germain used his position for personal gain. Despite finding violations of law and House rules, it recommended no sanction. A Republican faction led by Newt Gingrich, Ga., and Robert S. Walker, Pa., sought to revive the matter after a July 16 *Wall Street Journal* story raised new questions about both St Germain and the committee's inquiry.

A Spotlight on Democrats

The defeated resolution was part of the conservatives' ongoing effort to spotlight controversies involving a number of House Democrats, including Speaker Jim Wright of Texas. The GOP critics wanted to publicize what Duncan Hunter, R-Calif., called Democrats' "double standard" in zealously investigating administration officials, Wall Street financiers and religious broadcasters, while ignoring their colleagues' alleged sins.

In so doing, the conservatives hoped to blunt what was shaping up as a Democratic theme for the coming election year — public integrity.

While the strategy had made headlines, it had little House support. In a related challenge June 29, the House voted 77-297 against the group's proposal for an independent commission to review House ethics procedures.

On the latest vote, only one Democrat, Romano L. Mazzoli, Ky., voted for the resolution (H Res 244), while Republicans favored it 2-to-1, with 110 for it and 51 against. Of the 46 Banking members who voted, five — all Republicans — voted to investigate the chairman, who has a reputation for vindictiveness. St Germain was absent, and an aide said he would have no comment.

All 12 members of the ethics committee, six Democrats and six Republicans, voted "present," though several Democrats initially voted "no" and switched.

On Aug. 4, the committee had met privately in anticipation of the vote. Conservatives provoked the floor fight when the panel did not answer their July 28 letter seeking a response to the Journal's report that St Germain had used a credit card belonging to lobbyist James O. "Snake" Freeman of the U.S. League of Savings Institutions. The paper also said that St Germain may have exceeded House limits on gifts from lobbyists, and that the ethics committee avoided the matter in its inquiry and retreated from an attempt to question Freeman.

Committee Chairman Julian C. Dixon, D-Calif., insisted during floor debate that it was "absolutely untrue" that his committee dodged any allegations.

As for the new reports against St Germain, Dixon said, "It is the unanimous opinion of the members of the committee that the relevant material is entirely from one press account.... It is nothing more or less than rumor."

Dixon confirmed reports that St Germain was the subject of a Justice Department criminal investigation. His revelation was made to buttress a plea that the House not force his committee to break its policy of deferring to legal authorities when they have separate investigations under way.

Meanwhile, Justice subpoenaed the records of another lobby group, the Securities Industry Association, adding to those it sought earlier from the U.S. League and the American Bankers Association.

After the vote, Gingrich suggested his resolution lost because members were "rattled" by a story in that day's Journal questioning Wright's political and business ties to Texas developer George Mallick. The members, he said, did not want to call for an investigation of St Germain based on a single Journal story if that precedent could be used against the Speaker.

But Gingrich, during debate, also invoked Wright's name, claiming he was part of what Gingrich called a "a $50 billion scandal" in the savings and loan industry. Wright was criticized for his efforts to protect insolvent Texas thrifts and investors from regulators; $50 billion was the speculative estimate of the government's potential cost of bailing out depositors.

No Action on Boner Case

Meanwhile, it appeared the ethics committee might never resolve its longest-pending inquiry, an 18-month-old investigation into reports that Bill Boner, D-Tenn., grew rich in office by violating numerous House rules governing members' finances and conflicts of interest.

After narrowly winning the Sept. 22, 1987, mayoral race in Nashville, Boner made plans to vacate his seat that October. Boner's departure from Congress allowed him to escape any threat from an ethics committee investigation.

Typically, the ethics committee drops cases against members who leave the House, as it did for five members who were defeated or resigned after they were implicated in the 1980 Abscam bribery scandal.

The committee suspended its Boner inquiry in April 1986 at the request of the Justice Department, which was conducting a criminal investigation. Justice closed its case in March without seeking indictments.

At that time, ethics committee leaders said the department's decision was irrelevant to their responsibility to enforce House ethics rules, but they were silent on Boner's case.

An aide said Boner had no comment about the unresolved inquiry. He felt vindicated by the Justice Department's inaction, the aide said. ▮

Winners Have No Trouble Retiring Debts:

Senate Freshmen Rewarded By Post-Election PAC Giving

In politics, as in war, to the victor go the spoils. The Senate's class of 1986 had been meeting a lot of new campaign contributors recently, many of whom showed little interest in the newcomers before they were elected.

A Congressional Quarterly study of reports on file at the Federal Election Commission (FEC) indicated that the new senators elected Nov. 4, 1986, who had net campaign debts managed to retire those debts or significantly reduce them in the first six months of 1987. All but two of the new senators who had campaign surpluses at the end of 1986 added to them in 1987.

The freshmen's good fortune came courtesy of a number of sources, including political action committees (PACs) that had supported their opponents during the 1985-86 election cycle.

According to the FEC reports:

- Thirteen Senate freshmen raised a total of nearly $3.1 million from all sources between Jan. 1 and June 30, 1987.
- PACs provided $1.6 million, or 52.5 percent, of the freshmen's total receipts.
- More than half of the PAC money received by the freshmen came from groups that had supported the recipients' opponents prior to the election.

Switch-Hitting PACs

Reports filed with the FEC by candidates and PACs showed that PACs were eager to contribute to incumbent senators, even if they had been stalwart supporters of those senators' opponents in the past.

Of the $1,603,188 that the 13 freshmen reported receiving from PACs during the six-month period, at least $864,821 — 53.9 percent — was contributed by groups that had provided financial backing to the new senators' opponents.

Some $203,626 of the $864,821 was received from PACs that hedged their bets during the 1985-86 races and contributed to both sides.

But the newly elected senators received at least $661,195 from PACs that had not supported them before the election, contributing instead to their opponents.

"It's called 'correcting a mistake,'" said Larry J. Sabato, professor of government at the University of Virginia, who said he heard the term from PAC managers while he was researching a book on PACs.

"This is a natural complement to the tidal wave of incumbent money given by PACs in the last cycle," Sabato said. "You give the most money to incumbents to ensure access [to elected lawmakers], then in the few cases where incumbents lose, you give quickly to correct your mistakes."

PACs contributed $23.6 million to Senate incumbents running for reelection in 1985-86, compared with $10.1 million given to challengers. Nearly $11.3 million was given to open-seat candidates.

Most of the PACs that switched sides and contributed to the freshmen after the 1986 elections represented business or professional interests.

Among the "switch-hitters" in the Congressional Quarterly survey were PACs sponsored by the Aetna Insurance Company, the American Dental Association, the American Medical Association, Barnett Banks of Florida, Litton Industries, Lockheed Corp. and McDonald's Corp.

PACs that gave to both sides prior to the Senate elections included those sponsored by the National Association of Realtors, Coca-Cola Co., Federal Express Corp. and the J. C. Penney Co.

"I don't look at it as anything new," said Richard A. Armstrong, president of the Public Affairs Council, who nonetheless frowned on such double-giving. The council is an association of public-affairs officers that includes many PAC officials.

Armstrong said that a lot of the PACs that made post-election contributions were trying to "get on the good side" of the new incumbents and "buy some access."

"As a society, we love underdogs but we hate losers," he said. "People like to give to winners."

"Those types of contributions [double-giving] simply give ammunition to critics of PACs who say that PACs do nothing more than buy access, curry favor, or, at worst, buy votes."

—Mick Staton, manager of political action programs, U.S. Chamber of Commerce

Others pointed to the nature of the 1986 elections and the policies followed by PACs in channeling their contributions.

Bernadette A. Budde, director of political education for the Business-Industry Political Action Committee (BIPAC), said many of the races in 1986 featured candidates on both sides that corporate PACs could support. Whom to support in the election "was an agonizing decision for a lot of people in a lot of circumstances," she said.

The American Medical Association's AMPAC, for example, had what officials described as a "friendly incumbent policy," under which the group would support an incumbent with a pro-doctor voting record, even if the challenger also met the group's criteria for support. In the 1986 North

Carolina Senate race, incumbent Republican James T. Broyhill had a good record on the association's issues, so AMPAC gave him $2,000. Winner Sanford, a former governor, also was popular with doctors in the state. So AMPAC gave him $8,000 in January to help retire his debt.

Principles and Practice

Regardless of the reasons for giving to both sides during the campaign, or changing sides afterward, PACs that made such contributions ran the risk of undermining attempts by some pro-PAC groups to present a more positive image for PACs.

In 1986, for example, Armstrong's Public Affairs Council disseminated a set of principles for PACs suggesting, among other things, that they considered the appropriateness of double-giving before making such contributions.

That March, the U.S. Chamber of Commerce, a major defender of PACs, drafted a more explicit set of standards for PACs. The first recommendation was that PACs should "avoid contributing to opposing candidates in general elections." PACs also were urged to avoid helping retire the debts of candidates whose opponents they had supported during the election.

"Those types of contributions simply give ammunition to critics of PACs who say that PACs do nothing more than buy access, curry favor, or, at worst, buy votes," said Mick Staton, a former GOP representative from West Virginia (1981-83), who now is manager of political action programs for the Chamber. "It's tough for us to fight against that ... criticism," Staton said. Organizations such as the Chamber had felt a particular need to fight in 1987.

A Senate bill (S 2) that would limit the amount of money congressional candidates could accept from PACs was stalled by a Republican filibuster. Senate Majority Leader Robert C. Byrd, D-W.Va., a leading advocate of the legislation, said he would not bring the bill to the floor again in 1987, but that the Senate would "revisit" the issue in 1988. He expressed hope that the pressure of an election year would bring more support to his side in 1988.

The bill was viewed by most PACs as an affront and a threat to their activities. However, its presence on the Senate floor had not diminished the fervor of PACs to contribute, nor of incumbents to receive.

Campaign Debts Retired

What all this giving has meant for most of the new senators was an end to their campaign finance worries. On Dec. 31, 1986, nine of the 13 newcomers had net campaign debts; six months later, only four — Christopher S. "Kit" Bond, R-Mo., Thomas A. Daschle, D-S.D., Timothy E. Wirth, D-Colo., and Terry Sanford, D-N.C. — were still in the red.

Contributions received during the first six months of 1987 from all sources — individuals and PACs — transformed the freshmen's combined net debts from slightly more than $1 million on Dec. 31, 1986, to a net surplus of $363,609 on June 30, 1987.

By contrast, a majority of the candidates defeated by the 13 in 1986 were still in debt at the end of June, including former incumbents Broyhill, Mark Andrews, R-N.D., Paula Hawkins, R-Fla., and Mack Mattingly, R-Ga.

"You just simply attract more attention" as an incumbent, said the Chamber's Staton. "People want to be around ... members of Congress." ∎

Realtors Lead in 1985-86 PAC Giving

When Democratic Rep. James R. Jones was running for the Senate in Oklahoma in 1986, the 750,000-member National Association of Realtors decided to lend a hand. The association's political action committee, R-PAC, gave Jones $3,250 and launched an independent-expenditure campaign on his behalf that ended up costing the PAC $515,836.

Then, in the midst of the campaign, R-PAC made another contribution: $5,000 to Sen. Don Nickles, R-Okla., Jones' opponent.

R-PAC was the top contributor of all PACs in 1985-86, giving congressional candidates nearly $2.8 million. In addition, it spent almost $1.9 million in independent expenditures on behalf of its chosen candidates.

The Oklahoma contest was only one of a number of Senate races in which R-PAC gave money to both sides before the Nov. 4, 1986, election or switched candidates and supported the winner after the election.

In five races, R-PAC backed both candidates before the election. The PAC gave $5,000 each to Democrat John B. Breaux and Republican W. Henson Moore in Louisiana; $500 to Democrat Dale Bumpers and $10,000 to Republican Asa Hutchinson in Arkansas; $1,000 to Democrat Harry Reid and $10,000 to Republican Jim Santini in Nevada; and $10,000 to Democrat Richard C. Shelby and $9,500 to Republican Jeremiah Denton in Alabama.

In seven races, the PAC gave money to the winner after Election Day, having supported the loser during the campaign. The beneficiaries of this post-election giving were Brock Adams, D-Wash.; Thomas A. Daschle, D-S.D.; Wyche Fowler Jr., D-Ga.; Bob Graham, D-Fla.; Terry Sanford, D-N.C.; and Timothy E. Wirth, D-Colo.

According to Albert E. Abrahams, senior political consultant for the Realtors, the double-giving and post-election contributing by R-PAC were a matter of internal procedures rather than any set policy.

In the Jones-Nickles race, for example, Abrahams said that an independent panel created within R-PAC to run independent-expenditure campaigns decided to support Jones' candidacy based on the Democrat's support of Realtor issues as a House member. Other R-PAC officials were distressed by the move because Nickles was considered a "friendly incumbent." They authorized the $5,000 contribution to the Republican.

In other cases, Abrahams said that R-PAC's size and structure sometimes led to double-giving. The PAC had 1,900 local boards, which made recommendations to state panels. These, in turn, recommended candidates for support to the national PAC. The fact that the national PAC was supporting one candidate did not prohibit local PAC officials from contributing to other candidates if they were invited to a fund-raiser.

"You'd be surprised at all the factors that are weighed before our decisions are made," said Abrahams, adding that the PAC was reviewing some of its 1985-86 activities, notably double-giving and running independent-expenditure campaigns.

House Refuses to Block Nuclear Plant Openings

Passes Two-Year NRC Reauthorization

After an acrimonious debate and a large-scale lobbying effort, the House Aug. 5, 1987, turned back an effort to stop two nuclear power plants from starting operation.

The 160-261 vote came on an amendment by Edward J. Markey, D-Mass., to an otherwise routine re-authorization (HR 1315) of the National Regulatory Commission (NRC). After defeating the amendment, the House passed HR 1315 by a 389-20 vote.

The Markey amendment was aimed at the Shoreham nuclear plant in Long Island, N.Y., and another nuclear plant in Seabrook, N.H., 10 miles from Massachusetts. Both were complete, but had been unable to meet an NRC rule requiring state and local government agreement with evacuation plans for all people within a 10-mile radius.

The governors of Massachusetts and New York had argued that a mass evacuation in such heavily populated areas is impossible.

The Markey amendment would have barred the NRC from relaxing its rules to let Shoreham and Seabrook generate power. Supporters of the amendment, many of whom represented the plants' neighbors, called the reactors unsafe and said the NRC rule change would violate states' rights.

Opponents, backed by the nation's utilities and the Reagan administration, argued that the Markey amendment would set a precedent that could destroy the nuclear power industry. They said the national interest was at stake because nuclear power was needed to reduce American dependence on foreign oil.

The amendment drew scores of lobbyists and Markey blamed them for the defeat. "The most powerful lobbying group in the country was able to flex its muscles tonight," he said, but he warned that "it would be foolish to say that this is the end of the battle."

Further legislative efforts were planned, but supporters and opponents of the plants, said that the issue would probably be settled by the courts.

Passionate Debate

Proponents of the Markey amendment tried throughout the debate to prove that the bill was not anti-nuclear and would not affect the 107 nuclear plants now in operation. They said Seabrook and Shoreham were unique in that no emergency plan had been found to give local citizens as much protection as the neighbors of other nuclear plants receive.

The Federal Emergency Management Agency (FEMA) had not found satisfactory emergency plans to protect residents around either plant.

Nicholas Mavroules, D-Mass., a cosponsor of the Markey amendment, said Seabrook's location was "the worst geographic area anyone could select as a site for a nuclear power plant." The area has a large summer population served by a single crowded highway.

Supporters of the Markey amendment also complained that evacuees from the Shoreham plant would have to travel over the Long Island Expressway, a thoroughfare that, according to George J. Hochbrueckner, D-N.Y., was recently gridlocked for five hours because of an overturned mayonnaise truck.

State and local officials criticized the emergency plan developed by the owners of the Shoreham plant, the Long Island Illuminating Co. (Lilco). Under the plan, evacuees would go to Nassau Stadium, where they would shower and receive paper suits to replace their contaminated clothing.

Three Democrats from Long Island's Suffolk County — Hochbrueckner, Thomas J. Downey and Robert J. Mrazek — said every elected Suffolk County official and 85 percent of the county's population opposed the plant.

Republican Norman F. Lent, who represents neighboring Nassau County, led the battle against Markey's amendment. He raised the spectre of an energy crisis, asking, "Are our memories so short that we have forgotten the spectacle of President Carter on television wearing his sweater with the fireplace ablaze behind him?"

"We are playing into the hands of the Ayatollah, who, I am sure, is glued to C-SPAN right now, wherever he may be, rooting for the passage of the Markey amendment."

—Norman F. Lent, R-N.Y.

Markey called this argument spurious, and said less than 3 percent of the nation's electrical power comes from imported oil.

Lent attacked Hochbrueckner, who based his 1986 congressional campaign on opposition to Shoreham. "Many of us in this room were elected here on the basis of running against something," he said, "but after we get here a while we calm down a little bit and we try to become statesmen."

Hochbrueckner's predecessor, former GOP Rep. William Carney, was in Washington lobbying on behalf of the utilities during the vote. Carney did not seek re-election in 1986 after his strong support for the Shoreham plant had eroded his chances of winning.

States' Rights

Utility lobbyists and floor opponents of the Markey amendment complained that the affected state and local governments supported — or at least did not oppose — the nuclear reactors until after the utilities had made major investments in them.

Markey argued that the NRC had refused a hearing for 12 years to the state governments of Massachusetts, New Hampshire and New York. Although New Hampshire's government eventually accepted the plant, all three states had criticized the two locations in the early 1970s.

He said the NRC had denied repeatedly that it would be prejudiced by the utilities' investments in their plants, saying the investments were a risk those companies must bear.

However, Markey noted that the NRC is now using cost as a reason for changing its rules. In January of 1987 the NRC said, "A forced abandonment of a completed nuclear plant for which billions of dollars have been invested also poses obvious serious financial consequences to the utility ratepayers and taxpayers." The utilities had spent about $4.8 billion on the Seabrook plant and about $5 billion on Shoreham.

"It is just wrong to allow a federal agency packed with nuclear supporters to change the rules," said Markey.

Supporters of the amendment — most of whom were liberal Democrats — took on an unaccustomed role as defenders of states' rights. "Should this decision rest with millions of citizens through their highest elected state officials or with a handful of bureaucrats here in Washington?" asked Joseph E. Brennan, D-Maine, a former governor of that state.

Carlos J. Moorhead, R-Calif., summed up the opposition view, saying, "The debate . . . is being cast as a classic confrontation between state and federal rights; but the real issue is not rights. It is what to do when a clash of rights threatens the national interests, when compelling national interests must prevail."

Some linked the amendment to U.S. involvement in the Persian Gulf, which they said would not be necessary if the United States depended less on imported oil.

Lent said, "We are playing into the hands of the Ayatollah [Ruhallah Khomeini of Iran], who, I am sure, is glued to C-SPAN right now, wherever he may be, rooting for the passage of the Markey amendment."

Although most Republicans opposed the amendment, the issue raised more regional antagonisms than party conflicts.

Opponents of the Markey amendment said the populations around both nuclear plants should not be allowed to "export their garbage and import their energy."

When Don Ritter, R-Pa., expressed concern for the two areas' economies, should they be denied nuclear electricity, Markey observed that Massachusetts' unemployment rate is half Pennsylvania's. "We are doing quite well, thank you," he said.

Strong Lobbying

Among the Markey forces' appeals was a letter from eight Democratic presidential candidates supporting the amendment and calling the two plants unsafe. But the AFL-CIO, the National Association of Manufacturers and energy organizations opposed the amendment.

Lobbyists on both sides organized groups of "concerned citizens" to make their case to members of Congress. The amendment's proponents came Aug. 3, 1987. About 400 citizens from Massachusetts, New Hampshire and Long Island bent ears and arms in Congress, then held a rally on the Capitol steps.

On Aug. 4, it was the utilities' turn. Fourteen busloads of "Citizens for Shoreham Electricity," which paid for the trip, and 150 volunteers from Seabrook arrived on Capitol Hill with green folders full of photocopied letters for House members.

One group consisted of Roger Wilkinson and Bob Lawrence — both consultants employed by the Shoreham plant — as well as Mark and Jane Potkin with their three children. Mark Potkin, an engineer at the plant, said, "It's a good experience for the kids" to visit Washington. The Potkins' 9-year-old son explained that Shoreham was surrounded by sod-grass farms, not people. Their twin girls, proudly claiming the age of 5½, wore buttons reading, "America needs Shoreham" on their matching star-spangled blouses.

All had boarded a motor coach at 4:30 a.m. for the six-hour ride to Washington. On arrival, they hit the Cannon and Rayburn buildings until noon. Afterwards, most of the 800-odd citizen lobbyists waited to enter the House galleries in lines that stretched through the third-floor corridors nearly to the Senate chamber. The buses returned to Shoreham at one o'clock the following morning.

After the vote, both sides looked to the future. George Edwards, president of the United Illuminating (Seabrook's second largest owner), said the vote "sent a loud and clear message" that the Nuclear Regulatory Commission was in charge of public safety relating to nuclear power plants.

Edwards said Seabrook would submit its own safety plan to the NRC by mid-September, and the plant would probably begin selling power in the latter half of 1988.

Michael Phillips, counsel for the Union of Concerned Scientists, a group that supported the Markey amendment, said a decision Aug. 4 by the U.S. Court of Appeals for the District of Columbia set a precedent that may block the NRC rule. A three-judge panel held that the NRC may not consider the cost of safety features when it sets standards for a nuclear power plant. Instead, the court ruled, it must consider only safety factors.

Edwards said of the NRC rule, "I feel sure that the opponents of Seabrook will appeal anything that's done but that doesn't mean that stays [on the plant's operation] will be granted by the courts."

Both the Long Island Illumination Co. and Seabrook's major owner, the Public Service Co. of New Hampshire, said they were in financial trouble because of their investments in the nuclear plants. The Public Service Co. recently announced that it would raise rates and stop providing new electric hookups until it edges farther away from bankruptcy.

NRC Reauthorization

HR 1315 is a two-year reauthorization of the Nuclear Regulatory Commission. It authorizes $427.8 million for fiscal 1988 and $422.6 million for fiscal 1989.

By voice vote, the House adopted an amendment, by Jim Slattery, D-Kan., requiring nuclear plants to underwrite the entire NRC budget, instead of 75 percent of it, as proposed in the bill. That would mean paying an average of $3.3 million per nuclear plant. The House also approved by voice vote an amendment by Dennis E. Eckart, D-Ohio, to bar the NRC from closing meetings to the public.

HR 1315 was approved by the Interior and the Energy and Commerce Committees. Differences between the two committees' reports were resolved in HR 3037, a clean compromise measure that was then offered as a substitute for the text of HR 1315. ∎

Veterans' Lobbies Showing New Unity on Hill

From the front lines of the veterans' lobbying community came news of a cease-fire.

For much of the last decade, the groups that lobbied Congress on behalf of America's veterans had been torn by hostilities. The conflict — sometimes quiet, sometimes noisy — had pitted several of the oldest, most established pillars of the veterans' community against the Vietnam Veterans of America Inc. (VVA), the small but scrappy new kid on the block.

Leaders of the VVA had long accused the traditional organizations of failing to pay adequate attention to those who served in the military during the war in Vietnam.

Members of the traditional groups — most notably the American Legion, the Veterans of Foreign Wars (VFW) and the Disabled American Veterans (DAV) — disputed that claim, arguing instead that the VVA's leadership was unrepresentative of most Vietnam veterans. They also criticized the VVA for focusing solely on the veterans of one war.

New Unity Emerging

The divisions between the two sides had not entirely disappeared. But the political and cultural gaps that had separated the VVA and the old-line organizations were beginning to narrow. The result was a level of cooperation in the 100th Congress that few would have predicted.

"If they take a position that we consider controversial, we won't hesitate to criticize them," said retired Lt. Col. David J. Passamaneck, national legislative director of the American Veterans of World War II, Korea and Vietnam (AMVETS), a group founded in 1944. "But that hasn't happened recently. It looks like we have an uneasy peace."

"The old adversarial instincts have by and large disappeared," said Steven M. Champlin, a former director of the VVA's Washington, D.C., office who works as a floor assistant to Democratic Rep. Tony Coelho of California, the House majority whip. "We're in a new period now."

Several signposts of the new period emerged on Capitol Hill in 1987.

One example was the "beneficiary travel" bill (HR 2327), which would make certain veterans eligible for compensation if they had to travel to reach a Veterans Administration (VA) medical facility. The bill was approved by the Veterans' Affairs Committee in early June, then sailed through the House by 420-1.

"We talked to people from the American Legion and the Paralyzed Veterans of America on it," said Michael Leaveck, legislative director of the VVA. "Three or four years ago, the other organizations sort of pretended that we didn't exist ... but that kind of session showed that we definitely count these days."

John F. "Rick" Heilman, national legislative director of the DAV, said better communication among veterans' groups helped spur congressional action on legislation designed to improve management of veterans' employment, job training and counseling programs. The House and Senate passed different versions of such legislation (HR 1504, S 999) in 1987.

"I don't routinely call the VVA on an issue," Heilman said. "We're not that comfy yet ... but the kind of contact and rapport we're developing on things like employment issues will lead to knocking down the barriers and continue a spirit of cooperation."

Rep. G. V. "Sonny" Montgomery, D-Miss., chairman of the Veterans' Affairs Committee, agreed. "What I need is them pulling together," Montgomery said. "Lately, that's what they've been doing for the most part."

That kind of spirit will be necessary, lobbyists said, if the groups were to overcome their differences on two important issues on their agenda.

One was the fate of "vet centers," storefront counseling operations that cater primarily to Vietnam veterans. The VVA supported a continuation of the program, created in 1979 and au-

"The kind of contact and rapport we're developing on things like employment issues will lead to knocking down the barriers and continue a spirit of cooperation."

—John F. "Rick" Heilman, legislative director, Disabled American Veterans

"Three or four years ago, the other organizations sort of pretended that we didn't exist."

— Michael Leaveck, legislative director, Vietnam Veterans of America

Vietnam Vets a Growing Force in Congress

As Democratic Rep. David E. Bonior remembered it, the Vietnam-Era Veterans in Congress (VVIC) caucus was born during a meeting with a man in a wheelchair.

The man was Robert O. Muller, a veteran and activist who was paralyzed by a combat injury in Vietnam. "Muller came in to see me, and he laid out to me the [political] situation for Vietnam veterans on the Hill," said Bonior, a five-term House veteran from Michigan who served in the Air Force (1968-72) during the Southeast-Asian war, all of it stateside.

"He laid it out to me," Bonior continued, "and I thought, 'Jesus, this is something that needs to be done.'" Shortly thereafter, Bonior began seeking out fellow Vietnam-era veterans in Congress who were interested in promoting legislation addressing concerns of their fellow veterans.

That meeting took place nearly a decade ago. In the intervening years, the group of 11 members that Bonior helped assemble has more than quadrupled in size and amassed considerable influence.

"They started out as a small group with no seniority," said Steven M. Champlin, a top assistant to House Majority Whip Tony Coelho, D-Calif., who had worked as an aide to Bonior and as Washington office director for the Vietnam Veterans of America Inc. (VVA). "Now they're at 50 plus, and they have the chief deputy whip in the House [Bonior]. They're everywhere."

The VVIC's rise to prominence did not come easily. Founding members said that their early efforts to move legislation pertaining to Vietnam veterans were not well-received on Capitol Hill.

Rep. David E. Bonior

"We went around the [House] Veterans' Committee basically, because they weren't willing to deal with us," recalled Bonior. "[They saw us] as young guys, newer guys. . . . The attitude was, 'A lot of Vietnam veterans are just crybabies, they don't have real needs.'"

"We couldn't get any hearings, any attention," Bonior continued. "So we formed this caucus and we decided to put an agenda together and tried to get things done."

Since then, members of the VVIC managed to get quite a few things done. Aided by a shift in public attitudes and increased interest in Vietnam issues, both on the Veterans' Affairs committees and throughout Congress, the VVIC played a significant part in helping to pass legislation providing compensation to some veterans exposed to the herbicide Agent Orange (PL 98-542), establishing Vietnam readjustment centers (PL 96-22) and inaugurating programs providing Vietnam-era veterans with job training and job counseling (PL 98-77). *(1984 CQ Almanac p. 499; 1979 Almanac p. 522; 1983 Almanac p. 599)*

Only one of the caucus' major priorities had yet to yield a legislative victory: Bonior and a number of other VVIC members had pushed in vain for passage of legislation that would allow veterans to appeal to federal courts decisions by the Veterans Administration denying claims for benefits.

Although such legislation passed the Senate for the fourth time in 1985, it never made it through the House — in large part because of the opposition of Democratic Rep. G. V. "Sonny" Montgomery of Mississippi, chairman of the House Veterans' Affairs Committee. *(1985 Almanac p. 409)*

Not all Vietnam veterans who served in Congress were active in the VVIC. Republican Rep. Tom Ridge of Pennsylvania, who saw combat duty in Vietnam, was one who viewed the caucus somewhat critically.

Rep. Tom Ridge

"It's a little misleading because it would suggest all Vietnam veterans in Congress," Ridge said. "There's a difference between Vietnam-era veterans, and those who actually served there."

Ridge dealt with that distinction by taking matters into his own hands. Shortly after his arrival in the House in 1983, he began searching out fellow members who had seen combat duty in the war.

The result was an informal group of 17, some of whom also participated in the VVIC, that convened occasionally to discuss issues such as the plight of prisoners of war and the effects of Agent Orange from the combat veterans' point of view.

"I did it for no particular reason other than to occasionally get together and talk about mutual interests," Ridge said. "It's really a kindred spirit-type thing more than an attempt to be a prime mover politically."

Ridge bore no animosity toward the VVIC, and pointed out that he had worked with Democratic Rep. Lane Evans of Illinois, the VVIC chairman in the 100th Congress, in an ongoing effort to encourage Vietnam veterans to become more outspoken about Vietnam issues in state legislatures.

Still, some members who had been active in the caucus lament such splintering, and long for a more unified battle force.

"I don't find the cohesion I'd like to see among Vietnam veterans on the Hill," said Democratic Sen. Thomas A. Daschle of South Dakota, who served in the Air Force (in the United States) from 1969-72. "It's more like legislative guerrilla warfare. We take our shots where we can."

thorized through 1987.

Many of the traditional groups would like to bring the functions currently performed by storefront operations under the control of the VA.

Another contentious issue was legislation to give veterans the right to appeal to the federal courts VA decisions denying claims for benefits. The VVA, the only major veterans' group supporting the legislation, had made this judicial review proposal (HR 639) its top legislative priority. The bill had not moved in 1987.

VVA's lobbyists said judicial review would provide a needed check on decisions made by the VA and would ensure that veterans receive their rights of due process. But some traditional groups said that judicial review could create a litigious environment in which it would be more difficult for veterans to receive their benefits.

Decade-Old Conflict

The conflict within the veterans' community dated to 1978, when the Council for Vietnam Veterans was formed by a cadre of Vietnam vets who felt that their cohort had special needs deserving of special attention. A year later, the group's leaders organized chapters across the country, began recruiting members and changed the name to the VVA.

It was not until 1986 — when the VVA won its federal charter and the improved access to key committees and federal agencies that designation brings — that it really received its stamp of legitimacy.

The House initially approved legislation authorizing a VVA charter in 1984. But the Senate did not go along until 1986.

The charter marked the VVA's entry into a community not accustomed to new arrivals. No more than a handful of groups joined the pantheon of federally chartered veterans' groups since the early 1920s, and VVA was the only one focused on veterans of a single conflict.

"They weren't advocating for all veterans," said John Minnick, a spokesman for the American Legion. "They were advocating just for Vietnam-era veterans, to the exclusion of all others. That ... contributed to the hostility."

Political considerations also colored the VVA's initial reception into the veterans' community. The VVA's founder — Robert O. Muller, a Marine infantry lieutenant who was paralyzed as a result of combat in Vietnam — had once offended other veterans by traveling to Hanoi and laying a wreath upon the grave of North Vietnamese leader Ho Chi Minh.

To many, the incident was merely indicative of deeper differences in political philosophy. "The traditional groups ... generally lined up on the conservative side on foreign policy and defense issues," said Sen. John McCain, R-Ariz., a former Navy officer who spent nearly six years as a prisoner of war in Vietnam. "For the newer group of Vietnam veterans, that by and large was not the case."

Critics claimed that the VVA was unrepresentative of most Vietnam veterans, noting that groups such as the American Legion and the VFW have more Vietnam veterans than the 35,000-member VVA.

"If it makes them feel a little better that they can get better representation out there with their 30,000 members rather than with the 2 million we have, that's their privilege," said Cooper T. Holt, executive director of the VFW's Washington office. "It just doesn't make sense to me."

The VVA Viewpoint

But VVA sympathizers saw things differently. They felt strongly that the organization was needed to fill a void on a range of Vietnam-related issues — such as exposure to the herbicide Agent Orange and post-traumatic stress syndrome — created by the indifference of the traditionals.

"When I first arrived in Congress, there was no organization that articulated Vietnam issues," said Sen. Thomas A. Daschle, D-S.D., who served four years in the Air Force during the Vietnam War before his election to the House in 1978.

VVA supporters had different theories about why the group had had trouble fitting in.

"There was only so much in the veterans' budget pie," said Rep. David E. Bonior of Michigan, a founder of the Vietnam-era Veterans in Congress and chief deputy whip for House Democrats.

"We weren't a part of that pie ... and they weren't willing to share," Bonior added.

Another theory was more generational. "The old-line organizations viewed veterans of the Vietnam War as a pretty strange type," said Leaveck of the VVA. "We were a bunch of long-haired, dope-smoking baby killers. It wasn't a real war anyway, you know ... like World War II. In Vietnam, all you did was wander around and burn hooches."

Shifting Strategies

Several forces conspired to improve the climate in the veterans' community — not the least of which was the legislative accomplishments of the VVA. During its early years, the group succeeded in establishing readjustment centers targeted on the Vietnam veteran and getting the VA to recognize post-traumatic stress syndrome as a legitimate basis for veterans' benefit claims.

"At this point, a lot of what we're trying to do is maintain those gains," Leaveck said. "We as an organization are also broadening our perspective and getting into issues that apply to all veterans."

Further, the leaders of the VVA took steps to remove the organization from involvement in debate over defense and foreign policy. In 1985, they amended the group's constitution to prohibit the VVA from taking a position on any issues outside the realm of veterans' affairs. Both of those moves helped mute traditional groups' criticism.

At the same time, there was a gradual shift in the membership of the old-line veterans' organizations. Groups previously dominated by veterans of World War II and Korea were increasingly populated by Vietnam veterans.

Heilman of the DAV noted that roughly one-third of his organization's members were Vietnam veterans, as were "all of the fellows employed here in Washington."

That helped produce an enhanced appreciation of Vietnam-related issues.

"I think there was mutual mistrust that was overcome over time significantly by the selection of Vietnam veterans to head some of these national organizations," said McCain. "I think they have begun to identify."

As time and age took their toll on the veterans of more distant conflicts, that trend was likely to continue — and might someday erase the gap.

"We take them [Vietnam veterans] whether we like them or not," said Passamaneck of AMVETS. "Because the survivability of these organizations depends on them. Once that fact is faced, you can forget about all the other problems." ∎

Veteran Lobbyist Steps Into Another Nomination Fray

It had become almost as much a part of Washington life as cherry blossoms and five-star fund-raisers. A Republican administration seeking to steer a controversial nomination through the Senate turned once again to Tom C. Korologos.

When the genial, 54-year-old veteran lobbyist took his seat Sept. 15, 1987, at the Senate Judiciary Committee hearings on the confirmation of Supreme Court nominee Robert H. Bork, it would mark, by one estimate, his 25th nomination fight of the past seven years.

Nominations are just a sideline in Korologos' career: He is president of Timmons and Company, Inc., a top-flight corporate lobbying outfit. But he made his reputation as the man White House officials turned to when they needed help getting a nominee through the Senate.

That reputation was enhanced by the fact that he nearly always prevailed. He had suffered a nomination-battle defeat when the Senate Judiciary Committee rejected the nomination of William Bradford Reynolds as associate attorney general in 1985. But Korologos was not involved in another major nomination defeat of the Reagan administration, the 1986 rejection of Jefferson B. Sessions III, who was chosen to become a district court judge.

In the Bork fight, Korologos faced what was perhaps the toughest nomination challenge of his career — the most intensely fought Senate-confirmation battle since President Richard M. Nixon was rebuffed on two Supreme Court nominations nearly two decades ago.

With a majority of senators publicly declared against Bork, the outcome seemed preordained. And on Oct. 6, 1987, the Judiciary Committee voted 9-5 to send Bork's name to the floor with a recommendation that it be rejected.

The Bork Fight

Despite his extensive experience with confirmation battles, Korologos said he still marveled at the hue and cry raised over Bork. "The ferocity of the opposition and the supporters is remarkable," Korologos said. "I've never seen anything quite like it."

Korologos was widely credited with devising the administration's strategy of portraying Bork as a moderate, pragmatic man well within the mainstream of American jurisprudence. "He doesn't really have horns, and he's not a right-wing kook," he said. Korologos insisted the White House portrayal was nothing more than the actual Bork.

Though Korologos downplayed his role in helping to craft administration strategy on the Bork nomination, he had played a major role in helping the nominee prepare for the Judiciary Committee proceedings. He had been coaching Bork on how to handle himself and putting him through practice sessions, peppering him with a wide variety of questions that might come up during the hearings.

Korologos came to the Bork fray with a track record that had earned him respect and admiration among lobbyists, White House officials and members of Congress alike.

"I don't know anybody that's done it as he's done it," said former GOP Sen. Charles McC. Mathias Jr. of Maryland (1969-87), who served on the Judiciary Committee and felt Korologos' hand on his shoulder more than a few times. "He's extremely helpful in a variety of situations."

But along with the accolades came questions about his actions. Some of his colleagues expressed concern that Korologos' habit of moving so nonchalantly back and forth between private- and public-sector lobbying could present conflicts of interest. And because he was not officially employed by the White House, he was not subject to laws that restrict corporate lobbying by members of the administration even after they leave office.

Between Two Worlds

Some lobbyists said that it was precisely the practice of moving back and forth between the private and public worlds that accounted for Korologos' success at the nominations game. His position outside the inner circles of the White House gave him added credibility when lobbying on the administration's behalf, they said.

During an earlier battle, White House lobbyist Tom C. Korologos confers with Senate GOP leaders Robert Dole, Kan., center, and Alan K. Simpson, Wyo., right.

"He can say the same thing as the administration, and it's more effective," said one well-placed Republican. "You know it's not just the party line," he said. Others argued that Korologos' careful attention to the Senate was his most important asset.

"He works the Senate exclusively, day in and day out," said Thomas Hale Boggs Jr., himself a powerful Washington lobbyist who is more closely associated with the Democratic Party. "Not that many people do that as intensively as he does."

The fact that Korologos knew many members and administration officials personally — "I've known most of the Reagan team since they were born," he said — didn't hurt. Korologos had been involved in GOP politics in Washington since the early 1960s.

He began his career as a journalist, working for 10 years as a reporter for the Salt Lake *Tribune* in his home state of Utah. But in 1961, following a two-year stint with a Salt Lake City advertising and public relations firm, he signed on as press secretary to conservative Republican Sen. Wallace F. Bennett (1951-74).

He became Bennett's administrative assistant in 1965, and held that job until 1971, when he became a special assistant to President Nixon.

Korologos remained a lobbyist for the Nixon White House until the bitter end; after Nixon resigned in 1974, he assumed a similar position under Gerald R. Ford.

It was not until 1975 that Korologos left the public payroll, joining Timmons and Co., which was founded by former Nixon and Ford aide William E. Timmons. His job involved lobbying Congress on behalf of some of the largest corporate concerns in the country, including Chrysler Corp., Boeing Co., Northrop Corp. and the H. J. Heinz Co.

Korologos learned the ropes of nominations politics while he was still working for the government; in the early 1970s, he helped oversee administration efforts to win congressional approval of Vice Presidents Ford and Nelson A. Rockefeller. He also helped Henry A. Kissinger win confirmation as secretary of state.

During the Reagan era, Korologos shepherded through the Senate the nominations of Edwin Meese III as attorney general, Alexander M. Haig Jr. as secretary of state, William P. Clark as interior secretary, and Kenneth L. Adelman as director of the Arms Control and Disarmament Agency. In 1986, he helped the White House win Senate confirmation of William H. Rehnquist as chief justice of the United States, and aided Antonin Scalia in his bid to fill the associate justice's seat vacated by Rehnquist.

When William H. Rehnquist, left, was nominated in 1986 to become chief justice of the United States, the White House called on lobbyist Tom C. Korologos. Korologos coached Rehnquist through several days of difficult Judiciary Committee hearings.

Pay Is Increased Access

Korologos was fond of pointing out that he was not paid for his efforts on behalf of the White House. But some lobbyists believed he derived from his involvement in nominations benefits that were far more valuable than any salary or fee.

"It gives you an opportunity to renew contacts both within the administration and on the Hill, in a way where you're not hat in hand asking somebody for a favor," said a Republican consultant. "Doing something like that, people expect that at some point in the future their phone calls will be returned and that meetings will be easy to establish."

Others reacted more angrily to the practice, arguing that it was inappropriate for Korologos to approach senators on behalf of a corporate client one day and then on behalf of a White House nomination the next.

"It's outrageous," said Joseph L. Rauh, a longtime Democratic lobbyist who worked to help defeat Nixon Supreme Court nominees Clement F. Haynsworth Jr. and G. Harrold Carswell.

"The White House ought to have its own people doing the nominations," Rauh argued. "It's unethical for a guy who lobbies the White House on some things to be the lobbyist *for* the White House on judicial nominations."

"Extra care has to be taken that the conflict-of-interest question has been adequately resolved," added William Taylor, a civil rights lawyer who was working to defeat Bork's nomination. "We're dealing with a judicial nominee that may affect the interests of corporations or other interests that he [Korologos] may lobby for."

Korologos dismissed such concerns, saying he did not stand to gain any more access to the administration than he already had. "I've helped the White House during the other nominations, during the campaigns. . . . I don't need any more friends in the White House," he said.

The lobbyist's defenders scoffed at the notion that he was engaged in anything unethical.

"That's hogwash," said M. B. Oglesby Jr., former director of the Reagan administration's legislative affairs office. "Everybody has a Kitchen Cabinet. . . . There's nothing wrong with that. . . . Tom is just more visible because of the spotlight on the Bork nomination."

Mathias added, "He's perfectly open about it . . . and I think perhaps that's his saving grace. He never makes any bones about who he's working for. As long as it's all on the record, nobody can doubt where his particular bias is." ▮

SUPREME COURT

Power to Rule Legislation Unconstitutional Exerts Deterrent Effect

Under the United States' system of checks and balances, the Supreme Court stands at the pinnacle of the federal judicial structure as the final reviewing authority of congressional legislation and executive action.

However, as is implicit in a checks-and-balance system of government, the high court and the lower federal judiciary do not function with complete independence. On the one hand, the size, salaries and jurisdiction of the judicial branch are determined by the legislative branch. On the other hand, the membership of the judicial branch is selected by the executive branch.

Federal and State Courts

Two types of judicial systems, state and federal, provide forums for the resolution of disputes. The state judicial systems are composed of the state supreme court, or state court of appeals, intermediate appellate courts and trial courts with general jurisdiction over disputes where most cases of a serious nature begin. In addition, states usually have a group of lower courts, such as municipal, police and justice-of-the-peace courts, which are the lowest courts in the judicial hierarchy and have limited jurisdiction in both civil and criminal cases. The federal system forms a tri-level pyramid, comprised of district courts at the bottom, circuit courts of appeals in the middle, and the Supreme Court at the top. *(Chart, next page)*

Provision for a federal judiciary was made by Article III, Section 1, of the Constitution, which stated: "The judicial power of the United States shall be vested in one supreme court, and in such inferior courts as the Congress may from time to time ordain and establish." Thus, aside from the required "supreme court," the structure of the lower federal judicial system was left entirely to the discretion of Congress.

Congress and Federal Courts

The Judiciary Act of 1789 established the Supreme Court; 13 district courts, each with a single judge; and, above the district courts, three circuit courts, each presided over by one district and two Supreme Court judges. Thereafter, as the nation grew and the federal judiciary's workload increased, Congress established additional circuit and district courts. In 1987 there were 13 circuit courts of appeals, 91 district courts and three territorial courts. Supreme Court justices no longer presided over federal circuit courts; each level of courts had its own judges.

The influence of Congress over the federal judiciary goes beyond the creation of courts. Although the power to appoint federal judges resides with the president, by and with the Senate's advice and consent, the power to create judgeships to which appointments can be made resides with Congress. It is in this area that politics historically plays its most critical role in the federal judicial system. For example, in 1801 the Federalist Congress created additional circuit court judgeships to be filled by a Federalist president. However, in 1802, when the Jeffersonian Republicans came into power, the new posts were abolished.

As federal judges are appointed to serve during good behavior, the power of Congress to abolish judgeships is limited to providing that when one becomes vacant, it cannot be filled. The history of the Supreme Court's size provides the best illustration of the earlier habit of creating and abolishing judgeships. Originally, the Supreme Court was composed of six justices. Subsequently, however, its membership varied: seven justices, 1807-37; nine justices, 1837-63; 10 justices, 1863-66; seven justices, 1866-69; and nine justices since 1869.

Jurisdiction of Federal Courts

Article III, Section 2, of the Constitution vests in the Supreme Court original jurisdiction — the power to hear a case argued for the first time — over only a few kinds of cases. The most important of these are suits between two states, which might concern such issues as water rights or offshore lands. Article III, Section 2, also extends to the court "judicial power" over all cases arising under the Constitution, federal laws and treaties. This jurisdiction, however, is appellate (i.e., limited to review of decisions from lower courts) and is subject to "such exceptions and . . . regulations as Congress shall make."

Most of the high court's present jurisdiction is defined by the Judiciary Act of 1925, largely drafted by the court itself under Chief Justice William Howard Taft. This act made exercise of the court's appellate jurisdiction largely discretionary, giving the justices more leeway to refuse to review cases.

Except for certain limited types of cases in which the court is still "obligated" to take appeals, the court is allowed to decide whether the decisions from the lower courts present questions or conflicts important enough or of such a constitutional nature as to warrant the court's consideration on review.

But only in this way is the court able to control the issues with which it deals. Its power is limited by the fact that it cannot reach out to bring issues before it, but must wait until they are properly presented in a case which has made its way through the lower courts.

In the relationship between federal and state judicial systems, federal courts have jurisdiction over cases relating to federal rights or actions in which the parties are citizens of different states. The state courts, on the other hand, are concerned with cases generally involving citizens of that

Federal Judicial System

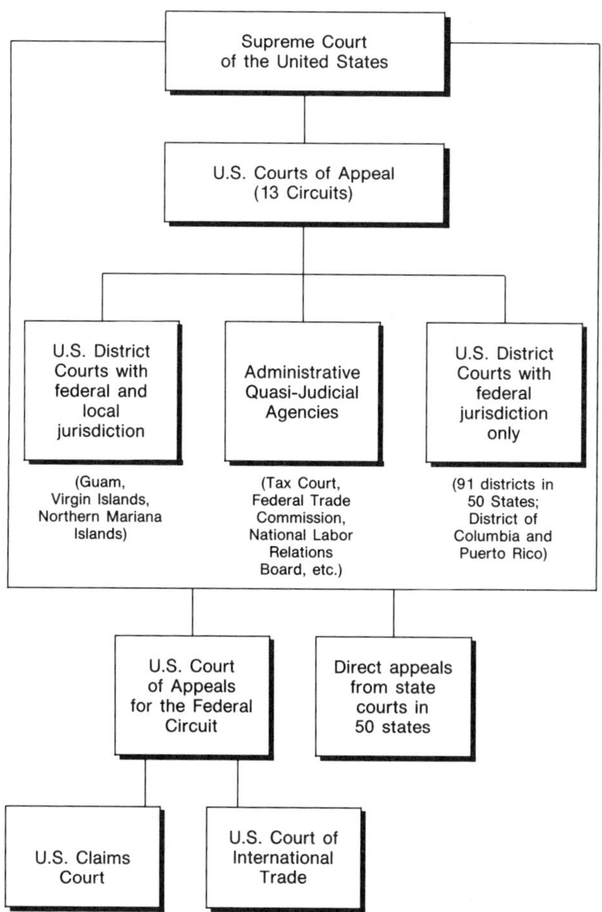

State Judicial System

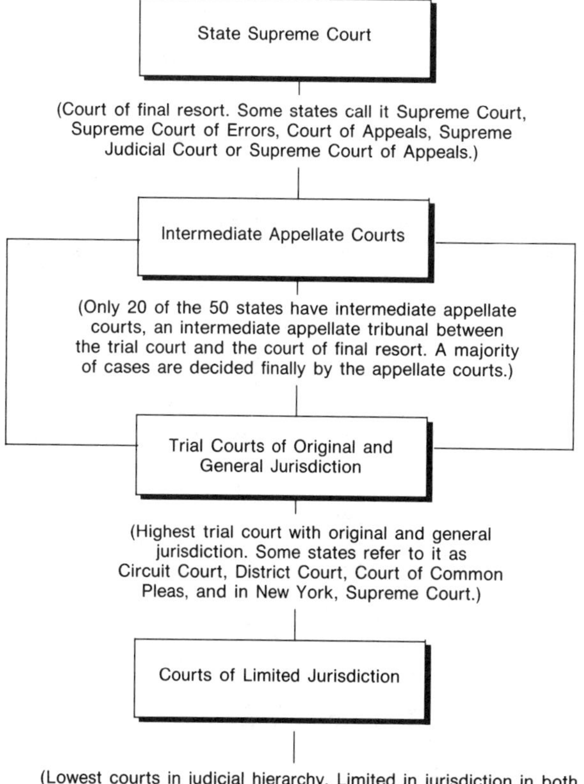

state and their own state laws. There is some overlap of jurisdiction. The state courts are empowered to hear litigation concerning some federal rights, and federal constitutional rights often form the basis of decisions in state court cases.

In the federal courts, where jurisdiction is based on a "diversity of citizenship" (i.e., the litigants are from different states), the court is obliged to apply the pertinent law of the state in which the court is sitting. In state court cases, similarly, in those few instances where a "federal question" might be resolved, the court is obliged to disregard its own precedents and apply appropriate federal law.

The Power of Judicial Review

The Supreme Court exerts a strong restraining influence upon Congress through its power to declare that certain of its legislative acts are unconstitutional and invalid. Although the Constitution does not expressly authorize the court to strike down acts it deems unconstitutional, the court assumed that important authority in 1803 through its own broad interpretation of its vested powers. Without this process, known as judicial review, there would be no assurance (not even in the president's veto) against domination of the government by runaway congressional majorities.

The court has been restrained in its exercise of this power; only a few more than 100 acts of Congress have been declared unconstitutional. Of those invalidated, many were relatively unimportant and others, such as the measures prohibiting the spread of slavery and those carrying out parts of Franklin D. Roosevelt's New Deal program, were replaced by legislation revised so as to pass muster with the Supreme Court.

Most constitutional scholars find the real significance of the Supreme Court's power of judicial review in the awareness of Congress that all of its acts are subject to a final veto by the Supreme Court. With a few exceptions, the court has interpreted the legislature's power to enact specific laws as broadly as it has viewed its own authority to sit in review of the statutes.

The court's traditional approach to its duty of judicial review was outlined in 1827 by one of its first members — Justice Bushrod Washington. Justice Washington observed that "it is but a decent respect due to the wisdom, the integrity and the patriotism of the legislative body, by which any law is passed, to presume in favor of its validity until its violation of the Constitution is proved beyond all reasonable doubt." Justices on almost every court since Justice Washington's day have reaffirmed that attitude.

Changes in Court's Philosophy

Because Supreme Court justices are appointed for life terms, changes in the court's philosophy occur less often than in the other two branches of the federal government.

For its first 150 years, the court served primarily as a bulwark against encroachment on property rights. Even in the 1930s, with the passage of the precedent-shattering legislation aimed at the nation's economic crisis, the court struck down 11 New Deal statutes — the heart of the recovery program. After his re-election in 1936, President Roosevelt threatened to "pack" the court with additional justices who presumably would favor his program. However, before Congress had turned to his proposal, a judicial about-face was under way. The court reinforced its new stance by sustaining re-enactment of much of the New Deal legislation it had previously found unconstitutional.

During the years Earl Warren was Chief Justice (1953-1969), the court consistently sustained individual and minority interests against what many citizens considered to be the best interests of the community. But with Warren's retirement, the pendulum began to swing back. The membership of the court changed. By 1987 only three Warren court justices remained. The court's rulings in the 1970s and 1980s were less protective of individual rights, making clear that they were rarely absolute.

Moreover, in 1976 the court held that Congress exceeded its authority to regulate commerce when it extended the coverage of federal wages and hours legislation to state and local government employees. The action was reminiscent of the court overturning New Deal legislation applying to the private sector of the economy and raised questions about whether the justices in future years would place additional limits on the power of Congress to control the actions of state and local governments.

Sources of Court's Power

Unlike the rebels who framed the Declaration of Independence, the men who met at Philadelphia in 1787 to shape the U.S. Constitution represented conservative financial interests. These interests had suffered heavily during the period of national confederation following the Revolution, when state legislatures, controlled mostly by agrarian interests, made repeated assaults on vested rights.

While the framers of the Constitution deprecated the excesses of the legislatures, they held a high respect for the courts, which gave judgments in favor of creditors and sent delinquent debtors to jail. As political scientist Charles A. Beard, a leading constitutional scholar, once put it in his book *The Supreme Court and the Constitution:* "The conservative interests, made desperate by the imbecilities of the Confederation and harried by the state legislatures, roused themselves from their lethargy, drew together in a mighty effort to establish a government that would be strong enough to pay the national debt, regulate interstate and foreign commerce, provide for national defense, prevent fluctuations in the currency created by paper emissions, and control the propensities of legislative majorities to attack private rights."

At the time the framers met, judicial review had not yet been instituted in any country in the world. And despite considerable discussion of some means to check the excesses of Congress, the matter of a judicial veto never came up for a direct vote. Wilfred E. Binkley and Malcolm C. Moos have pointed out in their book *A Grammar of American Politics* that there were matters the delegates "dared not baldly assert in the Constitution without imperiling its ratification, but they doubtless hoped that implications would eventually be interpreted to supply the thing desired." Judicial review appeared to be one of those things. Most other constitutional scholars have supported this view.

In *The Federalist,* a series of essays written to promote adoption of the Constitution, Alexander Hamilton made clear that the framers expected the judiciary to rule on constitutional issues. In Number 78 of *The Federalist,* Hamilton wrote: "The complete independence of the courts of justice is peculiarly essential in a limited constitution. By a limited constitution, I understand one which contains certain specified exceptions to the legislative authority, such for instance, as that it shall pass no bills of attainder, no ex post facto laws, and the like. Limitations of this kind can be preserved in practice no other way than through the courts of justice, whose duty it must be to declare all acts contrary to the manifest tenor of the Constitution void. Without this, all the reservations of particular rights or privileges would amount to nothing."

Asserting the power of judicial review for the first time, the court in the 1803 case of *Marbury v. Madison* struck down a portion of the same Judiciary Act that had granted it the power to review state court rulings. The offending section, wrote Chief Justice John Marshall, purported to enlarge the original jurisdiction of the court — and that Congress had no power to do.

The court's power to review the acts of Congress has since become firmly established in practice. Binkley and Moos asserted: "Whether or not the Supreme Court 'usurped' the practice of judicial review is now purely an academic question. So completely has the practice been woven into the warp and woof of our constitutional fabric that the garment could now scarcely endure its elimination."

Court-Curbing Proposals

Intermittently throughout American history, congressional critics of judicial power have sought to impose restrictions on the Supreme Court. The methods have ranged from proposed curbs on the court's authority to the Senate's rejection of court nominees.

Early Proposals

Charles Warren details the circumstances of the first move against the court in his study *The Supreme Court.* In 1802 the newly elected Congress dominated by Jeffersonian Republicans abolished the additional federal circuit courts set up the year before by the old Congress and staffed with 16 Federalist judges (the "midnight judges") appointed by President Adams on the eve of his departure from office. To delay a decision in the *Marbury* and other controversial cases, Congress also enacted legislation postponing the Supreme Court's term for 14 months, until February 1803. In 1805 Rep. John Randolph, a Virginia Republican, proposed a constitutional amendment providing for removal of Supreme Court justices by the president upon the approval of both houses of Congress. However, Randolph's proposal attracted little support and was dropped.

In the 1820s and early 1830s controversial decisions expanding the powers of the national government at the expense of state sovereignty led Congress to try unsuccessfully to remove the court's jurisdiction to hear cases challenging the validity of state laws. Repeal of this power would have prevented the court from reviewing the validity of any state law and would have resulted in conflict and confusion among the states. The proposals were, however, soundly defeated in the House in 1831.

In a later study, *Congress, The Constitution and Supreme Court,* Warren discusses another series of attacks on the court launched in the early 1900s by critics of the court's decisions protecting property rights. In 1923 Sen. William E. Borah, R-Idaho, introduced a bill to require concurrence by seven of the nine justices to invalidate an act of Congress. The following year Sen. Robert M. La Follette, R-Wis., proposed a constitutional amendment providing that a statute once struck down by the Supreme Court could be declared constitutional and immune from further court consideration by a two-thirds majority of both houses of Congress. Neither the Borah nor the La Follette proposal received serious consideration.

After Congress rejected the Roosevelt court-packing plan in 1937, the Supreme Court experienced a period of relatively placid relations with Congress until the Warren court launched on its course of judicial activism in the mid-1950s. The only proposed curb on the court that attracted much support from the mid-1930s to the early 1950s was a 1953 proposal to amend the Constitution to make retirement mandatory for all federal judges at age 75. The resolution proposing the amendment, suggested by the American Bar Association, was adopted by the Senate in 1954 but was shelved by the House.

Attacks on the Warren Court

Warren began his career on the court by writing the opinion declaring segregation in public schools unconstitutional. Under his guidance the court — often by narrow margins — sustained procedural rights for alleged wrongdoers and criminals, upheld the civil rights of blacks and other racial minorities, granted First Amendment protections to alleged subversives, narrowly defined what material was obscene and could therefore be banned, prohibited officially prescribed prayer and religious obsrvances in public schools and ordered state legislatures to reapportion on the basis of "one person, one vote."

Each of these decisions outraged some segment of the population. Responding to their constituents and their own more conservative political and social philosophies, several groups in Congress tried to curb the Warren court, but very few of these attempts were successful and even fewer had any real effect on the court. Efforts to cut back the court's jurisdiction to review certain kinds of federal and state legislation failed, as did several attempts to reverse specific decisions by legislation or constitutional amendment. Congress did succeed in reversing one decision relating to subversive activities and in modifying three decisions relating to criminal procedures in federal courts.

The court of the 1970s and 1980s had a significantly more consvative cast than the Warren court. Nonetheless, a few of the decisions in the 1970s, including acceptance of forced busing as a method to achieve racial segregation in public schools and its bar on state prohibition of abortions, have elicited loud but ineffective calls from Congress for statutory reversal and jurisdictional curbs on the court.

While Congress has rarely been successful — outside of reversing decisions by legislation — in directly pressuring the court, it is impossible to measure how much, if any, indirect pressure consideration of court-limiting proposals places on the court. Perhaps the overall impact of such congressional efforts has been not to weaken the court's authority but to strengthen it. Each time Congress attempts to curb the court and fails, the public perception is heightened that the court as an institution is unassailable and that its decisions, except in extreme circumstances, are final.

Congressional Reversals of Rulings

Of all its methods of influencing the Supreme Court, Congress has had the most success in reversing individual rulings either through adoption of a constitutional amendment or passage of legislation.

Four of the 26 amendments to the Constitution were adopted specifically to overrule the Supreme Court's interpretation of that document. The amendments reversed the court's rulings on the ability of citizens of one state to bring suit against another state, the status of blacks as citizens, the income tax and the 18-year-old vote.

But it is difficult and time-consuming to amend the Constitution. Each chamber of Congress must approve the proposed amendment by a two-thirds vote and it must then be ratified by three-fourths of all the states. Moreover, there is longstanding and deeply held sentiment that amendments to the Constitution should not be adopted every time there is a significant disagreement with a Supreme Court ruling. As a result, most proposals for such constitutional amendments never emerge from Congress.

The more frequent — and more successful — way of reversing the Supreme Court is for Congress to repass the offending statute after modifying it to meet the court's objections. This kind of reversal through simple legislation is easily accomplished if the court has interpreted a statute contrary to the construction intended by Congress. The House and Senate may then pass new legislation explicitly setting forth their intention. In many cases of this type, the court in its opinion will suggest the course the legislation should take to achieve its original purpose.

Reversal is not so easily accomplished when the court and Congress are at politically philosophical odds. Twice in the early 1900s Congress passed legislation to end child labor, for example, and twice the Supreme Court ruled that such legislation was not within Congress' power to enact. That its interpretation was based on philosophical differences rather than constitutional considerations was evident when the court reversed these two decisions several years later. In the mid-1930s it appeared that a similar confrontation would develop over New Deal legislation, but the court's re-examination of its position on congressional authority to regulate economic matters eased the crisis.

Not all attempts at congressional reversal are successful. In June 1984, the House approved legislation to overturn a court ruling on Title IX of the 1972 Education Amendments. On Feb. 28, 1984, the court stated that Title IX's general ban on sex discrimination does not apply to all school activities, but only to the particular program receiving funds. The legislation, however, failed to be approved by the Senate before adjournment of the 98th Congress.

Court Nominees

Congress exerts influence over the judiciary in another major way — through the Senate's prerogative to "advise and consent" in the president's selection of candidates for judicial offices, including not only Supreme Court justices but also other federal court judges.

Patronage

The power to name members of the federal judiciary — to well-paid, prestigious, lifetime posts — is perhaps the strongest patronage lever possessed by an incumbent president. As a result federal judgeships traditionally go to persons of the president's political party, despite the stated intention of almost every chief executive to make non-partisan judicial appointments.

In apparent contradiction of the American ideal of an independent non-partisan judiciary, the process of selecting federal judges is pure politics. No constitutional guidelines exist beyond the provision that the president "shall nominate, and by and with the advice and consent of the Senate, shall appoint . . . judges of the Supreme Court, and all other officers of the United States. . . ."

Only custom dictates that the president nominate and the Senate confirm federal judges below the Supreme Court level. Only tradition requires that federal judges reside in their districts or that they be attorneys.

The president has complete independence in selecting his Supreme Court nominees, but since 1840 tradition has awarded to senators of the president's party the prerogative of selecting persons for vacant or newly-created federal judgeships within their states. If there are no senators of the appropriate party from that state, the White House usually looks to its party organization in the state for suggested nominess.

Senatorial recommendations carry less weight in the choice of persons for seats on the courts of appeals, each of which has jurisdiction over cases from a number of states. On most circuit courts of appeals, however, it is traditional that each state have a certain representation on the court at all times.

Once the nomination is made, it is sent from the White House to the Senate, and referred to the Senate Judiciary Committee. Hearings are held on virtually every nomination, but they are rarely more than perfunctory proceedings of brief length. The Senate committee then routinely recommends that the Senate confirm the nominees, which usually occurs by voice vote and without debate.

Senatorial Courtesy

Prior to confirmation, a senator can object to a nominee for specific reasons or using the stock, but rare, objection that the nominee is "personally obnoxious" to him. The Senate is most reluctant to confirm a nominee who is repugnant to a senator of the nominee's home state. In this case, the other senators usually join in blocking confirmation out of courtesy to their colleague.

This practice of "senatorial courtesy" began as early as 1789 when the Senate refused to confirm Benjamin Fishbourn, nominated naval officer for the port of Savannah, Ga., by George Washington. More recently, in 1976, the Senate Judiciary Committee tabled, and thereby killed, President Ford's nomination of William B. Poff to a federal judgeship in Virginia, a selection objected to by Sen. William Lloyd Scott, R-Va.

Recess Appointments

Aside from the regular appointment route outlined above, a president can make a "recess" appointment to the Supreme Court or any other federal court vacancy. The Constitution states that "The President shall have the power to fill up all vacancies that may happen during the recess of the Senate, by granting commissions which shall expire at the end of their next session."

The president can fill a vacant post while Congress is not in session and the new judge can take his seat without confirmation. When Congress reconvenes, the president has 40 days within which to submit the recess appointee's name for confirmation. If he does not do so, the judge's pay is terminated. If the name is submitted, but Congress fails to confirm or reject the nomination during the session, the appointment is good until Congress adjourns.

Chief Justice Earl Warren and Justices William J. Brennan Jr. and Potter Stewart were the last three men to accept recess appointments to the Supreme Court.

Rejection of Nominees

Starting with George Washington, 16 presidents have seen 26 of their nominees for the Supreme Court fail to win Senate confirmation — among a total of 140 appointments. One nominee, Edward King, failed to be confirmed despite two attempts in 1844, for a total of 27 unsuccessful nominations. Twelve of the 27 nominations were rejected outright, and the others were withdrawn or allowed to lapse in the face of Senate opposition. In contrast, only eight Cabinet nominees have been rejected by the Senate. The last time a Cabinet nomination was rejected was in 1959, when Senate Democrats refused to approve President Eisenhower's selection of Lewis L. Strauss as secretary of commerce.

Although Congress also has authority to remove federal judges by impeachment, only one such attempt with respect to a Supreme Court justice has moved past the preliminary stage, and that attempt failed. In 1804 the House impeached Justice Samuel Chase, a staunch Federalist who had rankled Republicans with his partisan political statements and his vigorous prosecution of the Sedition Act, which had finally been repealed in 1802. But Chase was not convicted by the Senate even though his opponents obtained a majority on three of the eight articles of impeachment. (A total of 23 senators — two-thirds of the Senate — was necessary for conviction. The greatest number of votes for conviction on any of the articles was 19.) After the trial, President Jefferson, a strong foe of the Federalist-dominated court, criticized impeachment as "a bungling way of removing judges" and "a farce which will not be tried again" in a letter of Sept. 6, 1819, cited in Warren's book *The Supreme Court in United States History*.

Senate rejection of court nominations was common in the 19th century, when political ideology often colored the confirmation process. But from 1900 to 1968 the Senate refused a seat on the Supreme Court to only one man, John J. Parker in 1930. Then, in a 19-month period from late 1968 to early 1970, the Senate refused to approve four Supreme Court nominees — Abe Fortas and Homer Thornberry, nominated by President Johnson, and G. Harrold Carswell and Clement F. Haynsworth Jr. nominated by President Nixon.

Fortas, already an associate justice, had been nominated for chief justice. Thornberry was to take his place as an associate justice. The Senate's refusal to take up the

Fortas and Thornberry nominations resulted largely from Fortas' affirmative votes in some of the most controversial decisions of the Warren court and from the desire of Senate Republicans to have a Republican president name the new chief justice.

President Nixon's 1970 appointment of Carswell was rejected largely because of Carswell's mediocre judicial record. Haynsworth, although well-qualified judicially, was rejected in part because he appeared insensitive to ethical improprieties and participated in cases where his financial interest might have involved him in conflicts of interest.

In 1987 Robert H. Bork, nominated by President Reagan, became the first nominee to be rejected by the Senate since 1970.

Despite the low incidence of rejection for most of the 20th century, at least four other court nominations faced stiff opposition — those of Louis D. Brandeis in 1916, Harlan F. Stone in 1925, Charles Evans Hughes in 1930, Thurgood Marshall in 1967, and William Rehnquist in 1971.

Opposition to the Brandeis' nomination focused on his liberal economic, political and social posture. However, there is also evidence that much of the opposition was motivated by anti-Semitic prejudice.

At the time of his nomination, Stone was attorney general and was in the midst of concluding a prosecution in an oil-land fraud against Burton K. Wheeler, a recently elected and influential Democratic senator from Montana. Wheeler, although eventually acquitted of the charges, vigorously fought Stone's nomination on the Senate floor. Stone then personally appeared before the committee, something no previous Supreme Court nominee had done. Subjected to hostile questioning, Stones' performance was impressive, and the committee recommended that he be confirmed.

In 1967, President Johnson ran into stubborn opposition when he named Marshall to become the first black to sit on the Supreme Court. Influential southern senators argued that Marshall was a judicial activist whose liberal leanings would upset the court's balance. But the Southerners were in a minority and Marshall was confirmed.

Nixon ran into trouble when he named Rehnquist to the court in 1971. Liberals went on the attack, focusing on Rehnquist's conservative record on civil rights and civil liberties issues. Attention centered in particular on a memorandum Rehnquist wrote as a law clerk favoring separate but equal schools for blacks. But Rehnquist rebuted his critic's charges — insisting that the memo did not reflect his personal views — and Rehnquist was confirmed. The same criticisms were brought up when Rehnquist was nominated for chief justice by Reagan in 1986. Rehnquist was again confirmed but had more votes cast against him to be chief justice than any other successful Supreme Court nominee in the 20th century.

Senate Debates, Then Dispatches Bork, 42-58

The Senate Oct. 23, 1987, formally rejected the doomed Supreme Court nomination of Robert H. Bork after 23 hours of rhetoric that ranged from speeches on the history of the Constitution to acerbic denunciations of Bork's opponents. The vote was 42-58.

When the debate began, 54 senators had already declared their opposition to Bork. Thirty-nine had expressed support and only seven were officially uncommitted. Four of the uncommitted — Sam Nunn, D-Ga.; William Proxmire, D-Wis.; John C. Stennis, D-Miss.; and John W. Warner, R-Va. — voted against Bork, while three — Frank H. Murkowski, R-Alaska; William V. Roth Jr., R-Del.; and Dave Durenberger, R-Minn. — voted in favor of confirmation. *(Vote breakdown, p. 105)*

President Reagan quickly issued a statement expressing disappointment with the Bork vote and promising to appoint another nominee from the conservative mold. "My next nominee will share Judge Bork's belief in judicial restraint — that a judge is bound by the Constitution to interpret laws, not make them," he said.

On Oct. 29, Reagan nominated Judge Douglas H. Ginsburg to fill the seat of Justice Lewis F. Powell Jr., who retired June 26. Nine days later, Ginsburg, a federal appeals court judge in the District of Columbia, withdrew his nomination after disclosures that he had used marijuana while a law professor at Harvard.

Reagan's third choice for Powell's seat was Judge Anthony M. Kennedy. The 51-year-old Kennedy had been a judge on the U.S. 9th Circuit Court of Appeals for 12 years.

Judiciary Committee Democrats said it would be difficult to begin hearings before January 1988 because of the time required for the FBI check and a review of Kennedy's credentials by the American Bar Association.

After the Bork vote, Majority Leader Robert C. Byrd, D-W.Va., said it was time to "start the healing, to lower our voices." Bork's supporters said they were pleased that the debate had been held. "It was the correct thing," said Orrin G. Hatch, R-Utah. "There was a record made."

Bork's supporters had hoped that by taking their case to the Senate floor and questioning the entire confirmation process, they could convince senators that the political fight over Bork was inappropriate and should not be repeated. In doing so they hoped to ease the way for the next nominee.

But Democrats warned there would be no free rides. "This Senate is not going to buckle under because of political pressure," said Arizona Democrat Dennis DeConcini Oct. 22. "We are going to make our own judgments, and some outside this body are going to disagree with our judgment. But we are going to make it based on what we think is right."

Bork, a 60-year-old federal appeals court judge who was nominated by Reagan July 1, 1987, insisted on a Senate vote even though he said he had "no illusions" about the outcome. The Judiciary Committee voted 9-5 Oct. 6 to send his nomination to the floor with a recommendation that it be defeated. Bork became the first Supreme Court nominee to be rejected by the Senate since 1970.

By the time the Senate began its debate Oct. 21, the Bork nomination had been overtaken by more urgent concerns — the collapse on Wall Street and the escalating hostilities in the Persian Gulf. And the Bork debate seemed both irrelevant and anticlimactic.

Even Reagan, who had called the Bork nomination his highest priority, dropped out before the end. He made one five-minute speech about Bork Oct. 14, but then did not mention Bork's name again until he was asked about it at the end of his Oct. 22 news conference.

The debate that finally occurred on the Senate floor wasn't really a debate at all, but a succession of speeches by proponents and opponents.

The nominee's supporters spent most of their time focusing on events that happened outside the Senate, while Bork's opponents sought to confine their remarks to the 12 days of Judiciary Committee hearings and Bork's extensive writings and speeches.

Within moments of Bork's rejection, President Reagan promised to nominate another jurist who will "share Judge Bork's belief in judicial restraint."

William L. Armstrong, R-Colo., argued that concentration on events outside the Senate was appropriate because of a "deliberate, calculated strategy" by interest groups opposing Bork "to move the focus of the debate out of this chamber, out of the Senate, into the public arena."

Armstrong said he had no quarrel with groups getting involved in Senate matters, but, he said, "what is not proper is the vicious personal nature of that attack [on Bork] and the untruthfulness of it."

Armstrong and Bork's other supporters were referring to advertisements purchased by groups like Planned Parenthood Inc., the National Abortion Rights Action League (NARAL), and People for the American Way, a liberal interest group founded by television producer Norman Lear. These ads asserted that Bork's conservative views would threaten the advances made by women, blacks and other minorities over the past 20 years.

The ad distributed by People for the American Way, for example, was entitled "Robert Bork vs. the People," and charged that Bork supported a policy requiring workers to be sterilized, would deny disadvantaged individuals the right to file lawsuits and would eliminate the right to privacy.

Hatch claimed the ads were a campaign of "distortion and ridicule" that "mischaracterize, misconstrue and mislead." He said the NARAL ad, which talked about women's rights, had 84 inaccuracies, and the Planned Parenthood ad, which discussed the same general subject, had 99.

Other senators were equally harsh in their remarks. Steve Symms, R-Idaho, accused "liberal propagandists" of engaging in "character assassination" against Bork. Charles E. Grassley, R-Iowa, charged that the judge's detractors "spent millions to willfully smear an American citizen," and Gordon J. Humphrey, R-N.H., called them "a dozen clamoring special-interest groups with selfish agendas screaming for Judge Bork's scalp."

All of these groups defended their ads in point-by-point rebuttals that were distributed to senators. And during the evening of Oct. 21, in one of the few real exchanges between senators, Judiciary Chairman Joseph R. Biden Jr., D-Del., debated with Armstrong about the correctness of some of the ads.

Citing several public-opinion polls, Biden contended that the ads had little effect on the senators and on the general public. He noted that after Bork's testimony, which was televised live, the nominee's negative ratings with the public increased.

"All the money spent on advertising against Judge Bork could not have purchased one half of a day of the live coverage the networks gave to [Bork]," Biden said, "and they covered everything Judge Bork did live and in color. . . . I am told that tens of millions of people watched Judge Bork . . . unfiltered by any senator, unfiltered by the news media, and drew a conclusion."

Politics and the Court

When Republicans complained that the process had been "politi-

Vote on Bork

The Senate Oct. 23 rejected the nomination of Robert H. Bork to be an associate justice of the Supreme Court. The vote was 42-58.

VOTING FOR CONFIRMATION (42)

Democrats (2)

David L. Boren, Okla.
Ernest F. Hollings, S.C.

Republicans (40)

William L. Armstrong, Colo.
Christopher S. "Kit" Bond, Mo.
Rudy Boschwitz, Minn.
Thad Cochran, Miss.
William S. Cohen, Maine
Alfonse M. D'Amato, N.Y.
John C. Danforth, Mo.
Robert Dole, Kan.
Pete V. Domenici, N.M.
Dave Durenberger, Minn.
Daniel J. Evans, Wash.
Jake Garn, Utah
Phil Gramm, Texas
Charles E. Grassley, Iowa
Orrin G. Hatch, Utah
Mark O. Hatfield, Ore.
Chic Hecht, Nev.
John Heinz, Pa.
Jesse Helms, N.C.
Gordon J. Humphrey, N.H.
David Karnes, Neb.
Nancy Landon Kassebaum, Kan.
Bob Kasten, Wis.
Richard G. Lugar, Ind.
John McCain, Ariz.
James A. McClure, Idaho
Mitch McConnell, Ky.
Frank H. Murkowski, Alaska
Don Nickles, Okla.
Larry Pressler, S.D.
Dan Quayle, Ind.
William V. Roth Jr., Del.
Warren B. Rudman, N.H.
Alan K. Simpson, Wyo.
Ted Stevens, Alaska
Steve Symms, Idaho
Strom Thurmond, S.C.
Paul S. Trible Jr., Va.
Malcolm Wallop, Wyo.
Pete Wilson, Calif.

VOTING AGAINST CONFIRMATION (58)

Democrats (52)

Brock Adams, Wash.
Max Baucus, Mont.
Lloyd Bentsen, Texas
Joseph R. Biden Jr., Del.
Jeff Bingaman, N.M.
Bill Bradley, N.J.
John B. Breaux, La.
Dale Bumpers, Ark.
Quentin N. Burdick, N.D.
Robert C. Byrd, W.Va.
Lawton Chiles, Fla.
Kent Conrad, N.D.
Alan Cranston, Calif.
Thomas A. Daschle, S.D.
Dennis DeConcini, Ariz.
Alan J. Dixon, Ill.
Christopher J. Dodd, Conn.
J. James Exon, Neb.
Wendell H. Ford, Ky.
Wyche Fowler Jr., Ga.
John Glenn, Ohio
Albert Gore Jr., Tenn.
Bob Graham, Fla.
Tom Harkin, Iowa
Howell Heflin, Ala.
Daniel K. Inouye, Hawaii
J. Bennett Johnston, La.
Edward M. Kennedy, Mass.
John Kerry, Mass.
Frank R. Lautenberg, N.J.
Patrick J. Leahy, Vt.
Carl Levin, Mich.
Spark M. Matsunaga, Hawaii
John Melcher, Mont.
Howard M. Metzenbaum, Ohio
Barbara A. Mikulski, Md.
George J. Mitchell, Maine
Daniel Patrick Moynihan, N.Y.
Sam Nunn, Ga.
Claiborne Pell, R.I.
William Proxmire, Wis.
David Pryor, Ark.
Harry Reid, Nev.
Donald W. Riegle Jr., Mich.
John D. Rockefeller IV, W.Va.
Terry Sanford, N.C.
Paul S. Sarbanes, Md.
Jim Sasser, Tenn.
Richard C. Shelby, Ala.
Paul Simon, Ill.
John C. Stennis, Miss.
Timothy E. Wirth, Colo.

Republicans (6)

John H. Chafee, R.I.
Bob Packwood, Ore.
Arlen Specter, Pa.
Robert T. Stafford, Vt.
John W. Warner, Va.
Lowell P. Weicker Jr., Conn.

cized," Democrats retorted that it was Reagan who had injected politics into the judiciary, not the Senate.

They cited campaign speeches last year in the South in which Reagan urged voters to send Republicans to the Senate so they could help put conservative judges on the federal bench.

"Any politicizing has been driven by President Reagan's single-minded pursuit of a judiciary packed with those who are his ideological allies."

—Sen. Joseph R. Biden Jr., D-Del.

"Any politicizing has been driven by President Reagan's single-minded pursuit of a judiciary packed with those who are his ideological allies," Biden said.

George J. Mitchell, D-Maine, said the Bork nomination was not the first time the Senate had been embroiled in a political fight over judges. He referred to the 1968 fight over President Lyndon B. Johnson's nomination of Justice Abe Fortas to be chief justice.

Fortas was blocked by a filibuster, and, Mitchell said, a group of Republicans that year said flatly that no nominee was going to get through before the November elections. "For raw politics," Mitchell said, "this fight doesn't even come close to the Fortas fight."

Biden defended the committee process and said that senators cannot be blamed for things out of their control and out of the Senate.

He and his Democratic colleagues sought to focus on Bork's record. Biden maintained that his "antiseptic" view of the Constitution was unacceptable to the country.

Several senators repeatedly focused on Bork's criticism in 1963 — later retracted — of proposed open-housing legislation. Although Bork changed his view, senators contended that it was still important how he reacted when the issue was alive and hotly debated in Congress and the country.

They also focused on his now-famous 1971 Indiana University law review article proclaiming "neutral principles" for interpreting the Constitution and suggesting that only political speech was protected by the First Amendment.

Senators also expressed concern about Bork's criticism of Supreme Court decisions concerning abortion and contraceptives that were based on an implied right of privacy in the Constitution. Bork testified that he believed the Constitution covers certain privacy rights, but he insisted that the court had used faulty legal reasoning and that he could find no support for the decisions in the Constitution.

Malcolm Wallop, R-Wyo., took direct aim at his Democratic colleagues, especially those on the Judiciary Committee. He challenged a statement by Patrick J. Leahy, D-Vt., that after exhaustive hearings the committee had "come to a conclusion" about Bork. "I do not think that is the case," Wallop said. "I think the committee started with a conclusion and came to a justification."

Intimidation

Humphrey spent much of his time on the Senate floor charging that Bork opponents had intimidated pro-Bork witnesses. He called the alleged behavior scandalous and said it smacked of Ku Klux Klan tactics.

He was referring in particular to an incident involving a call from Linda Greene, a black aide to Howard M. Metzenbaum, D-Ohio, to a black law professor, John T. Baker, who had been scheduled to testify for Bork. Baker decided not to testify. Greene had known Baker for years as a friend and professional associate.

He is now an Indiana University Law School professor, but had previously been the dean of Howard University Law School. He left the school under controversial circumstances that involved a dispute over students' academic records.

Greene said she called Baker on her own as a friend to ask him, as she put it in an Oct. 19 letter to Metzenbaum, whether he was "fully prepared to respond to all the issues likely to be raised by his testimony." Greene told *The New York Times* that she told Baker that Democrats on the Judiciary Committee were playing "hardball" and were likely to raise some embarrassing questions about the controversy at Howard. But Greene maintained that she did not seek to keep him from testifying.

After inquiries from the Times, Baker wrote a letter to Metzenbaum stating that "I bear complete responsibility for my decision [not to testify]. I would resent any attempt to attribute my position on Judge Bork . . . to the influence of any other person."

Humphrey called the explanation of the event "perfectly preposterous. . . . Are we really to believe that the Senate aide considered a law-school professor incompetent to testify? Are we supposed to believe

The nomination was defeated by "a dozen clamoring special-interest groups with selfish agendas screaming for Judge Bork's scalp."

—Sen. Gordon J. Humphrey, R-N.H.

that excuse?" Humphrey asked for a Judiciary Committee investigation, which was begun immediately.

Metzenbaum defended Greene as an able, intelligent aide, saying at worst she made a judgment error. A White House official also said that administration people working on the nomination knew about the Baker matter, but decided there was "nothing to it." ▮

Partisans Debate a Complex Legal Mind

He is a scholar and an intellect, an advocate of judicial restraint who would not significantly change the balance on the Supreme Court.

He is a judicial activist who would use the Supreme Court to achieve conservative political ends, reversing decades of court decisions.

Who is Robert Bork? That question dominated the debate since President Reagan nominated the 60-year-old federal appeals court judge to the Supreme Court July 1, 1987, to replace Justice Lewis F. Powell Jr., a centrist and important swing vote on the court during his 16-year tenure.

Since Bork was nominated, there were more than a half-dozen exhaustive studies of his writings, speeches and court decisions. But they tended to obscure the record more than illuminate it. Supporters and critics looked at the same record and came to vastly different conclusions.

Bork's supporters portrayed him as a scholar who practices "judicial restraint" — the term used to describe a limited role for federal judges who generally defer to Congress and state legislatures except in the narrowest of circumstances. The right of elected bodies to make political choices is paramount.

Bork backers said his long legal career, including his tenure as a Yale law professor, solicitor general and a judge on the U.S. Court of Appeals for the District of Columbia, demonstrated his commitment to a strict interpretation of the Constitution. They contended that his record showed he would have defered to the choices made by the elected branches of government, eschewing the kind of judicial trailblazing that led to many controversial Supreme Court decisions over the past quarter-century.

Bork's opponents, on the other hand, thought his reputation for judicial restraint was undeserved. They said his speeches and writings as a teacher and scholar and his decisions as an appeals court judge revealed an appetite for conservative activism as extreme as any liberal's passion for judicially imposed change.

A study requested by Senate Judiciary Committee Chairman Joseph R. Biden Jr., D-Del., specifically refuted the White House view that Bork was a mainstream jurist and concluded that his addition to the court "would cement a five-vote majority for undoing much of the social progress of the last three decades."

Following is a discussion of Bork's record, based on his speeches and writings, on a briefing book supporting Bork's nomination issued by the White House and on several reports criticizing Bork, including the Biden study and others by the AFL-CIO, Public Citizen Litigation Group, the National Women's Law Center, People for the American Way and the American Civil Liberties Union (ACLU).

"I am convinced, as I think most legal scholars are, that* Roe v. Wade *is, itself, an unconstitutional decision, a serious and wholly unjustifiable judicial usurpation of state legislative authority."

—Robert H. Bork, 1981

Abortion

As a judge, Bork had never ruled directly on the issue of abortion. However, he had criticized the Supreme Court's landmark 1973 decision that made abortion legal. In *Roe v. Wade*, the court struck down a state law that made abortion a crime, basing its decision on an implied right of privacy in the Constitution. The statute, a majority said, interfered with a woman's right to privacy.

In 1981, a year before being named to the appeals court, Bork commented on *Roe* in congressional testimony on anti-abortion legislation. He said: "I am convinced, as I think most legal scholars are, that *Roe v. Wade* is, itself, an unconstitutional decision, a serious and wholly unjustifiable judicial usurpation of state legislative authority."

Bork's critics said his condemnation of *Roe v. Wade* and other high court decisions showed a lack of concern for individual rights. They contended that Bork would vote to overturn decades of important precedents.

The White House said Bork's comments meant nothing of the kind. "Judge Bork has never stated whether he would vote to overrule *Roe v. Wade*," the administration said in a briefing book on Bork distributed to Congress. "He has questioned only whether there is a right to abortion in the Constitution." The White House said if the high court determined there was no right to abortion in the Constitution, it would not make abortion illegal. It would simply leave it up to legislative bodies to decide whether abortion should be legal.

The White House went out of its way to stress that the opinions Bork expressed in private life did not presage how he would vote on particular issues. "As a law professor," the administration said in its briefing book, Bork "often criticized the reasoning of Supreme Court opinions; that is what law professors do. But as a judge, he has faithfully applied the legal precedents of both the Supreme Court and his own Circuit Court.... Judge Bork understands that in the American legal system, which places a premium on the orderly development of the law, the mere fact that one may disagree with a prior decision does not mean that that decision ought to be overruled."

The Biden study disputed that view, insisting that Bork would vote to overrule previous decisions. The study quotes a 1986 radio interview in which Bork said, "Teaching is very much like being a judge and you approach the Constitution in the same way."

Privacy Rights

In 1971, Bork criticized the Supreme Court's 1965 decision in *Griswold v. Connecticut*, which invalidated Connecticut's ban on the use of contraceptives. Bork said the decision could not be justified because a right to use contraceptive devices is not "covered specifically or by obvious implication in the Constitution.... Where the Constitution does not embody a moral or ethical choice, the judge has no basis other than his own values upon which to set aside the community judgment embodied in the statute. That, by definition, is an inadequate basis for judicial supremacy."

As a circuit court judge in 1984, Bork refused in *Droneburg v. Zech* to extend the right of privacy to homosexual sodomy in the Navy. Bork concluded that the Supreme Court had neither stated nor applied a principle that would cover a right to engage in homosexual conduct. "If it is in any degree doubtful that the Supreme Court should freely create new constitutional rights," he said, "we think it certain that lower courts should not do so."

In its analysis of Bork's record, the National Women's Law Center, a litigation and research organization in Washington, D.C., concluded that Bork's decisions and academic writings "demonstrate beyond question that he would allow governmental regulation of the most intimate aspects of sexual and family lives without recourse to the basic constitutional freedoms recognized by the Supreme Court for many decades."

The White House disagreed and said Bork's views were consistent with Supreme Court positions. It pointed out that his views were upheld in 1986 when the Supreme Court held in *Bowers v. Harwick* that the right to privacy does not confer upon homosexuals a right to engage in sodomy.

Criminal Justice

Bork is a defender of the death penalty and an opponent of broad interpretations of the exclusionary rule, which bars the use of evidence improperly gathered by police.

In a 1986 interview, Bork said of the death penalty, "the issue is almost concluded by the fact that the death penalty is specifically referred to, and assumed to be an available penalty, in the Constitution itself.... It is a little hard to understand how a penalty that the framers explicitly assumed to be available can somehow become unavailable because of the very Constitution the framers wrote."

Speaking of the exclusionary rule in the same interview, Bork said, "The only good argument [for the rule] rests on the deterrence rationale, and it's time we examine that with great care to see how much deterrence we are getting and at what cost."

The White House cited two decisions to bolster its argument that Bork would be tough on criminals. In *United States v. Mount*, Bork concurred in a decision affirming a defendant's conviction for lying on a passport application. Bork wrote that the court had no power to exclude evidence obtained from a search conducted in England by British police. The White House also cited *U.S. v. Singleton*, in which Bork overruled a district court order suppressing evidence in a defendant's retrial for robbery.

Other supporters, including several law enforcement groups, said this kind of approach was necessary to fight crime.

Critics said his record showed a fundamental disregard for Supreme Court precedents in criminal justice issues. The ACLU said, "Bork's approach to criminal appeals reflects little respect for the rights of the innocent who may be mistakenly accused, or for the role of the courts in protecting those rights."

First Amendment Issues

Bork had argued for strong protection of political speech, but had complained that some Supreme Court decisions have incorrectly broadened First Amendment protections to cover subversive or obscene speech.

In a 1977 speech, Bork argued, "Pornography and obscene speech can hardly be thought to lie at the center of the First Amendment's concerns. Indeed, to the degree the Amendment is about the health of a republican form of government, to that degree pornography and obscene speech run counter to its values."

On the question of subversive speech, he said, "Speech advocating the forcible destruction of democratic government or the frustration of such government through law violation has no value in a system whose basic premise is democratic rule."

The White House analysis of Bork's appeals court decisions concluded that they "reflect a strong concern for the freedom of the media and of citizens to express unpopular views."

In addition, the White House said, Bork's decisions "suggest a strong hostility to any form of government censorship."

The administration pointed to Bork's 1984 opinion in *Ollman v. Evans*, in which the court rejected a libel claim against columnists Rowland Evans Jr. and Robert D. Novak by a Marxist college professor who charged they had libeled him.

Bork said the upsurge in libel suits and large damage awards had "threatened to impose self-censorship on the press which can as effectively inhibit debate and criticism as would overt governmental regulation."

The White House also noted that Bork had extended First Amendment protections to new technologies not foreseen by the Founding Fathers, and in another case, *Lebron v. WMATA*, the White House said Bork protected the free-speech rights of an individual who had been told that he could not use advertising space on the Washington, D.C.-area subway to display a poster critical of Reagan.

Bork's critics found his First Amendment record less praiseworthy. Public Citizen, a consumer group founded by Ralph Nader, said that in the cases where Bork had upheld free speech, he had "emphasized its political aspects."

But, the report asserts, "Even when Judge Bork found that speech was 'political,' his opinions have not provided great protection to the speakers. Indeed we found no case in which he voted to uphold the right to engage in political demonstrations."

The AFL-CIO and Public Citizen cited three cases in which Bork ruled against an individual's right to demonstrate. One of those, *Boos v. Barry*, was before the Supreme Court in 1987. It challenges a Washington, D.C., ordinance barring certain types of demonstrations.

The AFL-CIO report said these cases were important to individuals "who must often rely on marches, picket lines and leaflets to express their views since they do not own their own presses or broadcast stations.... Judge Bork's record on these practical [F]irst [A]mendment questions is disturbing."

The AFL-CIO was also dubious about Bork's libel ruling in the *Ollman* case, calling it a "pro-defendant rule that primarily redounds to the benefit of large institutions, i.e. the institutional press."

Civil Rights

In a 1977 speech, Bork said, "Equality has always been a primary American value. But Americans have also always been rather ambivalent and ambiguous about its meaning. We were never entirely sure whether it meant equality of opportunity or equality of condition.... What is new, arising within the last decade or two, is a strong shift toward the assumption that the only truly moral society would be one in which outcomes were completely equal.... It is never stated that at a certain point sufficient equality would have been achieved and we could stop struggling for more."

The White House described Bork as a person who "has consistently advanced positions that grant minorities and females the full protection of civil rights laws."

Citing his years as solicitor general, the administration said Bork "has never advocated or rendered a judicial decision that was less sympathetic to minority or female plaintiffs than was the position ultimately adopted by either a majority of the Supreme Court or by Justice Powell."

As an appeals court judge, the White House said, Bork "has joined or authored opinions that established, for example, that the military branches are subject to judicial review of civil rights claims involving the selection of senior officers subject to Senate confirmation, that the State Department's Foreign Service was subject to the Equal Pay Act, that ... flight stewardesses may not be paid less than male pursers in jobs that are nominally different ... and that inferences of intentional discrimination can arise from statistics alone."

The administration added that Bork "has always emphasized his 'abhorrence of racial discrimination' and repeatedly praised the correctness and wisdom of the *[Brown v. Board of Education]* decision," which required desegregation of schools.

> ***"At their most specific, [the antitrust] laws say little, if anything, more than: Avoid monopoly, preserve competition. The task of making the rules to accomplish those results was delegated to the federal judiciary."***
>
> **—Robert H. Bork, 1981**

Although Bork once opposed the 1964 Civil Rights Act, he later repudiated that position, and noted that it was "not in any way premised on resistance to the principle of equal opportunity but on concerns that these laws probably exceeded Congress' ... authority and constituted legislating morality at the cost of personal freedom."

In addition to repudiating his past opposition, the White House said, Bork "has repeatedly demonstrated throughout his public career that he will fully enforce and uphold these laws."

The report prepared for Biden rejects almost all of the White House positions. It contended that Bork's "extensive record showed that he has opposed virtually every major civil rights advance on which he has taken a position, including such issues as the public accommodations bill, open housing, restrictive covenants, literacy tests, poll taxes and affirmative action."

The AFL-CIO claimed that Bork resisted interpreting the Constitution broadly to protect individual rights, saying he believed that to do so "is anti-democratic" because such protections infringe on the rights of the majority "to govern through the normal political process."

The Women's Center study was especially critical of Bork for his decisions and writings on laws designed to protect women's rights. It said Bork had consistently criticized the use of the Equal Protection Clause of the Constitution to protect women. They cited a 1982 address he made before the Federalist Society arguing that such protections for "groups that were historically not intended to be protected by that clause" amount to "nationalizations of morality, not justified by anything in the Constitution."

Business and Labor Issues

Bork's legal specialty is antitrust law, and considerable attention had been paid to his views on that subject, particularly his contention that the courts have broad discretionary authority in that area.

In a 1981 speech supporting the Justice Department's refusal to press forward with certain antitrust cases, Bork said, "A great body of wrong and damaging Supreme Court precedent remains on the books. This is what the senatorial critics refer to when they demand that the Department of Justice enforce 'the law'.... It is important to remember that the law, the effective law, under discussion was not made by Congress. That body did not gather, debate, make political and economic choices, and then write those choices into a statute.... At their most specific, those laws say little, if anything, more than: Avoid monopoly, preserve competition. The task of making the rules to accomplish those results was delegated to the federal judiciary."

The Biden study said in the antitrust area, "Bork has called for unprecedented judicial activism, proposing that the courts ignore almost 100 years of judicial precedents and congressional enactments."

The AFL-CIO also criticized Bork's treatment of antitrust issues, contending that he "is willing to completely subordinate the statutory texts [of the antitrust laws] to the abstractions of a particular economic theory."

Bork's critics accused him of a broad bias in favor of business, at the expense of consumers and taxpayers.

The AFL-CIO said Bork "follows an economic theory that would free business from a vast array of government regulations, for Bork's own bias against government regulation of business is extreme."

> ***"Pornography and obscene speech can hardly be thought to lie at the center of the First Amendment's concerns."***
>
> **—Robert H. Bork, 1977**

Both the AFL-CIO and Public Citizen cited cases before the D.C. circuit in which a utilities company, Jersey Central Power, attacked its rate schedule set by the Federal Energy Regulatory Commission (FERC).

Bork wrote that as long as the higher rates sought by the company did not exceed those charged by neighboring utilities, it would be an unjustified "taking" of property under the Constitution for the FERC to reject the increased rate.

In a harsh dissent, Judge Abner J.Mikva accused Bork of creating a new entitlement for the utility based on his own "sense of economic fairness." Mikva charged that this new right was created "virtually out of thin air; the majority just makes it up."

The White House saw a different Bork. "Despite Judge Bork's strong philosophical commitment to free market economics ... he has argued strenuously that the Constitution cannot fairly be read to include protection of economic rights not clearly contained in the text of that document."

Contrary to critics, the administration said Bork "has consistently voted to overturn 'pro-free-market' deregulatory initiatives when they ignored statutory requirements."

Separation of Powers

Bork's critics also objected to his views on the constitutional system of checks and balances. Public Citizen charged that "Bork has not been faithful to the doctrine of separate but equal branches" of government, but instead has "advocated the supremacy of the executive branch over the legislative and judicial branches, and he has disdained many of the checks that safeguard against the aggrandizement of the executive branch's power."

The group cited Bork's dissent in 1986 in *Reagan v. Abourezk*, in which Bork voted to uphold the government's right to deny entry to the United States to foreigners who it believed might act against national interest. It said Bork gave preference to the discretion of the State Department over legislative statutes.

The ACLU contended that in 1971, in a defense of President Nixon's decision to bomb Cambodia, Bork insisted Congress had no power to limit Nixon's discretion to stage the attack.

Watergate

Bork is perhaps most famous for his role in defending the powers of the president during the Watergate crisis.

Bork was solicitor general on Oct. 20, 1973, when Attorney General Elliot L. Richardson resigned and Deputy Attorney General William D. Ruckelshaus was fired after refusing Nixon's order to fire Archibald Cox, the Watergate special prosecutor. Bork then dismissed Cox.

In 1973, acting on President Richard M. Nixon's orders, then-Solicitor General Robert H. Bork, right, fired special Watergate prosecutor Archibald Cox.

Bork had said that after firing Cox, he offered to resign but was persuaded to stay on by Richardson to ensure continuity at the Justice Department. Bork had said that unlike Richardson and Ruckelshaus, he had made no pledge not to fire Cox. He also believed that the president had the constitutional right to dismiss Cox and that he had had no choice but to bow to the president's command.

People for the American Way, a liberal lobbying group, charged that in firing Cox, Bork "violated the Justice Department charter establishing the special prosecutor, under which Cox could be removed only for 'extraordinary impropriety.' " The group added, "Bork chose to follow a president who sought to obstruct justice rather than follow the rule of law."

The White House pointed out that after firing Cox, Bork persuaded Nixon to appoint another special prosecutor, Leon Jaworski, and that Nixon agreed he would not dismiss Jaworski without the concurrence of House and Senate leaders. "Although at the time Bork bore the brunt of criticism," the White House concluded, "commentators have since credited him for saving the Justice Department.... He preserved the Watergate investigation and protected the prosecutors from political pressure, thereby ensuring that justice was served." ∎

Would Justice Bork Have Made Much Difference?

Interest groups that supported or opposed Robert H. Bork's nomination to the Supreme Court solicited millions of dollars by portraying Bork's Senate confirmation as the Armageddon of the Reagan Revolution.

But legal scholars generally observe that one new justice does not a majority make, and even controversial appointees rarely cause the court to pirouette as predicted.

"No one vote [on the court] is going to change the history of civilization as we know it," said Walter F. Pratt Jr., a law professor at the University of Notre Dame and a former law clerk to former Chief Justice Warren E. Burger."Both sides [of the confirmation debate] are engaging in a bit too much hyperbole."

On the other hand, the state of the court's political balance was, as Geoffrey R. Stone of the University of Chicago Law School described it, "exquisitely divided" — lending unusual significance to Bork's moment in history.

Bork would have replaced retired Justice Lewis F. Powell Jr., who had been the fulcrum on which the majority most frequently turned. Some had even referred to the recent sessions of the court as the "Powell Court."

In brief, the conventional wisdom held that a new bird confined in a cage of sparrows was likelier to learn their song than to teach them its own.

The dissent held that the court was an aviary where the new birds needed but one more strong voice to drown the sparrows out.

One of Nine

If history teaches that a single justice takes time to make a mark or to move the court, theory suggests several reasons.

First, the court consists of nine members, each of whom operates, as one former clerk puts it, "pretty much as his own boss," even though the format of court operation is a collegial effort to reach consensus.

One vote, even in the hands of a strong-willed and persuasive individual, has often been a lonely instrument.

During the Civil War, Abraham Lincoln had the extraordinary opportunity to name three justices in one year (1862). Yet, in that same year he had to persuade Congress to expand the court to 10 justices so he could gain a working majority on issues affecting the war.

Even then, Lincoln could not finally count on the high bench supporting the Unionist view until the ailing Chief Justice Roger B. Taney, an advocate of states' rights and author of the *Dred Scott* decision, died near the end of the war.

In this century, Woodrow Wilson's appointment of Justices Louis D. Brandeis and John H. Clarke in the summer of 1916 was thought to be a turning point for the court.

When Louis D. Brandeis was named to the court in 1916, he was branded a radical who would radicalize the court. But like other justices who confounded both supporters and critics, Brandeis did nothing of the sort.

Brandeis, a social reform lawyer from Boston and the first Jewish appointee to the court, stirred a storm of opposition.

"The Boston establishment felt Brandeis would radicalize the court," said Joseph C. Sweeney, a Fordham University law professor who teaches Supreme Court history. "Of course," Sweeney added, "he did nothing of the sort."

Instead, the next seven justices after Clarke were appointed by Republican presidents. And Brandeis, who was eventually confirmed 47-22, had to wait more than two decades before President Franklin D. Roosevelt's appointments began swinging the balance of power his way.

By then, he was on the verge of retirement. But in the intervening years, Brandeis did demonstrate that one or two justices could identify a position and presage the court's future direction — as he and Justice Oliver Wendell Holmes did with respect to individual rights.

Slow to Change

A second reason a single judge might find it difficult to make a mark is that the court operates on a time base that is geologic in comparison with that of government, or life, in general.

At any point in time, the court consists of justices appointed by several presidents over several decades.

The 1987 court was appointed by six presidents who occupied the White House in such different eras that they seemed to have been elected by different nations.

In fact, half the people in the United States in 1987 had not yet been born when President Dwight D. Eisenhower appointed Justice William J. Brennan Jr., now the senior justice, in 1957.

The men named to the court by Roosevelt served a total of 141 years. One of them, Justice William O. Douglas, served 36 years. Operating on a plane of such underlying stability imparts a certain equilibrium.

Controversial Nominees Can Be 'Surprise Judges'

The appointment of Supreme Court justices, who serve for life, may well be a president's best opportunity to shape the nation's affairs beyond his own term in office. But presidents and pundits alike found predicting a given appointee's performance a terribly inexact science.

President Franklin D. Roosevelt, who appointed more justices than any president since George Washington, generally got what he wanted. But even his long list included a few surprises for the public, and for FDR himself.

He had to wait until his second term to name his first justice, Hugo Black, who promptly ran into trouble when it was learned he had been a member of the Ku Klux Klan.

"Black is an outstanding example of someone who was castigated as a red-necked demagogue," noted Richard B. Stewart, a professor at Harvard Law School.

"By the time he had grown to be a very distinguished justice, [Black] was making decisions no one would have expected."

Daniel J. Meador, a law professor at the University of Virginia who was a law clerk for Black, attributed the "surprise judge" phenomenon primarily to the intellectual and working atmosphere of the court.

"Most . . . come to function in terms of the court, its conventions and traditions," he said. "It works subtly. It's probably the saving grace of the system."

At the same time, Meador said, news media and political scientists were also responsible for the phenomenon because they often misrepresented the appointees and raised false expectations.

Justice Louis D. Brandeis was sometimes described as a youthful radical (one scholar called him "the Ralph Nader of his day") who ended his 22-year career on the court writing relatively conservative opinions — especially in defense of judicial restraint.

But it should be noted that, by then, judicial restraint meant leaving in place the programs of the New Deal. It had been the Republican-dominated court of Franklin Roosevelt's first term that struck down much of his program and prompted his ill-fated "court-packing" plan.

In the same vein, Brandeis had probably never been as radical as some of the clients he defended. And much of the talk about his politics now sounds like anti-Semitism in disguise.

Other, less celebrated cases had shown significant movement in a justice's orientation over the years.

Justice Felix Frankfurter, named in 1939 as Franklin Roosevelt's third addition to the court, was presumed to be another guardian of the New Deal. But in his 23 years on the court he moved notably toward the center-right.

In 1981, C. Neal Tate, then a professor of political science at North Texas State University, published an index of Supreme Court votes between 1946 and 1978 on civil liberties, civil rights and economics. By that index, Frankfurter approximated the mean for all justices on civil liberties and civil rights and was 30 percentage points more conservative than the mean on economic issues.

Conversely, Justice John M. Harlan was a Wall Street lawyer appointed by Dwight D. Eisenhower who was presumed to be pro-business. Yet his score on Tate's economic issues index was slightly more liberal than Frankfurter's.

But the champion "surprise justice" might well have been Chief Justice Earl Warren, a former governor of California appointed by Eisenhower in 1953 and confirmed the following spring.

Warren became the leader and symbol of an activist court that supported the rights of the accused in criminal procedure and advanced a social agenda that included school desegregation and other aspects of civil rights.

"Eisenhower actually said that Warren was one of the biggest mistakes he ever made," said Joseph C. Sweeney, a law professor teaching Supreme Court history at Fordham. "And I'd have to say he probably thought that [Justice William J.] Brennan was No. 2."

"In some sense, they're all surprises," said Kate Stith, a professor at Yale Law School.

"They cannot predict how they are going to be transformed — not so much by their colleagues as by the nature of the power they will have. There's nothing like it."

Politics at the Court

Finally, the high bench is difficult to alter overnight because it is an institution of ever-present political conflict, where battles are no less intense for being courtly.

As longtime Supreme Court scholar Arthur Selwyn Miller wrote in 1981: "The Supreme Court is now and always has been deeply immersed in politics. Indeed it would have little meaning or function outside of politics. . . . "

Miller was referring both to the justices' interest in the results of their opinions on the extralegal world and to their internal struggles to achieve those results.

Usually shielded from public view, these internal tuggings and haulings were only glimpsed in the opinions and dissents that emerged — and in the unpredictable alliances that formed and faded.

Thus a justice such as Brennan, with a gift for — and three decades of experience at — the inner workings of the court, might affect its decisions far more than his single vote would suggest.

And a leader of the court, such as Burger or Chief Justice William H. Rehnquist, might be hampered in exercising his apparent powers by a lack of negotiating skills — the sort of bargaining associated with legislative maneuvering.

This could be true even when one particular justice might be philosophically inimical to another. And two justices presumed to be allies might diverge.

In their 1979 book "The Brethren," Bob Woodward and Scott Armstrong described the personal help Brennan offered Justice Harry A. Blackmun, who was struggling with the historic *Roe v. Wade* opinion, the basis of current federal law on abortion.

They reported that Brennan even concurred in another Blackmun opinion, with which he did not agree, rather than offend Blackmun at a sensitive stage of the *Wade* deliberations.

Blackmun had come to the court as Burger's supposed "Minnesota Twin," but was quickly seen as resenting that label and all it implied. He moved away from Burger and closer to the consensus that had characterized the court in the past.

In doing so, he had been cited as another example of the "surprise justice" phenomenon, a topic of some debate in its own right. *(Box, p. 112)*

Reagan's Court

Fitting Bork into this environment required speculation. But such were the calculations by which justices were selected for appointment and, usually, sized up for confirmation.

Bork was President Reagan's third new appointment to the court, the others being Justices Sandra Day O'Connor (1981) and Antonin Scalia (1986). Both O'Connor and Scalia were considered conservatives, although O'Connor seemed insufficiently orthodox to some on the right and Scalia was only beginning to make his mark.

The 1987 court is led by Chief Justice Rehnquist, a 1971 appointment by Richard M. Nixon, whom Reagan elevated to chief justice upon Burger's retirement in 1986.

In other words, Bork would have given the court a solid core of four indisputably conservative votes if he had been confirmed.

Still, some scholars saw this formulation as too pat.

Another possibility advanced by scholars and observers of the court was that O'Connor, or even Scalia, could move away from the Reagan bloc — possibly to assume the powerful broker's role occupied by Powell (and also in the past by Justice Potter Stewart).

But Thomas C. Grey, a professor at Stanford Law School and a former law clerk to Justice Thurgood Marshall, saw the conservative bloc, with Bork, as reaching a critical mass.

"There are a lot of studies of group dynamics, like on juries, where one or two people can't hold out against the rest but three or four can," Grey said.

Moreover, this bloc of four could have become a majority by adding just one additional vote from among the three remaining "swing voters": Justices Blackmun, Byron R. White and John Paul Stevens.

White, 70, seemed the best candidate to join the bloc — especially on issues in criminal law. Having served on the court for 25 years, he had generally sided with conservatives on criminal law and with the liberal-to-moderate wing on economics.

It sometimes surprised people to learn that White was one of two justices named to the court by liberal Democratic President John F. Kennedy (they knew each other during World War II and in postwar Washington).

As for the future, the five justices not appointed (or promoted) by Reagan had an average age of 75 in 1987. The youngest among them, Stevens, was 67.

Thus the results of the 1988 presidential election would probably determine whether the year of the Bork nomination more closely resembled 1937 (the year Roosevelt began appointing justices) or 1916 (the year Brandeis began his long wait).

The answer was critical because at the right moment in time, as Raoul Berger, retired senior fellow at Harvard University in American legal history, had written: "The replacement of one or two justices may result in a complete reversal of the prevailing national conscience."

Berger used the common example of Chief Justice Earl Warren succeeding Chief Justice Fred M. Vinson. But other scholars suggested that so dramatic a shift at the helm was not needed to effect great change.

"It's not just Bork and his considerable persuasive powers," said Stone of Chicago, a former law clerk to Brennan. The court "is a seesaw that's leaning in one direction. Add one more stone to that end and that end hits the ground."

Stone also said one justice's vote could be critical even when it did not tip the balance of a 5-4 decision, arguing that "a six or seven-man majority will do things that a five-man [majority] would not." ▮

Supreme Court Term Hinges on Vacant Chair

The 1987-88 Supreme Court term opened on a note of uncertainty, with the outcome depending as much on the Senate as on the court.

The Senate could not settle the controversy over Supreme Court nominee Robert H. Bork before the Oct. 5, 1987, start of the new term, leaving an empty chair at the bench when the first oral arguments were heard. On Oct. 23, the Senate rejected Bork's nomination 58-42 to replace retired Justice Lewis F. Powell Jr.

Powell was a crucial swing vote. In the last three court terms, there were 75 5-4 decisions in which Powell sided with the majority. Many of these involved the court's most controversial issues, such as abortion and affirmative action.

Since Bork was rejected, the Powell seat could remain vacant for months, which could leave the court deadlocked 4-4 in important cases. When the court divides evenly, the lower court ruling is upheld, without setting a precedent.

The last time the court was reduced to eight justices — when Powell took three months off in 1985 to recuperate from surgery — the court found itself deadlocked eight times, including three controversial First Amendment cases.

The longest vacancy on the court lasted more than two years, from 1844 to 1846, after the Senate rejected four nominations by two presidents. After Justice Abe Fortas resigned under fire in 1969, his seat was vacant for 13 months until the confirmation of Harry A. Blackmun.

Old Laws up for Review

In the course of its work each year, the high court often provides a quick test for new congressional initiatives, but it is a review of some of the country's bedrock older laws that forms a sizable chunk of the high court's docket for the 1987-88 term.

Depending on how the court rules, its decisions on these statutes could have important consequences for consumers, environmentalists, veterans, businessmen and handicapped children.

Before leaving town for its summer 1987 recess, the court accepted more than 90 cases for the new term and another 60 or so were selected over the next few months. Among the laws at issue in cases already set for argument are the 1934 Securities and Exchange Act, the 1952 McCarren-Walter immigration law, the 1972 Clean Water Act and the 97-year-old Sherman Antitrust Act.

Members of Congress were already legislating in some of these areas, and the court's pronouncements could affect those efforts. In other areas, members would be watching the court closely, and if they were unhappy with its rulings, lawmakers might introduce legislation to overturn or at least modify the court's decisions.

Two perennially controversial issues — abortion and school prayer — would also be before the court in 1987. The justices agreed to hear an Illinois case involving a minor's right to abortion and another challenging the constitutionality of a New Jersey statute requiring a moment of silence in public schools. While there was no existing legislative drive in Congress on either of these issues, abortion and school prayer are so emotional that a high court pronouncement invariably has a ripple effect across the street at the Capitol.

Several other cases of potential interest to Congress might also be put on the docket this fall, including a challenge by former White House aide Michael K. Deaver to the independent

counsel law. This law, first enacted in 1978, provides for the appointment of special prosecutors to investigate alleged wrongdoing by high government officials. Deaver challenged the constitutionality of the law.

Securities Law

The scandals that rocked Wall Street, a rash of takeovers and an April Supreme Court decision, *CTS Corp. v. Dynamics Corp. of America*, affirming states' rights to enact anti-takeover laws, had already prompted the House and Senate to start tightening up the securities laws.

One focus was how to define "insider" trading — the term used to describe illegal stock transactions that make use of information about impending developments before they become public.

The court had accepted a case, *Carpenter v. U.S.*, that goes to the heart of the issue.

Former *Wall Street Journal* reporter R. Foster Winans was convicted of securities fraud after he disclosed information that was going to appear in his column, "Heard on Wall Street." Winans also used the information to make some trades of his own. (David Carpenter, the other defendant, also made use of Winans' information.)

Winans' attorneys said this was not insider trading because Winans did not work for any of the companies whose securities were involved. The 2nd U.S. Circuit Court of Appeals disagreed. So did Solicitor General Charles Fried, who told the court that Winans' interpretation of the law would leave "a large and illogical gap" in enforcement of the securities laws.

Legislation pending before the House and Senate would define what constitutes "insider" trading, but some members, including John D. Dingell, D-Mich., chairman of the House Energy and Commerce Committee, and Senate Banking Committee Chairman William Proxmire, D-Wis., worried that the proposed definition would leave too many loopholes.

Dingell was considering instead a provision that would make a securities firm liable for employee actions, even if the employee were trading for his or her personal benefit.

Another securities fraud case of interest to Congress is *Basic Inc. v. Levinson*, which focuses on what a company must disclose when asked about merger talks.

The 6th U.S. Circuit Court of Appeals ruled that preliminary merger talks were "material" — that is, significant enough under the law to require disclosure — whether or not there was an agreement in principle.

Basic Inc. argued that the 6th Circuit greatly expanded the fraud law and improperly characterized what were in fact very preliminary discussions between Basic and Combustion Engineering Inc. The effect of the appeals court ruling, Basic argued, was to require "disclosure of the most insignificant and inconclusive contacts. This is more confusing than helpful to investors."

Fried filed a friend-of-the-court brief siding with the 6th Circuit. "Concerns about affecting the course of negotiations do not justify allowing corporations to make materially false or misleading statements on which investors may rely," he wrote.

A provision in legislation drafted by Dingell and Edward J. Markey, D-Mass., (HR 2172), did not directly address the fraud issue in *Basic Inc. v. Levinson*, but it would revise current law by requiring a corporation to answer "yes" or "no" when asked by a stock exchange about takeover rumors that were causing substantial swings in the price of a company's stock. Critics said a "no comment" response often fuels speculation. *(Weekly Report pp. 1662, 835)*

Immigration Law

The government's right to keep foreigners out of the United States was behind another case on the court docket, *Reagan v. Abourezk*.

At issue was whether the government could prevent someone from entering the country because it feared the effect of the person's presence, rather than because it feared a particular action by the person.

The case concerns a provision of the 1952 McCarran-Walter Act allowing the exclusion of an alien when the government "has reason to believe" he or she wants to enter the country "solely, principally or incidentally to engage in activities that would be prejudicial to the public interest or endanger the welfare, safety or security of the United States."

Another section of that law bars people who are or have been members of the Communist Party or any other totalitarian party.

In the case before the court, the government denied visas to one person from Nicaragua, two from Cuba and one from Italy. In all four cases, the government, on the advice of the State Department, said the people should be excluded because of foreign policy concerns.

The groups that invited the individuals challenged the government's actions, claiming that people cannot be excluded from the country merely because of fears about their "presence" in the United States.

Their lawsuit, which was joined by several members of Congress, was thrown out by a U.S. district judge in Washington, D.C. A divided appeals court lifted the district court's order, and while it agreed that the government could use foreign policy concerns to exclude aliens, it sent the matter back to the district court for more information on whether mere presence justifies an exclusion.

The *Reagan v. Abourezk* case was discussed at length during the Bork confirmation hearings because Bork, who sat on the appeals court, dissented in the ruling, arguing that the majority's decision deprived the government "of much of the flexibility and nuance that are essential in the conduct of foreign relations." During the hearings, several Judiciary Committee members challenged Bork's views on the grounds that he gave too much discretion to the executive branch of government.

Rep. Barney Frank, D-Mass., had introduced a bill (HR 1119) that would resolve the issue by removing much of the government's discretion. It would allow an exclusion only for specified "dangerous" activities, such as gathering weapons for a terrorist attack or planning or organizing terrorist activities against the United States.

Consumers

The court had accepted two cases that could be particularly important to consumers. Both might affect the ability of shoppers to find discount merchandise.

One case, *K Mart Corp. v. Cartier Inc.*, involves the legality of "parallel imports." These are products made abroad with the approval of the trademark owner in the United States, but then imported — without the trademark owner's permission — by a third company.

The case involves a clash between the 1930 Tariff Act and U.S. Customs Service regulations developed under the 1930 law. These regulations allow the overseas products into the country in what is known as the "gray market," where brand-name goods are available at a lower price.

In this case, Cartier Inc., which makes expensive jewelry, and a coalition of other companies challenged the customs regulations, contending they undercut trademark protections and were in violation of the Tariff Act.

They argued that those who sell on the gray market get a "free ride" on the marketing and service associated with the trademarked product while selling goods of different quality from those manufactured for or in the United States.

The long-term result of this, the coalition argued, "will be to depreciate the value of the trademark owners' investment in the goodwill that his trademark represents."

The companies and the coalition sued the Treasury Department. The Customs Service and two well-known discount houses, K Mart Corp. and 47th Street Photo Inc., intervened as defendants.

The federal district court in Washington, D.C., found the customs regulations to be valid, but the appeals court reversed the decision, saying the regulations were not a "reasonable interpretation" of the Tariff Act provision.

Goverment lawyers and those representing K Mart and 47th Street Photo argued that the customs regulations were reasonable, particularly because Congress had not directly spoken to the issue.

Legislative efforts to change the tariff law — including one attempt to attach provisions to the omnibus trade bill (HR 3) — had been unsuccessful thus far. But a House Judiciary Committee aide said members and staffers were watching this case. "Regardless of who wins, we'll have to do something," he said.

The other case, *Business Electronics v. Sharp Electronics Corp.*, involves antitrust protections for discount dealers.

At issue was whether an agreement between a manufacturer — in this case Sharp — and a distributor to terminate an arrangement with a competing distributor that discounts the product violated the antitrust laws even though there was no agreement on a specific resale price level.

The 5th U.S. Circuit Court of Appeals found no violation because there was no direct price fixing.

But Business Electronics contended that the 5th Circuit misread previous court decisions that broadly define price fixing.

Fried intervened in this case, urging the high court to uphold the 5th Circuit decision. He conceded that an agreement to eliminate a competing dealer "may reduce intrabrand price competition." But he said, "such an agreement may serve the legitimate purpose of allowing dealers to charge prices that cover the cost of services necessary to the efficient distribution of the product."

The issue of vertical price restraints — those between manufacturer and distributor — was of concern to many members of Congress. They were at odds with the Justice Department over its interpretation of the antitrust laws, complaining that the department was too lax in policing what they perceive to be abuses.

The Senate Judiciary Committee Aug. 6, 1987, approved a bill (S 430) that makes it more difficult for a manufacturer to terminate a contract with a discounting distributor.

Handicapped Children

Members of Congress were also involved in a case focusing on the disciplining of handicapped children.

In *Honig v. Doe*, two handicapped students alleged that California's superintendent of public instruction and the San Francisco unified school districts violated the law by suspending the students for disrupting classes without following administrative and judicial procedures established in the 1975 Education for All Handicapped Children Act.

If there is an extended delay in confirming a successor to retired Justice Lewis F. Powell Jr., the court may deadlock, 4-4, on important issues.

Fifteen members of Congress, including six who were original sponsors of the Act, filed a friend-of-the-court brief supporting the children.

California officials contended the suspensions were proper and that the 9th U.S. Circuit Court of Appeals, which ruled against the school system, was wrong. In its brief, the state said that the appeals court decision requiring a child to be returned to the classroom after a short suspension "makes no sense. It would be contrary to the interests of the disruptive child as well as the interest of the children in the classroom. It could not have been what Congress intended."

The members disagreed. Their brief asserted that the legislative history of the act "makes clear that Congress did not want to leave decisions regarding [handicapped students'] placement in the discretion of school officials. The [act] was a congressional response to a shameful history of exclusion, segregation, inadequate education and expulsion of handicapped children."

Food Stamps

Food stamp advocates in the House and Senate would be closely watching a case challenging the law allowing the government to deny food stamps to a household when one member is on strike.

The case is *Lyng v. International Union, United Automobile Aerospace & Agricultural Implement Workers of America, UAW et al.*, and concerns the validity of the strike language, which was added to the Food Stamp Act in 1981. The highly controversial amendment floated around Congress for years and finally was adopted as part of a massive budget "reconciliation" bill (PL 97-35).

The federal district court in Washington, D.C., ruled the provision unconstitutional because it did not rationally further a legitimate governmental purpose.

Fried, arguing for the Agriculture Department, which handles the food stamp law, charged that the lower court "improperly second-guesses the complex choices made by Congress when it amended the Food Stamp Act." Fried said it was appropriate for Congress to "remove itself from labor disputes by withdrawing benefits that it thought were more appropriately provided by union strike funds."

If the high court upholds the strike provision, opponents in Congress were likely to introduce legislation to remove it from the Food Stamp Act.

Homosexual Rights

In another case of interest to Congress, the court in June agreed to review a decision that could help define the constitutional rights of homosexuals and the authority of the CIA director to fire people.

Members would be paying attention to this case for guidance on homosexual rights and, in the wake of the Iran-contra affair, the limits of accountability of the CIA.

The case, *Webster v. Doe,* involves the firing of a CIA employee, known only as John Doe, who told his superiors that he was a homosexual. He challenged his firing, claiming that he posed no security risk and noting that his work had been considered exemplary. He asked to be told why he was fired, but his request was refused.

The CIA claimed that Doe's case was not subject to judicial review, but the D.C. appeals court disagreed. The court sent the case back to the district court to gather more evidence about whether the CIA has a policy barring employment of someone who is a homosexual or because of homosexual conduct.

The government appealed to the Supreme Court contending that the CIA director's decision to fire someone was not reviewable. To allow judicial review, Fried said, would undermine the CIA director's ability to run his agency. But Doe contended the case was not about the director's discretion, but whether the CIA has a policy of denying work to homosexuals and whether this policy is unconstitutional.

Exclusionary Rule

The court last addressed the so-called "exclusionary rule" in 1984, when it created two exceptions to the general proposition that evidence gathered by police in violation of the Fourth Amendment must be excluded at a criminal trial. The Fourth Amendment bars unreasonable searches and seizures.

The exclusionary rule was first developed by the court in 1914 to deter police misconduct. For years, some law enforcement officers chafed under the doctrine, convinced it hampers police work and allows guilty people to go free.

Conservative members of Congress had sought to ease the rule, but had been unsuccessful.

The court took much of the energy out of the congressional debate in 1984, when it approved modifications to the rule. In one case it carved out a "good faith" exception in cases where an officer had obtained a warrant, seized evidence and then learned that the warrant was defective. In the other, it eased the rule in situations where the evidence improperly obtained would have inevitably been discovered anyway.

The justices accepted two drug cases for argument in 1987 that might offer a new refinement of the exclusionary rule. The issue in *Murray v. U.S.* and *Carter v. U.S.* is the legality of a search and seizure of property with a warrant when that warrant came after a previously illegal search.

In the cases, the police discovered evidence of drug offenses during an illegal search of a warehouse. After discovering the evidence, they went to a magistrate, obtained a warrant, researched the premises and seized bales of marijuana.

In appealing their convictions, the defendants argued that the evidence should have been thrown out. The government contended the convictions should stand because the seizure of evidence was based on a proper warrant and was independent of the previously illegal search.

Clean Water Act

The right of citizens to bring lawsuits to enforce the 1972 Clean Water Act was at issue in *Gwaltney of Smithfield Ltd. v. Chesapeake Bar Foundation, Inc.*

Chesapeake Bar, an environmental group, charged that a Gwaltney meatpacking plant in Smithfield, Va., had discharged effluent into the Pagan River in violation of the Clean Water Act. A federal court fined Gwaltney, a subsidiary of Smithfield Foods Inc., $1.3 million, the largest penalty ever assessed in a citizen suit.

Gwaltney appealed, contending that its violations were rectified and that the law did not permit lawsuits for past violations. The 4th U.S. Circuit Court of Appeals agreed with the district court, and Gwaltney took the case to the Supreme Court.

The company contended the law "precludes citizen suits seeking penalties for purely past violations." But the foundation asserted that there were "express statements" by sponsors of the legislation endorsing suits for past violations.

Fried filed a friend-of-the-court brief in support of the foundation's lawsuit. But Fried's brief said a citizen suit had to allege a "continuing violation," and he said those circumstances were met in the *Gwaltney* litigation.

Veterans' Benefits

In two companion cases it had accepted, the court was expected to decide whether a Veterans Administration (VA) regulation that defines alcoholism as "willful misconduct" discriminates against the handicapped and thus violates the Rehabilitation Act of 1973.

By designating alcoholism "willful misconduct," the VA denied to alcoholic veterans benefits that were available to veterans with problems considered to be handicaps.

Also at issue was whether a court could review a VA decision.

In one case, *Traynor v. Turnage,* the 2nd U.S. Circuit Court of Appeals ruled that judicial review of the VA's decision was not appropriate. It reversed a federal district court ruling finding that the VA had violated the Rehabilitation Act.

The other case, *McKelvey v. Turnage,* came from the D.C. Circuit, which determined that on the particular facts of the case, it was appropriate for the court to review the VA decision. It then decided that the VA regulation was reasonable because alcoholism, like drug addiction, is generally self-inflicted, absent any "underlying psychiatric disorder" leading to the alcoholism.

McKelvey and Traynor were challenging those respective rulings. They believed judicial review was appropriate, and that it was necessary to look at the VA regulations in the context of the 1973 anti-bias law.

Arguing for the VA, Fried contended that the VA decisions were not reviewable. Even if they were, he said, the 1973 rehabilitation law was not intended "to forbid differing treatment of different handicaps."

Veterans are a politically potent group, and depending upon the court's decision, members might decide to introduce legislation clarifying the benefits law. ∎

More Than 300 Appointees Make a Big Difference

Whatever happened to the Supreme Court nomination of Robert H. Bork, President Reagan had already made his mark on the federal judiciary.

In 6½ years in office, Reagan appointed more than 300 federal judges who were slowly but surely changing the tenor and behavior of the federal courts. Everyone seemd to agree on this; where they disagreed was on whether the change was a good thing.

Reagan supporters said the judges were having a beneficial effect, practicing judicial restraint, imposing stiff sentences on criminals who deserved to be behind bars, and protecting constitutional rights, such as the right to practice one's religion.

Critics argued that their impact had been negative — that individual rights were being denied, that civil rights victories of earlier decades were being eroded and that people with legitimate grievances were being turned away from federal courts.

These critics said Reagan's impact was apparent not only in the decisions his appointees handed down, but also in the cases they never saw.

The reason, said lawyers who specialize in individual rights litigation, was that they no longer turned so avidly to the federal courts to ask for broad enforcement of civil and constitutional rights. They feared Reagan judges would use such cases to limit enforcement. "We are afraid to give these judges issues that will allow them to reverse existing precedent," said one Chicago civil rights lawyer.

What was happening instead, said John Powell, national legal director of the American Civil Liberties Union (ACLU), was that lawyers were filing more cases in state courts or asking Congress to change the law.

And when there was no option but federal litigation, civil rights lawyers then spent more time looking around for a court where Reagan had made few appointments or where his selections were not perceived to be so conservative, such as the federal circuits in the West and Northeast.

While liberal lawyers lamented Reagan's influence on the courts, conservatives applauded it. They believed that Reagan's judges were doing precisely what they should be doing, and that the more disputes that went to state courts or to legislatures for resolution the better.

Looking at the Statistics

As of August 1987, the president had made 322 lifetime judicial appointments that had been confirmed.

Nine were to specialized courts that handle patent and trade matters. The remaining 313 appointments broke down this way: three to the Supreme Court (Associate Justices Sandra Day O'Connor and Antonin Scalia, and the elevation of William H. Rehnquist to chief justice); 69 appointments to the 12 regional federal appeals courts; and 241 appointments to the federal district courts.

Reagan's appointees in 1987 filled 16 district court positions and seven circuit court seats, including one on the federal circuit.

In terms of percentages, Reagan's imprint was significant. He appointed 32 percent of the 754 district court judges. (This included 535 full-time judges and another 219 in semi-retired status who still hear cases.)

The president had appointed 30.1 percent of the 226 regional appeals court judges. (This included 157 judges hearing cases full time and another 69 in semi-retired status.)

Reagan's appointments to the appeals courts were especially significant because in most instances they were the final arbiters of disputes. The Supreme Court took only about 110 cases per year of the thousands that were decided by the federal courts.

There was one existing vacancy on the Supreme Court, for which Appeals Court Judge Bork had been nominated, 46 vacancies at the district court level and 14 on the appeals courts.

Two Case Studies

Reagan's influence was particularly apparent on the Court of Appeals for the District of Columbia, and on the 7th U.S. Circuit Court of Appeals. On both courts, he had appointed seven of 11 judges. The 7th Circuit covers Illinois, Indiana and Wisconsin.

In the D.C. circuit especially, civil rights lawyers complained that the judges had repeatedly told them their grievances didn't belong in court. In one particularly controversial case, Haitian refugees challenged Reagan's program of interdicting boats to prevent illegal aliens from entering the United States.

The plaintiffs argued that Reagan's actions violated the Constitution and several laws relating to immigration. But the appeals court in 1987 rejected the claim, contending that the issue amounted to a political fight, not a legal one.

While Reagan critics fumed about this, conservative legal analyst Bruce Fein of the Heritage Foundation said the Reagan judges were doing exactly what they should be doing. "They are far more inclined to find barriers to any public interest group that wants to walk into court because they seem intellectually irritated," he said.

The 7th Circuit was fast earning a reputation as a place civil rights lawyers wanted to avoid. One public interest attorney in Washington, D.C., called this court "as inhospitable a circuit as you could find. We try to stay out of there if we can.... The police always win. The individual loses. Constitutional rights don't mean anything." The Washington lawyer, like most of the Reagan critics interviewed for this article, declined to be identified because he regularly argues cases in the federal courts.

Another attorney cited two cases over the last three years that he said illustrated the problems for civil rights litigants in the 7th Circuit. In both cases the appeals court ruled against the individuals filing civil rights claims after the plaintiffs had won in the district court.

One case involved a challenge to Justice Department guidelines for domestic spying, which the plaintiffs claimed violated a Justice Department consent decree on appropriate surveillance by the FBI.

The district court judge agreed and enjoined the FBI from implementing guidelines concerning domestic security and terrorism investigations.

But the appeals panel reversed the ruling and lifted the injunction, claiming there was no evidence that action by the FBI was imminent or that such surveillance would violate the guidelines.

The other case concerned a challenge to a Du Page County, Ill., zoning ordinance by a group of low- and moderate-income people and a non-profit housing organization. They charged that the local zoning ordinance was discriminatory because it had the effect of excluding low- and moderate-income housing from certain neighborhoods.

The district court agreed with the plaintiffs, but the appeals court threw out the case. The judges said neither the individuals nor the housing organization had the right — or "standing" — to sue. The court said there was no evidence presented by either the individuals or the organization that any low- or moderate-income project had been rejected, and thus there had not been any injury shown that resulted from the zoning ordinance. The plaintiffs' claim, the court said, was based on conjecture.

Judicial Restraint

While civil rights lawyers argued that Reagan's judges had twisted the law to satisfy their own ends, conservative legal analyst Peter J. Ferrara, a former White House policy adviser, issued a strong defense in "The Judges War," a book published by the Free Congress Foundation's Institute for Government and Politics.

Ferrara contended Reagan's appointees "have complied strictly with the limitations on their judicial authority."

Within the constraints imposed by past precedents and the Constitution, he said, "Reagan's appointees have taken a strongly conservative direction where the law allows, though not radically more conservative than the appointees of previous Republican presidents. Moreover, when the issues are examined closely, the positions taken by Reagan judicial appointees on the controversial issues generally seem to be supported by broad majorities of the American people."

Ferrara cited specifically a tendency by Reagan judges to impose stiff sentences on criminal defendants, to avoid finding procedural reasons to set these defendants free and a reluctance to find that such government activities as state laws allowing school prayer or the use of public facilities for religious activities violate the First Amendment bar to government establishment of religion.

Liberal critics of the Reagan bench, Ferrara asserted, "fear these judges may be able to use the courts to impose their personal political philosophies, as liberal activist judges do. The fear is clearly unfounded."

Stephen J. Markman, head of the Justice Department's Office of Legal Policy, which screens judicial nominees, insisted that fair-minded people should have no concern about a judiciary dominated by Reagan appointees. He said the administration used no litmus test for selecting appointees. "We are not looking for judges who are going to be reaching conservative policy results or any other kind of policy results," he said. "We want them to read the law and the Constitution as honestly as they can and come to whatever result is directed by that reading."

In 6½ years in office, Reagan has appointed more than 300 federal judges who are slowly but surely changing the tenor and behavior of the federal courts. Everyone seems to agree on this; where they disagree is on whether the change is a good thing.

Pace of the Process

While there were disagreements over Reagan's judicial selections, there also were disputes over the way the Senate handled them.

All judicial appointments go through the Senate Judiciary Committee, and after the Democrats took control in January, 1987, it didn't take Republicans long to complain about the pace of those proceedings.

Strom Thurmond, S.C., the ranking Republican, chided Chairman Joseph R. Biden Jr., D-Del., and Patrick J. Leahy, D-Vt., head of an ad hoc panel that screens judges, for not moving Reagan's nominations fast enough.

Leahy and Biden defended their procedures and said statistics proved that they were not treating Reagan judgeships any differently from the way the Republicans did.

As of Aug. 7, 1987, the committee had held nomination hearings for 31 judges. At the same time in 1985, which was the first year of the 99th Congress, the Republican-controlled panel had held hearings for 33 judges.

Two nominees pending in the committee in 1987 wre considered to be especially controversial. One of them was Bernard H. Siegan, a law professor at the University of San Diego and a former colleague of Attorney General Edwin Meese III. Siegan had been nominated for a seat on the 9th U.S. Circuit Court of Appeals.

Critics said Siegan's views of constitutional rights weare outside the spectrum of acceptable legal theory, but the Justice Department said that when Siegan has a chance to testify, he will allay members' misgivings.

The other controversial nominee is Susan W. Liebeler, who was selected for a seat on the federal circuit. Liebeler was then chaiman of the International Trade Commission (ITC).

Opponents were critical of her stewardship of the agency and contended that some of her actions, particularly the manner in which she handled a study of ITC operations, showed that she did not have the temperament to be on the federal bench.

Some critics also contended that her interpretations of the trade laws distorted congressional intent. But Markman said he believed she would be confirmed.

Conservative Critics

Not all of the criticism of Reagan's judicial nominees came from liberals. Some conservative supporters were also unhappy with his selections, primarily for district court seats.

With these appointments, the administration — like others before it — generally deferred to senators in selecting nominees. But on appeals court seats, the president had more of a free hand.

Patrick McGuigan, director of the Judicial Reform Project, said "about half" of Reagan's judges "are in the mold of Bork and Scalia in that they are very serious and principled in their philosophy and willing to apply it."

The other half, he said, "reflect strategic and political compromises the administration made with the members of the Senate and they run the full gamut from being pretty good to a handful of outright liberals."

Markman found the criticism unfair. "Every indication that I have is that the president's judicial selection process is working extremely well," he said. ∎

Biographies of Supreme Court Justices

The following are biographical sketches of each of the justices who currently serve on the Supreme Court.

William Hubbs Rehnquist

Reagan's appointment of William H. Rehnquist as chief justice clearly indicated that the president was hoping to shift the court to the right. Since his early years as an associate justice in the 1970s Rehnquist has been the court's most conservative justice. An ardent advocate of judicial restraint, he feels that the court should simply call a halt to unconstitutional policies — and stop at that. Innovation in public policy, he believes, is the prerogative of elected officials, not appointed judges.

Rehnquist, the fourth associate justice to become chief, is the only justice completely comfortable with the argument that the original intent of the framers of the Constitution and the Bill of Rights is the proper standard for interpreting those documents today. He also takes a literal approach to individual rights. These beliefs have led him to dissent from the court's rulings protecting a woman's privacy-based right to abortion, to argue that there is no constitutional barrier to school prayer, and to side with police and prosecutors on questions of criminal law.

Born in Milwaukee, Wis., Oct. 1, 1924, Rehnquist went west to college. At Stanford University, where he received both his undergraduate and law degrees, classmates recalled him as a brilliant student whose already well-entrenched conservative views set him apart from his more liberal classmates.

After graduating from law school in 1952, Rehnquist traveled east to Washington, D.C., to serve as a law clerk to Supreme Court Justice Robert H. Jackson. There in 1952, he wrote a memorandum that later would come back to haunt him during his Senate confirmation hearings. In the memorandum, Rehnquist favored separate but equal schools for blacks and whites. Asked about those views by the Senate Judiciary Committee in 1971, Rehnquist repudiated them, declaring that they were Justice Jackson's not his own.

Following his clerkship, Rehnquist decided to begin law practice in the Southwest. In 1953, Rehnquist moved to Phoenix, Ariz., and immediately became immersed in state Republican politics. From his earliest days in the state, he was associated with the party's most conservative wing. A 1957 speech denouncing the liberality of the Warren court typified his views at the time.

During the 1964 presidential campaign, Rehnquist campaigned ardently for Barry Goldwater. It was during the campaign that Rehnquist met and worked with Richard G. Kleindienst, who later as President Nixon's deputy attorney general, would appoint Rehnquist to head the Justice Department's Office of Legal Counsel as an assistant attorney general.

Controversy surrounded Rehnquist's 1986 nomination for chief justice. He was accused of acting as a challenger and harassing voters in Phoenix, Arizona. Charges were also raised against him for racial bias. His views on civil rights were questioned and he was found to have accepted anti-Semitic restrictions in a property deed to a Vermont home. In addition, his medical records were reviewed over concern about a chronic low-back problem.

More votes were cast against Rehnquist than against any other successful Supreme Court nominee in the twentieth century. He also tied for the second-highest number of negative votes when he was confirmed as an associate justice in 1971.

In 1971, the once-obscure Phoenix lawyer was nominated by President Nixon to the Supreme Court.

Rehnquist has been married since 1953 to Natalie Cornell. They have two daughters and a son.

Born Oct. 1, 1924, Milwaukee, Wis.; Stanford University B.A. (1948); Phi Beta Kappa; LL.B (1952); Harvard University M.A. (1949); law clerk to Justice Robert H. Jackson, U.S. Supreme Court 1952-53; married 1953; two daughters, one son; practiced law 1953-69; assistant U.S. attorney general, Office of Legal Counsel 1969-71; nominated as associate justice, U.S. Supreme Court, by President Nixon Oct. 21, 1971; confirmed Dec. 10, 1971; nominated as chief justice of the United States, by President Reagan June 17, 1986; confirmed Sept. 17, 1986.

William Joseph Brennan Jr.

As a member of the activist Warren court, William J. Brennan Jr. became known as an articulate judicial scholar, who framed some of the court's key decisions. On the more conservative Burger court, however, Brennan has been largely confined to writing dissents. But while he has been relegated to a minority voice on the court, Brennan has continued to rise in the esteem of legal scholars, some of whom characterize him as the court's most eminent jurist.

Brennan was born April 25, 1906, in Newark, N.J., the second of eight children of Irish parents who immigrated to the United States in 1890. Brennan displayed impressive academic abilities early in his life. He was an outstanding student in high school, an honors student at the University of Pennsylvania's Wharton School of Finance and graduated in the top 10 percent of his Harvard Law School class in 1931.

Following law school, Brennan returned to Newark, where he joined the law firm of Pitney, Hardin and Skinner. After several years of general practice and the passage of the Wagner Labor Relations Act in 1937, he began to specialize in labor law. With the outbreak of World War II, Brennan entered the Army, serving as a manpower trouble-shooter on the staff of Under Secretary of War Robert B. Patterson.

At the conclusion of the war, Brennan returned to his old law firm. But as his practice swelled, Brennan, a dedicated family man, began to resent the demands which it placed on his time. "My practice was bidding to kill me," he once recalled.

A desire to temper the pace of his work was one of the reasons which prompted Brennan to accept an appointment to the newly-created New Jersey Superior Court. Brennan had been a leader in the movement to establish the court as part of a larger program of judicial reform. Thus it was not surprising when Republican Governor Alfred E. Driscoll named Brennan, a registered, but inactive Democrat, to the Superior Court bench in 1949.

During his tenure on the Superior Court, Brennan's use of pretrial procedures to speed up the disposition of cases brought him to the attention of New Jersey Supreme Court Justice Arthur T. Vanderbilt. It was reportedly at Vanderbilt's suggestion that Brennan was moved first in 1950 to the appellate division of the Superior Court and then in 1952 to the state Supreme Court. Late in 1956, President Eisenhower gave Brennan a recess appointment to the United States Supreme Court, sending his nomination to Congress early in 1957 when the new Congress convened.

Brennan is a football fan and a walker. Aside from these diversions, he is committed to his family and the law. Brennan was married in 1928 to Marjorie Leonard and has three children. After his wife's death in 1982, he married Mary Fowler in March 1983.

Born April 25, 1906, in Newark, N.J.; University of Pennsylvania B.S. (1928); Harvard Law School LL.B (1931); married 1928; two sons, one daughter; practiced law Newark 1931-49; N.J. Superior Court judge 1949; appellate division 1951-52; associate justice N.J. Supreme Court 1952-56; received recess appointment as associate justice, U.S. Supreme Court, from President Eisenhower Oct. 16, 1956; nominated as associate justice by President Eisenhower Jan. 14, 1957; confirmed March 19, 1957.

Byron Raymond White

Byron R. White is noted for his quick and precise legal mind, and his peppery and incisive questioning during oral argument.

White was born June 8, 1917, in Fort Collins, Colo., but grew up in Wellington, a small town in a sugar beet growing area of the state. Ranking first in his high school class, White won a scholarship to the University of Colorado, which he entered in 1934.

At the university White earned his reputation as an outstanding scholar-athlete. He was first in his class, a member of Phi Beta Kappa and the winner of three varsity letters in football, four in basketball and three in baseball. By the end of his college career in 1938 he had been dubbed "Whizzer" White for his outstanding performance as a football player, a performance which earned him not only a national reputation but also a one-year contract with the Pittsburgh Pirates (now the Steelers). White had already accepted a coveted Rhodes Scholarship for study at Oxford, but decided to postpone his year in England.

Despite his success as a pro football player, at the end of the football season, White sailed for England to attend Oxford. When the European war broke out in September 1939, White returned to the United States and entered Yale Law School. But during 1940 and 1941, he alternated law study with playing football for the Detroit Lions.

After the United States entered the war, White served in the Navy in the South Pacific. There he renewed an old acquaintance with John F. Kennedy, whom he had met in England and who later would nominate White to the Supreme Court. After the war, White returned to Yale, earning his law degree *magna cum laude* in 1946. Following graduation, White served as law clerk to U.S. Chief Justice Fred M. Vinson. In 1947, he returned to his native Colorado, where for the next 14 years he practiced law with the Denver firm of Lewis, Grant and Davis.

White renewed his contact with Kennedy during the 1960 presidential campaign, leading the nationwide volunteer group, Citizens for Kennedy. After the election, Kennedy named White to the post of deputy attorney general, a position he held until his Supreme Court appointment in 1962.

White has been married since 1946 to Marion Stearns. They have one son and one daughter.

Born June 8, 1917, in Fort Collins, Colo.; University of Colorado B.A. (1938); Phi Beta Kappa; Rhodes scholar, Oxford University; Yale Law School LL.B *magna cum laude* (1946); married 1946; one son, one daughter; law clerk to Chief Justice Fred M. Vinson, U.S. Supreme Court 1946-47; practiced law, Denver, 1947-60; U.S. deputy attorney general 1961-62; nominated as associate justice, U.S. Supreme Court, by President Kennedy March 30, 1962; confirmed April 11, 1962.

Thurgood Marshall

Unlike some jurists who undergo striking philosophical changes once elevated to the Supreme Court, Thurgood Marshall has deviated little from his earlier convictions. For more than a quarter of a century, Marshall exemplified, through his work with the National Association for the Advancement of Colored People (NAACP), that part of the civil rights movement which sought change through legal processes. Once on the court, Marshall has continued to champion the rights of minorities. And as a member of the court's minority liberal wing, Marshall has persisted in his defense of individual rights.

Marshall was born July 2, 1908, in Baltimore, Md., the son of a primary school teacher and a club steward. In 1926, he left Baltimore to attend all-black Lincoln University in Chester, Pa., where he developed a reputation as an outstanding debater. After graduating *cum laude* in 1930, Marshall decided to study law, and in 1931 he entered Howard University in Washington, D.C.

During his law school years, Marshall began to develop an interest in civil rights. After graduating first in his law school class in 1933, Marshall commenced a long and historic involvement with the NAACP.

In 1940 Marshall became the head of the newly formed NAACP Legal Defense and Educational Fund, a position he held for more than 20 years.

Over the next two and one-half decades, Marshall coordinated the fund's attack on segregation in voting, housing, public accommodations and education. But the culmination of his career as a civil rights attorney came in 1954 as chief counsel in a series of cases grouped under the title *Brown v. Board of Education.* In that historic case, which Marshall argued before the court, civil rights advocates convinced the court to declare that segregation in public schools was unconstitutional.

In 1961, Marshall was appointed by President Kennedy to the U.S. Court of Appeals for the 2nd Circuit, but because of heated opposition from Southern Democratic senators, he was not confirmed until a year later.

Four years after he was named to the circuit court, Marshall was chosen by President Johnson to be the nation's first black solicitor general. During his years as the government's chief advocate before the Supreme Court, Marshall scored impressive victories in the areas of civil and constitutional rights. He won Supreme Court approval of the 1965 Voting Rights Act, voluntarily informed the court that the government had used electronic eavesdropping devices in two cases, and joined in a suit that successfully overturned a California constitutional amendment that prohibited open housing legislation.

On June 13, 1967, Marshall became the first black appointed to be a justice of the Supreme Court, chosen by President Johnson.

Marshall was married in 1955 to Cecelia A. Suyat. He has two sons by his first wife who died in 1955.

Born July 2, 1908, in Baltimore, Md.; Lincoln University B.A. (1930); Howard University LL.B (1933); practiced law 1933-37; assistant special counsel NAACP 1936-38; special counsel 1938-50; married 1955; two sons; director-counsel, NAACP Legal Defense and Educational Fund 1940-61; judge, U.S. Court of Appeals for the 2nd Circuit 1961-65; U.S. Solicitor General 1965-67; nominated as associate justice, U.S. Supreme Court, by President Johnson June 13, 1967; confirmed Aug. 30, 1967.

Harry Andrew Blackmun

During his first years on the court Harry A. Blackmun was frequently described as one of the "Minnesota Twins" along with the court's other Minnesota native, Chief Justice Warren E. Burger. Blackmun and Burger are lifelong friends who initially voted together on important court decisions.

However, Blackmun, who originally impressed observers as a modest, even meek, addition to the court's conservative bloc, has authored some of the court's most controversial decisions, among them its 1973 ruling upholding a woman's right to an abortion. And he has broken frequently enough with his conservative colleagues to earn a reputation as an independent, if still fundamentally conservative, justice.

Blackmun was born in Nashville, Ill., on November 12, 1908, but spent most of his early years in Minneapolis-St. Paul, where his father was an official of the Twin Cities Savings and Loan Co. It was in grade school that Blackmun began his lifelong friendship with Burger.

"A whiz at math," according to his mother, Blackmun went East after high school to attend Harvard College on a scholarship. At Harvard, Blackmun majored in mathematics and toyed briefly with the idea of becoming a physician.

But Blackmun chose the law instead. After graduating from Harvard in 1929, Phi Beta Kappa, Blackmun entered Harvard Law School, from which he graduated in 1932. During his law school years, Blackmun supported himself with a variety of odd jobs, including tutoring in math and driving the launch for the college crew team.

Following law school, Blackmun returned to St. Paul, where he served for a year-and-a-half as a law clerk to United States Circuit Court Judge John B. Sanborn, whom Blackmun succeeded 20 years later. He left the clerkship at the end of 1933 and joined the Minneapolis law firm of Dorsey, Colman, Barker, Scott and Barber. At the same time he taught for a year at William Mitchell College of Law in St. Paul, Chief Justice Burger's alma mater. In addition to his practice he also taught for two years during the 1940s at the University of Minnesota Law School.

In 1950 he accepted a post as "house counsel" for the world-famous Mayo Clinic in Rochester, Minn.

Among his colleagues at the clinic, Blackmun quickly developed a reputation as a serious man, totally engrossed in his profession.

The reputation followed him to the bench of the U.S. Court of Appeals for the 8th Circuit, to which Blackmun was appointed by Eisenhower in 1959. As a judge, he was known for his scholarly and thorough opinions.

Blackmun's total devotion to the law leaves little time for outside activities. He is an avid reader, delving primarily into judicial tomes. Over the years, he has also been active in Methodist church affairs. Before a knee gave out, Blackmun was a proficient squash and tennis player. It was on the tennis court that Blackmun met his future wife, Dorothy E. Clark. They were married in 1941 and have three daughters.

Born Nov. 12, 1908 in Nashville, Ill.; Harvard College B.A. (1929); Phi Beta Kappa; Harvard Law School LL.B. (1932); clerk, John Sanborn, U.S. Court of Appeals for the 8th Circuit, St. Paul 1932-33; practiced law, Minneapolis, 1934-50; married 1941; three daughters; resident counsel, Mayo Clinic, Rochester, Minn. 1950-59; judge, U.S. Court of Appeals for the 8th Circuit 1959-70; nominated as associate justice U.S. Supreme Court, by President Nixon April 14, 1970; confirmed May 12, 1970.

John Paul Stevens

When President Ford nominated federal appeals court Judge John Paul Stevens to the Supreme Court seat vacated by veteran liberal William O. Douglas in 1975, court-watchers and other observers struggled to pin an ideological label on the new nominee. The consensus which emerged was that Stevens was neither a doctrinaire liberal nor conservative, but a judicial "centrist," whose well-crafted, scholarly opinions made him a "judge's judge." His subsequent opinions bear out this description.

A soft-spoken, mild-mannered man who occasionally sports a bow tie under his judicial robes, Stevens had a long record of excellence in scholarship. A member of a prominent Chicago family, Stevens graduated Phi Beta Kappa from the University of Chicago in 1941. After a wartime stint in the Navy, during which he earned the Bronze Star, he returned to Chicago to enter Northwestern University Law School, from which he graduated *magna cum laude* in 1947. From there, Stevens left for Washington, where he served as a law clerk to Supreme Court Justice Wiley Rutledge. He returned to Chicago to join the prominent law firm of Poppenhusen, Johnston, Thompson and Raymond, which specialized in antitrust law. Stevens developed a reputation as a pre-eminent antitrust lawyer, and after three years with Poppenhusen, he left in 1952 to form his own firm, Rothschild, Stevens, Barry and Myers. He remained there, engaging in private practice and teaching part-time at Northwestern and the University of Chicago law schools, until his appointment by President Nixon in 1970 to the U.S. Court of Appeals for the 7th Circuit.

Stevens developed a reputation as a political moderate during his undergraduate days at the University of Chicago, then an overwhelmingly liberal campus. But although he is a registered Republican, he has never been active in partisan politics. Nevertheless, Stevens did serve as Republican counsel in 1951 to the House Judiciary Committee's Subcommittee on the Study of Monopoly Power. He also served from 1953 to 1955, during the Eisenhower administration, as a member of the Attorney General's National Committee to Study the Antitrust Laws.

An enthusiastic pilot, Stevens flies his own small plane. According to friends, he is also a creditable bridge player and golfer. Stevens underwent open heart surgery several years ago, from which he is said to have recovered fully. However, the operation did force him to give up the game of squash. In 1942, Stevens married Elizabeth Jane Sheeren. They have four children. They were divorced in 1979. Stevens subsequently married Maryan Mulholland Simon, a longtime neighbor in Chicago.

Born April 20, 1920, Chicago, Ill.; University of Chicago B.A. (1941); Phi Beta Kappa; Northwestern University School of Law J.D. (1947); *magna cum laude;* married 1942; three daughters, one son; divorced 1979; married Maryan Mulholland Simon 1980; law clerk to Justice Wiley Rutledge, U.S. Supreme Court 1947-48; practiced law Chicago, 1949-70; judge, U.S. Court of Appeals for the 7th Circuit 1970-75; nominated as associate justice, U.S. Supreme Court, by President Ford Nov. 28, 1975; confirmed Dec. 17, 1975.

Sandra Day O'Connor

Pioneering came naturally to Sandra Day O'Connor. Her grandfather left Kansas in 1880 to take up ranching in the desert land that would eventually become the state of Arizona. O'Connor, born in El Paso where her mother's parents lived, was raised on the Lazy B Ranch, the 162,000-acre spread that her grandfather had founded in southeastern Arizona near Duncan. She spent her school years in El Paso, living with her grandmother and attending the schools there. She graduated from high school at age 16 and then entered Stanford University.

Six years later, in 1952, Sandra Day had won degrees, with great distinction, both from the university, in economics, and from Stanford Law School. There she met John J. O'Connor III, her future husband, and was also a classmate of William H. Rehnquist, a future colleague on the Supreme Court. During her law school years, Sandra Day was an editor of the Stanford Law Review and a member of Order of the Coif, both reflecting her academic leadership.

But despite her outstanding law school record, she found it difficult to locate a job as an attorney in 1952 when relatively few women were practicing law. She applied, among others, to the firm in which William French Smith — attorney general in the Reagan administration — was a partner, only to be offered a job as a secretary.

After a short stint as deputy county attorney for San Mateo County (Calif.) while her new husband completed law school at Stanford, the O'Connors moved with the U.S. Army to Frankfurt, Germany. There Sandra O'Connor worked as a civilian attorney for the Army, while John O'Connor served his tour of duty.

In 1957, they returned to Phoenix to live. In the next eight years, their three sons were born and O'Connor's life was a mix of mothering, homemaking, volunteer work and some "miscellaneous legal tasks" on the side.

In 1965, O'Connor resumed her legal career full time, taking a job as an assistant attorney general for Arizona. After four years in that post, she was appointed to fill a vacancy in the state Senate, where she served on the judiciary committee. In 1970, she was elected to the Senate, and two years later was chosen its majority leader; the first woman in the nation to hold such a post.

O'Connor was active in Republican Party politics and was co-chairman of the Arizona Committee to Re-Elect the President in 1972.

In 1974, she was elected to the Superior Court for Maricopa County where she served for five years. Then in 1979, Gov. Bruce Babbitt — acting, some said, to remove a potential rival for the governorship — appointed O'Connor to the Arizona Court of Appeals. It was from that seat that President Reagan chose her as his first nominee to the Supreme Court, describing her as "a person for all seasons."

She was confirmed unanimously Sept. 21, 1981, by the Senate as the first woman associate justice of the U.S. Supreme Court.

Born March 26, 1930 in El Paso, Texas; Stanford University, B.A. (1950); *magna cum laude*; Stanford University Law School, LL.B. (1952); with high honors; deputy county attorney, San Mateo, Calif., 1952-53; assistant attorney general, Arizona, 1965-69; Arizona state senator, 1969-1975, Senate majority leader, 1972-75; judge, Maricopa County Superior Court, 1974-79; judge, Arizona Court of Appeals, 1979-81; married John J. O'Connor III, Dec. 20, 1952; three sons; nominated associate justice U.S. Supreme Court, by President Ronald Reagan Aug. 19, 1981, to replace Potter Stewart, who retired; confirmed by the U.S. Senate Sept. 21, 1981, by a vote of 99-0.

Antonin Scalia

When Warren Burger resigned and President Reagan named William Rehnquist to be the new chief justice, it was not surprising that he would appoint Antonin Scalia to the Supreme Court. On issues dear to Reagan, it was clear that Scalia met the president's tests for conservatism. Scalia, whom Reagan named to the U.S. Court of Appeals for the District of Columbia in 1982, became the first justice of Italian ancestry. A Roman Catholic, he has nine children and opposes abortion. He has also expressed opposition to "affirmative action" preferences for minorities.

The president is a strong advocate of deregulation, a subject of considerable interest to Scalia, a specialist in administrative law. Scalia was from 1977-82 editor of the magazine *Regulation,* published by the American Enterprise Institute for Public Policy Research.

In sharp contrast to the hours of floor debate over Rehnquist's nomination, only a few moments of speeches were held in opposition to the equally conservative Scalia before he was confirmed.

Born in Trenton, N.J., on March 11, 1936, Scalia grew up in Queens, N.Y. He graduated from Georgetown University in 1957 and from Harvard Law School in 1960.

He worked for six years at the firm of Jones, Day in Cleveland and then taught contract, commercial and comparative law at the University of Virginia Law School.

Scalia served as general counsel of the White House Office of Telecommunications Policy in 1971-72. He then headed the Administrative Conference of the United States, a group that advises the government on questions of administrative law and procedure. From 1974 through the Ford administration he headed the Justice Department's Office of Legal Counsel, a post Rehnquist held three years earlier. Scalia then returned to academia, to teach at the University of Chicago Law School.

Scalia has shown himself a hard worker, an aggressive interrogator and an articulate advocate. He has been impatient with what he sees as regulatory or judicial overreaching. In 1983, he dissented from an appeals court ruling requiring the Food and Drug Administration to consider whether drugs used for lethal injections met FDA standards as safe and effective. The Supreme Court agreed, reversing the appeals court in 1985.

Scalia was thought to be the principal author of an unsigned decision in 1986 that declared key portions of the Gramm-Rudman-Hollings budget-balancing act unconstitutional. The Supreme Court upheld the decision later in the year.

Born March 11, 1936, Trenton, N.J.; Georgetown University A.B. (1957); Harvard University, LL.B. (1960); practiced law in Cleveland, 1960-67; married to Maureen McCarthy; nine children; taught at the University of Virginia, 1967-71; general counsel, White House Office of Telecommunications Policy 1971-72; chairman Administrative Conference of the United States 1972-74; head Office of Legal Counsel 1974-77; taught at the University of Chicago Law School 1977-82; judge, U.S. Court of Appeals, District of Columbia; nominated as associate justice, U.S. Supreme Court June 17, 1986; confirmed Sept. 17, 1986.

Glossary of Congressional Terms

Act—The term for legislation once it has passed both houses of Congress and has been signed by the president or passed over his veto, thus becoming law. *(See below.)* Also used in parliamentary terminology for a bill that has been passed by one house and engrossed. *(See Engrossed Bill.)*

Adjournment Sine Die—Adjournment without definitely fixing a day for reconvening; literally "adjournment without a day." Usually used to connote the final adjournment of a session of Congress. A session can continue until noon, Jan. 3, of the following year, when, under the 20th Amendment to the Constitution, it automatically terminates. Both houses must agree to a concurrent resolution for either house to adjourn for more than three days.

Adjournment to a Day Certain—Adjournment under a motion or resolution that fixes the next time of meeting. Under the Constitution, neither house can adjourn for more than three days without the concurrence of the other. A session of Congress is not ended by adjournment to a day certain.

Amendment—A proposal of a member of Congress to alter the language, provisions or stipulations in a bill or in another amendment. An amendment usually is printed, debated and voted upon in the same manner as a bill.

Amendment in the Nature of a Substitute—Usually an amendment that seeks to replace the entire text of a bill. Passage of this type of amendment strikes out everything after the enacting clause and inserts a new version of the bill. An amendment in the nature of a substitute also can refer to an amendment that replaces a large portion of the text of a bill.

Appeal—A member's challenge of a ruling or decision made by the presiding officer of the chamber. In the Senate, the senator appeals to members of the chamber to override the decision. If carried by a majority vote, the appeal nullifies the chair's ruling. In the House, the decision of the Speaker traditionally has been final; seldom are there appeals to the members to reverse the Speaker's stand. To appeal a ruling is considered an attack on the Speaker.

Appropriations Bill—A bill that gives legal authority to spend or obligate money from the Treasury. The Constitution disallows money to be drawn from the Treasury "but in Consequence of Appropriations made by Law."

By congressional custom, an appropriations bill originates in the House, and it is not supposed to be considered by the full House or Senate until a related measure authorizing the funding is enacted; appropriations bills need not provide the full amount permissible under the authorization measures. Under the 1985 Gramm-Rudman-Hollings law, the House is supposed to pass by June 30 the last regular appropriations bill for the fiscal year starting the following Oct. 1. *(See also Authorization, Budget Process.)*

In addition to general appropriations bills, there are two specialized types. *(See Continuing Resolution, Supplemental Appropriations Bill.)*

Authorization—Basic, substantive legislation that establishes or continues the legal operation of a federal program or agency, either indefinitely or for a specific period of time, or which sanctions a particular type of obligation or expenditure. An authorization normally is a prerequisite for an appropriation or other kind of budget authority. Under the rules of both houses, the appropriation for a program or agency may not be considered until its authorization has been considered. An authorization also may limit the amount of budget authority to be provided or may authorize the appropriation of "such sums as may be necessary." *(See also Backdoor Spending.)*

Backdoor Spending—Budget authority provided in legislation outside the normal appropriations process. The most common forms of backdoor spending are borrowing authority, contract authority and entitlements. *(See below.)*

In some cases, such as interest on the public debt, a permanent appropriation is provided that becomes available without further action by Congress.

Bills—Most legislative proposals before Congress are in the form of bills and are designated by HR in the House of Representatives or S in the Senate, according to the house in which they originate, and by a number assigned in the order in which they are introduced during the two-year period of a congressional term. "Public bills" deal with general questions and become public laws if approved by Congress and signed by the president. "Private bills" deal with individual matters such as claims against the government, immigration and naturalization cases, land titles, etc., and become private laws if approved and signed. *(See also Concurrent Resolution, Joint Resolution, Resolution.)*

Bills Introduced—In both the House and Senate, any number of members may join in introducing a single bill or resolution. The first member listed is the sponsor of the bill, and all members' names following his are the bill's cosponsors.

Many bills are committee bills and are introduced under the name of the chairman of the committee or subcommittee. All appropriations bills fall into this category. A committee frequently holds hearings on a number of related bills and may agree to one of them or to an entirely new bill. *(See also Report, Clean Bill, By Request.)*

Bills Referred—When introduced, a bill is referred to the committee or committees that have jurisdiction over the subject with which the bill is concerned. Under the standing rules of the House and Senate, bills are referred by the Speaker in the House and by the presiding officer in the Senate. In practice, the House and Senate parliamentarians act for these officials and refer the vast majority of bills.

Borrowing Authority—Statutory authority that permits a federal agency to incur obligations and make payments for specified purposes with borrowed money.

Budget—The document sent to Congress by the president early each year estimating government revenue and expenditures for the ensuing fiscal year.

Budget Authority—Authority to enter into obligations that will result in immediate or future outlays involving federal funds. The basic forms of budget authority are appropriations, contract authority and borrowing authority. Budget authority may be classified by (1) the period of availability (one-year, multiple-year or without a time limitation), (2) the timing of congressional action (current or permanent), or (3) the manner of determining the amount available (definite or indefinite).

Budget Process—Congress in 1985 attempted to strengthen its 11-year-old budget process with the goal of balancing the federal budget by October 1980. The law, known as Gramm-Rudman-Hollings for its congressional sponsors, established annual maximum deficit targets and mandated across-the-board automatic cuts if the deficit goals were not achieved through regular budget and appropriations action.

The 1985 law also established an accelerated timetable for presidential submission of budgets and for congressional approval of budget resolutions and reconciliation bills, two mechanisms created by the Congressional Budget and Impoundment Control Act of 1974. Budget resolutions, due by April 15 annually, set guidelines for congressional action on spending and tax measures; they are adopted by the House and Senate but are not signed by the president and do not have the force of law. Reconciliation bills, due by June 15, actually make changes in existing law to meet budget resolution goals. *(See Budget Reconciliation)*

A special federal court found Gramm-Rudman's automatic spending cut mechanism to be unconstitutional. The mechanism was to be activated in mid-August each year if deficit re-estimates showed Congress and the president had not managed through conventional legislation to hold deficits below targets set by the statute. Absent the automatic device, the cuts necessitated by those estimates would take effect only if approved by Congress and the president. The Supreme Court July 7, 1986, upheld the lower court ruling that the automatic mechanism violated the separation-of-powers doctrine, because it assigned executive-type responsibilities to the General Accounting Office, which the court found to be a legislative branch entity. Under the remaining procedure deficit re-estimates will be made, but Congress and the president must approve any spending cuts.

Budget Reconciliation—The 1974 budget act provides for a "reconciliation" procedure for bringing existing tax and spending laws into conformity with the congressional budget resolutions. Under the procedure, Congress instructs designated legislative committees to approve measures adjusting revenues and expenditures by a certain amount. The committees have a deadline by which they must report the legislation, but they have the discretion of deciding what changes are to be made. The recommendations of the various committees are consolidated without change by the Budget committees into an omnibus reconciliation bill, which then must be considered and approved by both houses of Congress.

By Request—A phrase used when a senator or representative introduces a bill at the request of an executive agency or private organization but does not necessarily endorse the legislation.

Calendar—An agenda or list of business awaiting possible action by each chamber. The House uses five legislative calendars. *(See Consent, Discharge, House, Private and Union Calendar.)*

In the Senate, all legislative matters reported from committee go on one calendar. They are listed there in the order in which committees report them or the Senate places them on the calendar, but may be called up out of order by the majority leader, either by obtaining unanimous consent of the Senate or by a motion to call up a bill. The Senate also uses one non-legislative calendar; this is used for treaties and nominations. *(See Executive Calendar.)*

Calendar Wednesday—In the House, committees, on Wednesdays, may be called in the order in which they appear in Rule X of the House, for the purpose of bringing up any of their bills from either the House or the Union Calendar, except bills that are privileged. General debate is limited to two hours. Bills called up from the Union Calendar are considered in Committee of the Whole. Calendar Wednesday is not observed during the last two weeks of a session and may be dispensed with at other times by a two-thirds vote. This procedure is rarely used and routinely is dispensed with by unanimous consent.

Call of the Calendar—Senate bills that are not brought up for debate by a motion, unanimous consent or a unanimous consent agreement are brought before the Senate for action when the calendar listing them is "called." Bills must be called in the order listed. Measures considered by this method usually are non-controversial, and debate is limited to a total of five minutes for each senator on the bill and any amendments proposed to it.

Chamber—The meeting place for the membership of either the House or the Senate; also the membership of the House or Senate meeting as such.

Clean Bill—Frequently after a committee has finished a major revision of a bill, one of the committee members, usually the chairman, will assemble the changes and what is left of the original bill into a new measure and introduce it as a "clean bill." The revised measure, which is given a new number, then is referred back to the committee, which reports it to the floor for consideration. This often is a timesaver, as committee-recommended changes in a clean bill do not have to be considered and voted on by the chamber. Reporting a clean bill also protects committee amendments that might be subject to points of order concerning germaneness.

Clerk of the House—Chief administrative officer of the House of Representatives, with duties corresponding to those of the secretary of the Senate. *(See also Secretary of the Senate.)*

Cloture—The process by which a filibuster can be ended in the Senate other than by unanimous consent. A motion for cloture can apply to any measure before the Senate, including a proposal to change the chamber's rules. A cloture motion requires the signatures of 16 senators to be introduced, and to end a filibuster the cloture motion must obtain the votes of three-fifths of the entire Senate membership (60 if there are no vacancies), except that to end a filibuster against a proposal to amend the standing rules of the Senate a two-thirds vote of senators present and voting is required. The cloture request is put to a roll-call vote one hour after the Senate meets on the second day following introduction of the motion. If approved, cloture limits each senator to one hour of debate. The bill or amendment in question comes to a final vote after 100 hours of consideration (including debate time and the time it takes to conduct roll calls, quorum calls and other procedural motions). *(See Filibuster.)*

Committee—A division of the House or Senate that prepares legislation for action by the parent chamber or makes investigations as directed by the parent chamber. There are several types of committees. *(See Standing and Select or Special Committees.)* Most standing committees are divided into subcommittees, which study legislation, hold hearings and report bills, with or without amendments, to the full committee. Only the full committee can report legislation for action by the House or Senate.

Committee of the Whole—The working title of what is formally "The Committee of the Whole House (of Representatives) on the State of the Union." The membership is comprised of all House members sitting as a committee. Any 100 members who are present on the floor of the chamber to consider legislation comprise a quorum of the committee. Any legislation, however, must first have passed through the regular legislative or Appropriations committee and have been placed on the calendar.

Technically, the Committee of the Whole considers only bills directly or indirectly appropriating money, authorizing appropriations or involving taxes or charges on the public. Because the Committee of the Whole need number only 100 representatives, a quorum is more readily attained, and legislative business is expedited. Before 1971, members' positions were not individually recorded on votes taken in Committee of the Whole. *(See Teller Vote.)*

When the full House resolves itself into the Committee of the Whole, it supplants the Speaker with a "chairman." A measure is debated and amendments may be proposed, with votes on amendments as needed. *(See Five-Minute Rule.)* When the committee completes its work on the measure, it dissolves itself by "rising." The Speaker returns, and the chairman of the Committee of the Whole reports to the House that the committee's work has been completed. At this time members may demand a roll-call vote on any amendment *adopted* in the Committee of the Whole. The final vote is on passage of the legislation.

Committee Veto—A requirement added to a few statutes directing that certain policy directives by an executive department or agency be reviewed by certain congressional committees before they are implemented. Under common practice, the government department or agency and the committees involved are expected to reach a consensus before the directives are carried out. *(See also Legislative Veto.)*

Concurrent Resolution—A concurrent resolution, designated H Con Res or S Con Res, must be adopted by both houses, but it is not sent to the president for his signature and therefore does not have the force of law. A concurrent resolution, for example, is used to fix the time for adjournment of a Congress. It also is used as the vehicle for expressing the sense of Congress on various foreign policy and domestic issues, and it serves as the vehicle for coordinated decisions on the federal budget under the 1974 Congressional Budget and Impoundment Control Act. *(See also Bills, Joint Resolution, Resolution.)*

Conference—A meeting between the representatives of the House and the Senate to reconcile differences between the two houses on provisions of a bill passed by both chambers. Members of the conference committee are appointed by the Speaker and the presiding officer of the Senate and are called "managers" for their respective chambers. A majority of the managers for each house must reach agreement on the provisions of the bill (often a compromise between the versions of the two chambers) before it can be considered by either chamber in the form of a "conference report." When the conference report goes to the floor, it cannot be amended, and, if it is not approved by both chambers, the bill may go back to conference under certain situations, or a new conference must be convened. Many rules and informal practices govern the conduct of conference committees.

Bills that are passed by both houses with only minor differences need not be sent to conference. Either chamber may "concur" in the other's amendments, completing action on the legislation. Sometimes leaders of the committees of jurisdiction work out an informal compromise instead of having a formal conference. *(See Custody of the Papers.)*

Confirmations—*(See Nominations.)*

Congressional Record—The daily, printed account of proceedings in both the House and Senate chambers, showing substantially verbatim debate, statements and a record of floor action. Highlights of legislative and committee action are embodied in a Daily Digest section of the Record, and members are entitled to have their extraneous remarks printed in an appendix known as "Extension of Remarks." Members may edit and revise remarks made on the floor during debate, and quotations from debate reported by the press are not always found in the Record.

The Record provides a way to distinguish remarks spoken on the floor of the House and Senate from undelivered speeches. In the Senate, all speeches, articles and other matter that members insert in the Record without actually reading them on the floor are set off by large black dots, or bullets. However, a loophole allows a member to avoid the bulleting if he delivers any portion of the speech in person. In the House, undelivered speeches and other material are printed in a distinctive typeface.

Congressional Terms of Office—Normally begin on Jan. 3 of the year following a general election and are two years for representatives and six years for senators. Representatives elected in special elections are sworn in for the remainder of a term. A person may be appointed to fill a Senate vacancy and serve until a successor is elected; the successor serves until the end of the term applying to the vacant seat.

Consent Calendar—Members of the House may place on this calendar most bills on the Union or House Calendar that are considered to be non-controversial. Bills on the Consent Calendar normally are called on the first and third Mondays of each month. On the first occasion that a bill is called in this manner, consideration may be blocked by the objection of any member. The second time, if there are three objections, the bill is stricken from the Consent Calendar. If fewer than three members object, the bill is given immediate consideration.

A bill on the Consent Calendar may be postponed in

another way. A member may ask that the measure be passed over "without prejudice." In that case, no objection is recorded against the bill, and its status on the Consent Calendar remains unchanged. A bill stricken from the Consent Calendar remains on the Union or House Calendar.

Cosponsor—*(See Bills Introduced.)*

Continuing Resolution—A joint resolution drafted by Congress "continuing appropriations" for specific ongoing activities of a government department or departments when a fiscal year begins and Congress has not yet enacted all of the regular appropriations bills for that year. The continuing resolution usually specifies a maximum rate at which the agency may incur obligations. This usually is based on the rate for the previous year, the president's budget request or an appropriation bill for that year passed by either or both houses of Congress, but not cleared.

Contract Authority—Budget authority contained in an authorization bill that permits the federal government to enter into contracts or other obligations for future payments from funds not yet appropriated by Congress. The assumption is that funds will be available for payment in a subsequent appropriation act.

Controllable Budget Items—In federal budgeting this refers to programs for which the budget authority or outlays during a fiscal year can be controlled without changing existing, substantive law. The concept "relatively uncontrollable under current law" includes outlays for open-ended programs and fixed costs such as interest on the public debt, Social Security benefits, veterans' benefits and outlays to liquidate prior-year obligations.

Correcting Recorded Votes—Rules prohibit members from changing their votes after the result has been announced. But, occasionally hours, days or months after a vote has been taken, a member may announce that he was "incorrectly recorded." In the Senate, a request to change one's vote almost always receives unanimous consent. In the House, members are prohibited from changing their votes if tallied by the electronic voting system installed in 1973. If taken by roll call, it is permissible if consent is granted.

Current Services Estimates—Estimated budget authority and outlays for federal programs and operations for the forthcoming fiscal year based on continuation of existing levels of service without policy changes. These estimates of budget authority and outlays, accompanied by the underlying economic and policy assumptions upon which they are based, are transmitted by the president to Congress when the budget is submitted.

Custody of the Papers—To reconcile differences between the House and Senate versions of a bill, a conference may be arranged. The chamber with "custody of the papers" — the engrossed bill, engrossed amendments, messages of transmittal — is the only body empowered to request the conference. By custom, the chamber that asks for a conference is the last to act on the conference report once agreement has been reached on the bill by the conferees. Custody of the papers sometimes is manipulated to ensure that a particular chamber acts either first or last on the conference report.

Deferral—Executive branch action to defer, or delay, the spending of appropriated money. The 1974 Congressional Budget and Impoundment Control Act requires a special message from the president to Congress reporting a proposed deferral of spending. Deferrals may not extend beyond the end of the fiscal year in which the message is transmitted. A federal district court in 1986 struck down the president's authority to defer spending for policy reasons; the Justice Department planned to appeal. *(See also Rescission Bill.)*

Dilatory Motion—A motion made for the purpose of killing time and preventing action on a bill or amendment. House rules outlaw dilatory motions, but enforcement is largely within the discretion of the Speaker or chairman of the Committee of the Whole. The Senate does not have a rule banning dilatory motions, except under cloture.

Discharge a Committee—Occasionally, attempts are made to relieve a committee from jurisdiction over a measure before it. This is attempted more often in the House than in the Senate, and the procedure rarely is successful.

In the House, if a committee does not report a bill within 30 days after the measure is referred to it, any member may file a discharge motion. Once offered, the motion is treated as a petition needing the signatures of 218 members (a majority of the House). After the required signatures have been obtained, there is a delay of seven days. Thereafter, on the second and fourth Mondays of each month, except during the last six days of a session, any member who has signed the petition must be recognized, if he so desires, to move that the committee be discharged. Debate on the motion to discharge is limited to 20 minutes, and, if the motion is carried, consideration of the bill becomes a matter of high privilege.

If a resolution to consider a bill is held up in the Rules Committee for more than seven legislative days, any member may enter a motion to discharge the committee. The motion is handled like any other discharge petition in the House.

Occasionally, to expedite non-controversial legislative business, a committee is discharged by unanimous consent of the House, and a petition is not required. *(Senate procedure, see Discharge Resolution.)*

Discharge Calendar—The House calendar to which motions to discharge committees are referred when they have the required number of signatures (218) and are awaiting floor action.

Discharge Petition—*(See Discharge a Committee.)*

Discharge Resolution—In the Senate, a special motion that any senator may introduce to relieve a committee from consideration of a bill before it. The resolution can be called up for Senate approval or disapproval in the same manner as any other Senate business. *(House procedure, see Discharge a Committee.)*

Division of a Question for Voting—A practice that is more common in the Senate but also used in the House, a member may demand a division of an amendment or a motion for purposes of voting. Where an amendment or motion can be divided, the individual parts are voted on separately when a member demands a division. This procedure occurs most often during the consideration of conference reports.

Division Vote—*(See Standing Vote.)*

Enacting Clause—Key phrase in bills beginning, "Be it enacted by the Senate and House of Representatives. . . ." A successful motion to strike it from legislation kills the measure.

Engrossed Bill—The final copy of a bill as passed by one chamber, with the text as amended by floor action and certified by the clerk of the House or the secretary of the Senate.

Enrolled Bill—The final copy of a bill that has been passed in identical form by both chambers. It is certified by an officer of the house of origin (clerk of the House or secretary of the Senate) and then sent on for the signatures of the House Speaker, the Senate president pro tempore and the president of the United States. An enrolled bill is printed on parchment.

Entitlement Program—A federal program that guarantees a certain level of benefits to persons or other entities who meet requirements set by law, such as Social Security or unemployment benefits. It thus leaves no discretion with Congress on how much money to appropriate.

Executive Calendar—This is a non-legislative calendar in the Senate on which presidential documents such as treaties and nominations are listed.

Executive Document—A document, usually a treaty, sent to the Senate by the president for consideration or approval. Executive documents are identified for each session of Congress as Executive A, 97th Congress, 1st Session; Executive B, etc. They are referred to committee in the same manner as other measures. Unlike legislative documents, however, treaties do not die at the end of a Congress but remain "live" proposals until acted on by the Senate or withdrawn by the president.

Executive Session—A meeting of a Senate or House committee (or occasionally of either chamber) that only its members may attend. Witnesses regularly appear at committee meetings in executive session — for example, Defense Department officials during presentations of classified defense information. Other members of Congress may be invited, but the public and press are not allowed to attend.

Expenditures—The actual spending of money as distinguished from the appropriation of funds. Expenditures are made by the disbursing officers of the administration; appropriations are made only by Congress. The two are rarely identical in any fiscal year. In addition to some current budget authority, expenditures may represent budget authority made available one, two or more years earlier.

Filibuster—A time-delaying tactic associated with the Senate and used by a minority in an effort to prevent a vote on a bill or amendment that probably would pass if voted upon directly. The most common method is to take advantage of the Senate's rules permitting unlimited debate, but other forms of parliamentary maneuvering may be used. The stricter rules used by the House make filibusters more difficult, but delaying tactics are employed occasionally through various procedural devices allowed by House rules. *(Senate filibusters, see Cloture.)*

Fiscal Year—Financial operations of the government are carried out in a 12-month fiscal year, beginning on Oct. 1 and ending on Sept. 30. The fiscal year carries the date of the calendar year in which it ends. (From fiscal year 1844 to fiscal year 1976, the fiscal year began July 1 and ended the following June 30.)

Five-Minute Rule—A debate-limiting rule of the House that is invoked when the House sits as the Committee of the Whole. Under the rule, a member offering an amendment is allowed to speak five minutes in its favor, and an opponent of the amendment is allowed to speak five minutes in opposition. Debate is then closed. In practice, amendments regularly are debated more than 10 minutes, with members gaining the floor by offering pro forma amendments or obtaining unanimous consent to speak longer than five minutes. *(See Strike Out the Last Word.)*

Floor Manager—A member who has the task of steering legislation through floor debate and the amendment process to a final vote in the House or the Senate. Floor managers are usually chairmen or ranking members of the committee that reported the bill. Managers are responsible for apportioning the debate time granted supporters of the bill. The ranking minority member of the committee normally apportions time for the minority party's participation in the debate.

Frank—A member's facsimile signature, which is used on envelopes in lieu of stamps, for the member's official outgoing mail. The "franking privilege" is the right to send mail postage-free.

Germane—Pertaining to the subject matter of the measure at hand. All House amendments must be germane to the bill being considered. The Senate requires that amendments be germane when they are proposed to general appropriation bills, bills being considered once cloture has been adopted, or, frequently, when proceeding under a unanimous consent agreement placing a time limit on consideration of a bill. The 1974 budget act also requires that amendments to concurrent budget resolutions be germane. In the House, floor debate must be germane, and the first three hours of debate each day in the Senate must be germane to the pending business.

Grandfather Clause—A provision exempting persons or other entities already engaged in an activity from rules or legislation affecting that activity. Grandfather clauses sometimes are added to legislation in order to avoid antagonizing groups with established interests in the activities affected.

Grants-in-Aid—Payments by the federal government to states, local governments or individuals in support of specified programs, services or activities.

Guaranteed Loans—Loans to third parties for which the federal government in the event of default guarantees, in whole or in part, the repayment of principal or interest to a lender or holder of a security.

Hearings—Committee sessions for taking testimony from witnesses. At hearings on legislation, witnesses usually include specialists, government officials and spokesmen for persons or entities affected by the bill or bills under study. Hearings related to special investigations bring forth a variety of witnesses. Committees sometimes use their subpoena power to summon reluctant witnesses. The public and press may attend open hearings, but are barred from closed, or "executive," hearings. The vast majority of hearings are open to the public. *(See Executive Session.)*

Hold-Harmless Clause—A provision added to legislation to ensure that recipients of federal funds do not receive less in a future year than they did in the current year if a new formula for allocating funds authorized in the legislation would result in a reduction to the recipients. This clause has been used most frequently to soften the impact of sudden reductions in federal grants.

Hopper—Box on House clerk's desk where members deposit bills and resolutions to introduce them. *(See also Bills Introduced.)*

Hour Rule—A provision in the rules of the House that permits one hour of debate time for each member on amendments debated in the House of Representatives sitting as the House. Therefore, the House normally amends bills while sitting as the Committee of the Whole, where the five-minute rule on amendments operates. *(See Committee of the Whole, Five-Minute Rule.)*

House—The House of Representatives, as distinct from the Senate, although each body is a "house" of Congress.

House as in Committee of the Whole—A procedure that can be used to expedite consideration of certain measures such as continuing resolutions and, when there is debate, private bills. The procedure only can be invoked with the unanimous consent of the House or a rule from the Rules Committee and has procedural elements of both the House sitting as the House of Representatives, such as the Speaker presiding and the previous question motion being in order, and the House sitting as the Committee of the Whole, such as the five-minute rule pertaining.

House Calendar—A listing for action by the House of public bills that do not directly or indirectly appropriate money or raise revenue.

Immunity—The constitutional privilege of members of Congress to make verbal statements on the floor and in committee for which they cannot be sued or arrested for slander or libel. Also, freedom from arrest while traveling to or from sessions of Congress or on official business. Members in this status may be arrested only for treason, felonies or a breach of the peace, as defined by congressional manuals.

Impoundments —Any action taken by the executive branch that delays or precludes the obligation or expenditure of budget authority previously approved by Congress. *(See also Deferral, Rescission Bill.)*

Joint Committee—A committee composed of a specified number of members of both the House and Senate. A joint committee may be investigative or research-oriented, an example of the latter being the Joint Economic Committee. Others have housekeeping duties such as the joint committees on Printing and on the Library of Congress.

Joint Resolution—A joint resolution, designated H J Res or S J Res, requires the approval of both houses and the signature of the president, just as a bill does, and has the force of law if approved. There is no practical difference between a bill and a joint resolution. A joint resolution generally is used to deal with a limited matter such as a single appropriation.

Joint resolutions also are used to propose amendments to the Constitution in Congress. They do not require a presidential signature, but become a part of the Constitution when three-fourths of the states have ratified them.

Journal—The official record of the proceedings of the House and Senate. The *Journal* records the actions taken in each chamber, but, unlike the *Congressional Record*, it does not include the substantially verbatim report of speeches, debates, etc.

Law—An act of Congress that has been signed by the president or passed over his veto by Congress. Public bills, when signed, become public laws, and are cited by the letters PL and a hyphenated number. The two digits before the number correspond to the Congress, and the one or more digits after the hyphen refer to the numerical sequence in which the bills were signed by the president during that Congress. Private bills, when signed, become private laws. *(See also Slip Laws, Statutes at Large, U.S. Code.)*

Legislative Day—The "day" extending from the time either house meets after an adjournment until the time it next adjourns. Because the House normally adjourns from day to day, legislative days and calendar days usually coincide. But in the Senate, a legislative day may, and frequently does, extend over several calendar days. *(See Recess.)*

Legislative Veto—A procedure, no longer allowed, permitting either the House or Senate, or both chambers, to review proposed executive branch regulations or actions and to block or modify those with which they disagreed.

The specifics of the procedure varied, but Congress generally provided for a legislative veto by including in a bill a provision that administrative rules or action taken to implement the law were to go into effect at the end of a designated period of time unless blocked by either or both houses of Congress. Another version of the veto provided for congressional reconsideration and rejection of regulations already in effect.

The Supreme Court June 23, 1983, struck down the legislative veto as an unconstitutional violation of the law-making procedure provided in the Constitution.

Lobby—A group seeking to influence the passage or defeat of legislation. Originally the term referred to persons frequenting the lobbies or corridors of legislative chambers in order to speak to lawmakers.

The definition of a lobby and the activity of lobbying is a matter of differing interpretation. By some definitions, lobbying is limited to direct attempts to influence lawmakers through personal interviews and persuasion. Under other definitions, lobbying includes attempts at indirect, or "grass-roots," influence, such as persuading members of a group to write or visit their district's representative and state's senators or attempting to create a climate of opinion favorable to a desired legislative goal.

The right to attempt to influence legislation is based on the First Amendment to the Constitution, which says Congress shall make no law abridging the right of the people "to petition the government for a redress of grievances."

Majority Leader—The majority leader is elected by his party colleagues. In the Senate, in consultation with the minority leader and his colleagues, the majority leader directs the legislative schedule for the chamber. He also is his party's spokesman and chief strategist. In the House, the majority leader is second to the Speaker in the majority party's leadership and serves as his party's legislative strategist.

Majority Whip—In effect, the assistant majority leader, in either the House or Senate. His job is to help marshal majority forces in support of party strategy and legislation.

Manual—The official handbook in each house prescribing in detail its organization, procedures and operations.

Marking Up a Bill—Going through the contents of a piece of legislation in committee or subcommittee, considering its provisions in large and small portions, acting on amendments to provisions and proposed revisions to the language, inserting new sections and phraseology, etc. If the bill is extensively amended, the committee's version may be introduced as a separate bill, with a new number, before being considered by the full House or Senate. *(See Clean Bill.)*

Minority Leader—Floor leader for the minority party in each chamber. *(See also Majority Leader.)*

Minority Whip—Performs duties of whip for the minority party. *(See also Majority Whip.)*

Morning Hour—The time set aside at the beginning of each legislative day for the consideration of regular, routine business. The "hour" is of indefinite duration in the House, where it is rarely used.

In the Senate it is the first two hours of a session following an adjournment, as distinguished from a recess. The morning hour can be terminated earlier if the morning business has been completed.

Business includes such matters as messages from the president, communications from the heads of departments, messages from the House, the presentation of petitions, reports of standing and select committees and the introduction of bills and resolutions.

During the first hour of the morning hour in the Senate, no motion to proceed to the consideration of any bill on the calendar is in order except by unanimous consent. During the second hour, motions can be made but must be decided without debate. Senate committees may meet while the Senate conducts morning hour.

Motion—In the House or Senate chamber, a request by a member to institute any one of a wide array of parliamentary actions. He "moves" for a certain procedure, the consideration of a measure, etc. The precedence of motions, and whether they are debatable, is set forth in the House and Senate manuals. *(See some specific motions above and below.)*

Nominations—Presidential appointments to office subject to Senate confirmation. Although most nominations win quick Senate approval, some are controversial and become the topic of hearings and debate. Sometimes senators object to appointees for patronage reasons — for example, when a nomination to a local federal job is made without consulting the senators of the state concerned. In some situations a senator may object that the nominee is "personally obnoxious" to him. Usually other senators join in blocking such appointments out of courtesy to their colleagues. *(See Senatorial Courtesy.)*

One-Minute Speeches—Addresses by House members at the beginning of a legislative day. The speeches may cover any subject but are limited to one minute's duration.

Override a Veto—If the president disapproves a bill and sends it back to Congress with his objections, Congress may try to override his veto and enact the bill into law. Neither house is required to attempt to override a veto. The override of a veto requires a recorded vote with a two-thirds majority in each chamber. The question put to each house is: "Shall the bill pass, the objections of the president to the contrary notwithstanding?" *(See also Pocket Veto, Veto.)*

Oversight Committee—A congressional committee, or designated subcommittee of a committee, that is charged with general oversight of one or more federal agencies' programs and activities. Usually, the oversight panel for a particular agency also is the authorizing committee for that agency's programs and operations.

Pair—An voluntary arrangement between two lawmakers, usually on opposite sides of an issue. If passage of the measure requires a two-thirds majority vote, a pair would require two members favoring the action to one opposed to it. Pairs can take one of three forms — specific, general and live. The names of lawmakers pairing on a given vote and their stands, if known, are published in the *Congressional Record.*

The specific pair applies to one or more votes on the same subject. On special pairs, lawmakers usually specify how they would have voted.

A general pair in the Senate, now rarely used, applies to all votes on which the members pairing are on opposite sides. It usually does not specify the positions of the senators pairing. In a general pair in the House, no agreement is involved. A representative expecting to be absent may notify the House clerk he wishes to make a "general" pair. His name then is paired arbitrarily with that of another member desiring a pair, and the list is published in the *Congressional Record.* He may or may not be paired with a member taking the opposite position. General pairs in the House give no indication of how a member would have voted.

A live pair involves two members, one present for the vote, the other absent. The member present casts his vote and then withdraws it and votes "present." He then announces that he has a live pair with a colleague, identifying how each would have voted on the question. A live pair subtracts the vote of the member in attendance from the final vote tabulation.

Petition—A request or plea sent to one or both chambers from an organization or private citizens' group asking support of particular legislation or favorable consideration of a matter not yet receiving congressional attention. Petitions are referred to appropriate committees.

Pocket Veto—The act of the president in withholding his approval of a bill after Congress has adjourned. When Congress is in session, a bill becomes law without the president's signature if he does not act upon it within 10 days, excluding Sundays, from the time he gets it. But if Congress adjourns sine die within that 10-day period, the bill will die even if the president does not formally veto it.

The Supreme Court in 1986 agreed to decide whether the president can pocket veto a bill during recesses and between sessions of the same Congress or only between Congresses. The justices in 1987 declared the case moot, however, because the bill in question was invalid once the case reached the Court. *(See also Veto.)*

Point of Order—An objection raised by a member that the chamber is departing from rules governing its conduct of business. The objector cites the rule violated, the chair sustaining his objection if correctly made. Order is restored by the chair's suspending proceedings of the chamber until it conforms to the prescribed "order of business."

President of the Senate—Under the Constitution, the vice president of the United States presides over the Senate. In his absence, the president pro tempore, or a senator designated by the president pro tempore, presides over the chamber.

President Pro Tempore—The chief officer of the Senate in the absence of the vice president; literally, but loosely, the president for a time. The president pro tempore is elected by his fellow senators, and the recent practice has been to elect the senator of the majority party with the longest period of continuous service.

Previous Question—A motion for the previous question, when carried, has the effect of cutting off all debate, preventing the offering of further amendments, and forcing a vote on the pending matter. In the House, the previous question is not permitted in the Committee of the Whole. The motion for the previous question is a debate-limiting device and is not in order in the Senate.

Printed Amendment—A House rule guarantees five minutes of floor debate in support and five minutes in opposition, and no other debate time, on amendments printed in the *Congressional Record* at least one day prior to the amendment's consideration in the Committee of the Whole. In the Senate, while amendments may be submitted for printing, they have no parliamentary standing or status. An amendment submitted for printing in the Senate, however, may be called up by any senator.

Private Calendar—In the House, private bills dealing with individual matters such as claims against the government, immigration, land titles, etc., are put on this calendar. The private calendar must be called on the first Tuesday of each month, and the Speaker may call it on the third Tuesday of each month as well.

When a private bill is before the chamber, two members may block its consideration, which recommits the bill to committee. Backers of a recommitted private bill have recourse. The measure can be put into an "omnibus claims bill" — several private bills rolled into one. As with any bill, no part of an omnibus claims bill may be deleted without a vote. When the private bill goes back to the House floor in this form, it can be deleted from the omnibus bill only by majority vote.

Privilege—Relates to the rights of members of Congress and to the relative priority of the motions and actions they may make in their respective chambers. The two are distinct. "Privileged questions" deal with legislative business. "Questions of privilege" concern legislators themselves.

Privileged Questions—The order in which bills, motions and other legislative measures are considered by Congress is governed by strict priorities. A motion to table, for instance, is more privileged than a motion to recommit. Thus, a motion to recommit can be superseded by a motion to table, and a vote would be forced on the latter motion only. A motion to adjourn, however, takes precedence over a tabling motion and thus is considered of the "highest privilege." *(See also Questions of Privilege.)*

Pro Forma Amendment—*(See Strike Out the Last Word.)*

Public Laws—*(See Law.)*

Questions of Privilege—These are matters affecting members of Congress individually or collectively. Matters affecting the rights, safety, dignity and integrity of proceedings of the House or Senate as a whole are questions of privilege in both chambers.

Questions involving individual members are called questions of "personal privilege." A member rising to ask a question of personal privilege is given precedence over almost all other proceedings. An annotation in the House rules points out that the privilege rests primarily on the Constitution, which gives him a conditional immunity from arrest and an unconditional freedom to speak in the House. *(See also Privileged Questions.)*

Quorum—The number of members whose presence is necessary for the transaction of business. In the Senate and House, it is a majority of the membership. A quorum is 100 in the Committee of the Whole House. If a point of order is made that a quorum is not present, the only business that is in order is either a motion to adjourn or a motion to direct the sergeant-at-arms to request the attendance of absentees.

Readings of Bills—Traditional parliamentary procedure required bills to be read three times before they were passed. This custom is of little modern significance. Normally a bill is considered to have its first reading when it is introduced and printed, by title, in the *Congressional Record*. In the House, its second reading comes when floor consideration begins. (This is the most likely point at which there is an actual reading of the bill, if there is any.) The second reading in the Senate is supposed to occur on the legislative day after the measure is introduced, but before it is referred to committee. The third reading (again, usually by title) takes place when floor action has been completed on amendments.

Recess—Distinguished from adjournment *(see above)* in that a recess does not end a legislative day and therefore does not interrupt unfinished business. The rules in each house set forth certain matters to be taken up and disposed of at the beginning of each legislative day. The House usually adjourns from day to day. The Senate often recesses, thus meeting on the same legislative day for several calendar days or even weeks at a time.

Recognition—The power of recognition of a member is lodged in the Speaker of the House and the presiding officer of the Senate. The presiding officer names the member who will speak first when two or more members simultaneously request recognition.

Recommit to Committee—A motion, made on the floor after a bill has been debated, to return it to the committee that reported it. If approved, recommittal usually is considered a death blow to the bill. In the House, a motion to recommit can be made only by a member opposed to the bill, and, in recognizing a member to make the motion, the Speaker gives preference to members of the minority party over majority party members.

A motion to recommit may include instructions to the committee to report the bill again with specific amendments or by a certain date. Or, the instructions may direct that a particular study be made, with no definite deadline given for further action.

If the recommittal motion includes instructions to "report the bill back forthwith" and the motion is adopted, floor action on the bill continues; the committee does not actually reconsider the legislation.

Reconciliation—*(See Budget Reconciliation.)*

Reconsider a Vote—A motion to reconsider the vote by which an action was taken has, until it is disposed of, the effect of putting the action in abeyance. In the Senate, the motion can be made only by a member who voted on the prevailing side of the original question or by a member who did not vote at all. In the House, it can be made only by a member on the prevailing side.

A common practice in the Senate after close votes on an issue is a motion to reconsider, followed by a motion to table the motion to reconsider. On this motion to table, senators vote as they voted on the original question, which allows the motion to table to prevail, assuming there are no switches. The matter then is finally closed and further motions to reconsider are not entertained. In the House, as a routine precaution, a motion to reconsider usually is made every time a measure is passed. Such a motion almost always is tabled immediately, thus shutting off the possibility of future reconsideration, except by unanimous consent.

Motions to reconsider must be entered in the Senate within the next two days of actual session after the original vote has been taken. In the House they must be entered either on the same day or on the next succeeding day the House is in session.

Recorded Vote—A vote upon which each member's stand is individually made known. In the Senate, this is accomplished through a roll call of the entire membership, to which each senator on the floor must answer "yea," "nay" or, if he does not wish to vote, "present." Since January 1973, the House has used an electronic voting system for recorded votes, including yea-and-nay votes formerly taken by roll calls.

When not required by the Constitution, a recorded vote can be obtained on questions in the House on the demand of one-fifth (44 members) of a quorum or one-fourth (25) of a quorum in the Committee of the Whole. *(See Yeas and Nays.)*

Report—Both a verb and a noun as a congressional term. A committee that has been examining a bill referred to it by the parent chamber "reports" its findings and recommendations to the chamber when it completes consideration and returns the measure. The process is called "reporting" a bill.

A "report" is the document setting forth the committee's explanation of its action. Senate and House reports are numbered separately and are designated S Rept or H Rept. When a committee report is not unanimous, the dissenting committee members may file a statement of their views, called minority views and referred to as a minority report. Members in disagreement with some provisions of a bill may file additional or supplementary views. Sometimes a bill is reported without a committee recommendation.

Adverse reports occasionally are submitted by legislative committees. However, when a committee is opposed to a bill, it usually fails to report the bill at all. Some laws require that committee reports — favorable or adverse — be made.

Rescission Bill—A bill rescinding or canceling budget authority previously made available by Congress. The president may request a rescission to reduce spending or because the budget authority no longer is needed. Under the 1974 budget act, however, unless Congress approves a rescission bill within 45 days of continuous session after receipt of the proposal, the funds must be made available for obligation. *(See also Deferral.)*

Resolution—A "simple" resolution, designated H Res or S Res, deals with matters entirely within the prerogatives of one house or the other. It requires neither passage by the other chamber nor approval by the president, and it does not have the force of law. Most resolutions deal with the rules or procedures of one house. They also are used to express the sentiments of a single house such as condolences to the family of a deceased member or to comment on foreign policy or executive business. A simple resolution is the vehicle for a "rule" from the House Rules Committee. *(See also Concurrent and Joint Resolutions, Rules.)*

Rider—An amendment, usually not germane, that its sponsor hopes to get through more easily by including it in other legislation. Riders become law if the bills embodying them are enacted. Amendments providing legislative directives in appropriations bills are outstanding examples of riders, though technically legislation is banned from appropriations bills.

The House, unlike the Senate, has a strict germaneness rule; thus, riders usually are Senate devices to get legislation enacted quickly or to bypass lengthy House consideration and, possibly, opposition.

Rules—The term has two specific congressional meanings. A rule may be a standing order governing the conduct of House or Senate business and listed among the permanent rules of either chamber. The rules deal with duties of officers, the order of business, admission to the floor, parliamentary procedures on handling amendments and voting, jurisdictions of committees, etc.

In the House, a rule also may be a resolution reported by its Rules Committee to govern the handling of a particular bill on the floor. The committee may report a "rule," also called a "special order," in the form of a simple resolution. If the resolution is adopted by the House, the temporary rule becomes as valid as any standing rule and lapses only after action has been completed on the measure to which it pertains. A rule sets the time limit on general debate. It also may waive points of order against provisions of the bill in question such as non-germane language or against certain amendments intended to be proposed to the bill from the floor. It may even forbid all amendments or all amendments except those proposed by the legislative committee that handled the bill. In this instance, it is known as a "closed" or "gag" rule as opposed to an "open" rule, which puts no limitation on floor amendments, thus leaving the bill completely open to alteration by the adoption of germane amendments.

Secretary of the Senate—Chief administrative officer of the Senate, responsible for overseeing the duties of Senate employees, educating Senate pages, administering oaths, handling the registration of lobbyists, and handling other tasks necessary for the continuing operation of the Senate. *(See also Clerk of the House.)*

Select or Special Committee—A committee set up for a special purpose and, usually, for a limited time by resolution of either the House or Senate. Most special committees are investigative and lack legislative authority — legislation is not referred to them and they cannot report bills to their parent chamber. *(See also Standing Committees.)*

Senatorial Courtesy—Sometimes referred to as "the courtesy of the Senate," it is a general practice — with no written rule — applied to consideration of executive nominations. Generally, it means that nominations from a state are not to be confirmed unless they have been approved by the senators of the president's party of that state, with other senators following their colleagues' lead in the attitude they take toward consideration of such nominations. *(See Nominations.)*

Sequester Order—The Gramm-Rudman-Hollings law of 1985 established an automatic budget-cutting procedure that the Supreme Court declared unconstitutional a year later. Under that procedure, the Congressional Budget Office (CBO) and the Office of Management and Budget (OMB) must separately calculate deficits for an upcoming fiscal year and the across-the-board cuts that would be needed to meet the deficit fixed by the statute. The General Accounting Office (GAO) would review, and could revise, the CBO-OMB numbers. GAO would then submit the final figures to the president, who must issue a "sequester order" making the cuts. Although the Supreme Court invalidated the automatic feature, another section of the law provided that the cuts would take effect if the president and Congress approved them. *(See Budget Process.)*

Sine Die—*(See Adjournment Sine Die.)*

Slip Laws—The first official publication of a bill that has been enacted and signed into law. Each is published separately in unbound single-sheet or pamphlet form. *(See also Law, Statutes at Large, U.S. Code.)*

Speaker—The presiding officer of the House of Representatives, selected by the caucus of the party to which he belongs and formally elected by the whole House.

Special Session—A session of Congress after it has adjourned sine die, completing its regular session. Special sessions are convened by the president.

Spending Authority—The 1974 budget act defines spending authority as borrowing authority, contract authority and entitlement authority *(see above),* for which budget authority is not providedby appropriation acts.

Sponsor—*(See Bills Introduced.)*

Standing Committees—Committees permanently established by House and Senate rules. The standing committees of the House were last reorganized by the committee reorganization of 1974. The last major realignment of Senate committees was in the committee system reorganization of 1977. The standing committees are legislative committees — legislation may be referred to them and they may report bills and resolutions to their parent chambers. *(See also Select or Special Committees.)*

Standing Vote—A non-recorded vote used in both the House and Senate. (A standing vote also is called a division vote.) Members in favor of a proposal stand and are counted by the presiding officer. Then members opposed stand and are counted. There is no record of how individual members voted.

Statutes at Large—A chronological arrangement of the laws enacted in each session of Congress. Though indexed, the laws are not arranged by subject matter, and there is not an indication of how they changed previously enacted laws. *(See also Law, Slip Laws, U.S. Code.)*

Strike From the Record—Remarks made on the House floor may offend some member, who moves that the offending words be "taken down" for the Speaker's cognizance, and then expunged from the debate as published in the *Congressional Record.*

Strike Out the Last Word—A motion whereby a House member is entitled to speak for five minutes on an amendment then being debated by the chamber. A member gains recognition from the chair by moving to "strike out the last word" of the amendment or section of the bill under consideration. The motion is pro forma, requires no vote and does not change the amendment being debated.

How a Bill Becomes Law

Note: Parliamentary terms used below are defined in the glossary.

Introduction of Bills

A House member (including the resident commissioner of Puerto Rico and non-voting delegates of the District of Columbia, Guam, the Virgin Islands and American Samoa) may introduce any one of several types of bills and resolutions by handing it to the clerk of the House or placing it in a box called the hopper. A senator first gains recognition of the presiding officer to announce the introduction of a bill. If objection is offered by any senator, the introduction of the bill is postponed until the following day.

As the next step in either the House or Senate, the bill is numbered, referred to the appropriate committee, labeled with the sponsor's name, and sent to the Government Printing Office so that copies can be made for subsequent study and action. Senate bills may be jointly sponsored and carry several senators' names. Until 1978, the House limited the number of members who could cosponsor any one bill; the ceiling was eliminated at the beginning of the 96th Congress. A bill written in the executive branch and proposed as an administration measure usually is introduced by the chairman of the congressional committee that has jurisdiction.

Bills—Prefixed with "HR" in the House, "S" in the Senate, followed by a number. Used as the form for most legislation, whether general or special, public or private.

Joint Resolutions—Designated H J Res or S J Res. Subject to the same procedure as bills, with the exception of a joint resolution proposing an amendment to the Constitution. The latter must be approved by two-thirds of both houses and is thereupon sent directly to the administrator of general services for submission to the states for ratification rather than being presented to the president for his approval.

Concurrent Resolutions—Designated H Con Res or S Con Res. Used for matters affecting the operations of both houses. These resolutions do not become law.

Resolutions—Designated H Res or S Res. Used for a matter concerning the operation of either house alone and adopted only by the chamber in which it originates.

Committee Action

A bill is referred to the appropriate committee by a House parliamentarian in the Speaker's order, or by the Senate president. Sponsors may indicate their preferences for referral, although custom and chamber rule generally govern. An exception is the referral of private bills, which are sent to whatever group is designated by their sponsors. Bills are technically considered "read for the first time" when referred to House committees.

When a bill reaches a committee it is placed on the group's calendar. At that time it comes under the sharpest congressional focus. Its chances for passage are quickly determined — and the great majority of bills falls by the legislative roadside. Failure of a committee to act on a bill is equivalent to killing it; the measure can be withdrawn from the group's purview only by a discharge petition signed by a majority of the House membership on House bills, or by adoption of a special resolution in the Senate. Discharge attempts rarely succeed.

The first committee action taken on a bill usually is a request for comment on it by interested agencies of the government. The committee chairman may assign the bill to a subcommittee for study and hearings, or it may be considered by the full committee. Hearings may be public, closed (executive session), or both. A subcommittee, after considering a bill, reports to the full committee its recommendations for action and any proposed amendments.

The full committee then votes on its recommendation to the House or Senate. This procedure is called "ordering a bill reported." Occasionally a committee may order a bill reported unfavorably; most of the time a report, submitted by the chairman of the committee to the House or Senate, calls for favorable action on the measure since the committee can effectively "kill" a bill by simply failing to take any action.

When a committee sends a bill to the chamber floor, it explains its reasons in a written statement, called a report, which accompanies the bill. Often committee members opposing a measure issue dissenting minority statements that are included in the report.

Usually, the committee "marks up" or proposes amendments to the bill. If they are substantial and the measure is complicated, the committee may order a "clean bill" introduced, which will embody the proposed amendments. The original bill then is put aside and the "clean bill," with a new number, is reported to the floor.

The chamber must approve, alter, or reject the committee amendments before the bill itself can be put to a vote.

Floor Action

After a bill is reported back to the house where it originated, it is placed on the calendar.

There are five legislative calendars in the House, issued in one cumulative calendar titled *Calendars of the United States House of Representatives and History of Legislation.* The House calendars are:

The Union Calendar to which are referred bills raising revenues, general appropriations bills and any measures directly or indirectly appropriating money or property. It is the Calendar of the Committee of the Whole House on the State of the Union.

The House Calendar to which are referred bills of public character not raising revenue or appropriating money or property.

The Consent Calendar to which are referred bills of a non-controversial nature that are passed without debate when the Consent Calendar is called on the first and third Mondays of each month.

The Private Calendar to which are referred bills for relief in the nature of claims against the United States or private immigration bills that are passed without debate when the Private Calendar is called the first and third Tuesdays of each month.

The Discharge Calendar to which are referred motions to discharge committees when the necessary signatures are signed to a discharge petition.

There is only one legislative calendar in the Senate and one "executive calendar" for treaties and nominations submitted to the Senate. When the Senate Calendar is called, each senator is limited to five minutes' debate on each bill.

Debate. A bill is brought to debate by varying procedures. If a routine measure, it may await the call of the calendar. If it is urgent or important, it can be taken up in the Senate either by unanimous consent or by a majority vote. The policy committee of the majority party in the Senate schedules the bills that it wants taken up for debate.

In the House, precedence is granted if a special rule is obtained from the Rules Committee. A request for a special rule is usually made by the chairman of the committee that favorably reported the bill, supported by the bill's sponsor and other committee members. The request, considered by the Rules Committee in the same fashion that other committees consider legislative measures, is in the form of a resolution providing for immediate consideration of the bill. The Rules Committee reports the resolution to the House where it is debated and voted upon in the same fashion as regular bills. If the Rules Committee should fail to report a rule requested by a committee, there are several ways to bring the bill to the House floor — under suspension of the rules, on Calendar Wednesday or by a discharge motion.

The resolutions providing special rules are important because they specify how long the bill may be debated and whether it may be amended from the floor. If floor amendments are banned, the bill is considered under a "closed rule," which permits only members of the committee that first reported the measure to the House to alter its language, subject to chamber acceptance.

When a bill is debated under an "open rule," amendments may be offered from the floor. Committee amendments are always taken up first, but may be changed, as may all amendments up to the second degree; i.e., an amendment to an amendment to an amendment is not in order.

Duration of debate in the House depends on whether the bill is under discussion by the House proper or before the House when it is sitting as the Committee of the Whole House on the State of the Union. In the former, the amount of time for debate is determined either by special rule or is allocated with an hour for each member if the measure is under consideration without a rule. In the Committee of the Whole the amount of time agreed on for general debate is equally divided between proponents and opponents. At the end of general discussion, the bill is read section by section for amendment. Debate on an amendment is limited to five minutes for each side.

Senate debate is usually unlimited. It can be halted only by unanimous consent by "cloture," which requires a three-fifths majority of the entire Senate except for proposed changes in the Senate rules. The latter requires a two-thirds vote.

The House sits as the Committee of the Whole when it considers any tax measure or bill dealing with public appropriations. It can also resolve itself into the Committee of the Whole if a member moves to do so and the motion is carried. The Speaker appoints a member to serve as the chairman. The rules of the House permit the Committee of the Whole to meet with any 100 members on the floor, and to amend and act on bills with a quorum of the 100, within the time limitations mentioned previously. When the Committee of the Whole has acted, it "rises," the Speaker returns as the presiding officer of the House and the member appointed chairman of the Committee of the Whole reports the action of the committee and its recommendations (amendments adopted).

Votes. Voting on bills may occur repeatedly before they are finally approved or rejected. The House votes on the rule for the bill and on various amendments to the bill. Voting on amendments often is a more illuminating test of a bill's support than is the final tally. Sometimes members approve final passage of bills after vigorously supporting amendments that, if adopted, would have scuttled the legislation.

The Senate has three different methods of voting: an untabulated voice, a standing vote (called a division) and a recorded roll call to which members answer "yea" or "nay" when their names are called. The House also employs voice and standing votes, but since January 1973 yeas and nays have been recorded by an electronic voting device, eliminating the need for time-consuming roll calls.

Another method of voting, used in the House only, is the teller vote. Traditionally, members filed up the center aisle past counters; only vote totals were announced. Since 1971, one-fifth of a quorum can demand that the votes of individual members be recorded, thereby forcing them to take a public position on amendments to key bills. Electronic voting now is commonly used for this purpose.

After amendments to a bill have been voted upon, a vote may be taken on a motion to recommit the bill to committee. If carried, this vote removes the bill from the chamber's calendar. If the motion is unsuccessful, the bill then is "read for the third time." An actual reading usually is dispensed with. Until 1965, an opponent of a bill could delay this move by objecting and asking for a full reading of an engrossed (certified in final form) copy of the bill. After the "third reading," the vote on final passage is taken.

The final vote may be followed by a motion to reconsider, and this motion itself may be followed by a move to lay the motion on the table. Usually, those voting for the bill's passage vote for the tabling motion, thus safeguarding the final passage action. With that, the bill has been formally passed by the chamber. While a motion to reconsider a Senate vote is pending on a bill, the measure cannot be sent to the House.

Action in Second House

After a bill is passed it is sent to the other chamber. This body may then take one of several steps. It may pass the bill as is — accepting the other chamber's language. It may send the bill to committee for scrutiny or alteration, or reject the entire bill, advising the other house of its actions. Or it may simply ignore the bill submitted while it continues work on its own version of the proposed legislation. Frequently, one chamber may approve a version of a bill that is greatly at variance with the version already passed by the other house, and then substitute its amendments for the language of the other, retaining only the latter's bill designation.

A provision of the Legislative Reorganization Act of 1970 permits a separate House vote on any non-germane amendment added by the Senate to a House-passed bill and requires a majority vote to retain the amendment.

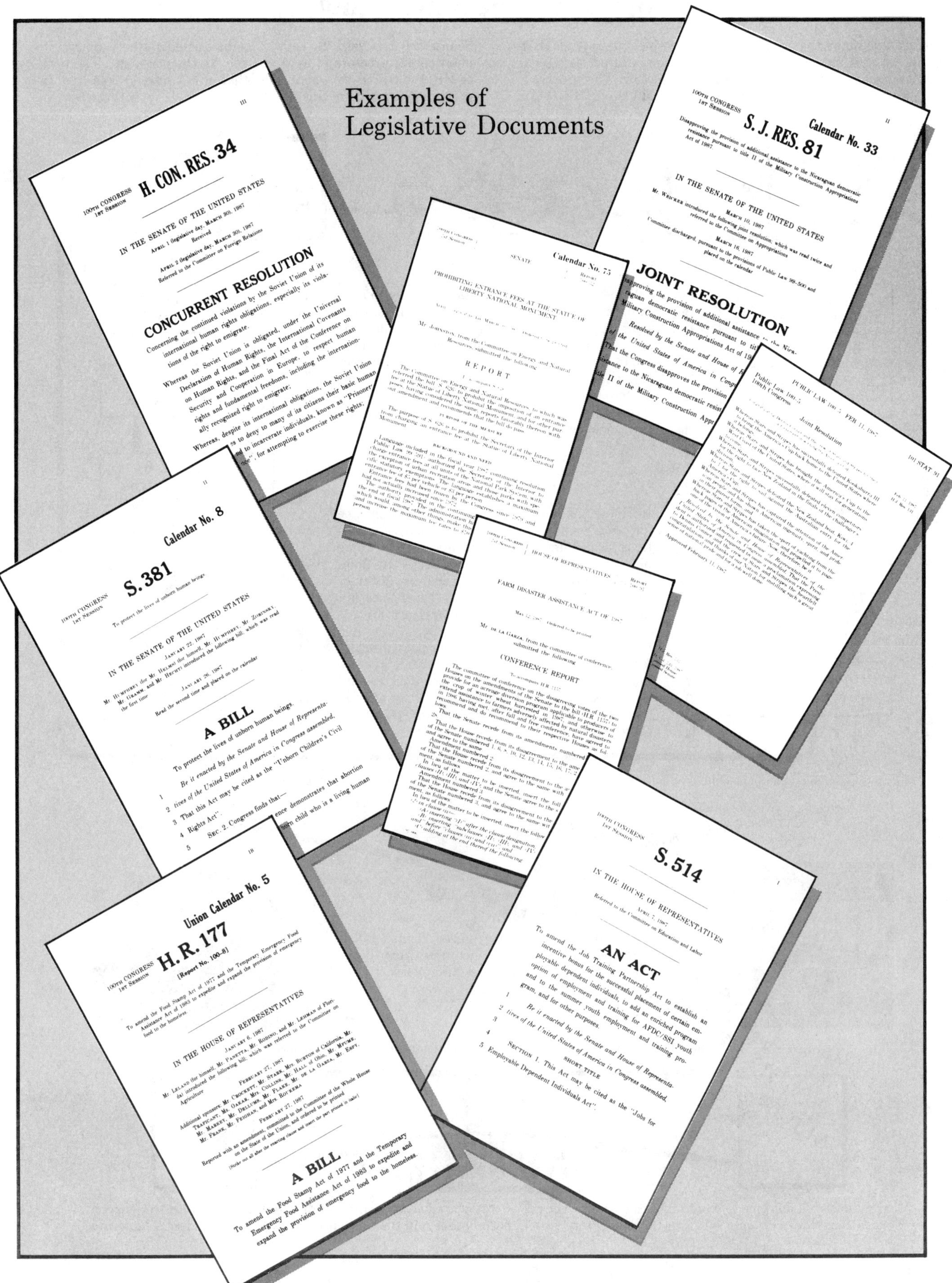
Examples of Legislative Documents
H. CON. RES. 34
CONCURRENT RESOLUTION
S. J. RES. 81
Calendar No. 33
JOINT RESOLUTION
Calendar No. 75
REPORT
Calendar No. 8
S. 381
A BILL
CONFERENCE REPORT
Union Calendar No. 5
H. R. 177
A BILL
S. 514
AN ACT

How a Bill Becomes Law

This graphic shows the most typical way in which proposed legislation is enacted into law. There are more complicated, as well as simpler, routes, and most bills never become law. The process is illustrated with two hypothetical bills, House bill No. 1 (HR 1) and Senate bill No. 2 (S 2). Bills must be passed by both houses in identical form before they can be sent to the president. The path of HR 1 is traced by a solid line, that of S 2 by a broken line. In practice most bills begins as similar proposals in both houses.

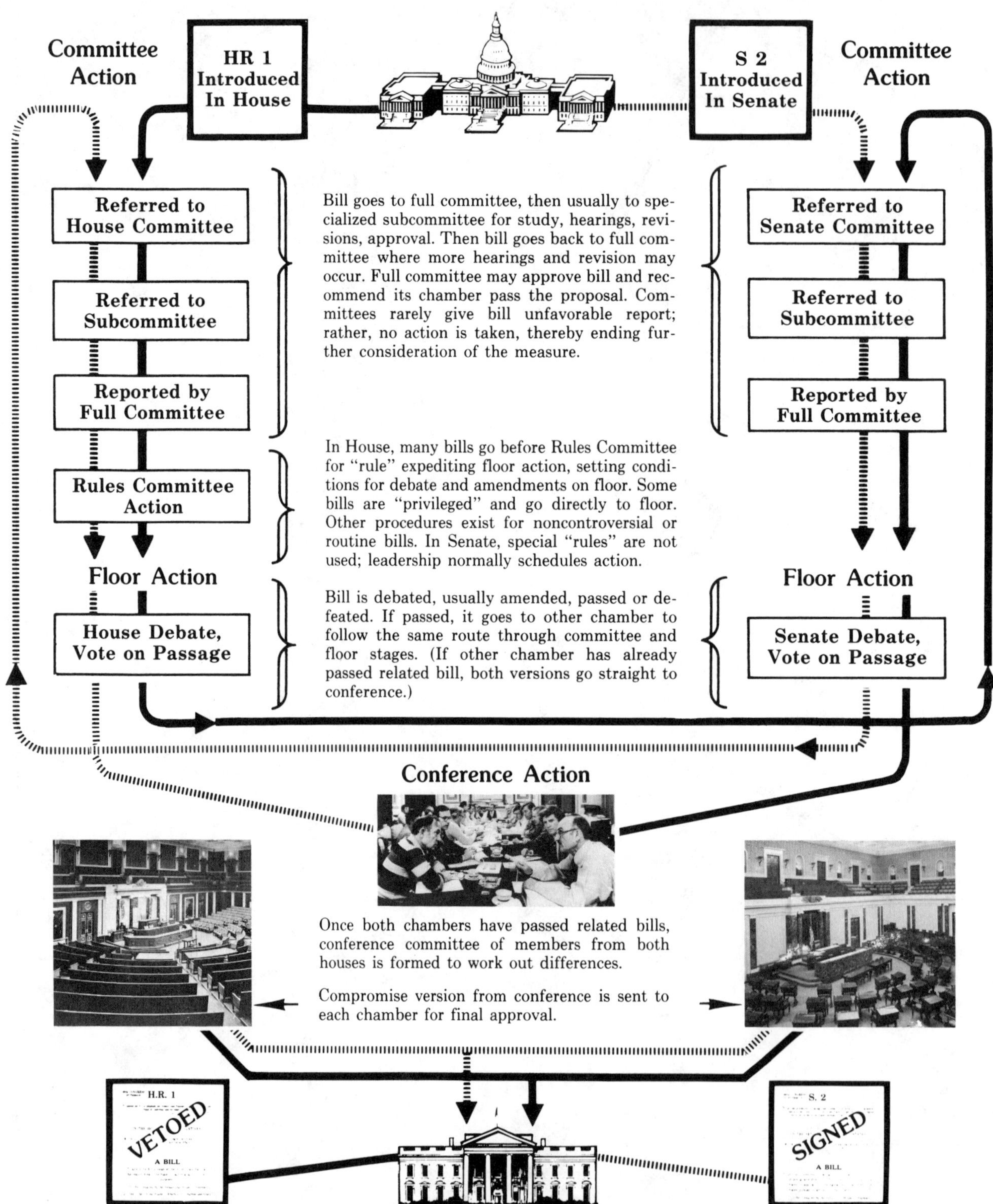

Compromise bill approved by both houses is sent to the president, who can sign it into law or veto it and return it to Congress. Congress may override veto by a two-thirds majority vote in both houses; bill then becomes law without president's signature.

Previously the House was forced to act on the bill as a whole; the only way to defeat the non-germane amendment was to reject the entire bill.

Often the second chamber makes only minor changes. If these are readily agreed to by the other house, the bill then is routed to the White House for signing. However, if the opposite chamber basically alters the bill submitted to it, the measure usually is "sent to conference." The chamber that has possession of the "papers" (engrossed bill, engrossed amendments, messages of transmittal) requests a conference and the other chamber must agree to it. If the second house does not agree, the bill dies.

Conference, Final Action

Conference. A conference undertakes to harmonize conficting House and Senate versions of a legislative bill. The conference is usually staffed by senior members (conferees), appointed by the presiding officers of the two houses, from the committees that managed the bills. Under this arrangement the conferees of one house have the duty of trying to maintain their chamber's position in the face of amending actions by the conferees (also referred to as "managers") of the other house.

The number of conferees from each chamber may vary, the range usually being from three to nine members in each group, depending upon the length or complexity of the bill involved. There may be five representatives and three senators on the conference committee, or the reverse. But a majority vote controls the action of each group so that a large representation does not give one chamber a voting advantage over the other chamber's conferees.

Theoretically, conferees are not allowed to write new legislation in reconciling the two versions before them, but this curb sometimes is bypassed. Many bills have been put into acceptable compromise form only after new language was provided by the conferees. The 1970 Reorganization Act attempted to tighten restrictions on conferees by forbidding them to introduce any language on a topic that neither chamber sent to conference or to modify any topic beyond the scope of the different House and Senate versions.

Frequently the ironing out of difficulties takes days or even weeks. Conferences on involved appropriations bills sometimes are particularly drawn out.

As a conference proceeds, conferees reconcile differences between the versions, but generally they grant concessions only insofar as they remain sure that the chamber they represent will accept the compromises. Occasionally, uncertainty over how either house will react, or the positive refusal of a chamber to back down on a disputed amendment, results in an impasse, and the bills die in conference even though each was approved by its sponsoring chamber.

Conferees sometimes go back to their respective chambers for further instructions, when they report certain portions in disagreement. Then the chamber concerned can either "recede and concur" in the amendment of the other house, or "insist on its amendment."

When the conferees have reached agreement, they prepare a conference report embodying their recommendations (compromises). The reports, in document form, must be submitted to each house.

The conference report must be approved by each house. Consequently, approval of the report is approval of the compromise bill. In the order of voting on conference reports, the chamber which asked for a conference yields to the other chamber the opportunity to vote first.

Final Steps. After a bill has been passed by both the House and Senate in identical form, all of the original papers are sent to the enrolling clerk of the chamber in which the bill originated. He then prepares an enrolled bill, which is printed on parchment paper. When this bill has been certified as correct by the secretary of the Senate or the clerk of the House, depending on which chamber originated the bill, it is signed first (no matter whether it originated in the Senate or House) by the Speaker of the House and then by the president of the Senate. It is next sent to the White House to await action.

If the president approves the bill, he signs it, dates it and usually writes the word "approved" on the document. If he does not sign it within 10 days (Sundays excepted) and Congress is in session, the bill becomes law without his signature.

However, should Congress adjourn before the 10 days expire, and the president has failed to sign the measure, it does not become law. This procedure is called the pocket veto.

A president vetoes a bill by refusing to sign it and before the 10-day period expires, returning it to Congress with a message stating his reasons. The message is sent to the chamber that originated the bill. If no action is taken there on the message, the bill dies. Congress, however, can attempt to override the president's veto and enact the bill, "the objections of the president to the contrary notwithstanding." Overriding of a veto requires a two-thirds vote of those present, who must number a quorum and vote by roll call.

Debate can precede this vote, with motions permitted to lay the message on the table, postpone action on it, or refer it to committee. If the president's veto is overridden by a two-thirds vote in both houses, the bill becomes law. Otherwise it is dead.

When bills are passed finally and signed, or passed over a veto, they are given law numbers in numerical order as they become law. There are two series of numbers, one for public and one for private laws, starting at the number "1" for each two-year term of Congress. They are then identified by law number and by Congress — i.e., Private Law 21, 97th Congress; Public Law 250, 97th Congress (or PL 97-250).

REFERENCE GUIDES

Congress and Legislation

Current Government Documents

Bills and Resolutions—All legislation is printed daily after it is introduced. (Available from members of Congress)

Biographical Directory of the American Congress 1774-1971—Data on all members who have served in Congress. (Available from Government Printing Office)(GPO)

Calendar of the House of Representatives—Published daily, the calendar lists all bills—Senate and House—which have been reported: gives report numbers, dates of passage in each chamber, dates of enactments, etc. Cumulative. Indexed on Mondays only. (Clerk of the House)

Cannon's Procedure in the House of Representatives—This volume condenses the eleven volumes of Hinds' and Cannon's Precedents of the House of Representatives. (GPO)

Committee Prints—These documents are usually committee staff studies and research papers issued by committees; they range from compilation of laws on particular subjects to studies of foreign policy problems. (Generally available from the issuing committee)

Committee Reports—A report accompanies each piece of legislation when it goes to the floor. It generally analyzes the bill, describes its purposes, and states the views of the members of the committee as to the desirability of enactment. (Available from committees)

Congressional Directory—Published each year, it contains brief biographical sketches of each member, lists committee memberships, committee assignments by member, maps of all congressional districts. It also lists major executives of all government agencies, members of the diplomatic corps, and members of the press accredited to the press galleries. A pocket edition of the Directory contains pictures of each member of Congress. (GPO)

Congressional Record (Bound)—Since 1789, the proceedings of Congress have appeared under four different titles: *Annals of Congress,* 1789-1824; *The Register of Debates,* 1824-1837; *Congressional Globe,* 1833-1873; *The Congressional Record* has been published since 1873. The bound sets consist of 15 to 20 parts per year, including separate index and (since 1947) *Daily Digest* volumes. (GPO)

Constitution, Jefferson's Manual and Rules of the House of Representatives—The House's rules and regulations. (GPO)

Digest of Public General Bills and Resolutions—A compilation giving a brief description of each public bill introduced during the session. It is cumulative, in approximately five issues per year. Indexed by subject. (GPO)

Hearings—Copies of all testimony taken by committees in open session are printed by the GPO and made available by the issuing committee.

Hinds' and Cannon's Precedents of the House of Representatives Including References to Provisions of the Constitution, the Laws and Decisions of the United States Senate—Eleven-volume set contains the constitutional provisions, established rules and procedures, with explanation and documentation, governing the House of Representatives. (GPO)

Public and Private Laws—Copies of all laws enacted are printed with citations to the statutes that are amended or deleted by the legislation. (GPO)

Report of the Clerk of the House of Representatives—Semiannual report includes salaries of representatives, staffs, committee staffs, officers and employees of the House; statement of expenditures and allowances. (GPO)

Report of the Secretary of the Senate—Contains salaries of senators, staffs, committee staff members, officers and employees of the Senate; statements of expenditures and gross salaries of senators; issued semiannually. (GPO)

Senate Manual—The Manual contains "standing rules, orders, laws and regulations..." of the Senate. (GPO)

United States Code—The 50 titles of the code include all the general and permanent laws of the U.S. The Code is published every six years, with annual supplements until the next publication. (Available from GPO, 14-volumes and supplements)

Privately Published Materials

Almanac of American Politics—Contains biographies, group ratings, committee assignments, voting records and lobby interests of members, and political, demographic and economic makeup of congressmen's state or district. (Published by National Journal)

CIS Index—A monthly, quarterly, and annual index to hearings, reports, documents and other congressional papers by subject, committee and witness. (Published by Congressional Information Service)

CIS Microfiche Library—Complete texts of congressional hearings, reports and documents in microform; issued monthly. (Published by Congressional Information Service)

Commerce Clearing House Congressional Index—This weekly, loose-leaf index is a guide to all legislation by subject, author and bill number. (Published by C.C.H., Chicago, Ill.)

Congress and the Nation, Vol. I (1945-64), *Vol. II* (1965-68), *Vol. III* (1969-72), *Vol. IV* (1973-76), *Vol. V* (1977-80), *Vol. VI* (1981-84), Congressional Quarterly. The 6,600-page-six-volume set documents legislative actions and national political campaigns, 1945-84.

Congressional Digest—Monthly coverage of major legislative issues in pro-con format. (Published by Congressional Digest)

Congressional Monitor—Daily report on congressional committee and floor actions, including advance schedule of committee hearings, weekly listing of status of major legislation and documents. (Published by Congressional Quarterly)

Congressional Quarterly Almanac—Published each year since 1945, the Almanac presents a thorough review of legislative and political activity for each session of Congress. (Available separately with regular CQ service)

Congressional Quarterly Weekly Report—A weekly report of major congressional actions on the House and Senate floors and in committees. The Report contains roll-call votes and weekly political coverage. Carries rosters, updated committee and subcommittee assignments, presidential texts, etc.

Congressional Quarterly's Guide to Congress—A 1,000-page volume documenting the origins, development and operations of the U.S. Congress. Explains how Congress works, its powers and the pressures upon it.

Congressional Staff Directory—Published annually, the Directory contains biographical sketches of many members of Congress' staffs; lists employees of members and committees; lists all cities of 1,500 or more population by congressional districts. (Available from Congress Staff Directory, Alexandria, Va.)

National Journal—Weekly report of congressional and executive actions and programs, and reports on issues. (Published by National Journal Inc.)

Politics in America—Profiles of all members of Congress, including biographical data, committee assignments, campaign finances, election returns, key votes and interest group ratings. Also provides maps and detailed descriptions of each state and congressional district. (Published by CQ Press)

United States Code Congressional and Administrative News—This monthly service of the West Publishing Co., St. Paul, gives the full text of all public laws, and, in many cases, includes committee reports on the legislation.

Supreme Court

Current Government Documents

The Constitution of the United States of America: Analysis and Interpretation—Discussion of each phrase of the Constitution and annotations of cases decided by the Supreme Court. (GPO)

The United States Reports—Official record of Supreme Court decisions and proceedings; issued daily in "slip opinions"; cumulative volumes issued annually. (GPO)

Privately Published Materials

Biographical Directory of the Federal Judiciary—Biographical data on judges of the Supreme Court, Courts of Appeals, District Courts, Court of Claims; statistical data on religious and political persuasions. Detroit, Michigan, Gale Research Corp., 1983.

Black's Law Dictionary edited by Henry C. Black—Definitions of terms and phrases of American and English jurisprudence. St. Paul, Minnesota, West Publishing Co., 1979.

Congressional Quarterly's Guide to the U.S. Supreme Court—A 1,000-page volume documenting the development and working of the court. Includes summaries of major decisions and biographies of all justices. Washington, D.C., Congressional Quarterly Inc., 1979.

Court and Constitution in the Twentieth Century by William F. Swindler—Two-volume history of the court from 1889 through 1968. Indianapolis, Bobbs-Merrill, 1969.

Justices and Presidents: A Political History of Appointments to the Supreme Court by Henry J. Abraham—History of appointments to the Supreme Court from George Washington through Lyndon Johnson. New York, Oxford University Press, 1974.

The Justices of the United States Supreme Court: Their Lives and Major Opinions, edited by Leon Friedman and Fred Israel—Five volumes on the lives and major opinions of the Supreme Court justices from 1789 through 1971. New York, R. R. Bowker.

Landmark Briefs and Arguments of the Supreme Court of the United States: Constitutional Law, edited by Philip B. Kurland and Gerhard Casper—Includes briefs, transcripts of oral arguments and decisions of the Supreme Court on major constitutional law cases from 1793 through 1973. Washington, D.C., University Publications of America Inc., 1975.

Lawyer's Edition of the United States Supreme Court—Weekly report of court opinions, summary of arguments, digest of court decisions; bound volumes issued annually. Rochester, N.Y., Lawyer's Cooperative Publishing Co.

Significant Decisions of the Supreme Court by Bruce E. Fein—Annual review of all major opinions and analyses since 1969. Washington, D.C., American Enterprise Institute for Public Policy Research.

The Supreme Court by Lawrence Baum—Analysis of the Supreme Court's policy-making role. Washington, D.C., CQ Press, 1985.

The Supreme Court in United States History by Charles Warren—Two-volume history covers the period 1789 through 1918. Boston, Little, Brown and Co., 1922.

A Different Justice by Elder Witt—Examination of President Reagan's influence on the Supreme Court. Washington, D.C., Congressional Quarterly Inc., 1985.

Supreme Court Practice by Robert L. Stern and Eugene Gressman. Washington, D.C., Bureau of National Affairs, 1978.

Supreme Court Reporter—Bimonthly coverage of Supreme Court decisions and proceedings; bound cumulative reports issued annually. St. Paul, Minnesota, West Publishing Co.

The United States Law Week—Digest and analysis of current developments, opinions and rulings of the Supreme Court. Washington, D.C., Bureau of National Affairs.

Constitution of the United States

We the People of the United States, in Order to form a more perfect Union, establish Justice, insure domestic Tranquility, provide for the common defence, promote the general Welfare, and secure the Blessings of Liberty to ourselves and our Posterity, do ordain and establish this Constitution for the United States of America.

ARTICLE I

Section 1. All legislative Powers herein granted shall be vested in a Congress of the United States, which shall consist of a Senate and House of Representatives.

Section 2. The House of Representatives shall be composed of Members chosen every second Year by the People of the several States, and the Electors in each State shall have the Qualifications requisite for Electors of the most numerous Branch of the State Legislature.

No Person shall be a Representative who shall not have attained to the age of twenty five Years, and been seven Years a Citizen of the United States, and who shall not, when elected, be an Inhabitant of that State in which he shall be chosen.

[Representatives and direct Taxes shall be apportioned among the several States which may be included within this Union, according to their respective Numbers, which shall be determined by adding to the whole Number of free Persons, including those bound to Service for a Term of Years, and excluding Indians not taxed, three fifths of all other Persons.][1] The actual Enumeration shall be made within three Years after the first Meeting of the Congress of the United States, and within every subsequent Term of ten Years, in such Manner as they shall by Law direct. The Number of Representatives shall not exceed one for every thirty Thousand, but each State shall have at Least one Representative; and until such enumeration shall be made, the State of New Hampshire shall be entitled to chuse three, Massachusetts eight, Rhode-Island and Providence Plantations one, Connecticut five, New-York six, New Jersey four, Pennsylvania eight, Delaware one, Maryland six, Virginia ten, North Carolina five, South Carolina five, and Georgia three.

When vacancies happen in the Representation from any State, the Executive Authority thereof shall issue Writs of Election to fill such Vacancies.

The House of Representatives shall chuse their Speaker and other Officers; and shall have the sole Power of Impeachment.

Section 3. The Senate of the United States shall be composed of two Senators from each State, [chosen by the Legislature thereof,][2] for six Years; and each Senator shall have one Vote.

Immediately after they shall be assembled in Consequence of the first Election, they shall be divided as equally as may be into three Classes. The Seats of the Senators of the first Class shall be vacated at the Expiration of the second Year, of the second Class at the Expiration of the fourth Year, and of the third Class at the Expiration of the sixth Year, so that one third may be chosen every second Year; [and if Vacancies happen by Resignation, or otherwise, during the Recess of the Legislature of any State, the Executive thereof may make temporary Appointments until the next Meeting of the Legislature, which shall then fill such Vacancies.][3]

No Person shall be a Senator who shall not have attained to the Age of thirty Years, and been nine Years a Citizen of the United States, and who shall not, when elected, be an Inhabitant of that State for which he shall be chosen.

The Vice President of the United States shall be President of the Senate, but shall have no Vote, unless they be equally divided.

The Senate shall chuse their other Officers, and also a President pro tempore, in the Absence of the Vice President, or when he shall exercise the Office of President of the United States.

The Senate shall have the sole Power to try all Impeachments. When sitting for that Purpose, they shall be on Oath or Affirmation. When the President of the United States is tried the Chief Justice shall preside: And no Person shall be convicted without the Concurrence of two thirds of the Members present.

Judgment in Cases of Impeachment shall not extend further than to removal from Office, and disqualification to hold and enjoy any Office of honor, Trust or Profit under the United States: but the Party convicted shall nevertheless be liable and subject to Indictment, Trial, Judgment and Punishment, according to Law.

Section 4. The Times, Places and Manner of holding Elections for Senators and Representatives, shall be prescribed in each State by the Legislature thereof; but the Congress may at any time by Law make or alter such Regulations, except as to the Places of chusing Senators.

The Congress shall assemble at least once in every Year, and such Meeting shall [be on the first Monday in December],[4] unless they shall by Law appoint a different Day.

Section 5. Each House shall be the Judge of the Elections, Returns and Qualifications of its own Members, and a Majority of each shall constitute a Quorum to do Business; but a smaller Number may adjourn from day to day, and may be authorized to compel the Attendance of absent Members, in such Manner, and under such Penalties as each House may provide.

Each House may determine the Rules of its Proceedings, punish its Members for disorderly Behaviour, and, with the Concurrence of two thirds, expel a Member.

Each House shall keep a Journal of its Proceedings, and from time to time publish the same, excepting such Parts as may in their Judgment require Secrecy; and the Yeas and Nays of the Members of either House on any question shall, at the Desire of one fifth of those Present, be entered on the Journal.

Neither House, during the Session of Congress, shall, without the Consent of the other, adjourn for more than three days, nor to any other Place than that in which the two Houses shall be sitting.

Section 6. The Senators and Representatives shall receive a Compensation for their Services, to be ascertained by Law, and paid out of the Treasury of the United States. They shall in all Cases, except Treason, Felony and Breach of the Peace, be privileged from Arrest during their Attendance at the Session of their respective Houses, and in going to and returning from the same; and for any Speech or Debate in either House, they shall not be questioned in any other Place.

No Senator or Representative shall, during the Time for which he was elected, be appointed to any civil Office under the Authority of the United States, which shall have been created, or the Emoluments whereof shall have been encreased during such time; and no Person holding any Office under the United States, shall be a Member of either House during his Continuance in Office.

Section 7. All Bills for raising Revenue shall originate in the House of Representatives; but the Senate may propose or concur with amendments as on other Bills.

Every Bill which shall have passed the House of Representatives and the Senate, shall, before it become a Law, be presented to the President of the United States; If he approve he shall sign it, but if not he shall return it, with his Objections to that House in which it shall have originated, who shall enter the Objections at large on their Journal, and proceed to reconsider it. If after such Reconsideration two thirds of that House shall agree to pass the Bill, it shall be sent, together with the Objections, to the other House, by which it shall likewise be reconsidered, and if approved by two thirds of that House, it shall become a Law. But in all such Cases the Votes of both Houses shall be determined by yeas and Nays, and the Names of the Persons voting for and against the Bill shall be entered on the Journal of each House respectively. If any Bill shall not be returned by the President within ten Days (Sundays excepted) after it shall have been presented to him, the Same shall be a Law, in like Manner as if he had signed it, unless the Congress by their Adjournment prevent its Return, in which Case it shall not be a Law.

Every Order, Resolution, or Vote to which the Concurrence of the Senate and House of Representatives may be necessary (except on a question of Adjournment) shall be presented to the President of the United States; and before the Same shall take Effect, shall be approved by him, or being disapproved by him, shall be repassed by two thirds of the Senate and House of Representatives, according to the Rules and Limitations prescribed in the Case of a Bill.

Section 8. The Congress shall have Power To lay and collect Taxes, Duties, Imposts and Excises, to pay the Debts and provide for the common Defence and general Welfare of the United States; but all Duties, Imposts and Excises shall be uniform throughout the United States;

To borrow Money on the credit of the United States;

To regulate Commerce with foreign Nations, and among the several States, and with the Indian Tribes;

To establish an uniform Rule of Naturalization, and uniform Laws on the subject of Bankruptcies throughout the United States;

To coin Money, regulate the Value thereof, and of foreign Coin, and fix the Standard of Weights and Measures;

To provide for the Punishment of counterfeiting the Securities and current Coin of the United States;

To establish Post Offices and post Roads;

To promote the Progress of Science and useful Arts, by securing for limited Times to Authors and Inventors the exclusive Right to their respective Writings and Discoveries;

To constitute Tribunals inferior to the supreme Court;

To define and punish Piracies and Felonies commited on the high Seas, and Offences against the Law of Nations;

To declare War, grant Letters of Marque and Reprisal, and make Rules concerning Captures on Land and Water;

To raise and support Armies, but no Appropriation of Money to that Use shall be for a longer Term than two Years;

To provide and maintain a Navy;

To make Rules for the Government and Regulation of the land and naval Forces;

To provide for calling forth the Militia to execute the Laws of the Union, suppress Insurrections and repel Invasions;

To provide for organizing, arming, and disciplining, the Militia, and for governing such Part of them as may be employed in the Service of the United States, reserving to the States respectively, the Appointment of the Officers, and the Authority of training the Militia according to the discipline prescribed by Congress;

To exercise exclusive Legislation in all Cases whatsoever, over such District (not exceeding ten Miles square) as may, by Cession of Particular States, and the Acceptance of Congress, become the Seat of the Government of the United States, and to exercise like Authority over all Places purchased by the Consent of the Legislature of the State in which the Same shall be, for the Erection of Forts, Magazines, Arsenals, dock-Yards, and other needful Buildings; — And

To make all Laws which shall be necessary and proper for carrying into Execution the foregoing Powers, and all other Powers vested by this Constitution in the Government of the United States, or in any Department or Officer thereof.

Section 9. The Migration or Importation of such Persons as any of the States now existing shall think proper to admit, shall not be prohibited by the Congress prior to the Year one thousand eight hundred and eight, but a Tax or duty may be imposed on such Importation, not exceeding ten dollars for each Person.

The Privilege of the Writ of Habeas Corpus shall not be suspended, unless when in Cases of Rebellion or Invasion the public Safety may require it.

No Bill of Attainder or ex post facto Law shall be passed.

No capitation, or other direct, Tax shall be laid, unless in Proportion to the Census of Enumeration herein before directed to be taken.[5]

No Tax or Duty shall be laid on Articles exported from any State.

No Preference shall be given by any Regulation of Commerce or Revenue to the Ports of one State over those of another; nor shall Vessels bound to, or from, one State, be obliged to enter, clear or pay Duties in another.

No Money shall be drawn from the Treasury, but in

Consequence of Appropriations made by Law; and a regular Statement and Account of the Receipts and Expenditures of all public Money shall be published from time to time.

No Title of Nobility shall be granted by the United States: And no Person holding any Office of Profit or Trust under them, shall, without the Consent of the Congress, accept of any present, Emolument, Office, or Title, of any kind whatever, from any King, Prince or foreign State.

Section 10. No State shall enter into any Treaty, Alliance, or Confederation; grant Letters of Marque and Reprisal; coin Money; emit Bills of Credit; make any Thing but gold and silver Coin a Tender in Payment of Debts; pass any Bill of Attainder, ex post facto Law, or Law impairing the Obligation of Contracts, or grant any Title of Nobility.

No State shall, without the Consent of the Congress, lay any Imposts or Duties on Imports or Exports, except what may be absolutely necessary for executing it's inspection Laws: and the net Produce of all Duties and Imposts, laid by any State on Imports or Exports, shall be for the Use of the Treasury of the United States; and all such Laws shall be subject to the Revision and Controul of the Congress.

No State shall, without the Consent of Congress, lay any Duty of Tonnage, keep Troops, or Ships of War in time of Peace, enter into any Agreement or Compact with another State, or with a foreign Power, or engage in War, unless actually invaded, or in such imminent Danger as will not admit of delay.

ARTICLE II

Section 1. The executive Power shall be vested in a President of the United States of America. He shall hold his Office during the Term of four Years, and, together with the Vice President, chosen for the same Term, be elected, as follows.

Each State shall appoint, in such Manner as the Legislature thereof may direct, a Number of Electors, equal to the whole Number of Senators and Representatives to which the State may be entitled in the Congress: but no Senator or Representative, or Person holding an Office of Trust or Profit under the United States, shall be appointed an Elector.

[The Electors shall meet in their respective States, and vote by Ballot for two Persons, of whom one at least shall not be an Inhabitant of the same State with themselves. And they shall make a List of all the Persons voted for, and of the Number of Votes for each; which List they shall sign and certify, and transmit sealed to the Seat of the Government of the United States, directed to the President of the Senate. The President of the Senate shall, in the Presence of the Senate and House of Representatives, open all the Certificates, and the Votes shall then be counted. The Person having the greatest Number of Votes shall be the President, if such Number be a Majority of the whole Number of Electors appointed; and if there be more than one who have such Majority, and have an equal Number of Votes, then the House of Representatives shall immediately chuse by Ballot one of them for President; and if no Person have a Majority, then from the five highest on the list the said House shall in like Manner chuse the President. But in chusing the President, the Votes shall be taken by States, the Representation from each State having one Vote; a quorum for this Purpose shall consist of a Member or Members from two thirds of the States, and a Majority of all the States shall be necessary to a Choice. In every Case, after the Choice of the President, the Person having the greatest Number of Votes of the Electors shall be the Vice President. But if there should remain two or more who have equal Votes, the Senate shall chuse from them by Ballot the Vice President.][6]

The Congress may determine the Time of chusing the Electors, and the Day on which they shall give their Votes; which Day shall be the same throughout the United States.

No Person except a natural born Citizen, or a Citizen of the United States, at the time of the Adoption of this Constitution, shall be eligible to the Office of President; neither shall any Person be eligible to that Office who shall not have attained to the Age of thirty five Years, and been fourteen Years a Resident within the United States.

In Case of the Removal of the President from Office, or of his Death, Resignation, or Inability to discharge the Powers and Duties of the said Office,[7] the Same shall devolve on the Vice President, and the Congress may by Law provide for the Case of Removal, Death, Resignation or Inability, both of the President and Vice President, declaring what Officer shall then act as President, and such Officer shall act accordingly, until the Disability be removed, or a President shall be elected.

The President shall, at stated Times, receive for his Services, a Compensation, which shall neither be encreased nor diminished during the Period for which he shall have been elected, and he shall not receive within that Period any other Emolument from the United States, or any of them.

Before he enter on the Execution of his Office, he shall take the following Oath or Affirmation: — "I do solemnly swear (or affirm) that I will faithfully execute the Office of President of the United States, and will to the best of my Ability, preserve, protect and defend the Constitution of the United States."

Section 2. The President shall be Commander in Chief of the Army and Navy of the United States, and of the Militia of the several States, when called into the actual Service of the United States; he may require the Opinion, in writing, of the principal Officer in each of the executive Departments, upon any Subject relating to the Duties of their respective Offices, and he shall have Power to grant Reprieves and Pardons for Offenses against the United States, except in Cases of Impeachment.

He shall have Power, by and with the Advice and Consent of the Senate, to make Treaties, provided two thirds of the Senators present concur; and he shall nominate, and by and with the Advice and Consent of the Senate, shall appoint Ambassadors, other public Ministers and Consuls, Judges of the supreme Court, and all other Officers of the United States, whose Appointments are not herein otherwise provided for, and which shall be established by Law: but the Congress may by Law vest the Appointment of such inferior Officers, as they think proper, in the President alone, in the Courts of Law, or in the Heads of Departments.

The President shall have Power to fill up all Vacancies that may happen during the Recess of the Senate, by granting Commissions which shall expire at the End of their next Session.

Section 3. He shall from time to time give to the Congress Information of the State of the Union, and recommend to their Consideration such Measures as he shall judge necessary and expedient; he may, on extraordinary Occasions, convene both Houses, or either of them, and in Case of Disagreement between them, with Respect to the Time of Adjournment, he may adjourn them to such Time as he shall think proper; he shall receive Ambassadors and other public Ministers; he shall take Care that the Laws be faithfully executed, and shall Commission all the Officers of the United States.

Section 4. The President, Vice President and all Civil Officers of the United States, shall be removed from office on Impeachment for, and Conviction of, Treason, Bribery, or other high Crimes and Misdemeanors.

ARTICLE III

Section 1. The judicial Power of the United States, shall be vested in one supreme Court, and in such inferior Courts as the Congress may from time to time ordain and establish. The Judges, both of the supreme and inferior Courts, shall hold their Offices during good Behaviour, and shall, at stated Times, receive for their Services, a Compensation, which shall not be diminished during their Continuance in Office.

Section 2. The judicial Power shall extend to all Cases, in Law and Equity, arising under this Constitution, the Laws of the United States, and Treaties made, or which shall be made, under their Authority; — to all Cases affecting Ambassadors, other public Ministers and Consuls; — to all Cases of admiralty and maritime Jurisdiction; — to Controversies to which the United States shall be a Party; — to Controversies between two or more States; — between a State and Citizens of another State;[8] — between Citizens of different States; — between Citizens of the same State claiming Lands under Grants of different States, and between a State, or the Citizens thereof, and foreign States, Citizens or Subjects.[8]

In all Cases affecting Ambassadors, other public Ministers and Consuls, and those in which a State shall be Party, the supreme Court shall have original Jurisdiction. In all the other Cases before mentioned, the supreme Court shall have appellate Jurisdiction, both as to Law and Fact, with such Exceptions, and under such Regulations as the Congress shall make.

The Trial of all Crimes, except in cases of Impeachment, shall be by Jury; and such Trial shall be held in the State where the said Crimes shall have been committed; but when not committed within any State, the Trial shall be at such Place or Places as the Congress may by Law have directed.

Section 3. Treason against the United States, shall consist only in levying War against them, or in adhering to their Enemies, giving them Aid and Comfort. No Person shall be convicted of Treason unless on the Testimony of two Witnesses to the same overt Act, or on Confession in open Court.

The Congress shall have Power to declare the Punishment of Treason, but no Attainder of Treason shall work Corruption of Blood, or Forfeiture except during the Life of the Person attainted.

ARTICLE IV

Section 1. Full Faith and Credit shall be given in each State to the public Acts, Records, and judicial Proceedings of every other State. And the Congress may by general Laws prescribe the Manner in which such Acts, Records and Proceedings shall be proved, and the Effect thereof.

Section 2. The Citizens of each State shall be entitled to all Privileges and Immunities of Citizens in the several States.

A Person charged in any State with Treason, Felony, or other Crime, who shall flee from Justice, and be found in another State, shall on Demand of the executive Authority of the State from which he fled, be delivered up, to be removed to the State having Jurisdiction of the Crime.

[No Person held to Service or Labour in one State, under the Laws thereof, escaping into another, shall, in Consequence of any Law or Regulation therein, be discharged from such Service or Labour, but shall be delivered up on Claim of the Party to whom such Service or Labour may be due.][9]

Section 3. New States may be admitted by the Congress into this Union; but no new State shall be formed or erected within the Jurisdiction of any other State; nor any State be formed by the Junction of two or more States, or Parts of States, without the Consent of the Legislatures of the States concerned as well as of the Congress.

The Congress shall have Power to dispose of and make all needful Rules and Regulations respecting the Territory or other Property belonging to the United States; and nothing in this Constitution shall be so construed as to Prejudice any Claims of the United States, or of any particular State.

Section 4. The United States shall guarantee to every State in this Union a Republican Form of Government, and shall protect each of them against Invasion; and on Application of the Legislature, or of the Executive (when the Legislature cannot be convened) against domestic Violence.

ARTICLE V

The Congress, whenever two thirds of both Houses shall deem it necessary, shall propose Amendments to this Constitution, or, on the Application of the Legislatures of two thirds of the several States, shall call a Convention for proposing Amendments, which, in either Case, shall be valid to all Intents and Purposes, as Part of this Constitution, when ratified by the Legislatures of three fourths of the several States, or by Conventions in three fourths thereof, as the one or the other Mode of Ratification may be proposed by the Congress; Provided [that no Amendment which may be made prior to the Year One thousand eight hundred and eight shall in any Manner affect the first and fourth Clauses in the Ninth Section of the first Article; and][10] that no State, without its Consent, shall be deprived of its equal Suffrage in the Senate.

ARTICLE VI

All Debts contracted and Engagements entered into, before the Adoption of this Constitution, shall be as valid against the United States under this Constitution, as under the Confederation.

This Constitution, and the Laws of the United States which shall be made in Pursuance thereof; and all Treaties made, or which shall be made, under the Authority of the United States, shall be the supreme Law of the Land; and the Judges in every State shall be bound thereby, any

Thing in the Constitution or Laws of any State to the Contrary notwithstanding.

The Senators and Representatives before mentioned, and the Members of the several State Legislatures, and all executive and judicial Officers, both of the United States and of the several States, shall be bound by Oath or Affirmation, to support this Constitution; but no religious Test shall ever be required as a Qualification to any Office or public Trust under the United States.

ARTICLE VII

The Ratification of the Conventions of nine States, shall be sufficient for the Establishment of this Constitution between the States so ratifying the Same. Done in Convention by the Unanimous Consent of the States present the Seventeenth Day of September in the Year of our Lord one thousand seven hundred and Eighty seven and of the Independence of the United States of America the Twelfth In witness whereof We have hereunto subscribed our Names, George Washington, President and deputy from Virginia.

New Hampshire:	John Langdon, Nicholas Gilman.
Massachusetts:	Nathaniel Gorham, Rufus King.
Connecticut:	William Samuel Johnson, Roger Sherman.
New York:	Alexander Hamilton
New Jersey:	William Livingston, David Brearley, William Paterson, Jonathan Dayton.
Pennsylvania:	Benjamin Franklin, Thomas Mifflin, Robert Morris, George Clymer, Thomas FitzSimons, Jared Ingersoll, James Wilson, Gouverneur Morris.
Delaware:	George Read, Gunning Bedford Jr., John Dickinson, Richard Bassett, Jacob Broom.
Maryland:	James McHenry, Daniel of St. Thomas Jenifer, Daniel Carroll.
Virginia:	John Blair, James Madison Jr.
North Carolina:	William Blount, Richard Dobbs Spaight, Hugh Williamson.
South Carolina:	John Rutledge, Charles Cotesworth Pinckney, Charles Pinckney, Pierce Butler.
Georgia:	William Few, Abraham Baldwin.

[The language of the original Constitution, not including the Amendments, was adopted by a convention of the states on Sept. 17, 1787, and was subsequently ratified by the states on the following dates: Delaware, Dec. 7, 1787; Pennsylvania, Dec. 12, 1787; New Jersey, Dec. 18, 1787; Georgia, Jan. 2, 1788; Connecticut, Jan. 9, 1788; Massachusetts, Feb. 6, 1788; Maryland, April 28, 1788; South Carolina, May 23, 1788; New Hampshire, June 21, 1788.

Ratification was completed on June 21, 1788.

The Constitution subsequently was ratified by Virginia, June 25, 1788; New York, July 26, 1788; North Carolina, Nov. 21, 1789; Rhode Island, May 29, 1790; and Vermont, Jan. 10, 1791.]

Amendments

Amendment I

(First ten amendments ratified Dec. 15, 1791.)

Congress shall make no law respecting an establishment of religion, or prohibiting the free exercise thereof; or abridging the freedom of speech, or of the press; or the right of the people peaceably to assemble, and to petition the Government for a redress of grievances.

Amendment II

A well regulated Militia, being necessary to the security of a free State, the right of the people to keep and bear Arms, shall not be infringed.

Amendment III

No Soldier shall, in time of peace be quartered in any house, without the consent of the Owner, nor in time of war, but in a manner to be prescribed by law.

Amendment IV

The right of the people to be secure in their persons, houses, papers, and effects, against unreasonable searches and seizures, shall not be violated, and no Warrants shall issue, but upon probable cause, supported by Oath or affirmation, and particularly describing the place to be searched, and the persons or things to be seized.

Amendment V

No person shall be held to answer for a capital, or otherwise infamous crime, unless on a presentment or indictment of a Grand Jury, except in cases arising in the land or naval forces, or in the Militia, when in actual service in time of War or public danger; nor shall any person be subject for the same offence to be twice put in jeopardy of life or limb; nor shall be compelled in any criminal case to be a witness against himself, nor be deprived of life, liberty, or property, without due process of law; nor shall private property be taken for public use, without just compensation.

Amendment VI

In all criminal prosecutions, the accused shall enjoy the right to a speedy and public trial, by an impartial jury of the State and district wherein the crime shall have been committed, which district shall have been previously ascertained by law, and to be informed of the nature and cause of the accusation; to be confronted with the witnesses against him; to have compulsory process for obtaining witnesses in his favor, and to have the Assistance of Counsel for his defence.

Amendment VII

In Suits at common law, where the value in controversy shall exceed twenty dollars, the right of trial by jury shall be preserved, and no fact tried by a jury, shall be otherwise re-examined in any Court of the United States, than according to the rules of the common law.

Amendment VIII

Excessive bail shall not be required, nor excessive fines imposed, nor cruel and unusual punishments inflicted.

Amendment IX

The enumeration in the Constitution, of certain rights, shall not be construed to deny or disparage others retained by the people.

Amendment X

The powers not delegated to the United States by the Constitution, nor prohibited by it to the States, are reserved to the States respectively, or to the people.

Amendment XI *(Ratified Feb. 7, 1795)*

The Judicial power of the United States shall not be construed to extend to any suit in law or equity, commenced or prosecuted against one of the United States by Citizens of another State, or by Citizens or Subjects of any Foreign State.

Amendment XII *(Ratified June 15, 1804)*

The Electors shall meet in their respective states and vote by ballot for President and Vice-President, one of whom, at least, shall not be an inhabitant of the same state with themselves; they shall name in their ballots the person voted for as President, and in distinct ballots the person voted for as Vice-President, and they shall make distinct lists of all persons voted for as President, and of all persons voted for as Vice-President, and of the number of votes for each, which lists they shall sign and certify, and transmit sealed to the seat of the government of the United States, directed to the President of the Senate; — The President of the Senate shall, in the presence of the Senate and House of Representatives, open all the certificates and the votes shall then be counted; — The person having the greatest number of votes for President, shall be the President, if such number be a majority of the whole number of Electors appointed; and if no person have such majority, then from the persons having the highest numbers not exceeding three on the list of those voted for as President, the House of Representatives shall choose immediately, by ballot, the President. But in choosing the President, the votes shall be taken by states, the representation from each state having one vote; a quorum for this purpose shall consist of a member or members from two-thirds of the states, and a majority of all the states shall be necessary to a choice. [And if the House of Representatives shall not choose a President whenever the right of choice shall devolve upon them, before the fourth day of March next following, then the Vice-President shall act as President, as in the case of the death or other constitutional disability of the President —][11] The person having the greatest number of votes as Vice-President, shall be the Vice-President, if such number be a majority of the whole number of Electors appointed, and if no person have a majority, then from the two highest numbers on the list, the Senate shall choose the Vice-President; a quorum for the purpose shall consist of two-thirds of the whole number of Senators, and a majority of the whole number shall be necessary to a choice. But no person constitutionally ineligible to the office of President shall be eligible to that of Vice-President of the United States.

Amendment XIII *(Ratified Dec. 6, 1865)*

Section 1. Neither slavery nor involuntary servitude, except as a punishment for crime whereof the party shall have been duly convicted, shall exist within the United States, or any place subject to their jurisdiction.

Section 2. Congress shall have power to enforce this article by appropriate legislation.

Amendment XIV *(Ratified July 9, 1868)*

Section 1. All persons born or naturalized in the United States and subject to the jurisdiction thereof, are citizens of the United States and of the State wherein they reside. No State shall make or enforce any law which shall abridge the privileges or immunities of citizens of the United States; nor shall any State deprive any person of life, liberty, or property, without due process of law; nor deny to any person within its jurisdiction the equal protection of the laws.

Section 2. Representatives shall be apportioned among the several States according to their respective numbers, counting the whole number of persons in each State, excluding Indians not taxed. But when the right to vote at any election for the choice of electors for President and Vice President of the United States, Representatives in Congress, the Executive and Judicial officers of a State, or the members of the Legislature thereof, is denied to any of the male inhabitants of such State, being twenty-one years of age,[12] and citizens of the United States, or in any way abridged, except for participation in rebellion, or other crime, the basis of representation therein shall be reduced in the proportion which the number of such male citizens shall bear to the whole number of male citizens twenty-one years of age in such State.

Section 3. No person shall be a Senator or Representative in Congress, or elector of President and Vice President, or hold any office, civil or military, under the United States, or under any State, who, having previously taken an oath, as a member of Congress, or as an officer of the United States, or as a member of any State legislature, or as an executive or judicial officer of any State, to support the Constitution of the United States, shall have engaged in insurrection or rebellion against the same, or given aid or comfort to the enemies thereof. But Congress may by a vote of two-thirds of each House, remove such disability.

Section 4. The validity of the public debt of the United States, authorized by law, including debts incurred for payment of pensions and bounties for services in suppressing insurrection or rebellion, shall not be questioned. But neither the United States nor any State shall assume or pay any debt or obligation incurred in aid of insurrection or rebellion against the United States, or any claim for the loss or emancipation of any slave; but all such debts, obligations and claims shall be held illegal and void.

Section 5. The Congress shall have power to enforce, by appropriate legislation, the provisions of this article.

Amendment XV *(Ratified Feb. 3, 1870)*

Section 1. The right of citizens of the United States to vote shall not be denied or abridged by the United States or by any State on account of race, color, or previous condition of servitude.

Section 2. The Congress shall have power to enforce this article by appropriate legislation.

Amendment XVI *(Ratified Feb. 3, 1913)*

The Congress shall have power to lay and collect taxes

on incomes, from whatever source derived, without apportionment among the several States, and without regard to any census or enumeration.

Amendment XVII *(Ratified Apr. 8, 1913)*

The Senate of the United States shall be composed of two Senators from each State, elected by the people thereof, for six years; and each Senator shall have one vote. The electors in each State shall have the qualifications requisite for electors of the most numerous branch of the State legislatures.

When vacancies happen in the representation of any State in the Senate, the executive authority of such State shall issue writs of election to fill such vacancies: *Provided,* That the legislature of any State may empower the executive thereof to make temporary appointments until the people fill the vacancies by election as the legislature may direct.

This amendment shall not be so construed as to affect the election or term of any Senator chosen before it becomes valid as part of the Constitution.

[Amendment XVIII *(Ratified Jan. 16, 1919)*

Section. 1. After one year from the ratification of this article the manufacture, sale, or transportation of intoxicating liquors within, the importation thereof into, or the exportation thereof from the United States and all territory subject to the jurisdiction thereof for beverage purposes is hereby prohibited.

Section 2. The Congress and the several States shall have concurrent power to enforce this article by appropriate legislation.

Section 3. This article shall be inoperative unless it shall have been ratified as an amendment to the Constitution by the legislatures of the several States, as provided in the Constitution, within seven years from the date of the submission hereof to the States by the Congress.][13]

Amendment XIX *(Ratified Aug. 18, 1920)*

The right of citizens of the United States to vote shall not be denied or abridged by the United States or by any State on account of sex.

Congress shall have power to enforce this article by appropriate legislation.

Amendment XX *(Ratified Jan. 23, 1933)*

Section 1. The terms of the President and Vice President shall end at noon on the 20th day of January, and the terms of Senators and Representatives at noon on the 3d day of January, of the years in which such terms would have ended if this article had not been ratified; and the terms of their successors shall then begin.

Section 2. The Congress shall assemble at least once in every year, and such meeting shall begin at noon on the 3d day of January, unless they shall by law appoint a different day.

Section 3.[14] If, at the time fixed for the beginning of the term of the President, the President elect shall have died, the Vice President elect shall become President. If a President shall not have been chosen before the time fixed for the beginning of his term, or if the President elect shall have failed to qualify, then the Vice President elect shall act as President until a President shall have qualified; and the Congress may by law provide for the case wherein neither a President elect nor a Vice President elect shall have qualified, declaring who shall then act as President, or the manner in which one who is to act shall be selected, and such person shall act accordingly until a President or Vice President shall have qualified.

Section 4. The Congress may by law provide for the case of the death of any of the persons from whom the House of Representatives may choose a President whenever the right of choice shall have devolved upon them, and for the case of the death of any of the persons from whom the Senate may choose a Vice President whenever the right of choice shall have devolved upon them.

Section 5. Sections 1 and 2 shall take effect on the 15th day of October following the ratification of this article.

Section 6. This article shall be inoperative unless it shall have been ratified as an amendment to the Constitution by the legislatures of three-fourths of the several States within seven years from the date of its submission.

Amendment XXI *(Ratified Dec. 5, 1933)*

Section 1. The eighteenth article of amendment to the Constitution of the United States is hereby repealed.

Section 2. The transportation or importation into any State, Territory or possession of the United States for delivery or use therein of intoxicating liquors, in violation of the laws thereof, is hereby prohibited.

Section 3. This article shall be inoperative unless it shall have been ratified as an amendment to the Constitution by conventions in the several States, as provided in the Constitution, within seven years from the date of the submission hereof to the States by the Congress.

Amendment XXII *(Ratified Feb. 27, 1951)*

Section 1. No person shall be elected to the office of the President more than twice, and no person who has held the office of President, or acted as President, for more than two years of a term to which some other person was elected President shall be elected to the office of the President more than once. But this Article shall not apply to any person holding the office of President when this Article was proposed by the Congress, and shall not prevent any person who may be holding the office of President, or acting as President, during the term within which this Article become operative from holding the office of President or acting as President during the remainder of such term.

Section 2. This Article shall be inoperative unless it shall have been ratified as an amendment to the Constitution by the legislatures of three-fourths of the several States within seven years from the date of its submission to the States by the Congress.

Amendment XXIII *(Ratified March 29, 1961)*

Section 1. The District constituting the seat of Government of the United States shall appoint in such manner as the Congress may direct:

A number of electors of President and Vice President equal to the whole number of Senators and Representatives in Congress to which the District would be entitled if it were a State, but in no event more than the least populous State; they shall be in addition to those appointed by the States, but they shall be considered, for the purposes of the election of President and Vice President, to be electors appointed by a State; and they shall meet in the District and perform such duties as provided by the twelfth article of amendment.

Section 2. The Congress shall have power to enforce this article by appropriate legislation.

Amendment XXIV *(Ratified Jan. 23, 1964)*

Section 1. The right of citizens of the United States to vote in any primary or other election for President or Vice President, for electors for President or Vice President, or for Senator or Representative in Congress, shall not be denied or abridged by the United States or any State by reason of failure to pay any poll tax or other tax.

Section 2. The Congress shall have power to enforce this article by appropriate legislation.

Amendment XXV *(Ratified Feb. 10, 1967)*

Section 1. In case of the removal of the President from office or of his death or resignation, the Vice President shall become President.

Section 2. Whenever there is a vacancy in the office of the Vice President, the President shall nominate a Vice President who shall take office upon confirmation by a majority vote of both Houses of Congress.

Section 3. Whenever the President transmits to the President pro tempore of the Senate and the Speaker of the House of Representatives his written declaration that he is unable to discharge the powers and duties of his office, and until he transmits to them a written declaration to the contrary, such powers and duties shall be discharged by the Vice President as Acting President.

Section 4. Whenever the Vice President and a majority of either the principal officers of the executive departments or of such other body as Congress may by law provide, transmit to the President pro tempore of the Senate and the Speaker of the House of Representatives their written declaration that the President is unable to discharge the powers and duties of his office, the Vice President shall immediately assume the powers and duties of the office as Acting President.

Thereafter, when the President transmits to the President pro tempore of the Senate and the Speaker of the House of Representatives his written declaration that no inability exists, he shall resume the powers and duties of his office unless the Vice President and a majority of either the principal officers of the executive department or of such other body as Congress may by law provide, transmit within four days to the President pro tempore of the Senate and the Speaker of the House of Representatives their written declaration that the President is unable to discharge the powers and duties of his office. Thereupon Congress shall decide the issue, assembling within forty-eight hours for that purpose if not in session. If the Congress, within twenty-one days after receipt of the latter written declaration, or, if Congress is not in session, within twenty-one days after Congress is required to assemble, determines by two-thirds vote of both houses that the President is unable to discharge the powers and duties of his office, the Vice President shall continue to discharge the same as Acting President; otherwise, the President shall resume the powers and duties of his office.

Amendment XXVI *(Ratified July 1, 1971)*

Section 1. The right of citizens of the United States, who are eighteen years of age or older, to vote shall not be denied or abridged by the United States or by any State on account of age.

Section 2. The Congress shall have power to enforce this article by appropriate legislation.

Notes

1. The part in brackets was changed by section 2 of the Fourteenth Amendment.
2. The part in brackets was changed by section 1 of the Seventeenth Amendment.
3. The part in brackets was changed by the second paragraph of the Seventeenth Amendment.
4. The part in brackets was changed by section 2 of the Twentieth Amendment.
5. The Sixteenth Amendment gave Congress the power to tax incomes.
6. The material in brackets has been superseded by the Twelfth Amendment.
7. This provision has been affected by the Twenty-fifth Amendment.
8. These clauses were affected by the Eleventh Amendment.
9. This paragraph has been superseded by the Thirteenth Amendment.
10. Obsolete.
11. The part in brackets has been superseded by section 3 of the Twentieth Amendment.
12. See the Twenty-sixth Amendment.
13. This Amendment was repealed by section 1 of the Twenty-first Amendment.
14. See the Twenty-fifth Amendment.

Source: U.S. Congress, House, Committee on the Judiciary, *The Constitution of the United States of America, As Amended Through July 1971,* H. Doc. 93-215, 93rd Cong., 2nd sess., 1974.

INDEX

Abortion, 107, 114
Abscam, 27, 84
Adams, Brock, D-Wash., 46-47
AFL-CIO, 107-109
Agent Orange, 94
AIDS
policy on, 22
Airlines
deregulation, 46, 48-50
American Civil Liberties Union (ACLU), 110
American Enterprise Institute, 86
Americans for Democratic Action, 84
Antitrust laws, 109
Arms Export Control Act, 16, 25
Armstrong, William L., R-Colo., 104-105

Baker, James, 21
Basic Inc. v. Levinson, 115
Bentsen, Lloyd, D-Texas, 19, 20, 21
Biden, Joseph R. Jr., D-Del., 105-106, 107, 119
Black vote, 78
Blackmun, Harry A., 112-113, 122
Boll Weevils. *see* Conservative coalition
Boner, Bill, D-Tenn., 88
Bonior, David, D-Mich., 94
Boren, David L., D-Okla., 19
Bork, Robert H., 41, 96, 107-110, 111-113, 114, 118-119
Boschwitz, Rudy, R-Minn., 61, 64-65
Bowen, Otis, 22
Bowers v. Harwick, 108
Brandeis, Louis D., 111, 112, 113
Brennan, William J., 112, 120-121
Bribery of congressmen, 84
Brown v. Board of Education, 109
Budget
control of, 23-24, 52-53
see also Office of Management and Budget (OMB)
Burger, Warren, 112
Bush, George, 17, 19
Business Electronics v. Sharp Electronics Corp., 112
Byrd, Robert C., D-W.Va., 28-33, 35, 41, 90, 104

Campaign spending, 80
Carpenter v. U.S., 115
Carter, Jimmy, 55, 70
Central Intelligence Agency (CIA), 5-9, 14, 16
firing of homosexuals, 117
Civil rights, 108-109
Clean Water Act, 117
Coelho, Tony, D-Calif., 36-37, 70, 93, 94
Commerce
regulation of, 24
Committee on Political Education (COPE), 85
Committee on Standards of Official Conduct, 88
Common Cause, 82, 84
Congress
budget control, 23-24
control of, 28-33
ethics, 26-27
foreign policy powers, 24-25
members' salaries, 27
powers of, 23-27
regulation of commerce, 24
see also Senate; House

Congressional Election Calendar, 68
Conservative Caucus, 84
Conservative coalition, 73-79
Constitution, U.S.
amendments, 26
election of president, 26
impeachment, 25-26
on foreign relations, 24-25
on legislative powers, 23
on trade matters, 21
text, 142-149
Consumer Federation of America (CFA), 49
Covert operations, 14-16

Danforth, John C., R-Mo., 46, 51
Dannemeyer, William E., R-Calif., 22
DeConcini, Dennis, D-Ariz., 104
Defense
SDI funding, 17
de la Garza, E. Kika, D-Texas, 82
Delegate selection, 59-60
Democratic Congressional Campaign Committee (DCCC), 69-72
Democratic Party
primaries, 56
see also Elections
Democratic Senatorial Campaign Committee (DSCC), 61-65
Deregulation, 46-51
Dole, Elizabeth H., 47
Dole, Robert, R-Kan., 21
Douglas, William O., 111
Droneburg v. Zech, 108
Durenberger, Dave, R-Minn., 104

Education for All Handicapped Children Act, 116
Elections
delegate selection, 59-60
presidential primaries, 54-60
spending limits, 58
El Salvador, 4-5
Energy and Commerce Committee, 22
English, Glenn, D-Okla., 47
Equal Rights Amendment (ERA), 84
Ethics panel, 88
Executive branch, 23
Executive privilege, 15

Federal Elections Commission, 89
Federal Emergency Management Agency (FEMA), 91
Federal Regulation of Lobbying Act, 87
Filibusters, 40-45
First Amendment rights, 108, 109
Foley, Thomas S., D-Wash., 36-37
Food Research and Action Center, 84
Foreign interest lobbies, 84
Frankfurter, Felix, 112

Gephardt, Richard, D-Mo., 21
Ghorbanifar, Manucher, 6-7, 9
Gibbons, Clifford, 82
Gibbons, Sam, D-Fla., 80-82
Gingrich, Newt, R-Ga., 71
Ginsburg, Douglas H., 104
GOP. *see* Republican Party
Gramm-Rudman-Hollings, 24, 37, 52-53
Griswold v. Connecticut, 107

Harlan, John, 112
Hatch, Orrin, R-Utah, 104
Hollings, Ernest F., D-S.C., 24, 52, 76
Holmes, Oliver Wendell, 111
Homosexual rights, 108, 117
Honig v. Doe, 116
House of Representatives
elections, 69-72
Ethics Committee, 88
Intelligence Committee, 11, 16
Ways and Means Committee, 52-53
see also Congress

Immigration law, 115
Inouye, Daniel K., D-Hawaii, 11, 32
Insider trading, 115
Iran-contra affair, 4-13

Jaworski, Leon, 110
Jones, James R., D-Okla., 90
Judicial restraint, 119
Judiciary
powers, 23
Reagan nominations, 96-97, 118-119
see also Supreme Court
Justice Department. *see* Judiciary; Supreme Court

Kennedy, Edward M., D-Mass., 48-49
Kerry, John, D-Mass., 61
Khomeini, Ayatollah, 91-92
K Mart Corp. v. Cartier, 115-116
Korologos, Tom, 96-97

LaFollette, Robert M., 54
League of Women Voters, 84
Leahy, Patrick J., D-Vt., 119
Lobbies, 83-87
gifts from, 88
nuclear energy, 91-92
regulation, 87
veterans, 93-95
see also Political Action Committees (PACs)
Long Island Illumination Company (Lilco), 91-92
Lyng v. International Union, United Automobile Aerospace & Agricultural Implement Workers of America, UAW, et al., 116

Mackay, Buddy, D-Fla., 75
Markey, Edward J., D-Mass., 91-92
Marshall, Thurgood, 121-122
Mathias, Charles McC., R-Md., 96
McCurdy, Dave, D-Okla., 75, 79
McFarlane, Robert C., 5-10
Meese, Edwin III, 10, 16, 25, 97
Metzenbaum, Howard, D-Ohio, 106
Mitchell, George, D-Maine, 106
Montgomery, G. V. "Sonny", D-Miss., 93, 94
Moral Majority, 84
Muller, Robert O., 94-95
Murkowski, Frank, R-Alaska, 104

Nader, Ralph, 84
National Abortion Rights Action League (NARAL), 105
National Conference of Catholic Bishops, 84
National Low Income Housing Coalition, 84
National Republican Congressional Committee (NRCC), 69-72
National Republican Senatorial Committee (NRSC), 61-63, 66, 70
National Rifle Association (NRA), 85-86
National Security Council (NSC), 4-8, 10, 12, 14, 16
Nicaragua, 4-5, 7
Nickles, Don, R-Okla., 90
Nixon, Richard, 110, 113
North, Lt. Col. Oliver, 4-13
Nuclear energy lobby, 91-92
Nuclear Regulatory Commission (NRC), 91-92
Nunn, Sam, D-Ga., 104

O'Connor, Sandra Day, 113, 118, 123-124
Office of Management and Budget (OMB), 23, 24, 52-53
Ollman v. Evans, 108
O'Neill, Thomas P., D-Mass., 34-35, 38-39

People for the American Way, 105, 107
Persian Gulf, 18
Planned Parenthood, 105
Poindexter, Adm. John M., 5, 6, 10, 12-13
Political action committees (PACs), 69, 71, 89-90
see also Lobbies
Powell, Lewis F., 104, 111, 114
Presidency
budget cuts, 52-53
covert operations, 14-16
judiciary appointments, 118
powers of, 1-3
see also Reagan, Ronald
Presidential nominating process, 56-61
Primaries, 54-60
Privacy rights, 107-108
Proxmire, William, D-Wis., 104
Public Citizen, 110
Public interest lobbies, 84

Quayle, Dan, D-Ind., 43
Quillen, James H., R-Tenn., 81

Railroads
deregulation, 46, 48, 50-51
Reagan, Ronald
AIDS policy, 22
budget cuts, 52-53
"coattails" of, 67
covert operations, 14-16
firing air traffic controllers, 48
judiciary appointments, 118
management style, 5-6
nominations of, 96
struggles with Congress, 17-19
see also Presidency
Reagan v. Abourezk, 110, 115
Rehnquist, William H., 97, 112, 118, 120
Republican Party
and Southern Democrats, 78-79
bid to gain Senate seats, 61-68
primaries, 57
see also Elections

Index

Ridge, Tom, R-Pa., 94
Roe v. Wade, 107, 112
Roosevelt, Franklin D., 112, 113
Roth, William V., R-Del., 104

St Germain, Fernand J., D-R.I., 88
Scalia, Antonin, 113, 118, 124
School prayer, 114
SDI funding, 17-19
Search and seizure, 117
Senate
approval of presidential nominations, 25
bids for seats, 61-68
Bork rejection, 104-106
control of, 28-33, 66
filibusters in, 40-45
Intelligence Committee, 11, 13, 14
Judiciary Committee, 96, 104, 116, 119
majority control, 66
party caucuses, 30
see also Congress
Shoreham nuclear plant, 91
Southern Democrats, 73-79
Spratt, John M., D-S.C., 75, 79
Stennis, John C., D-Miss., 104
Stevens, John Paul, 113, 123
Super Tuesday, 56-57
Supreme Court
abortion, 107, 114
appointments of justices, 112
antitrust laws, 109
Bork vote, 104-106
Gramm-Rudman-Hollings, 24
homosexuality, 108, 117
judicial review, 99-100
jurisdiction, 98-99
legislative veto, 25
nominees, 102-103, 104
overview, 98-193
school prayer, 114
see also Judiciary

Taxation, 23
Telephone system
deregulation, 46, 48, 51
Thurmond, Strom, R-S.C., 40-43, 45, 119
Tower Commission, 5-6, 11-12
Tower, John, R-Texas, 5, 16
Trade policy, 20-21
Transportation, 46-51
Trucking industry
deregulation, 50

United States v. Mount, 108
United States v. Singleton, 108

Vander Jagt, Guy, R-Mich., 69-72
Veterans, 93-95, 117
Vietnam Veterans of America, 93-95

Walker, Robert S., R-Pa., 88
Warner, John, R-Va., 104
War Powers Resolution, 3, 18
Warren, Earl, 112, 113
Watergate, 110
Waxman, Henry, D-Calif., 22
White, Byron R., 113, 121
Wright, Jim, D-Texas, 20, 28, 29, 34-39, 74, 82, 88

Yeutter, Clayton, 21